This crosslinguistic collection looks at changes and developments in language involving gain or loss in structural complexity or utility. The dynamics of these processes of progression and regression are examined at the societal and the individual level, and the two are compared. In the former, the focus is on the social and cultural forces that influence groups of speakers to create new languages or abandon old ones. In the latter, the acquisition and attrition of both first and second languages are considered. Questions raised include: Can parallel structural patterning be observed in whole languages and in the individual's version of a language? Is there parallelism between progression and regression? Can changes occurring in progression and regression be interpreted in a typological framework? These are addressed from the perspectives of sociology, neuropsychology, and linguistics.

Progression and regression in language

Progression & regression in language

Sociocultural,
neuropsychological,
& linguistic
perspectives

Edited by
Kenneth Hyltenstam
and Åke Viberg

Centre for Research
on Bilingualism,
Stockholm University

CAMBRIDGE
UNIVERSITY PRESS

Published by the Press Syndicate of the University of Cambridge
The Pitt Building, Trumpington Street, Cambridge CB2 1RP
40 West 20th Street, New York, NY 10011-4211, USA
10 Stamford Road, Oakleigh, Melbourne 3166, Australia

First published 1993

Printed in Great Britain by Woolnough Bookbinding Ltd,
Irthlingborough, Northamptonshire.

A catalogue record for this book is available from the British Library

Library of Congress cataloguing in publication data

Progression and regression in language: sociocultural,
neuropsychological, and linguistic perspectives/edited by Kenneth
Hyltenstam and Åke Viberg.
   p. cm.
Papers presented at a conference held August 1990. Botkyrka, Sweden.
Includes bibliographical references and index.
ISBN 0 521 43290 1 (hardback). – ISBN 0 521 43874 8 (paperback)
1. Linguistic change – Congresses.   2. Code switching
(Linguistics) – Congresses.   3. Language acquisition – Congresses.
4. Language attrition – Congresses.   I. Hyltenstam, Kenneth.
II. Viberg, Åke.
P142.976   1993
401'.93 – dc20
92-46241
CIP

ISBN 0 521 43290 1 hardback
ISBN 0 521 43874 8 paperback

VN

Contents

List of contributors   *page* xi
Preface   xiii

INTRODUCTION   I

1   Linguistic progression and regression: an
    introduction   3
    KENNETH HYLTENSTAM and ÅKE VIBERG

    THE SOCIOCULTURAL SETTING   37

2   The role of pidgin and creole languages
    in language progression and regression   39
    PETER MÜHLHÄUSLER

3   Structure and practice in language shift   68
    JANE H. HILL

4   Growing up monolingual in a multilingual
    community: how language socialization
    patterns are leading to language shift in Gapun
    (Papua New Guinea)   94
    DON KULICK

vii

5   Language change in a creole continuum:
    decreolization?   122
    CHARLENE J. SATO

    PSYCHO- AND NEUROLINGUISTIC
    ASPECTS   145

6   Neurolinguistic aspects of first language
    acquisition and loss   147
    JEAN BERKO GLEASON

7   Neurolinguistic aspects of second language
    development and attrition   178
    LORAINE K. OBLER

8   Second language acquisition as a function of age:
    research findings and methodological issues   196
    MICHAEL H. LONG

9   Second language regression in Alzheimer's
    dementia   222
    KENNETH HYLTENSTAM AND
    CHRISTOPHER STROUD

    THE LINGUISTIC PERSPECTIVE 1:
    DISCOURSE, GRAMMAR, AND LEXIS   243

10 Crosslinguistic perspectives on native
    language acquisition   245
    RUTH A. BERMAN

11 Syntactic development in Danish L2   267
    ANNE HOLMEN

12 The weaker language in bilingual
    Swedish–French children   289
    SUZANNE SCHLYTER

13 Four operating principles and input distribution
    as explanations for underdeveloped and mature
    morphological systems   309
    ROGER W. ANDERSEN

14 Crosslinguistic perspectives on lexical
    organization and lexical progression   340
    ÅKE VIBERG

15 Attrition or expansion? Changes in the lexicon
    of Finnish and American adult bilinguals in
    Sweden   386
    SALLY BOYD

    THE LINGUISTIC PERSPECTIVE 2:
    PHONOLOGY   413

16 The development of phonological abilities   415
    HENNING WODE

17 The course of development in second language
    phonology acquisition: a natural path or
    strategic choice?   439
    BJÖRN HAMMARBERG

18 Sociolinguistic factors in loss and acquisition of phonology 463
ROY C. MAJOR

Index 479

Contributors

Roger W. Andersen
TESL/Applied Linguistics
University of California,
Los Angeles

Ruth A. Berman
Department of Linguistics
Tel-Aviv University

Sally Boyd
Department of Linguistics
University of Göteborg and
Centre for Research in International
Migration and Ethnic Relations
Stockholm University

Jean Berko Gleason
Department of Psychology
Boston University

Björn Hammarberg
Department of Linguistics
Stockholm University

Jane H. Hill
Department of Anthropology
University of Arizona

Anne Holmen
Department of Nordic Philology
Copenhagen University

Kenneth Hyltenstam
Centre for Research on Bilingualism
Stockholm University

Don Kulick
Department of Child Studies
University of Linköping

Michael H. Long
Department of English as
a Second Language
University of Hawai'i at Mānoa

Roy C. Major
Department of English
Washington State University

Peter Mühlhäusler
Linguistics CLTR
University of Adelaide

Loraine K. Obler
Speech and Hearing Sciences
City University of New York
Graduate School

Charlene J. Sato
Department of English as
a Second Language and *Center for*
Second Language Classroom Research
University of Hawai'i at Mānoa

xi

Suzanne Schlyter
Department of Romance
Languages
Lund University

Christopher Stroud
Centre for Research on Bilingualism
Stockholm University

Åke Viberg
Centre for Research on Bilingualism
Stockholm University

Henning Wode
Englisches Seminar
Christian-Albrechts-Universität
zu Kiel

Preface

This book is the result of a conference with invited participants around the theme of Progression and Regression in Language, held in August 1990 at Botkyrka in the vicinity of Stockholm. The conference was organized by the *Centre for Research on Bilingualism*, Stockholm University, in co-operation with the *Swedish Immigration Institute and Museum* at Botkyrka. The idea of a conference was originally proposed by representatives of the Institute, and the conference was set up as part of the *Summer University of Södertörn* programme. We would like to express our gratitude to the Institute and Summer University for the generous financial support which made the conference possible. In particular, we would like to thank the director of the Institute, Leif Magnusson, and Ingrid Lundberg, also from the Institute, for valuable and much appreciated help with the organization.

Among our colleagues at the Centre for Research on Bilingualism, we would first like to thank Maria Wingstedt for efficiently performing the frequently arduous duties requested of a conference secretary, and for her contribution to the creation of an inspiring and relaxed atmosphere during the meeting. We also owe special thanks to Christopher Stroud for his many fruitful suggestions on the organization and themes of the conference and for the insightful comments and the work he put into our introductory chapter of this book.

· Introduction ·

1 · Linguistic progression and regression: an introduction

KENNETH HYLTENSTAM
AND ÅKE VIBERG

BASIC ASSUMPTIONS

The dynamics of language

Our physical and social environment has provided a rich source of metaphors for linguistics. Most of us, for example, are familiar with ways of talking about languages where they are depicted as living organisms – languages are born, they grow, develop, and die. We may conceive of languages as being more or less distantly related to each other – they have parents and sisters – and they share no genetics with unrelated languages.

Also other, and perhaps more abstract, characteristics of language can be highlighted and brought to the forefront of linguistic consciousness through the use of metaphors. The linguistic phenomenon that is the topic of this volume is often characterized as *dynamism*. Dynamism, of course, is a metaphor taken from natural sciences. In parallel with air or water (aerodynamics, hydrodynamics), language can be seen as inherently dynamic, something that exhibits change and flux, and is characterized by motion resulting from 'natural' forces. Only languages such as Latin, that have ceased to 'live', are static and fossilized. Living languages are in a continuous motion, adapting to the social contexts in which they are used; they take form as different registers or lects, they appear in the written or spoken mode, and, above all, they move with time, changing chronologically. A specific instance of chronological change occurs in the individual. When languages are acquired or lost, they adapt to the successively changing constraints of the speaker's mind and to the conditions of the social environment. In general, this book can be seen as the result of current interest in how different manifestations of linguistic dynamism relate to each other.

One condition for talking about linguistic dynamism is the occurrence of linguistic heterogeneity, i.e. languages use a variety of forms for the expression of the same referential content. These features of heterogeneity make up the potential for the dynamics of language. Heterogeneity can come about in various ways. One important source of heterogeneity is *language contact*. In a language contact situation, the structures of two − or more − languages are available to speakers and can thus be used in dynamic processes. Since language contact is central to the issue of dynamism, it is also a central theme in many of the chapters of this book.

Space does not allow us to delve too deeply into a discussion of what a focus on dynamism has meant for current linguistic theory. Suffice it to say that an interest in variability has been a central component of popular and productive "directions" that originate from empirical linguistic concerns, i.e. directions in which naturally occurring data are accounted for theoretically. The most salient area that springs to mind is, of course, that of sociolinguistics and dialectology (e.g. Labov, 1969), but also the study of creole languages (e.g. Bickerton, 1973) and second language acquisition (for an overview, see Tarone, 1988) have provided important contributions in developing variation theory generally. An up-to-date treatment of these perspectives can be found in work by, for example, Silva-Corvalán (1991) and Rickford (1991).

Progression and regression in speech communities and in individuals

The title we have chosen for this book, *Progression and regression in language*, reflects our attempt to capture various manifestations of the dynamics of accretion and decrement of language on the societal and individual levels.

Among the various forms in which linguistic dynamism can be found, language change is, as hinted at above, maybe the most salient one. Obviously, all languages change over time. Languages change from the moment they are born until they are no longer used as means of communication in a speech community, i.e. until they have become obsolete. Seen in the perspective of the life-cycle of languages, one might want to talk about the earliest period of development, when a language comes into being, as a period of *progression*. Similarly, one might want to speak of the period when a language ceases to be a full-fledged medium of communication, and subsequently withers away and dies as its phase of *regression*.

But progression and regression are found not only within the life cycle of a whole language. These phases are created anew every time a language is learnt or lost by an individual. All individuals experience the phase of progression when they acquire their native language(s). Many repeat this experience as they acquire additional languages. In first language acquisition (L1A), if it occurs in a monolingual environment, the progression phase proceeds in a non-contact situation. Bilingual first language acquisition (BL1A) and second language acquisition (L2A) prototypically take place in a situation where more than one language is present in the social context, but obviously L2A can also be found in a monolingual L2 environment, as for example, in those cases when foreign children are adopted into a new host community. From the perspective of the psycholinguistic reality of the learner, this situation is also, however, an example of language contact.

Many individuals also experience the phase of regression. A first language may regress because another language has come to replace it as the person's normal and regular means of communication. It may also regress for pathological reasons, as in the case of aphasia or when a person suffers from dementia. Second or foreign languages may regress for the same reasons. Typical examples of regression fundamentally due to the non-use of a language comprise such cases as when an immigrant remigrates to his/her native country or when a person ceases to study a foreign language. In all these examples of regression, except the one caused by pathology in monolinguals, regression takes place in a language contact situation. This also reflects the fact that the prime reason for giving up a language is an extensive functional reallocation of this language in relation to another.

The theoretical interest in linguistic dynamism as a phenomenon has, from time to time, been accompanied by an awareness of similar patterning in different manifestations of dynamism. This was the case, for example, with work by Jakobson (1941; English translation in 1968), who compared phonological progression (in child language) to regression (in aphasia) and saw these as manifestations of universal regularities in the sound systems of natural languages. In the present book, we explore parallels of this kind, although the basic assumption is not, as it was in Jakobson's case, that regression will turn out to be a mirror of progression. More recent research (see below) has shown that the relationship is much more complex than was once thought to be the case.

Structural and registral correlates of progression and regression

Although the linguistic changes that take place under phases of progression and regression are in principle similar to those occurring in ordinary language change, they often specifically involve an increase and decrease, respectively, in degree of linguistic complexity. The phase of progression even includes a qualitative change that marks the transition from non-language to language. In the transition from a pidgin to a creole, children who belong to the first monolingual speaker generation of their parents' contact language develop a new language through adding to the pidgin the essential features that characterize a natural language (an example study is Sankoff and Laberge, 1973). In the individual's progression we find parallel changes. Proceeding from an 'under-two-stage', which in Bickerton's (1990) view ought not to be considered language proper, children individually construct a natural language through a process of complexification, adding those linguistic features that are definitional of natural languages. In Bickerton's terminology both types of speaker thus take the step from protolanguage to language. Protolanguage is used by 'trained apes, children under two, adults who have been deprived of language in their early years, and speakers of pidgin' and is 'a mode of linguistic expression that is quite separate from normal human language' (1990:122). In normal human language, but not in protolanguage, (1) differences in syntactic constituent order are 'constrained by general principles' and have specific meanings, (2) null elements appear in a principled way so that it is possible to infer that a constituent is notionally present, although it is not explicitly expressed, (3) verbs subcategorize for one, two, or three arguments, (4) phrases are expanded through recursive principle, and (5) bound morphemes and other grammatical forms are present (122ff.).

When a language is on its way to becoming obsolete, the linguistic distinctions made in relation to those found in the fully developed form of the language become fewer. However, to the best of our knowledge, there are no accounts of dying languages that single out and describe protolanguage systems at this end of the continuum. We might want to conjecture that stable stages of this kind do not exist. Since language obsolescence, as we noted above, generally occurs in a contact situation where the speakers shift from a minority language – the language undergoing obsolescence – to a majority language, the speakers already have another communication instrument at their disposal, and there may be no motivation for using an obsolete language with severely limited means of expression.

In the process of individual language attrition it is clear that some types of linguistic distinctions are affected more often than others. Indeed, it has been pointed out in some cases that these distinctions involve features that can be considered marked from a typological point of view (see e.g. Sharwood Smith, 1989; Seliger, 1989), and that attrition thus can be seen as a process of 'demarking'. It is also obvious, however, that the various manifestations of attrition at the individual level are extremely complex phenomena, where the interplay between process and knowledge levels needs to be investigated in more detail. For example, in the different types of pathological attrition, such process aspects as lexical access or knowledge aspects such as the semantics of alternative word orders may be differentially affected.

An interesting example of aphasic attrition is that of agrammatism, i.e. 'a language disorder due to acquired brain damage, characterized by slow, halting speech, by short and/or fragmentary sentences, and by limited output use of the syntactic and morphological resources of language' (Menn and Obler, 1990: 3). In this case, the remaining language might be better characterized as protolanguage than natural language according to Bickerton's criteria that were mentioned above. This means that a protolanguage stage is feasible in principle also in regression, although in practice it is probably manifested only at the individual level.

From the point of view of language structure, a number of specific issues relating to progression and regression can be studied. A recurrent theme in much of the work included in the present volume (particularly in the last two sections) is the search for psycholinguistically valid subsystems. Even if traditional distinctions in terms of discourse, lexicon, grammar (morphosyntax), and phonology are useful as general reference points, it is obvious that these broad divisions do not pattern in a uniform way in linguistic progression and regression. Alternative frameworks such as the components of communicative competence distinguished by Canale and Swain (1980) and submitted to large-scale empirical testing in the study presented in Harley, Allen, Cummins and Swain (1990) are probably also too broad. In order to understand progression and regression, global levels and components must be broken down into smaller, functionally integrated, subsystems which cut across these broader divisions.

At a more general level, data from different types of progression and regression can be used to test the validity of current models of linguistic structure. Such models can roughly be characterized as *formal,* represented primarily by Government and Binding (GB) (Chomsky, 1981), or *functional,* represented by several overlapping frameworks such as Dik's (1989) Functional Grammar, Foley and van Valin's (1984) Role and Reference Grammar, or Givón's (1984, 1990) Functional Typological Syntax. In the present volume, both formal and functional approaches are represented among the contributions, with a certain predominance for functional perspectives.

Within the formal approach, questions such as whether the principles of universal grammar are available to L2 as well as L1 learners have been a clear focus of research interest for a number of years (cf. Schlyter's contribution). Within the functional approach, progression and regression can be addressed at different levels. We might ask what consequences the learner's expanding communicative requirements might have for the development of discourse functions and syntax (Berman, Holmen), or, what biases (or frequency of occurrence) in input distributions of morphological and lexical elements might mean for language acquisition (Andersen, Viberg).

Another correlate of progression and regression both at the societal and at the individual level is that of registral and stylistic variability. Furthermore, at the societal level, functions such as context of use (Mühlhäusler) and the symbolic value of forms of speech (Hill) are central determinants of dynamism. In the process of progression, styles and registers are developed as speakers articulate new identities by means of lectal variation. Likewise in regression, such registral variability becomes successively more restricted as speakers re-enact themselves in other languages.

The socio-cultural framework

Returning momentarily to the conception of language as a living organism, we may note that different authors have extended and elaborated this metaphor to incorporate the ties between language as a life form and its environment. One famous example is Haugen's (1972) notion of *ecology of language.* The obvious socio-cultural framing of language change has occasionally become the explicit research focus of such branches of linguistics as the nineteenth-century philological tradition that studied texts in order to understand the cultural setting in which these texts were produced (cf. Malmberg, 1967), or the recent developments in historical linguistics that emphasize the social context for an understanding of historical change (Thomason and Kaufman, 1988). The socio-cultural – or socio-political – framing has been one of the foci in a number of recent influential large-scale studies of language regression and shift (Gal, 1979; Dorian, 1981; Schmidt, 1985; Hill and Hill, 1986; Woolard, 1989; Kulick, 1992) as well as in studies of progression (Ochs, 1988; Schieffelin, 1990). Especially in research taking an ethnographic perspective, such as many of the studies just mentioned, cultural relativism is explored in search of a comprehensive account of the particular manifestations of progression and regression under different societal conditions. Researchers may sometimes be accused of being shackled in their understanding of the cultural determinants of variability. Some critics would claim that they are of necessity bound by the conceptions of the world they hold, specific to their own cultural background (and not least by the assumptions behind their theoretical constructs) (cf. Duranti, 1988; Stroud, 1992). However, the growing cross-cultural sensitivity in studies of progression and regression, paralleled by the cross-linguistic perspectives currently prevailing in studies of both first and second language acquisition and loss (Slobin, 1985; Berman, 1984; Kellerman and Sharwood Smith, 1986; Andersen, 1982; Sharwood Smith, 1989), has a lot to promise for the future development of these research areas. This does not, of course, mean that issues of cultural variability need no further examination. On the contrary, the flood of recent research on this topic permits us to pose even more questions of even greater specificity. In this book we have incorporated a section which focuses directly on questions about the relationship between socio-cultural framing and linguistic dynamism such as, for example, what factors in the socio-cultural framework contribute to the diversity between and within speech communities. And at what socio-cultural level or combination of levels should we address our theoretical accounts of dynamism? At the level of global distribution of power (as in Mühlhäusler's contribution), at the social network level (Boyd), at the level of ethnic identity employing notions such as stigmatization, prestige, discrimination or solidarity (Sato), at the level of ideology (Kulick), or at the level of linguistic practice, where languages are seen as pools of resources (Hill).

The neuropsychological framework

For a fuller understanding of progression and regression, however, it is also necessary to take the individual's mind and brain into account. The constraints of the human brain in processing linguistic dynamism certainly places limits on the variation in patterns that can be found across cultures. Accordingly, biological, cognitive, or maturational perspectives, as well as language processing aspects have become especially important over the last 2 or 3 decades in studies of progression (Walsh and Diller, 1981; Long, 1990; McLaughlin, 1987:133ff.), and work on individual regression has also, naturally, incorporated such perspectives (Bates, Wulfeck and MacWhinney, 1991). Among the most salient and extensively treated issues from these perspectives is that of universal developmental sequences for both first and second language acquisition, and one of the most influential proposals for accounting for these sequences from a psycholinguistic point of view is, of course, that formulated in terms of operating principle and perceptual strategies (Slobin, 1973; Bever, 1970; Clahsen, Meisel and Pienemann, 1983). (Psycholinguistically oriented explanations, however, are not the only ones, as is evident from the section on structure above.)

It is well known that there is a diversity in the manner in which progression and regression are manifested linguistically. A natural question, therefore, is to what extent universal accounts must be revised. In what ways are, for example, differences between L1A and L2A − or L2A at different ages − dependent on the neuropsychological substrate that control linguistic perception and production (Wode, Long, Schlyter)? What are the cerebral correlates of typical, as opposed to atypical, language acquisition (Gleason) and of attrition (Gleason, Obler)? In order to handle questions such as these, this book also includes a section on biological, neurological, and psychological perspectives on progression and regression.

The so-called *regression hypothesis*, formulated explicitly by Jakobson, i.e. whether linguistic distinctions that develop later are more vulnerable to early loss in aphasia, has exerted considerable theoretical influence and comprised the basis for scrutinizing aphasic data in pursuit of answers to more specific questions. Because the bulk of this research on aphasia has addressed psycho- and neurolinguistic issues, it is reasonable to provide a short note on the regression hypothesis in this section.

One volume where the contributions specifically address the regression hypothesis, using aphasia data is Caramazza and Zurif (1978). In their preface, the editors are forced to conclude that the hypothesis 'simply does not bear close scrutiny' (p. x). Further- more, they state that 'where there is correspondence, it can be maintained in most instances only at a superficial level', with the exception of segmental speech perception (ibid.). However, as noted by Jordens, de Bot, and Trapman (1989:180), the comparison of child language and aphasia may not be the best option for investigating the regression hypothesis. A necessary condition in order to study regression is that the process ought to be gradual, something which is definitely not the case with aphasia, although it *is* the case with dementia (see the contribution by Hyltenstam and Stroud). Another problem is that the assumption behind comparing children with aphasics may be askew. Aphasia comprises a range of very specific linguistic manifestations that all depend upon the localization, type, and extent of brain trauma, whereas the development of language in the child is a composite effect of a global increase of many cognitive and linguistic skills.

The regression hypothesis has, however, also been attractive for comparisons of other kinds: first language acquisition and healthy first language attrition, second/foreign language acquisition and attrition etc. Over the last decade or so, this area of research has taken the step from a hypothesis formulation stage (e.g. Andersen, 1982; Gleason, 1978) to initial attempts at empirical validation (e.g. Olsthain, 1989; Jordens, de Bot, and Trapman, 1989). At this point in time, the large-scale support for the hypothesis still remains to be demonstrated.

Although Jakobson's typological perspective was not particularly influential in later research on the regression hypothesis, it is presently an important framework in much second language acquisition research (cf. Greenberg, 1991). Typology seems to have a large potential also for other types of progression or regression studies, or, rather, for the whole area of language dynamics. A typological perspective plays a role in several contributions of this volume, such as those by Viberg, Andersen, Wode, and Berman.

REVIEW OF CONTENTS

While the first two sections of the book are organized around the socio-cultural (chapters 2–5) and the neuro-/psycholinguistic (chapters 6–9) conditions for language progression and regression, the organizing principle behind the last two sections is that of linguistic levels. The third section (chapters 10–15) centers around the levels of discourse, grammar, and lexis, and the 3 chapters of the last section (chapters 16–18) treat phonological issues. All four sections comprise both contributions that give overviews and make comparisons between different settings and contributions that are of a more case study character.

The socio-cultural setting

Mühlhäusler, in his chapter, examines the role pidgin and creole languages can play in accelerating the transition from traditional vernaculars to modernized languages. He is critical of the view that sees the role of pidgins merely as that of auxiliary languages enabling speakers of different linguistic backgrounds to communicate with one another. Among other things, they are also instruments of power in the processes of missionization, colonization, and modernization. Mühlhäusler situates both pidgins and creoles in a developmental framework where these languages can serve a variety of roles at different stages. As pidgins progress structurally and functionally, the languages into whose ecology they are making inroads tend to regress and disappear. In virtually all instances their replacement by a creole or their modernization is only a temporary phenomenon. Over longer periods of time, the superimposed metropolitan language takes over.

Hill discusses three cases of language shift presented in the literature from the perspective of a theory of linguistic practice, drawing on the work of authors such as Bakhtin, Bourdieu, and Williams. The examples comprise the shift from Dyirbal to English in Australia, from Mexicano (Nahuatl) to Spanish in central Mexico, and from Vasco to English in the Warm Springs Reservation in Oregon, US. On the basis of a comparison of these cases, she concludes that multilingualism, language shift, and language loss can be regarded as types of deployment in practice of semiotic materials from a locally constructed diversity of 'languages', with shifting and contested symbolic significance and 'value'. In this view, linguistic practice is one component of a broader range of social practices like the construction of identity and the struggle for political economic resources, both material and symbolic. Yet from the point of view of a theory of languge structure, these practices are ultimately constrained by cognitive limitations on the possible forms of human languages and by functional limitations on the forms of discourse. It is shown how these two approaches, usually developed in isolation from one another, might complement each other to yield both theoretical refinement and more rigorous description.

The chapter by *Kulick* presents an in-depth ethnographic examination of language socialization patterns in a shift situation, a topic that has not formerly been addressed systematically in research. Kulick's research site is a small, rural, relatively isolated village, called Gapun, near the northern coast of Papua New Guinea. The main aim of the analysis is to reveal the mechanisms which are giving rise to language shift in this particular cultural setting. Adults in Gapun all value their vernacular, Taiap, and they want their children to learn it. They cannot understand why children no longer command Taiap, and they go as far as to blame pre-verbal infants for the shift to Tok Pisin.

Kulick asks what makes it seem reasonable for the villagers of Gapun to blame their babies for the demise of the village vernacular, and argues for the following answer: the villagers' notions of self, of language, of knowledge and of children structure, and are structured through, language in such a way that caregiver talk to children is unconsciously, yet very systematically, biased towards Tok Pisin. The result is that when children begin to talk, they do so in Tok Pisin. Underlying assumptions about the nature of children, of learning, and of language make up the interpretative frame within which the children themselves can be seen as the agents of shift.

Sato's chapter reports on one of the few studies to examine real-time decreolization in individuals. Findings from a longitudinal study in Hawai'i are presented to demonstrate differences in the rate and course of change of a range of linguistic and discoursal features. Lack of extensive decreolization is interpreted in light of comparisons of decreolization with second language acquisition. Results are also discussed with reference to legal and educational controversies in Hawai'i, which have revealed competing sociolinguistic trends: (1) continued adherence to stereotypical attitudes toward Hawaiian Creole English (HCE) and standard US English by some segments of the community and (2) a growing militancy in other groups in support of HCE use.

Psycho- and neurolinguistic aspects

Gleason begins her overview chapter on the neurolinguistic aspects of first language progression and regression with a discussion of the normal course of first language development in humans. Her point of departure is that linguistic capacity relies upon, among other things, neuroanatomical structures that are unique to our species. Infants' cognitive and affective propensities, assuming an intact neurological system, lead them to acquire language relatively rapidly during the first few years of life, and with remarkable similarity across languages. At the same time, a first language is not acquired solely through activity on the part of the child: the adult caregiver provides specialized child directed input, thus compensating for the child's limited processing capacities.

Next, Gleason discusses what we can learn about the neuro-psychological bases for linguistic dynamism from atypical language development. Atypical language development occurs under varying circumstances – either as an isolated phenomenon present in an otherwise 'normal' individual, or as part of a larger constellation of atypical characteristics. Whether typical or atypical in its course, first language development is characterized by variation as well as universality.

Loss, or regression of language skills, which is treated in the final part of the chapter, can occur for various 'environmental' reasons or through a change in the neurolinguistic underpinnings of language, as, for example, in aphasia. Aphasia in children and adults is quite different, however, even if the brain damage appears identical. The chapter concludes with a discussion of the neuropsychological implications of these adult/child differences.

In the next chapter, *Obler* gives a corresponding overview of current knowledge of neurolinguistic aspects of second language progression and regression. Three sets of neurolinguistic data bear on discussions of these issues: lateral dominance for cerebral organization, intrahemispheric specialization for language processing, and critical periods in brain maturation.

In brief, data from aphasic bilinguals suggest overall similarities in lateral dominance between bilinguals and monolinguals, but instrumental data on lateral organization for language in bilinguals may be construed to indicate greater right hemisphere participation in at least early stages of bilingual language processing as compared to monolingual language processing. Studies on the development of laterality in bilinguals are few and inconclusive; those on subjects with declining skills appear nonexistent.

Within the left hemisphere, the data of Ojemann and Whitaker (1978) suggest a fair degree of overlap for representation of the two languages of the mature adult bilingual. To the extent that there is some differentiation of sites outside the core language area, however, one may assume a certain degree of differential development of each of the languages.

Various neurological developmental phenomena pertain to questions of a critical period for second language acquisition. It becomes clear from what data there are that certain aspects of second language acquisition appear to be governed by maturational rules, while others are less constrained.

With respect to several other psycholinguistic phenomena (the bilingual monitor, lexical access, and syntactic transfer during acquisition and attrition), Obler claims, the neurolinguistic discussions must remain speculative at this time.

The question of critical or sensitive periods for language learning, or maturational constraints, is treated at depth on the basis of second language data in *Long*'s chapter. He also discusses the methodological problems inherent in this area.

Long concludes that research on the relationships between the age at which the acquisition of a second language or dialect is begun and subsequent performance supports four claims. (1) Initial learning rate and ultimate attainment are partly a function of age of onset. (2) Language development is governed by sensitive periods, during which the acquisition of different linguistic abilities is successful and after which it is irregular and incomplete. (3) The loss in learning capacity is not a catastrophic one-time event, but cumulative, affecting first one linguistic domain and then another. (4) The deterioration begins as early as age 6 in some individuals, not at puberty, as is often claimed.

Despite the emergence of some clear patterns in the findings to date, research on these and related phenomena in first and second language acquisition and loss still presents a number of methodological challenges. These include: the definition and operationalization of acquisition (or loss); the identification of comparable native speaker base-line data, especially when the target variety is highly variable; the choice of elicitation measures for use with subjects who vary in age, are poorly educated, illiterate and test-naive and/or when the language variety concerned is unwritten or has an orthography with which subjects are unfamiliar; the difficulty level and discrimination value of test items; variability due to task, topic, interlocutor and setting.

The chapter by *Hyltenstam and Stroud* presents results from research on language regression in bilingual demented speakers. The authors suggest that the specific type of language performance that can be observed in such speakers provides unique insights into bilingual processing and language processing generally. Three questions were specifically focused upon in this research. (1) Is bilingual speakers' ability to separate their linguistic codes affected in dementia? (2) Does their ability to choose an appropriate language in conversation with a monolingual speaker break down? (3) Is the second language less accessible in language processing than the first?

From their study of six bilingual (Finnish/Swedish) subjects with Alzheimer's disease, Hyltenstam and Stroud conclude that language separation problems and language choice problems are abundant in the group. However, the individual differences in the manifestation of these problems are large. For some patients the second language is not accessible for production. Accordingly, language separation and language choice problems do not seem to be simply, or directly, related to the stage of linguistic dissolution in which the patient finds him-/herself. The data rather suggest that it is the interaction between the stage of dissolution and the level of premorbid proficiency in the second language that determines the nature of the problems.

The linguistic perspective 1: discourse, grammar and lexis

Berman opens her review of 'Crosslinguistic perspective on native language acquisition' with a discussion of various motivations for crosslinguistic studies of L1A. These include psycholinguistic questions concerning mechanisms and principles guiding acquisition, attempts to provide evidence for particular theories of grammar or a concern for linguistic functions, in particular with reference to discourse and language use. From the last perspective, which is the central one for Berman's own approach, development can be examined in terms of the interaction between language-general functions and language-specific forms, for example, how children acquiring different languages learn to express certain discourse-anchored notions such as agency or simultaneity. Essential in this connection is the notion 'linguistically central' in the sense of the special status carried by systems which are of critical importance within a particular language or language-type – from the point of view of how much informational weight they carry and/or how wide a range of grammatical structure they impinge upon (e.g. auxiliaries in English, clitics in French, or inflectional markers in languages with highly developed systems of agreement). A schematic representation is presented of the general path of language acquisition, which is conceived of in terms of progression along a number of parameters integrating various subsystems of language structure and language use. In particular, three broad developmental phases are distinguished, from Pregrammar, via Linguistic Structures and Relations, to Thematically Organized Discourse. As mentioned earlier, language-specific factors play an increasing role in this development.

Holmen's study on syntactic development in Danish L2 combines the interlanguage framework for L2 development with functional theories of language structure such as Dik's functional grammar and Givón's functional syntax. The analysis is based on longitudinal conversational data from six adolescent learners with Albanian, English, and Vietnamese as L1:s. Early syntactic development is dealt with in formal as well as functional terms. On the basis of both quantitative and qualitative analyses, a common developmental sequence for the acquisition of Danish syntax and morphology is presented. The progression along the sequence is related to changes in information structure, which are considered to be the primary force in the development of formal features. Thus a steadily increasing amount of information in the learners' utterances is found together with qualitative changes in the kind of information expressed at different points in the acquisition process. This process may be seen as a complexification of the interlanguage involving grammaticization as well as an extension of the semantic potential. Even if the common developmental sequence is the main finding of the study, variation in the acquisitional rate, which varies widely between learners, is also taken into consideration.

Studies on bilingual children often presuppose a balanced bilingualism, or concentrate on children whose two languages seem to be equally strong. Recently, strong evidence has been presented in Meisel (1990) that in cases such as this each language develops in the same way as in monolingual L1A. *Schlyter*, in her contribution, concentrates on the relatively neglected case of unbalanced bilingual acquisition, where one of the two languages is weaker than the other. What is the nature of the weaker language? Does it develop like an ordinary L1 or rather like an L2? Data are presented from a study in progress on six bilingual Swedish–French speaking children, who were followed for two years starting around age two. The development of certain grammatical phenomena such as finiteness, pronominal subject, word order, and negation are charted in both languages, and the course of development of these items is related to five general stages along the lines of Clahsen's profile analysis. The general conclusion is that the stronger language exhibits all characteristics of normal first language acquisition, whereas the weaker language exhibits great variation with respect to the phenomena studied in a way that is reminiscent of second language acquisition. This finding is discussed in the context of the present debate among adherents of GB theory, as to whether the principles of Universal Grammar (UG) which determine L1A are available even to second language learners. The result of Schlyter's study clearly indicate that this is not the case. However, there also seem to be individual differences in the speed and accuracy of the acquisition of certain features, in particular finiteness.

Morphological systems are treated in *Andersen*'s contribution, in particular the underdeveloped nature of verb morphology for tense and aspect in language acquisition. In studies of first language acquisition, two conflicting positions are found. One is that children are guided by the inherent aspect of verbs, while the opposite position is that children have access to abstract grammatical categories from a very young age. Using data from second language acquisition, for which similar claims have been made, Andersen approaches the acquisition of tense and aspect from another direction, namely that there is a distributional bias in the native input that would lead the learner to the same (incorrect) conclusion that each inflection is used with a different semantic class of verbs. This is referred to as The Distributional Bias Principle, which is also supported with analyses of native language data from several different languages.

Viberg presents a general framework for studying the organization and acquisition of the basic lexicon from a crosslinguistic perspective. Theoretical reference points for his section on lexical structure are semantic field analysis, typological markedness in the tradition of Jakobson and Greenberg, and lexicalization hierarchies. Viberg concentrates on basic verbs. Within each basic verbal semantic field, it is possible to isolate just one or a few meanings which can be shown to lexicalize as nuclear verbs across a wide range of languages, for example: 'go' (field: Motion), 'give' and 'take'

(Possession), 'see' (Perception) and 'say' (Verbal communication). Nuclear verbs combine a number of unmarked characteristics such as high frequency, syntactic prototypicality, and semantic dominance in hierarchies of polysemy.

The section on lexical acquisition presents data from a study of the acquisition of Swedish L2 by six-year-old preschoolers. Nuclear verbs which represent unmarked features of the target language tended to be favoured, when compared to the usage of native controls of the same age, while basic verbs representing language-specific semantic patterning tended to be avoided or used in a way that neutralized language-specific semantic contrasts. A review of related studies of lexical progression in L2 and L1 turned up several parallels to these findings, but also some complicating factors. In general, nuclear verbs turned out to play a similar central role in L1 and L2. Different types of language-specific factors are discussed with respect to four lexical parameters: (1) conflation, (2) semantic differentiation, (3) polysemy, and, (4) grammaticalization. In most cases, language-specific features begin to emerge very early in first language acquisition, while such features have a strong tendency to be avoided or neutralized in second language acquisition (unless the learner's L1 happens to be congruent with the L2).

The next paper is also focused on the lexicon, but, at first glance at least, *Boyd*, in contrast to the other contributors to this section, looks at regression and not at progression. However, as is implied by the title of her paper 'attrition or expansion?', the changes she considers have a dual nature, as is often the case with contact-induced change. An examination is given of the contrasting patterns of incorporation of Swedish-origin lexemes into the English and the Finnish of adult bilinguals living in the town of Göteborg in Western Sweden. As a background, the central notions of borrowing and code-switching as presented in the literature are critically discussed, and Boyd questions the universality of certain code-switching constraints, and the predictability of patterns of code-switching or borrowing based on the structure of the languages in contact are both seriously questioned. Particularly interesting is Boyd's claim that the pattern of lexical incorporation can more directly be related to the social network structure of the Finnish as compared to the American informant group as a whole. An attempt is also made to distinguish different informants within each minority group, and to relate their particular pattern of incorporation to their place within a social network of other minority language speakers.

The linguistic perspective 2: Phonology

The last section is devoted to phonology. *Wode*'s contribution is centered around the development of speech perception and the consequences of findings within this area for our understanding of the Universal Theory of Language Acquisition (UTA). A major issue is the continuity vs. discontinuity of the abilities underlying different acquisitional types such as L1A, BL1A, child and adult L2A, re-learning of an L2 etc. Wode argues strongly for the continuity view (cf., for contrast, Long's and Schlyter's contributions), i.e. that the learning abilities remain essentially the same, despite obvious differences in the surface data in certain cases. Empirical data are drawn primarily from a number of experimental studies on speech perception comparing different age-groups, from pre-speech infants to adults. Particularly interesting is the discussion of perception in the categorial (all-or-none) mode, which is crucial for language processing. The emerging picture is that the original categorical abilities remain available, but become increasingly difficult to access. With age in L2A, similar though not identical elements present difficulties, since the areas of sensitivity have already been occupied by elements from the L1. The continuity view is supported also by data from ongoing sound change. In Labov's classical studies from New York and Martha's Vineyard, middle-aged speakers and not children were most sensitive to change. The preservation across the life span of the ability to adjust to ongoing sound change presupposes an intact ability to perceive changes in pronunciation.

Hammarberg's contribution focuses on the initial stages of L2 phonological progression. The presentation is based on data from a study of the acquisition of Swedish pronunciation by 5 adult Germans, who were observed at 3 points of time. There is, as Hammarberg points out, an inherent dualism in current approaches to L2 phonology. On the one hand, the learner is seen as a creative and strategic actor, on the other hand, development is seen as a uniform natural route along which variational patterns change gradually over time, restricted by inherent linguistic constraints. In particular, this linear character of development is questioned. Examples of variational patterns are given, in which the occurring variants are not possible to order in any obvious way. Restricting factors vary in strength and leave room for strategic choice to different degrees. One such factor has to do with the type of phonological regularity that comes into play. A phonetically motivated, low-level regularity which the learner has acquired earlier (e.g. in L1) constrains the learner more severely than one which lacks direct phonetic motivation. There is also an interesting discussion of the clash between phonetically based and lexically based solutions. A certain target sound is more likely to be influenced by L1 when it appears in Swedish words having a German cognate with similar form. This is a parallel at the phonological level to 'holophrastic' acquisition of unanalyzed items at the syntactic level.

Major presents the findings of a study profiling the sociolinguistic factors correlated with the phonological acquisition of a second language and the concomitant loss in the first language. The study included 5 adult native speakers of English who were immigrants to Brazil. VOT (voice onset time) of the subjects' Portuguese and English voiceless stops was examined, since there is good evidence that VOT is highly correlated with global foreign accent. In general, it was found that degree of integration into Brazilian culture and proficiency in Portuguese were correlated with loss of English proficiency. The correlation between L1 loss and L2 mastery on the one hand, and integration into L2 culture on the other was striking. For example, the VOTs for one subject whose overall command of Portuguese was marginal, diverged markedly from that of monolingual Portuguese controls, while her English production was equivalent to monolingual English controls residing in the US; another subject who passed for native Brazilian diverged clearly from native values in English. Her loss of native English pronunciation was further confirmed by her self-report that during her visits to the US many did not believe she was a native speaker of English. Two speakers were significantly different from native speakers in both English and Portuguese and thus appeared to be native speakers of neither language. Two different styles were also studied in L1. The casual style (conversation) turned out to be more affected than the formal style (word and sentence lists). The results are discussed within the framework of accommodation theory. The learning of a second language (or dialect) can be thought of as long-range accommodation in distinction to short-range accommodations to interlocutor.

TOWARDS A UNITARY PICTURE OF PROGRESSION AND REGRESSION

In our opinion, this short review of the contents of the individual chapters clearly shows that there are many parallels between the fields brought together in this volume, even if it still remains an open question as to how far this parallelism goes. The view that progression and regression simply represent the mirror image of one another must be refuted, at least in its most general form. However, change involves the same functional and formal parameters of linguistic structure, and is embedded in the same matrix of socio-cultural and neuropsychological determining factors irrespective of the direction of the change. It would be premature to try to strike a balance between the many different perspectives represented by the authors of the individual chapters, but it seems to be possible to indicate some major phenomena that a general theory

Table 1.1. *Major types of progression and regression at the
individual level*

PROGRESSION

First language acquisition (L1 A)
Typical L1A
Atypical L1A

Bilingual first language acquisition (BL1 A)
Balanced BL1A
Unbalanced BL1A

Second language acquisition (L2A)
Naturalistic L2A
Instructed L2A

Literacy acquisition
Literacy in L1
Literacy in L2

REGRESSION

Temporary regression
Reduced performance of normal subjects due to noise, stress etc

Environmental attrition
Deactualization of L1
Deactualization of L2: Naturalistic L2 / Instructed L2

Pathological attrition
Dementia: Monolingual / Bilingual dementia
Aphasia: Monolingual / Bilingual asphasia

Old age related attrition
Attrition of L1
Attrition of L2

of progression and regression in language should cover. We will
start with the individual level, since it is best understood. A
taxonomy of the major types of progression and regression at that
level are shown in Table 1.1. Here, at the individual level,
progression is identical to language acquisition (and development),

while regression covers attrition and loss. In addition to the familiar division between first language acquisition and second language acquisition, we might want to view the more or less simultaneous acquisition of two languages as a special type of progression, which is referred to as bilingual first language acquisition. The most extensive research on language acquisition has been concerned with what Gleason refers to as 'typical' L1A, and this type of progression has often been treated as the prototype against which all other types of language acquisition can be compared. With respect to bilingual first language acquisition, balanced BL1A which is most similar to typical L1A has been regarded as the normal case, in spite of the fact, as mentioned with reference to Schlyter's chapter, that unbalanced BL1A is as common or perhaps even more common. With respect to second language acquisition, instructed L2A has often been re-garded as less 'natural' than naturalistic L2A, which like L1A does not involve instruction. There is also a growing literature on various forms of atypical L1A – by learners such as deaf or blind children, mentally retarded or autistic children – which shed light on the existence of various linguistic subsystems, as Berko Gleason shows in her contribution. The acquisition of oral proficiency in the first language does not typically involve instruction. Reading and writing and related skills are, however, acquired through teaching. This is one of the primary reasons for regarding *literacy acquisition* as a specific type of language acquisition. Another reason is that, contrary to the acquisition of oral proficiency, the acquisition of literacy is not universal.

Turning now to regression, *temporary regression* can occur in normal subjects due to impoverished input (e.g. noise) or cognitive overload. Kilborn (1991) has shown how noise manipulation of stimuli presented to normal subjects can result in processing difficulties which are similar in certain respects to aphasic disturban-ces. Most studies of regression, however, have been concerned with more lasting, but not necessarily permanent, disturbances, which indicate a reduction of the underlying knowledge or processing ability (or both). We will use *attrition* as the general term for all types of non-temporary regression, since the most commonly used alternative term 'loss' seems to imply irreversibility. Attrition, then, covers a continuum from mild access problems (in particular word finding) to partial forgetting and complete loss of a language. *Pathological attrition* covers all types of aphasic disturbances and also more severe changes due to ageing, such as dementia. Regression can also result from reduced use of a language. Since this in general is combined with a change of environment (in a broad sense), we propose *environmental attrition* as a general term for such cases. Except for young children, such attrition seems to be a rather slow and reversible process. Deactualization due to lack of use of L1 can be experienced by immigrants, as in the cases treated in Boyd's and Major's contributions. With respect to the deactualization of L2, it is reasonable to make a major distinction between naturalistic and an instructed L2 similar to what was done for acquisition, even if further subdivisions are possible such as foreign language attrition (deactualization of an instructed L2 in an L1 environment), which is already an established area in its own right (see Weltens, 1987, for a review). Research over the last two decades or so has shown that, on average, even though there is large individual variation, language changes that can be characterized as attrition take place in elderly adults' L1 (Obler and Albert, 1985; Kemper, 1988) and L2 (Pietilä, 1989). We call this *old age related attrition*.

At the societal level, the general picture still resembles a mosaic where most of the pieces are missing. What should be regarded as progression or regression is also more problematic at this level. The spread of one language often implies the contraction and perhaps ultimate death of one or more other languages, at least in the long run. One scientist's language spread is another's glottophagy. There are a number of partly overlapping perspectives, which can be regarded as concerned primarily with progression or regression. The most important ones are tentatively presented in Table 1.2. *Language spread* (Cooper, 1982) takes the progressing language as the point of departure, while *language maintenance and language shift* (Fishman, 1972) is concerned on the other hand with the threatened or

Table 1.2. *Some types of progression and regression at the societal level*

PROGRESSION
Language spread
Pidginization and Creolization ('Language birth')
Planned progression: Language planning
REGRESSION
Language maintenance and language shift
Language decay and Language death
Decreolization, Dialect levelling

regressing language. Central within these perspectives are the communicative functions and usage patterns of a language. Cooper defines language spread as 'an increase, over time, in the proportion of a communication network that adopts a given language or language variety for a given communicative function' (1982:6). Important types of communicative functions are used for between- and within-group purposes and for horizontal versus vertical integration. Within Cooper's perspective, linguistic form is treated at a global level such as different varieties of a spreading language or the relatedness between the spreading language and the original language(s). What happens to the language structure is treated in depth within two other perspectives, which can also be compared to one another in a similar way. The first one, *pidginization* and *creolization* can be regarded as progressive functional expansion and structural elaboration from incipient lingua francas to full-blown first languages. This perspective is the motivation behind a term such as *language birth* (Foley, 1988). The other, contrasting perspective is *language decay* and *language death*. Structural changes induced by language contact are often quite dramatic in both progression and regression. One of the earliest and most conspicuous types of such change is borrowing, which, however, as mentioned in relation to Boyd's contribution, has a dual nature. In a language maintenance situation, borrowing often fills lexical gaps and it is motivated to talk about *borrowing as enrichment*. In a language shift situation, on the other hand, traditional words are being replaced by words from the encroaching language which motivates the expression *borrowing as interference*. (See Thomason and Kaufman, 1988, for a more general treatment of contact-induced change from such perspectives.)

The processes discussed this far can be characterized as naturalistic changes. However, progression, at least, can also be the result of planned intervention or *language planning* (e.g. Ferguson, 1983), which partly represents the equivalent of literacy acquisition at the individual level. *Status planning* is concerned with the functional allocation of languages and involves such matters as the status as an official language, medium of instruction, and vehicle of mass communication, while the planning of changes in the structure of language varieties is referred to as *corpus planning*, which can involve the introduction of a writing system, standardization and elaboration (e.g. the creation of technical and other specialized vocabulary). Related, even if not quite parallel, are *decreolization* and *dialect levelling*, which involves the convergence and ultimate disappearance of a creole or dialect as the result of influence from a dominating standard variety.

CONCLUSION

What we have been eager to stress in this introductory chapter is that linguistic progression and regression occur in response to specific social conditions, and are simultaneously determined by constraints on human biology. The linguistic or structural manifestations of these processes, therefore, are obviously part and parcel of such framing. We hope that this volume will contribute to making a good case for a view that sees progression and regression as different reflections of parallel types of processes, although the similarities are not always immediate and clear cut. Considering the amount and quality of research that is presently available on progression and regression, and, indeed, on the parallels between the two – as demonstrated in this volume – we believe that future theoretical models of linguistic dynamism cannot neglect any of the components of the ecology of language.

It is also useful to consider the topic of language progression and regression in its variety of manifestations from a more practical point of view. In the present situation of intense international communication, both in physical and verbal terms, and of immense political changes affecting the linguistic scene, language progression and regression are the stuff of ideologies and central concerns in the exercise of political agendas of states. The current political and economic changes in Europe, for example, have made the issue of language teaching more central than ever. In the former Soviet Union, where a multitude of languages will acquire new functions, for example as official languages, we can expect to see increased activities in language planning, involving standardization of these languages. Language regression, similarly, is a central issue for governments throughout the world that have to consider the situation of minority languages and how best to support the maintenance of these languages. Language obsolescence is, of course, a widespread phenomenon, although for various reasons, the disappearance of small languages has not been very salient in the global context until recently. If we take the European Community as an example again, we can see that the various linguistic minorities make up considerable proportions of the populations in the EC countries. EC's Bureau for Lesser Used Languages is an example of how the language progression/regression issue gains a political importance in the developments the world is currently experiencing. We can only hope that a theoretical understanding of progression and regression can help in the solving of practical questions of this nature.

REFERENCES

Andersen, R. W. (1982), Determining the linguistic attributes of language attrition. In Lambert, R. D., and Freed, B. F. (eds.), *The loss of language skills*. Rowley, Mass.: Newbury House.

Bates, E., Wulfeck, B. and MacWhinney, B. (1991), Cross-linguistic research in aphasia: An overview. *Brain and Language*, 41, 123–48.

Bever, T. G. (1970), The cognitive basis for language structures. In Hayes, J. R. (ed.), *Cognition and the development of language*. New York: Wiley.

Berman, R. A. (1984), Cross-linguistic first language perspectives on second language acquisition research. In: Andersen, R. W. (ed.), *Second languages. A cross-linguistic perspective*. Rowley, Mass.: Newbury House.

Bickerton, D. (1975), *Dynamics of a creole system*. Cambridge: Cambridge University Press.

(1990), *Language and species*. Chicago: University of Chicago Press.

Canale, M. and Swain, M. (1980), Theoretical bases of communicative approaches to second language teaching and testing. *Applied Linguistics*, 1, 1–47.

Caramazza, A. and Zurif, E. B. (1978) (eds.), *Language acquisition and language breakdown. Parallels and divergencies*. Baltimore: The Johns Hopkins University Press.

Clahsen, H., Meisel, J. M. and Pienemann, M. (1983), *Deutsch als Zweitsprache. Der Spracherwerb ausländischer Arbeiter*. Tübingen: Gunter Narr.

Chomsky, N. (1981), *Lectures on government and binding*. Dordrecht: Foris.

Cooper, R. L. (1982), A framework for the study of language spread. In Cooper, R. L. (ed.), *Language spread. Studies in diffusion and social change*. Bloomington: Indiana University Press.

Dik, S. (1989), *The theory of functional grammar. Part I: The structure of the clause*. Dordrecht: Foris.

Dorian, N. C. (1981), *Language death: The life cycle of a Scottish Gaelic dialect*. Philadelphia: University of Pennsylvania Press.

Duranti, A. (1988), Intentions, language and social action in a Samoan context. *Journal of Pragmatics*, 12, 13–33.

Fishman, J. (1972), Language maintenance and language shift as a field of inquiry: revisited. In Dil, A. S. (ed.), *Language in sociocultural change*. Stanford: Stanford University Press.

Foley, W. A. (1988), Language birth: the process of pidginization and creolization. In Newmeyer, F. J. (ed.), *Linguistics: The Cam-*

bridge survey. IV. Language: The socio-cultural context. Cambridge: Cambridge University Press.

Foley, W. and Van Valin, R. (1984), *Functional syntax and universal grammar.* Cambridge: Cambridge University Press.

Gal, S. (1979), *Language shift: Social determinants of linguistic change in bilingual Austria.* New York: Academic Press.

Gleason, J. Berko (1978), The acquisition and dissolution of the English inflectional system. In Caramazza and Zurif (eds.), *Language acquisition and language breakdown.*

Greenberg, J. H. (1991), Typology/universals and second language acquisition. In Huebner and Ferguson (eds.), *Crosscurrents in second language acquisition and linguistic theories.*

Givón, T. (1984, 1990), *Syntax. A functional–typological introduction.* I (1984), II (1990). Amsterdam: John Benjamins.

Harley, B., Allen, P., Cummins, J. and Swain, M. (1990) (eds.), *The development of second language proficiency.* Cambridge: Cambridge University Press.

Haugen, E. (1972), The ecology of language. In Dil, A. S. (ed.), *The ecology of language.* Stanford: Stanford University Press.

Hill, J. H. and Hill, K. C. (1986), *Speaking Mexicano.* Tucson: University of Arizona Press.

Huebner, T. and Ferguson, C. A. (1991) (eds.), *Crosscurrents in second language acquisition and linguistic theories.* Amsterdam: John Benjamins.

Hyltenstam, K. and Obler, L. K. (1989) (eds.), *Bilingualism across the lifespan. Aspects of acquisition, maturity, and loss.* Cambridge: Cambridge University Press.

Jakobson, R. (1941), *Kindersprache, Aphasie und allgemeine Lautgesetze.* Uppsala: Almqvist and Wiksell.

(1968) *Child language, aphasia and phonological universals.* The Hague: Mouton.

Jordens, P., de Bot, K. and Trapman, H. (1989), Linguistic aspects of regression in German case marking. *Studies in Second language Acquisition,* 11, 179–204.

Kellerman, E. and Sharwood Smith, M. A. (1986), (eds.), *Crosslinguistic influence in second language acquisition.* Oxford: Oxford University Press.

Kemper, S. (1988), Geriatric psycholinguistics: syntactic limitations of oral and written language. In Light, L. L. and Burke, D. M. (eds.), *Language, memory, and ageing*. Cambridge: Cambridge University Press.

Kilborn, K. (1991), Selective impairment of grammatical morphology due to induced stress in normal listeners: implications for aphasia. *Brain and Language*, 41, 275–88.

Kulick, D. (1992), *Language shift and cultural reproduction: socialization, syncretism and self in a Papua New Guinean village*. Cambridge: Cambridge University Press.

Labov, W. (1969), Contraction, deletion, and inherent variability of the English copula. *Language*, 45, 715–62.

Long, M. H. (1990), Maturational constraints on language development. *Studies in Second Language Acquisition*, 12, 251–85.

Malmberg, B. (1967), *Structural linguistics and human communication*. 2nd edn. Berlin: Springer.

McLaughlin, B. (1987), *Theories of second-language learning*. London: Edward Arnold.

Meisel, J. (1990) (ed.), *Two first languages. Early grammatical development in bilingual children*. Dordrecht: Foris.

Menn, L. and Obler, L. K. (1990), Theoretical motivations for the cross-language study of agrammatism. In Menn, L. and Obler, L. K. (eds.), *Agrammatic aphasia. A cross-language narrative sourcebook*. Amsterdam: John Benjamins.

Obler, L. K. and Albert, M. L. (1985), Language skills across adulthood. In Birren, J. and Schaie, K. W. (eds.), *Handbook of the psychology of ageing*. New York: Van Nostrand Reinhold.

Ochs, E. (1988), *Culture and language development: language acquisition and language socialization in a Samoan village*. New York: Academic Press.

Ojeman, N. and Whitaker, G. K. (1978), The bilingual brain. *Archives of Neurology*, 35, 409–12.

Olshtain, E. (1989), Is second language attrition the reversal of second language acquisition? *Studies in Second Language Acquisition*, 11, 151–65.

Pietilä, P. (1989), *The English of Finnish-Americans with reference to social and psychological background factors and with special reference to age*. Turku: Turun Yliopisto.

Rickford, J. R. (1991), Variation theory: implicational scaling and critical age limits in models of linguistic variation, acquisition and change. In Huebner and Ferguson (eds.), *Crosscurrents in second language acquisition and linguistic theories*.

Sankoff, G. and Laberge, S. (1973), On the acquisition of native speakers by a language. In DeCamp, D. and Hancock, I. F. (eds.), *Pidgins and creoles. Current trends and perspectives*. Washington, D.C.: Georgetown University Press.

Schieffelin, B. B. (1990), *The give and take of everyday life. Language socialization of Kaluli children*. Cambridge: Cambridge University Press.

Schmidt, A. (1985), *Young people's Dyirbal. An example of language death from Australia*. Cambridge: Cambridge University Press.

Seliger, H. (1989), Deterioration and creativity in childhood bilingualism. In Hyltenstam and Obler (eds.), *Bilingualism across the lifespan*.

Sharwood, Smith, M. A. (1989), Crosslinguistic influence in language loss. In Hyltenstam and Obler (eds.), *Bilingualism across the lifespan*.

Silva-Corvalán, C. (1991), Cross-generational bilingualism: theoretical implications of language attrition. In Huebner and Ferguson (eds.), *Crosscurrents in second language acquisition and linguistic theories*.

Slobin, D. I. (1973), Cognitive prerequisites for the development of grammar. In: Ferguson, C. A. and Slobin, D. I. (eds.), *Studies of language development*. New York: Holt, Rinehart and Winston.

Slobin, D. I. (1985) (ed.), *The cross-linguistic study of language acquisition*. 2 vols. Hillsdale, N.J.: Lawrence Erlbaum.

Stroud, C. (1992), The problem of intention and meaning in code-switching. *Text*, 12, 127–55.

Tarone, E. (1988), *Variation in interlanguage*. London: Edward Arnold.

Thomason, S. G. and Kaufman, T. (1988), *Languages contact, creolization, and genetic linguistics*. Berkeley: University of California Press.

Walsh, T. M. and Diller, K. C. (1981), Neurolinguistic considerations on the optimum age for second language acquisition. In Diller, K. C. (ed.), *Individual differences and universals in language learning aptitude*. Rowley, Mass.: Newbury House.

Weltens, B. (1987), The attrition of foreign language skills: a literature review. *Applied Linguistics*, 8, 22–38.

Woolard, K. (1989), *Double talk: Bilingualism and the politics of ethnicity in Catalonia*. Palo Alto: Stanford University Press.

The Sociocultural Setting

2 · The role of pidgin and creole languages in language progression and regression

PETER MÜHLHÄUSLER

INTRODUCTION

On surveying the literature on the social role of pidgins and creoles, one finds surprisingly little information about their place in the decline, progression, and disappearance of other languages. Let me expand upon this:

It is widely acknowledged that pidgins can temporarily push back indigenous languages on plantations where recruits from many different parts of the world have come together. Thus, on the sugar plantations of Queensland, Melanesians from diverse linguistic backgrounds used Kanaka English rather than their first language for a few years. However, on their return home, they resumed speaking their old vernacular. Reinecke (1937: 121) called pidgin development 'the result of temporary cultural isolation'.

Of course, there are many other documented instances of permanent displacement of populations. The many million Africans who were taken to the plantations of North and South America all ended up speaking a creolized version of the plantation language and losing their home language. Not necessarily in the first generation, but over several generations, this seems an inevitable process. This did not mean, however, that those who were left behind in Africa did not continue speaking their own vernacular. Forced immigration may have weakened some vernaculars, but it did not usually result in their death or replacement. My concern in this paper is a special subclass of pidgins and creoles, i.e. those that were employed in

39

horizontal communication in established multilingual areas, particularly Melanesia, Australia, and West Africa. Their effect differs from
that of pidgins and creoles in new societies such as Hawai'i or
Mauritius.

The standard view of pidgins therefore, has been that of Reinecke
(1964: 537), of a 'supplementary tongue for special forms of
intercourse', i.e. languages supplementary to existing languages.
Their main function was seen as being to enable communication
between insiders and outsiders (for instance 'visiting' Europeans
and indigenous populations) or between indigenous groups brought
into closer contact by a colonial administration, contact described as
the result of 'pax germanica, pax britanica', and so forth, rather than
taking over the functions of local languages.

One can understand this view in the light of the history of pidgin
and creole studies, the first large sociological analysis of pidgin and
creoles being carried out by Reinecke (1937) and Schultze (1933). At
that time, the main function of pidgins was indeed supplementary.
However, it was already becoming clear in the 1930s (for instance in
Reinecke 1937:124) that pidgins were very much a phenomenon
associated with linguistic and cultural transition.

In short, the trade jargons are the product of frontier trade conditions, and
as the frontier disappears and is replaced by closer association of the groups
concerned, a more adequate linguistic accommodation is made. And the
present Western régime, with its rapid transportation and its schools, is
rapidly restricting frontier conditions.

When considering individual languages such as Tok Pisin we find
that even in the more recent past, this dynamic character, its
progression, and its becoming complementary rather than supplementary to existing languages has often been under-emphasized.
Literal (1975:158ff.) portrays the relationship between local vernaculars, Tok Pisin, other lingua francas and English in Papua New
Guinea as being largely complementary (Figure 2.1).

Similarly, Sankoff (1972:3ff.) provides an atemporal (synchronic)

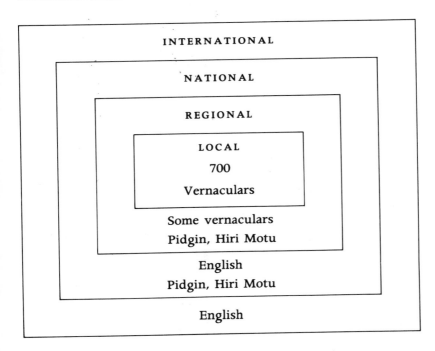

Figure 2.1   Communicative networks of Papua New Guinea

account of the components of speech events that determine the choice of Yabem (the mission lingua franca), Tok Pisin or Buang among Buang speakers (Figure 2.2).

In this chapter I shall try to replace the many static accounts of the linguistic and social role of pidgins and creoles with a dynamic one that considers their role, both in replacing other languages and in facilitating their own eventual replacement by lexically related standard languages.

NEW METAPHORS FOR LANGUAGE DEATH

What I would like to do in this section is to move away from the observation of individual cases at a particular point in time and present a more comprehensive, top-down, and pantemporal picture of pidgin and creole progression and vernacular regression. Before

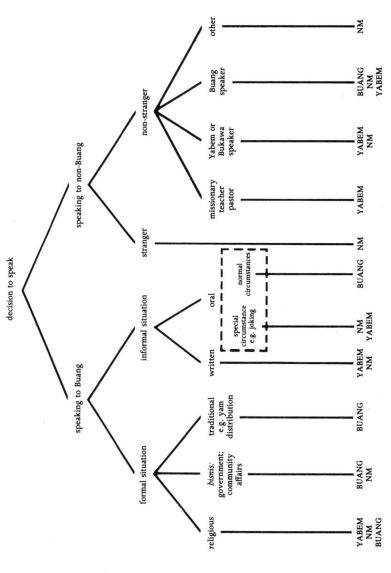

Figure 2.2 Factors constraining code choice for the Buang (NM = Neo-Melanesian; Neo-Melanesian = Tok Pisin or New Guinea Pidgin English)

doing this, a word of warning: it would be grossly simplistic, for example, to seek simple causal connections between pidgin progression and vernacular disappearance. Both processes are integral parts of a much more general phenomenon of modernization and Westernization. Pidgins came into being for social reasons rather than social change as a consequence of pidginization. Nevertheless, once brought into being, pidgins can assume their own dynamics and, in some instances, indeed fulfil a causal role in language shift.

In dealing with the question in the proposed manner it is necessary to create a language appropriate to the perceived subject matter. Reinecke, (1937:124) in his analysis, favoured metaphors derived from the wave view of linguistic innovation. For instance, he compared the spread of pidgins to the effect of the pebble thrown into a pond:

Pidgin English and *petit nègre* in West Africa seem to be expanding, but they are the outer ripples of European speech; hard on them follow adequate, school-taught knowledge of English and French.

I would like to adopt a more complex metaphor, that of the linguistic ecology pioneered by writers such as Haugen (1964), and more recently by the contributors to Enninger (1983). I have found a consideration of European imperialism particularly helpful as an additional perspective and have been most impressed by recent attempts (particularly Crosby, 1986), to combine ecological and historical considerations into a model of ecological imperialism that studies the biological consequences of European expansion.

In using the metaphor of ecology to discuss language ecology, it is necessary to search for more specific secondary metaphors to gain an understanding of more restricted ecological changes. In addressing the topic of how pidgins and creoles have affected the overall linguistic ecology in the Pacific I have chosen the metaphor of a weed. A weed in the technical sense is (Crosby, 1986:149):

any plant that spreads rapidly and outcompetes others in disturbed soil.

Analogous to this definition, we can regard pidgins as languages that spread rapidly and outcompete others in a disturbed language ecology. This view of pidgins really shifts the focus from their being supplementary, auxiliary interlanguages to their being both consequences and agents of linguistic change. It focuses our attention upon the rarely mentioned weakening of the indigenous language ecology before their spread, and provides reasons for their dynamic character.

The second characteristic of weeds is their being transitional between indigenous species and imported cultural species. They occupy the interim period during which the old equilibrium has not as yet been replaced by a new one. They are both transitional and indices of larger transitions.

A third characteristic of weeds concerns their spread. They spread together with introduced feral animals and introduced diseases which move much faster than the boundaries of European colonization, thus, there are many reports of pidgins having spread to areas not yet contacted by Europeans, reports that parallel the spread of introduced germs and weeds.

The weed metaphor may also be useful in the context of the history of value judgements. More or less right from their inception, pidgins were held in very low esteem by the speakers of metropolitan source languages, and their eradication and replacement by the standard languages was at times compared to weeding out. When going back to the original definition of weeds, we note that 'weed' is a subjective cultural definition; attitudes to them, and their economic usefulness, may shift. Thus Crosby (1986:149f.) points out:

Weeds are not always unlikeable. Rye and oats were once weeds; now they are crop plants. Can a crop plant shift the other way and become a weed? Yes. Amaranth and crabgrass were prehistoric crops in America and Europe, respectively, both treasured for their nourishing seeds, and now both have been demoted to weeds. (Amaranth may be on its way back to respectability in the crop category again.) Are weeds, while in that category, always a bane and torment to everyone? No, indeed. Bermuda grass, one of the most irrepressible tropical weeds, was extolled a century and a half ago as a stabilizer of levees along the lower Mississippi at the same

time that farmers not far from that river were calling it devilgrass. Weeds
are not good or bad; they are simply the plants that tempt the botanist to use
such anthropomorphic terms as aggressive and opportunistic.

Though occasional cases where pidgins creolize and become
self-sufficient cultural languages, Bislama in the New Hebrides and
Sranan in Surinam being examples, such cases do not invalidate the
more general rule that pidgins tend to be transitional phenomena.
From the perspective of the indigenous vernaculars, the outcome is
the same, thus both pidgin and creole development, either as the
outcome or as the intermediate stage, lead to the weakening of their
role and their eventual regression. There is a further interesting
parallel between the introduction of weeds into the Neo-Europes
and European colonies and the introduction of pidgins. Both
processes were unintentional, and in both instances entities that had
developed in other environments were transplanted into a new one.
Pidgin languages thrived in frontier situations in spite of negative
attitudes on the part of Government and missions. Pidgin languages
are also very rarely separate developments, but rather local
adaptations of solutions to cross-linguistic communication developed elsewhere. Thus, New South Wales Aboriginal Pidgin may
have been influenced by the forms of speech used in communication
between speakers of Gaelic and English in Ireland. Much of Tok
Pisin's development took place in Samoa, while Solomon Pijin and
Bislama can trace their origins to Queensland.

Those who have commented on the weakening and disappearance
of vernaculars have typically concentrated on disappearance among
first language users. Much less has been written about the perhaps
equally important decline in vernacular multilingualism. What
Laycock (1979:87) says for Papua New Guinea:

It is apparent that the [non-traditional] *lingue franche* are making progress at
the expense of multilingualism in vernacular languages

can also be observed in many other regions. This phenomenon
(particularly the disappearance of indigenous pidgins) will be dealt

with in a separate section, as will be the transitional character of any multilingualism involving languages of differential power. The picture I would like to present is one of several overlapping phases of progression and regression, leading in the long term to monolingualism in one of the small number of privileged world languages.

The dynamic changes I have tried to portray would seem to be pointers to the future language ecology of hitherto highly multilingual areas. What I have presented is a hypothesis about a very complex phenomenon. Predicting in the human sciences is a very hazardous business, and the development anticipated here may well turn out to move in a different direction. Still, I feel that what I have presented here is supported by enough evidence to deserve to be taken seriously.

THE ROLE OF TOK PISIN IN LANGUAGE SHIFT IN PAPUA NEW GUINEA. A CASE STUDY

The case of Tok Pisin is particularly interesting for a number of reasons.

1 In the short period of about 100 years we can observe a large variety of different types of language progression and regression involving Tok Pisin.
2 The external history of this language and its competitors is very well documented.
3 Some of the linguistic consequences of Tok Pisin's progression are also well documented.
4 Many of the processes accompanying the expansion of Tok Pisin appear to have close parallels in other languages.

I have been accused of having promoted Tok Pisin and the sociolinguistic situation in Papua New Guinea to that of a canonical case (Keesing, 1987). My reason for doing this is that we continue to have better documentation for Tok Pisin and Papua New Guinea than for any other comparable situation. I have tried, over the last five years, to accumulate data for other pidgins and creoles in Asia and the Pacific, but thus far have been unable to come up with anything approximating what I have been able to get for Tok Pisin, and I am not optimistic that I will ever be able to do so. Consequently, I see no reason not to continue using evidence from Tok Pisin in Papua New Guinea as the basis of generalizations on language change and pidgin progression and regression.

It is rare that one gets proper data on the progression of any pidgin language. For the most part we have to rely on estimates and indirect evidence. Not so for Tok Pisin. Right from the start people have written down observations that are extremely valuable in helping us to understand the external fate of this language. In 1880 there were probably no more than a few hundred Papua New Guineans who had any knowledge of a pidginized type of English. However, with the commercial exploitation of New Britain and the Duke of York Islands from 1873 onwards, a dramatic change appears to have taken place. Hersheim, a trader at Matupit observed that in 1873 (reported in Schuchardt, 1979:20):

No native understood any European languages. Now (this would be 1883) everybody and particularly children spoke that English in question. I had often heard natives using this jargon and talking about the white men and their matters.

By 1890 the number of speakers of Pidgin English in New Guinea was probably around 1,000, located mainly around Rabaul. From there the languages gradually spread to the new Government, mission, and plantation settlements on the New Guinea mainland coast. The number of Tok Pisin speakers during German times grew from a few hundred to about 15,000, more than a third of whom had acquired the language in German Samoa. Assuming that the population of German New Guinea was around half a million, this acounts for 3% of the total population.

After the First World War, under Australian administration, the plantation labour system was greatly expanded and new industries, in particular gold mining, were added to the existing ones. Between 1930 and 1938 the number of black contract labourers rose from around 25,000 to 40,000. Basing his estimates on labour contracts made between 1921 and 1936, Reid (1943:284) comes to the conclusion that around 85,000 additional workers had acquired Tok Pisin, bringing the total number of speakers to about 100,000, or $\frac{1}{5}$th of the population. Because of the disruption during the Second World War, this number probably did not increase significantly, although after 1945 another spectacular rise in the number of speakers occurred. By 1966 when the first census was carried out, 530,000, or 36% of the population of Papua New Guinea, spoke Tok Pisin. By the time of the next census in 1971 this had risen to 700,000, or 44% of the population. As the census questions have since been changed, no comparable data are available for the 1980 census, so it is estimated that in excess of 50% of the entire population of Papua New Guinea, including Papua which was formerly not a Tok Pisin speaking part of the new nation, now speaks Tok Pisin. Represented in graphic form, this development looks like an S curve.

Before we leave such quantative considerations, let us consider briefly the rise of English. The picture here is similar to the spread of Tok Pisin, but occurs much later. Again, we seem to be dealing with an S curve beginning with a very slow increase in English speakers between 1920 and 1945, a more significant increase up to 1970, and a rather more accelerated one ever since. The statistical information is revealing.

Between 1966 and 1971 the percentage of the total population 10 years and older who could speak English rose from 13.3% to 20.4%. The increase of English is most significant in areas that have been under colonial control longest, such as East New Britain (40%) Central District of Papua (45%) or Manus (46%). On the other hand, in the most recently opened up area of the southern highlands only 7.1% of the population claimed to be able to speak English. In one district, the Milne Bay district, more speakers use English as their lingua franca than either Tok Pisin or Hiri Motu.

When we look at the increase in those who speak English only, we

Table 2.1. *Population ten years of age and over speaking each of the official languages in 1966 and 1971 (expatriates excluded).*

Language		Male	Female	Total	Percentage of total population 10 years and older
English	1971	211,651	112,115	323,766	20.40
	1966	130,429	62,908	193,337	13.3
Tok Pisin	1971	469,770	237,355	707,125	44.5
	1966	369,855	161,835	531,690	36.5
Hiri Motu	1971	103,016	47,636	150,652	9.5
	1966	86,665	31,910	118,575	8.3

Note:
Data abstracted from Papua New Guinea census bulletins.
(*Source:* Sankoff, 1980:123)

can observe a very moderate change from 2.67% to 3.13% of the population between 1966 and 1971. If we consider those who had acquired English in addition to skills in other languages then the picture looks very different. There is a spectacular increase of 7.1% in only five years, which is shown to be even more spectacular if we contrast the total of 193,000 in 1966 with that of 323,000 in 1971, i.e. 66% more speakers in five years. In 1971 the national percentage of those who knew English had reached 20%. It is interesting to compare such data with the knowledge of Tok Pisin. There seems to be some correlation between an increase in English and a decrease in Tok Pisin skills, though it is not a very clear one.

Now to turn to regression. Data on this matter are virtually impossible to come by, and we have to rely on more or less indirect and anecdotal evidence. A reasonably reliable basis would seem to be the figures for speakers who did not know any of the three major lingua francas, Tok Pisin, Hiri Motu or English. That figure dropped from 55% in 1966 to 47% in 1971. As regards the non-statistical information on regression, we can concentrate on three areas:

1   The replacement of both indigenous pidgins and indigenous forms of multilingualism.
2   Structural changes in local vernaculars
3   Functional narrowing and replacement of vernaculars

As little was known about multilingualism in Papua New Guinea until very recently, not much has been written about the topic. In the pioneer studies of Salisbury (1965), Laycock (1979), and Sankoff (1972, 1980), this topic is not properly addressed. The descriptions given are either purely synchronic, or else regard bilingualism involving Tok Pisin as simply additional to traditional forms of bi- and multilingualism. More recently there are a growing number of reports emphasizing the replacive character of Tok Pisin. Thurston (1987: 6–27), in speaking about multilingualism in Western New Britain, remarks:

As stated earlier, because Tok Pisin is so useful as a lingua franca, it has supplanted the former high degree of multilingualism that was characteristic of the area. Though this trend is cause for concern among some of the elders, most young people, particularly in the coastal villages which speak a language of the Sisasi group, are content to speak only their own vernacular and Tok Pisin. On the other hand, it is notable that in those villages where language death is occurring, it is not Tok Pisin that is replacing the moribund language, but another vernacular. Though people recognise the utility of Tok Pisin as a lingua franca, they nevertheles maintain that it is important for everyone to have a distinct vernacular as a badge of group membership. There are small hints that a new pattern may be developing in which the children of people who live outside the village are unable to speak the vernacular. Though this may mark the beginning of a new linguistic era, at present, the phenomenon is still insignificant.

We can appeal to our weed metaphor for an explanation. Traditional forms of multilingualism were destroyed by a number of factors introduced by the colonial administration, including:

1   The replacement of local trade and trade contacts by mission and private traders.

2 Resettlement of populations.
3 The non-use of local languages by the powerful representatives of the missions and government.
4 New contacts between language groups that had not been in contact previously.

As the ground was cleared for the introduction of a new form of interlanguage contact, namely Pidgin English, very much the same also occurred in the case of local pidgins and lingua francas. Greenberg (1965:52) remarked, on the spread of lingua franca, 'the only thing that is likely to arrest its spread is a rival lingua franca'. This observation needs to be elaborated in several regards.

1 A distinction should be made between static and spreading lingua franchas.
2 Lingua francas can contract without being replaced by other lingua francas. A well-known example being the decline of Latin and the Greek *koiné*.
3 Hopping rather than even spread is a characteristic of expansion.

When we look at the precolonial situation in Australia and the Pacific area in detail, it becomes abundantly clear that the often commented on linguistic compartmentalization, the proverbial Tower of Babel, was only in the eyes of the European beholder. In actual fact there was a great deal of cultural exchange, intermarriage, and trade as well as quite a few linguistic solutions to the problems of intercultural communication. I have written about these in detail elsewhere (Mühlhäusler, 1987). Among them there were a number of pidgins and lingua francas whose existence is only gradually becoming better known. Thus, in the Sepik area of New Guinea there were dozens of small inter-village pidgins of the type described by Foley (1986) and Williams (1990). Whereas, in other parts of Papua New Guinea, there were interregional trade languages such as Dobu and the Motu trade language described by Dutton (1983). The fate of these local pidgins is interesting.

1   Virtually all the inter-village pidgins have been replaced by Tok
    Pisin within a couple of generations. Pidgins that were func-
    tional in the 1930s are now functionally dead.

2   Some of the traditional inter-regional lingua francas became
    administration or mission languages for a short period of time,
    thereby undergoing a considerable change in structural and
    functional character. Examples are Dobu, which was used in the
    Kula trading cycle of the Milne Bay Province, and Saua, that was
    used in the Maileu–East Papua–Aroma trade cycle, which both
    extended their geographical area as mission languages. Another
    example is simplified Motu which was adopted first as the
    language of the Police Force as Police Motu and later as the
    language of wider communication in Papua as Hiri Motu.

3   Both mission lingua franca and Hiri Motu have come under
    threat from Tok Pisin, their English-'based' competitor in the
    recent past. The case of Police/Hiri Motu is particularly
    interesting. When considering the census figures of 1966 and
    1971 we can see that, whereas the percentage of the population
    speaking Hiri Motu has grown from 8.3% to 9.5%, the jump in
    the knowledge of Tok Pisin is much greater (36.5% to 44.5%).
    More significantly in the case of Hiri Motu, its knowledge in its
    original homeland around Port Moresby declined from 78% to
    71%, whilst that of Tok Pisin grew from 55% to 61%. The
    increase in the knowledge of Hiri Motu thus is restricted to less
    modernized outlying rural areas, whilst in the town it is Tok
    Pisin that is beginning to prevail.

Sankoff (1976:293) remarks:

Hiri Motu, however, is very closely identified with Motu, with Port
Moresby, and with Papua generally. In the minds of the majority of
non-Hiri Motu speakers, 'Hiri Motu' and 'Motu' are indistinguishable,
being the Tok Ples of the Motu people of the Port Moresby area. This close
regional identification detracts somewhat from one of the usual advantages
of a lingua franca which is no-one's native language – its neutrality.

For most New Guineans, Tok Pisin is such a neutral language. Being, in the view of most New Guineans, no-one's Tok Ples, it is thereby in the public domain and can be learned with impunity. That is, learning it will not succeed in improving the fortunes of some other (its native) group. On the other hand to many Papuans, this is exactly the connotation of Tok Pisin, which, as the lingua franca of New Guinea, is viewed as a threat to the use and status of Hiri Motu. Despite the antagonism of Papuan nationalists, however, Tok Pisin appears to be making definite inroads. Though many of the 25,630 Tok Pisin speakers in the Central District are New Guinean migrants resident in the Port Moresby area, an increasing number of Papuans are also learning Tok Pisin. On a visit to Port Moresby in 1973, I was surprised to note the increase in the use of Tok Pisin by Papuans conversing with New Guineans, a situation which had changed considerably since my last visit in 1971.

Similarly, most mission lingua francas such as Yabem, Kâte or Dobu are gradually being replaced by English or Tok Pisin. Let us briefly return to the three points I raised earlier in this section. We find that:

1   Static inter-village pidgins tend to be the first victims of replacement by more dynamic, inter-regional pidgins. Thus, the diversity of solutions to problems of intercultural communication gives way to a uniform solution triggered and promoted by European presence.

2   Brief mention should be made of the pre-existing lingua francas that were replaced by non-lingua francas. This phenomenon can be found wherever colonial boundaries cut across pre-existing trade or bisect the currency of a lingua franca. Fijians and Tongans, who used to communicate in Pidgin Fijian, today communicate in English. Villages situated on either side of the Indonesian/Papua New Guinea border have a greatly reduced ability to intercommunicate following the demise of New Guinea Malay in Papua New Guinea, and their cousins, the North Australian Aborigines, no longer communicate by means of a Maccassanese Pidgin that was in use a long time before the arrival of the first white settlers in Australia's far north. Again,

Aborigines there now intercommunicate via English or an English derived creole.

3   The data that we have briefly considered here suggest that the replacement of lingua francas tends to hop from large urban centres to other urban centres. Thus, Tok Pisin did not gradually expand its sphere of influence across the Papua New Guinea border but established itself in Port Moresby from where it spread to other areas of Papua.

The replacement of local small pidgins by big pidgins is only one episode in the process that leads to the replacement of traditional vernaculars by a metropolitan language. It is neither a necessary nor a sufficient explanation for the process I am analysing here, but rather one of its numerous symptoms. This is not to say that the loss of smaller pidgins and lingua francas is not a sad one. A study of these varieties affords many insights into the diversity of solutions to problems of intercultural communication. A particularly sad phenomenon is the replacement of egalitarian solutions with non-egalitarian ones, i.e. half-way pidgins between two villages by pidgins reflecting the lexicon of the economically and politically dominant group. Another loss, which I cannot go into detail about here, is that we associate many of the traditional pidgins with highly ritualized exchange cycles, extraordinary encounters rather than day to day transaction. The many ritual interpersonal and emotional experiences accompanying the use of the traditional trade pidgins have been replaced by a monodimensional transactional form of communication. As big fish eat little fish, so would big pidgins seem to have a tendency to eat the little ones.

I will now turn to the effect of the progression of Tok Pisin on traditional languages. Again, this topic is one that has received attention only in the very recent past, and one which is documented in a rather patchy manner.

An interesting study by a native speaker of Abu, a language spoken in the Sepik area of Papua New Guinea is that of Neketeli (1984). Neketeli documents the very rapid change from the traditional situation where all villagers spoke Abu and were competent in one or more nearby languages, to one where Tok Pisin has become the primary language of the village. A similar situation has been reported for the more remote village of Gapun by Kulick and Stroud (1987).

Other cases are reported in Dutton and Mühlhäusler (1989). The total replacement of small languages by Tok Pisin appears to be an ever-growing trend. Larger, more viable languages, on the other hand, tend to borrow extensively from Tok Pisin, both lexically and grammatically, and may be replaced more gradually. What is remarkable about this process is its very recent nature: vernaculars that seemed viable only 20 years ago are now in danger of disappearing. The functional roles of vernaculars and Tok Pisin have been reversed. Use of Tok Pisin is normal in most contexts, whilst that of the traditional languages is supplementary for specially marked circumstances.

The case studies considered thus far have been concerned with the rural situation. I shall now consider processes of language progression and regression in urban contexts.

THE ROLE OF URBANISATION

Those who have applied the metaphor of Babel to the multilingual situation in Australia and the Pacific have tended to ignore the fact that Babel was an urban and not a rural phenomenon. The traditional rural areas as we have seen, did not, in fact, suffer from any great communication problems, and where problems arose, a diversity of solutions to them developed. It was the development of non-traditional settlements, particularly urban ones, that brought into being the Babylonic dimensions of linguistic diversity. Modern urban multilingualism in the Pacific and elsewhere in the Third World is qualitatively totally different from traditional rural multilingualism.

Jourdan (1985:126) has characterized the shift from traditional vernaculars to Solomon Pijin in urban Honiara as follows:

In this tower of Babel-like town, many people are married into another language group, and have neighbours, friends and colleagues belonging to other language groups. Pijin is not only the cement of this culture in the making, it is as well the cement of many families, when parents do not share the same language and raise their children through and with it. Pijin is then, for these families the only medium that will ensure communication, both at the generation level (between siblings for instance) and at the cross-generation level (between parents and children, or grand-parents and grand-children). Multilingualism is a natural environment for Pijin usage to which nobody pays attention; it is taken for granted and, so to speak, never considered to be an impairment to social interaction, probably because Pijin is there to fall back on in case of sociolinguistic difficulties.

Very much the same characterization could be given for the larger towns of Papua New Guinea, Vanuatu, and indeed most of the Third World: Town Bemba in Zambia, Pidgin Sango in Bangui (Central African Republic), and so forth. In most coastal towns of north-western Australia, Aborigines from different language backgrounds have settled either for a single Aboriginal lingua franca or for Creole or Black English. The reason rural people move to the towns of the Third World are many. The desire to give up their vernacular in most cases is not one of them. But it seems an almost inevitable consequence. It neither had a language ecology to support it, nor do urban dwellers in the Third World countries have the material resources to cultivate their small languages in an urban environment.

Whereas the plantation system in the Pacific was:

a   temporary, restricted to five or six years of indenture
b   restricted to the male population only (Tok Pisin used to be called Tok Boi)

and hence ideal for the development of a stable working pidgin, urbanisation is a much more permanent phenomenon, and, more importantly, involves members of all generations and both sexes. The solution to these urban communication problems thus has to be a permanent one. The cases surveyed suggest that the first stage is creolization (in the wider sense of adopting a pidgin as a primary language, such as Pijin in Honiara, Tok Pisin in Lae, or Sango in Banjui), followed by a gradual shift to a metropolitan language in most instances. The reasons for this are easy to see: educational facilities in the metropolitan languages, jobs that require their knowledge and social access to the 'target' are most developed in the big towns. Thus, with regard to urban Honiara, Jourdan (1985:234f.) writes:

As more and more people are marrying into different language groups, and as more and more of the social life in town is being conducted in Pijin, one might imagine that will come a time, *mutatis mutandis*, when most of the children being born in town will be raised in Pijin only. Through school they will acquire the superstrate language as they do today; they might or might not use it in their adult lives. If education (under its present form) becomes more widely available to the Honiara children, more and more will be exposed to English from an early age. This is already taking place, but as there is no English speaking Melanesian community as such and as English plays no practically significant role in Honiara beyond its status bearing function (to the exclusion of the expatriate community and some members of the elite), the children do not master it even after six years of primary education, during which they are taught English two hours a day, five days a week. The result of this is that children who are now brought up in Pijin only acquire English as a second language, whereas the old and more generalized pattern in town used to be and still is: vernacular as a first language and Pijin as a second language. Loosening of ties with the village and loosening of ties with the wantok system will only contribute to reinforce the pattern.

The latest (1980) census data for Papua New Guinea are similarly suggestive of such a development. English is the third largest language used at home or in the markets in urban areas, with Tok Pisin a clear first and Motu a poor second. The dramatic increase of English can best be seen in the comparison of the 1966 and 1971 figures of language use in urban centres quoted from Sankoff (1980: 126).

Table 2.2. *Language distribution in the several largest towns of Papua New Guinea. Note that percentages are calculated on the population over ten years old, whereas the total population includes all age groups.*

Major towns of Papua New Guinea	% of Tok Pisin speakers		% of English speakers		% of Hiri Motu speakers		Total population (expatriates excluded)	
	1966	1971	1966	1971	1966	1971	1966	1971
Port Moresby (Central)	54.9	61.0	64.4	64.6	77.8	71.1	31.983	59.563
Lae (Morobe)	94.2	95.1	36.1	43.8	14.8	12.9	13.341	32.076
Rabaul (East New Britain)	97.1	94.0	37.4	51.4	11.9	7.3	6.925	22.292
Madang (Madang)	96.2	97.4	30.8	47.4	8.0	7.2	7.398	14.696
Wewak (East Sepik)	96.2	97.0	27.8	52.8	5.2	6.9	7.967	13.837
Goroka (E. Highlands)	89.6	85.9	31.6	41.4	14.3	9.1	3.890	10.509
Mt Hagen (W. Highlands)	82.7	76.8	27.0	37.3	13.5	7.1	2.764	9.257
Total							74.268	162.23

Source: (Sankoff 1980:126).

Similar tendencies have been reported from other countries where the transition from vernacular to a metropolitan language is in evidence. Thus, with regard to the Central African Republic, Samarin (1986:380) reports:

We would like to know what role the French language has today. It is acquired by many more Centralafricans than in the colonial period. Education has been made available to a much higher percentage of the young people, more of them go on to secondary schools, and a very significant number get training at the university level in French. There are several working in their own country with professional doctorates. In 1962, by contrast, only twelve young people had passed their *premier baccalauréat* and sat the *deuxième* ... The large number of French-speaking young people are projecting a new identity. Living mostly in the urban centers, they are at some remove from their ancestral rural centers of focus. Identifying themselves with the whole body of *fonctionnaires* in the country, they are *engaged* in a new kind of life, only part of which is political.

In Zambia, the urban educated classes speak creolized Town Bemba and English, with a similar distribution of linguistic knowledge being reported for English and Swahili in urban Kenya. The African data just mentioned would seem to be important enough to warrant some additional remarks on language progression and regression of African pidgins and creoles.

LANGUAGE PROGRESSION AND REGRESSION IN SOME AFRICAN COUNTRIES

This chapter is concerned primarily with the linguistic situation in Melanesia. However, I would like to make a few suggestions as to how evidence from Africa might be relevant to a better understanding of the Melanesian situation. The reasons why African data are of such relevance include:

i   Having been colonized and decolonized earlier than the Pacific area, African states often anticipate developments that are only just emerging in Melanesia.
ii Policy decisions in African countries are often replicated in Melanesia. Whilst it is not possible to do full justice to the many observations on the African situation, a few generalizations seem possible.
iii Like Melanesia, but unlike North America or Australia, most parts of Africa were not permanently settled by Europeans.

We are in the fortunate position of having at our disposal extensive accounts of the sociolinguistic role of pidgins and lingua francas in Africa, notably in the work of Bernd Heine (e.g. 1970). A brief perusal of the African sources reveals some interesting parallelism with Melanesia, particularly:

1   During this century there has also been a drastic reduction in

both the numbers of vernaculars and the numbers of monolingual or primary speakers of vernaculars.

2   A large number of pidgins and lingua francas in use around the turn of the century has been replaced by a much smaller number of pidgins, creoles, and metropolitan languages.

3   Urbanization and regional mobility are the main focus favouring the adoption of 'modern' lingua francas and the abandonment of vernaculars.

4   The small number of indigenous pidgins such as Linguala, Swahili and Sango have developed into official and national languages in a number of countries.

5   The adoption of African based lingua francas by and large did little to arrest the progress of metropolitan languages such as English and French.

The first clear statement of the last development can be found in Reinecke's Ph.D. thesis (1937:116). Reinecke is rather dismissive of what he refers to as (p. 115) 'the romantic regard for the tribal vernaculars' and predicts that in the wake of emerging regionalism and nationalism they will be replaced by a creole:

In addition to an undeveloped folk sentiment for a dialect, a true spirit of nationalism (or at least strong regionalism) should be superadded, some of the creole dialects or trade pidgins might become true national languages.

This will very likely happen to the Lingala-Bangala, if the present direction of development is continued. A congeries of small tribal languages is the next best thing to a *tabula rasa* for the establishment of a national lingua franca, no matter how unorthodox its origin.

Reinecke's predictions are borne out by the observations of Heine (1970). Lingala, which had developed from a pre-colonial regional lingua franca into a colonial working pidgin used by the (p. 74) 'crews of river steamers and the soldiers and the labourers at the stations and the trading posts' had become the most widely used lingua franca by the time Belgian control over the Congo ended in 1960. It became one of the principal vehicles of African nationalism and the language of urban Kantrasa and other big towns.

Heine (p. 76) comments on the fact that, in the towns, immigrants from rural areas switched to Lingala as their primary language after a few years of town life, that after ten years or so they began using Lingala with their children, and that (p. 77) 'the children borne in Kinshasa grew up with Lingala as their only language'.

As in other post-colonial societies, there is another trend of language shift. In the towns (p. 80) 'French is becoming a competitor of Lingala ... French is also spreading in the police force and amongst the soldiers and thereby penetrates into the domains of Lingala.'

In contrast, the importance of Lingala in the interior of the country is increasing. This is not the place to survey the excellent case studies that Heine presents in his survey. However, many of them support the more general point I would like to make: *that pidgins tend to prepare the way for the eventual imposition of metropolitan languages, by weakening and replacing smaller local vernaculars.* Whether or not we are dealing with pidgins derived from European languages such as Nigerian Pidgin English or so-called 'indigenous' pidgins such as Lingala makes little difference. Virtually all present day indigenous pidgins were triggered by European colonial activities and can lay little claim to being traditional or even 'indigenous'. A lot remains to be done by way of comparative work, for instance, an examination of the role of languages such as the Lingua Gerale of Brazil in the disappearance of Brazilian Indian languages, or the role of Red Indian pidgins in the regression of those languages. The conclusions I can offer therefore, will have to remain tentative.

CONCLUSIONS

In making predictions in the area of the social sciences, the problem of knowing, let alone controlling, all the parameters needed to do a proper job is an immense one. In 1937 (p. 116) Reinecke could write:

There is a bare possibility of Pidgin English becoming the medium of a unified regional or racial feeling in Melanesia-Papua before the true English is established firmly – a possibility more fascinating to speculate with than profitable to analyze.

In 1945 Höltker, addressing the same topic, suspected that the Second World War had brought an end to this possibility; on the eve of independence many writers on Tok Pisin predicted its total downfall. In 1985 Laycock was suggesting a different scenario: the survival of some major regional lingua francas and standard English and the gradual disappearance of Tok Pisin over the next decades.

I would also like to mention, in the context of declining regression, the numerous studies at the turn of the century that predicted the inevitable disappearance of the Melanesians as a race. Such predictions seemed indeed reasonable in the case of inhabitants of New Caledonia, for example, for the fifty years between French annexation in 1853 and 1903, when its Melanesian population declined from 50,000 to about 28,000, a figure which remained static until 1930 (Lyons, 1986:83). During this period very considerable damage was done to New Caledonia's linguistic ecology and the subsequent increase in the indigenous population to over 60,000 in 1980 did nothing to reverse the sociolinguistic decline. This suggests an important difference between the survival of populations and the survival of languages. Populations can grow in many socio-economic and cultural settings. They get transmitted biologically: perpetuating one's race can be a fairly easy thing. Languages depend (for their survival and transmission) on much more complex constellations of cultural factors. To account for such developments a simple weed metaphor is of course insufficient.

An important consideration is the relationship between different political, economic and technological systems and language size. The very small languages of Melanesia, for instance, were ideally matched to the egalitarian, democratic organization of small populations. There were no powerful empires, no great asymmetries in the strengths of most populations, and no great technological differences. Linguistic diversity, as pointed out by Laycock (1982), was both an index of, and a means to, maintaining cultural and political diversity.

Power differentials within those small societies were often closely correlated with multilingual abilities; being proficient in a number of languages was the sign of being a big man (compare Salisbury, 1965; Sankoff, 1980). The diversity of local languages was a liability, rather than an asset, for a colonial administration that sought to establish larger homogeneous administrative areas, such as councils, districts, and provinces. Languages employed by the colonizers, in particular the colonial pidgins, were the only ones suitable for this purpose. Consequently, traditional multilingualism became much reduced in its relevance as a sign of power, and competence in the colonial pidgin became the new index of status and social mobility. Young men who had worked in the white men's towns and plantations and acquired a knowledge of such a pidgin could rise to powerful positions in their home villages without traditional linguistic skills. Just as modern administrative units are not tolerant of linguistic diversity, the media that were introduced by the colonizers were equally intolerant. Whilst oral societies can accommodate any number of linguistic variations, literacy, and particularly the printed word, is economical only in a standardized form in at least medium-sized languages. Radio broadcasts can be produced only for relatively large language groups (less than 10% of the languages of Papua New Guinea are represented on broadcast), whilst film, television, video, and computers are practical only for a single international language. In the case of the Pacific, Australia, and much of Africa, this language is English.

Another way of interpreting the processes discussed here is to regard them as a progression from contextualized to context-free forms of linguistic communication. The traditional languages of Australia and Melanesia are highly context sensitive. Many Australian languages, for instance, are used only in certain locations, reserved to purely defined subgroups and similarly, many languages in Melanesia are used only in esoteric functions, whilst others are reserved for exoteric communication with outsiders. Special sublanguages for hunting, food collecting, and other ritual purposes abound. Similarly, we find much of the social structure of small societies linguistically encoded, kinship and pronoun systems, for example, status in lexical choice and so forth. As a contrast, pidgin languages such as Tok Pisin quickly developed out of a contextualized language (for use with external cultures on the plantations among men only) into languages that were neutral. Not only were they neutral with regard to their user groups, they were also neutral as regards encoding social distinctions. There are no compulsory markers of social differences, no gender indications with nouns or pronouns, no special vocabulary for ritual purposes. It was often pointed out in the past that pidgin languages provided the neutral ground on which Europeans and indigenous populations could communicate. Meanwhile, as we are approaching a post-modern era, this neutral ground has expanded dramatically.

As yet, English and other metropolitan languages are contextually marked. They are the sign of urbanity and sophistication. However, their neutral character as languages of international communication and technology is also in evidence, and with larger numbers attending schools it is likely that these metropolitan languages will become contextually neutral. It is interesting in this context to remind oneself of what Samarin wrote about the knowledge of French in the Central African Republic (1986:2):

We must not, of course, limit ourselves to the young in talking about people with this identity. All of the educated must be included. It is important to observe that they see themselves as different from the majority of Central Africans, whom they identify as *paysans*. It would appear that today peasants represent the marked social category for the educated, whereas in the colonial era the marked category for both whites and blacks was the *évolué*. This change is bound to have its linguistic effects.

We have thus reached a state of affairs where speaking vernacular is the marked case, and speaking the metropolitan language is becoming increasingly unmarked, as where speaking a second language or creolized pidgin is the unmarked case.

The account I have given here is a dynamic one. Beginning with the erosion and destruction of the indigenous language ecology, the penetration of non-static pidgins and creoles into the empty space, and their eventual replacement by cultural metropolitan languages. The role of pidgins in this process seems a crucial one. They are adopted in preference to indigenous solutions to linguistic and interlinguistic communication because they have many perceived advantages: greater geographic coverage, prestige neutrality, agents of modernization, means of acquiring European type cargo such as wealth and education, and so on. Whilst the colonial pidgins were indeed ideal means of modernization and nation building in the initial phase, their suitability to a transition to Western technological modes of living is much smaller. The cost of developing and maintaining even well-established creoles and semi creoles such as Haitian Creole or Afrikaans in the face of rapid internationalization and post-modern life styles is large. Whilst the social stigma of pidgins and creoles no longer exists, this in itself is not sufficient reason for their survival. Their ultimate role may be that of providing substratum features for shallow differences in the variants of large metropolitan languages such as World English or World French.

REFERENCES

Crosby, A. W. (1986), *Ecological imperialism*. Cambridge: Cambridge University Press.
Dutton, T. E. (1983), *Hiri Motu: Iena Sivarai*. Port Moresby: University of Papua New Guinea Press.
Dutton, T. E. and Mühlhäusler, P. (1989), Language decline in Papua New Guinea. Paper presented at the Annual Meeting of the Linguistic Society of Papua New Guinea.
Enninger, W. and Haynes, L. M. (1984), *Studies in language ecology*. Wiesbaden: Steiner.
Foley, W. A. (1986), Language Birth: the process of pidginization and creolization. MS. Australia National University.

Greenberg, J. H. (1965), Urbanism, migration and language. In H. Kuper (ed.) *Urbanization and migration in West Africa*. Berkley and Los Angeles: University of California Press.

Haugen, E. (1972), Language ecology. In Dil, A. S. (ed.) *The ecology of language*. Essays by Einar Haugen. Stanford, Stanford University Press.

Heine, B. (1970), *Status and use of African lingua francas*. Munich: Weltforum.

Höltker, G. (1945), Das Pidgin-English als sprachliches Missionsmittel in Neuguinea. *Neue Zeitschrift für Missionswissenschaft*, 1, 44–63.

Jourdan, C. (1985), *Sapos Yumi Mitim Yumi: urbanization and creolization in the Solomon Islands*. Ph.D. thesis, Australian National University.

Keesing, R. M. (1988), *Melanesian Pidgin and the oceanic substrate*. Stanford: Stanford University Press.

Kulick, D. and Stroud, C. (1987), Christianity, cargo and ideas of self: patterns of literacy in a Papua New Guinea Village. *Man*, 25, 286–304.

Laycock, D. C. (1979), Multilingualism: linguistic boundaries and unsolved problems in Papua New Guinea. In Wurm, S. A. (ed.) *New Guinea and neighbouring areas: a sociolinguistic laboratory*, pp. 81–94. The Hague: Mouton.

(1982), Melanesian linguistic diversity. In May, R. J. and Nelson, H. (eds.) *Melanesia beyond diversity*, pp. 263–47. Canberra: Research School of Pacific Studies.

(1985), The Future of Tok Pisin. In Wurm, S. A., and Mühlhäusler, P. (eds.), *Handbook of Tok Pisin*, c. 70, pp. 665–8. Canberra, Pacific Linguistics.

Literal, R. (1975), A Proposal for the use of Pidgin in Papua New Guinea's Educational system. In McElhanon, K. A. (ed.), *Tok Pisin i Go We?* pp. 155–64. Port Moresby: Dept. Languages UPNG.

Lyons, M. (1986), *The totem and the tricolour*. Kensington: New South Wales University Press.

Mühlhäusler, P. (1988), Intercultural communication in the Pacific area in precolonial days. Paper delivered at the Fifth International Conference in Austronesian Linguistics, Auckland.

Neketeli, O. M. (1984), Language planning in Papua New Guinea: A nationalist viewpoint. *Yagl-Ambu*, 11: 1, 1–24.

Reed, S. W. (1943), *The making of modern New Guinea*. Philadelphia: American Philosophical Society.

Reinecke, J. F. (1937), *Marginal languages*. Ph.D. thesis, Yale University.

(1964), Trade jargons and creole dialects as marginal languages. In Hymes, D. (ed.), *Language in culture and society*, pp. 534–42. New York: Harper and Row.

Salisbury, R. F. (1972), Notes on bilingualism and linguistic change in New Guinea. In J. B. Pride and J. Holmes (eds.), *Sociolinguistics*, pp. 52–64

Samarin, W. J. (1986), French and Sango in the Central African Republic. *Anthropological Linguistics*, 28, 379–87.

(1986), Sango of the Central African Republic. Paper presented at the International Group for Study of Language Standardization, York.

Sankoff, G. (1972), Language use in multilingual societies: some alternative approaches. In Pride, J. B. and Holmes, J. *Sociolinguistics*, pp. 33–51. Harmondsworth: Penguin.

(1976), Political power and linguistic inequality in Papua New Guinea. In O'Barr, W. M. and O' Barr, F. (eds.), *Language and politics*, pp. 283–310. The Hague: Mouton.

(1980), *The social life of language*, Philadelphia: University of Pennsylvania Press.

Schuchardt, H. (1979), *The ethnography of variation, selected writings on pidgins and creoles*. Translated by T. L. Markey. Ann Arbour, Mich.: Karoma.

Schultze, E. (1933), Sklaven und Dienersprachen. *Sociologus*, 9, 378–418.

Thurston, W. R. (1987), Processes of change in the languages of north western New Britain. *Pacific Linguistics*. 13–99.

Williams, J. P. (1990), A preliminary survey of Papuan-based pidgins. Paper presented at the 3rd International Conference on Pidgins and Creoles in Melanesia, Lae.

3 · Structure and practice in language shift

JANE H. HILL

INTRODUCTION

During the last 20 years anthropologists have focused their attention on how human cultures are produced and reproduced through the 'interested action of historic agents' (Sahlins, 1985), often glossed as 'practice.'[1] They have shown that neither the mental 'rules' explored by structuralist scholarship, nor the 'hegemonic forces' proposed by students of political economy, seem to be determinant on these practices.

Students of language death have shown that two sets of phenomena that we might describe as 'structural' are frequently linked: the profound subordination of a minority population at the political-economic level, and a set of linguistic phenomena including attrition of form through rule loss and simplification until productivity is lost, and functional attrition until what was once the dominant language of the group is no longer acquired by children. A central problem is: How can political economy articulate with language? No matter how powerful the agents of oppression, we have no evidence that they can enforce practices like 'freeze derivation in the fifth position of verbal prefixation' or 'shift from ergative to nominative-accusative marking of arguments' or 'use honorific marking only in direct address'. Except in especially pathological situations (boarding-schools, for instance), we have no evidence of direct regulation of functional allocation of the minority language either: The agents of oppression may say 'do not speak your language any more', but they certainly do not say, 'restrict use of your language to the recitation of myths', or 'use it only to tease other people your own age'. Yet such outcomes are familiar in the contexts that we study. Recent anthropological theory suggests that the articulations that yield them must be produced at least partly through the practices of the minority population. I intend to explore what these might be, and how they might be constrained.

Following Bakhtin ((1929) 1973; (1935) 1980), I propose to begin by suspending my linguist's presuppositions about the inventory of systems: the 'languages' in some community of interest. Instead, we should assume that speakers confront 'heteroglossia', which is not necessarily sorted out into a clearly delineated system of codes. Such codes emerge and are reproduced (or not) through what speakers do as they create and deploy a set of interpretive and productive practices that are 'interested', exploiting the available symbolic materials to try to create those conjunctions of forms and meanings that may be most advantageous. While these practices will lead to the definition of 'languages' (that may or may not correspond well with a linguist's definition), in Bakhtinian terms speakers are constructing 'voices': ways of speaking that represent particular interested positions and identities.[2]

Negotiations over code differentiation and code contextualization – over what will 'count' as a 'language' in some context in some community – occur in all speech communities. But, in the contexts of subordination of the community and pressure on its boundaries that occur in language obsolescence, these negotiations may take on exaggerated importance, contextualizing and reproducing basic lines of cleavage. In these cases, attention to code differentiation and contextualization can initiate feedback loops that yield the rapid 'tip' in language death recently documented by Dorian (1986) and Mohan and Zador (1986). Such negotiations, thus, seem to be a site where the structures of oppression and the structures of language are articulated through local practice.

THREE CASE STUDIES

In order to exemplify how negotiations over code definition and contextualization might help us understand the articulation between political economy and language structure and use seen in language shift, I will discuss three cases: Dyirbal, based on the work of Annette Schmidt (1985); Mexicano (Nahuatl), based on my own work (cf. Hill and Hill, 1986), and Wasco, using especially the work of Robert Moore (1988). The three cases are culturally and geographically diverse, and illustrate three different levels of language moribundity. Yet certain common threads can be seen in the practices through which people in all three communities attempt to shape heteroglossia into 'voices' that will constitute a community identity and permit engagement with others on the most favourable possible grounds. In all cases, these practices have encouraged both formal and functional attrition of the indigenous language.

Code defining and contextualizing in the Dyirbal of Jambun, Queensland

The community of Jambun in Queensland, Australia was founded in 1977 when a grant of land from the Australian government permitted surviving members of two Dyirbal dialect groups to form a separate aboriginal community, rather than living scattered as labourers on the ranches of local whites. Jambun Dyirbal have become increasingly isolated from the surrounding white Australian community. Whites perceive this isolation as due to 'shyness' and 'shame'. Aboriginals (including people who lived among whites until 1977) describe themselves as avoiding contact with them because they 'aren't used to' interacting with white people.

Schmidt (1985) recognizes four codes at Jambun. These include traditional Dyirbal (TD), young people's Dyirbal (YD), Jambun English, and Standard Australian English (SAE). Both within the community, and between the community and the surrounding white population, there is dispute about which codes 'count' for which purposes, and about what type of speaking 'counts' as a particular labelled code.

Dyirbal is stigmatized by most whites as a primitive and childish 'lingo'. Schmidt reports that Dyirbal continues to be strongly discouraged by white speakers; while the use of isolated words on the playground is apparently now tolerated by teachers, Dyirbal speakers feel that whites dislike Dyirbal, and many employers do not permit its use. One man characterized how this situation is experienced:

> talking Guwal [everyday Dyirbal] to a waybala [white man] – it's like singing an' you're ashamed of your voice. (Schmidt, 1985:18)

By the time of Schmidt's field work, Jambun English was the dominant language at Jambun, used both within the aboriginal community and to assert aboriginal identity with outsiders. Jambun English is differentiated from SAE by a number of creole elements, but especially by the use of Dyirbal lexical items, which are exploited by aboriginal school children to tease white children on the playground. Local whites see Jambun English not as a language system, but as a collection of mistakes and distortions of SAE. Jambun people, though, see it as the appropriate English for use within the community. Many can speak SAE, but they regard it as 'flash' and restrict its use to contacts with officialdom.

The domains in which Dyirbal is used are increasingly restricted, and Schmidt (1985) resports differentiation within Dyirbal into traditional (TD) and 'young' (YD) varieties. TD is spoken only by people over 35 years of age, who use it with one another and to younger speakers. YD, the focus of Schmidt's work, is used by young speakers only in 'vertical' communication with TD speakers with whom YD speakers have special relationships, and internally to close-knit networks of intimates. Schmidt studied two such net-works among young women, the 'Rock-and-Rollers' and the 'Buckaroos'.

Negotiation over what counts as Dyirbal takes place between older and younger speakers, and among younger speakers as well.

Speakers do not recognize YD as a separate language; they consider it a broken-down variant of Dyirbal. TD speakers constantly correct young speakers for deviations from TD grammar and, especially, for using English words while speaking Dyirbal. They accuse young speakers of being 'half English,' 'all mixed up,' and 'wrong.' Young speakers evaluate their own usage as inadequate, and say that they prefer to speak Jambun English to elders in order to avoid the constant corrections. Elders concur that young people mainly speak English to them.

This attention to correctness by Dyirbal elders continues in a new context an old tradition of purism. Traditionally, purism was deployed in the construction of dialect boundaries (and almost certainly in negotiation over access to and ownership of 'country'). Thus Dixon (1972) reported that, in the 1960s, speakers emphasized differences among its various dialects and held strong opinions about their own dialect as 'correct'.

Schmidt reports that YD usage is a valued marker of membership in networks of intimates. However, even in this context there is negotiation about what will 'count' as Dyirbal. Schmidt heard Buckaroos censure each other for using too much English. The dynamic of usage internal to network of young speakers is especially interesting. Schmidt found that elicitation and testing of a 'careful' register from members of the Buckaroos showed considerable differences in Dyirbal proficiency among them. However, an analysis of speech used within the in-group revealed that they accommodated their Dyirbal to the speech of the least-proficient member; more precisely, Schmidt says, 'the norm of each in-group is similar to the careful Dyirbal style of the least-fluent member' (p. 146). This 'monitoring down' was quite self-conscious. Schmidt reports that when she began to use Dyirbal within the group, her traditional usage was censured as 'too flash'. Further, some of this accommodation was in the direction of using English words, the practice most condemned by TD speakers, and one which YD speakers themselves view negatively as well. Schmidt found that Buckaroos averaged 47.8% English words in speech within the in-group, with the highest percentage, 53%, reported precisely for the Buckaroo member whose Dyirbal Schmidt judged most proficient in careful speech.

Schmidt reports that Dyirbal parents no longer speak Dyirbal with their young children. She believes that this is mainly because parents want to be sure children are ready for school, but she cites speakers who seem to believe that Dyirbal is more appropriate for older children:

'we jus' want them to grow up a bit more, then they know what we talkin' about [when we teach them Dyirbal]'

'till he gets older, enough to understand . . .'   (Schmidt, 1985:25)

Such remarks suggest a refunctionalization of Dyirbal as not an everyday affair, but as a somewhat difficult 'heritage,' perhaps functionally equivalent in the local theory of learning a ritual tradition (as we will see below, Moore argues that Wasco has been refunctionalized along these lines). Brandt (1988) has reported similar attitudes about the 'difficulty' of indigenous languages in some Native American communities.

Code defining and contextualizing in the Mexicano of the Malinche region

Mexicano or Nahuatl, a Uto-Aztecan language, is spoken in towns in the Malinche Volcano region of the states of Puebla and Tlaxcala in central Mexico. Some of these towns date to the pre-conquest era, but most were probably founded in the seventeenth century as scattered rural populations were 'congregated' into planned communities by the Spanish colonial government. During the late 1940s and 1950s the development of the regional infrastructure encouraged many men to seek regular wage labour in factories, although, with the assistance of female relatives, they continue to practise maize cultivation, the traditional subsistence base in the region.

Code differentiation on the Malinche is an important issue.

Legítimo mexicano, a Mexicano without Spanish influence that community members don't believe exists in their area, is idealized. All speakers believe that their own Mexicano speech is imperfect, that it is 'mixed' because of Spanish loans. This view is shared by local Spanish speakers, who believe that Malinche Mexicano is an uncivilized jargon. The Nahuatl valued publicly in Mexico is a folklorized set of fixed usages, such as place names and personal names that are believed to date from before the conquest: Spanish-speaking 'experts' can publicly exhibit the ability to parse and interpret these, but the knowledge of native speakers of the language has almost no value in the local linguistic market.

Mexicano on the Malinche until quite recently was universally used between community members, including bilinguals. However, a coding continuum within Mexicano was constructed through adjusting the proportion of Spanish words and expressions. Relatively hispanized versions of Mexicano constituted a 'power code', used especially by senior men in public interactional arenas like politics and religion. This coding variety, which clearly 'counts' as Mexicano in its context, can exhibit an extremely high frequency of Spanish loans, often ranging around 50% of lexical items in running speech. This coding variety is recognizable in legal documents from the mid-seventeenth century. A relatively unhispanized Mexicano was a 'solidarity code', used by younger people and women, and associated with domestic activities, agriculture, and the like. Bilinguals, who were mainly men, used Spanish itself only outside the community.

By the time my field work began in 1974, men[3] who drew most of their income from factory work (the 'workers') had largely replaced the Mexicano 'power code' with Spanish itself, restricting Mexicano to occasions for solidarity. Their Mexicano usage was different in many ways from that of men who were dominantly cultivators. For instance, workers exhibited sharply decreased frequencies of complex sentences in narrative (Hill, 1989a). Yet at the same time they were more 'individualistic' than cultivators, as revealed through their choice of involvement strategies in narrative (Hill,

1989b), and because they were less likely than cultivators to speak of themselves in the first person as 'we' (Hill, 1988). 'Workers' exhibited a sharp retreat in the use of the complex system of 'honorifics' through which community-internal distance and deference were signalled; the honorific system had virtually disappeared from their speech in its referential function. Even in face-to-face address where such usages were required, as with ritual kin and parents, these men increasingly used Spanish. This did not go unnoticed. While the cultivators in the Malinche region seemed unable to describe exactly what was going on, we heard frequently from them that people no longer spoke with 'respect'.

The workers countered diffuse charges of 'lack of respect' with exhibitions of purism. Certain grammatical and phonological *loci* that had been defined as sites where 'Mexicano' versus 'Spanish' could be marked were highly monitored in their speech. Cultivators did not exhibit such monitoring, and seemed to be unaware of worker shibboleths. While all speakers believed that Mexicano was 'mixed up', only worker purists made negative comments about the speech of specific others. They corrected other people in their presence, and enjoyed giving 'vocabulary tests' on shibboleth items to innocent victims. The interviews that we conducted during our fieldwork, which sometimes involved groups of people, provided these speakers with a context for exhibiting purism, and we heard considerable negotiation over whether a particular grammatical usage or a Nahuatlized Spanish loan word could 'count' as Mexicano. Their critical remarks were often focused on the speech of the young, which tended to exhibit a great deal of Spanish influence that people did not view in a positive light. Our teenaged interviewer, who came from a conservative community where purism was still in its infancy, was several times challenged by middle-aged purists in other towns. But it seems very likely that the objection to hispanisms on the part of purist 'workers' had a covert target, the local political dominance of elderly cultivators, who used highly hispanized Mexicano within the ritual system through which community resources are distributed.

There is no register of Malinche Spanish that is comparable to Jambun English, or to the 'Indian English' of the Warm Springs Reservation to be discussed below. There are Mexicano-dominant bilinguals whose Spanish exhibits heavy interference (Hill, 1987a), and this usage is strongly stigmatized and often parodied by urbanites. But Spanish-dominant bilinguals do not emulate any of its features. Young people even avoid rusticisms such as *ansi* (for *así*) 'thus' and *muncho* (for *mucho*) 'much' that occur in the speech of their elders. Most Malinche Spanish, while slightly accented and 'rustic', exhibits no Mexicano lexical material beyond what is normally present in the rural Spanish of central Mexico. While Malinche people trade in Spanish-speaking cities almost daily, their needs seldom require them to interact with speakers of cultivated varieties of Spanish. Still, they feel that their Spanish is inadequate; they say that they make *cuatros*, dumb mistakes. The few Malinche people I know who do move in middle-class circles are quite self-conscious about their inadequacies in Spanish, in spite of their high levels of education.

In spite of ambivalence about the meanings of Spanish and insecurity in its use, at the time of my fieldwork in the late 1970s speakers in many communities had shifted almost entirely to the use of Spanish. On the Malinche the most 'shifted' towns restricted Mexicano to two quite distinct realms.[4] Mexicano prayers and blessings were felt to be appropriate at certain ceremonies, and elderly men served as *huehuetlahtohqueh* 'old speakers', who came forward on these occasions to utter the appropriate formulae in a highly hispanized register. At the opposite pole, young men challenged apparent outsiders with Mexicano obscenities; this might happen as one walked on the road leading to the town, or bought a drink in a *cantina*. We heard often that the main reason it was important to know Mexicano was to be able to reply to these challenges appropriately. Even in the most conservative and 'unshifted' town, young people who regarded themselves as relatively sophisticated preferred to use Spanish with one another. They did use Mexicano in teasing, joking, and in 'field chatter' while playing football. Thus the register of the most casual intimacy among them was marked by code-switching into Mexicano in which outsiders cannot participate, and such teasing and joking does occur in the workplace where Spanish monolinguals are present.[5]

Even in the most conservative community many young parents, including mothers whose Spanish is quite marginal, use a great deal of Spanish in speaking to pre-school children. While children attend schools in their communities through the sixth grade, primary schooling is entirely in Spanish, and only a handful of teachers know any Mexicano. Those who do still discourage its use in school. Children in most Malinche communities arrive in kindergarten speaking mainly Spanish; in the only community where many children are still Mexicano-dominant, school officials pressure parents strongly to change family practices.

Code defining and contextualizing in the Wasco-Wishram of Warm Springs, Oregon

Wasco (sometimes called Kiksht) is a Chinookan language spoken on the Warm Springs Reservation in Oregon. The upper Chinookan groups were among the great trading peoples of the Columbia River; the Wasco controlled the flow of goods around the Celilo Falls at The Dalles. However, they failed to maintain their importance in white-dominated economic systems that emerged in the nineteenth century, and, in 1858, their population decimated by epidemics, they accepted relocation away from the river to the Warm Springs Reservation. They shifted rapidly to a mixed economy that included farming and ranching, lumbering, and wage labour. Warm Springs is a relatively prosperous reservation community, with some indigenous industry, especially in lumbering and service to tourists. However, people there are emphatically disadvantaged economically compared to surrounding whites. Philips (1983) states that Warm Springs Indians interact very little with local whites. Schoolchildren segregate themselves on the playground, and adult interaction between Indian and Anglo groups is restricted to commercial transactions and official occasions. Warm Springs people feel that local whites are very racist.

'Indian English' is the dominant language of the Warm Springs community. Philips (personal communication) reports that young people especially are under considerable pressure to avoid standard English in favour of this local variety. Not only is this code marked by locally distinctive phonological and syntactic features, but Philips (1983) has described it as very indigenous at the discourse level, including the use of silence, principles of topic continuity and turn-taking, and the interaction between speech and gaze. She believes that these differences in discourse management are part of the pattern of strong separation and mutual dislike between Indians and whites in the region. Yet apparently neither group considers their difficulties to be 'linguistic'; even schoolteachers don't single out language as the source of the problems Warm Springs children have in school, but instead talk about behaviours like 'not paying attention'.

Three indigenous American languages are spoken on the Warm Springs Reservation: Wasco,[6] spoken by survivors of Columbia River Chinookan groups, Sahaptin (a Plateau 'Penutian' language once spoken by hunting-and-gathering groups in the Warm Springs region), and Northern Paiute (a Uto-Aztecan language). Sahaptin is the most 'alive' of the indigenous languages, with a number of middle-aged speakers. While there has been extensive intermarriage among the groups on the reservation, and an increasing tendency for people to define themselves simply as 'Warm Springs' Indians (Philips, 1983), French (1961) found considerable attention to ethnic differentiation among the groups. Wascos were thought by all to be skilled economically, and they occupy the dominant positions in the business ventures of the Warm Springs Confederation. Yet French found that Wascos used Sahaptins as a 'reference group' for the construction of 'Indian' identity.

Moore (1988), working in the early 1980s, identified three groups of speakers among people who think of themselves as 'Wasco'. A group of people over 75 years of age use 'real Wasco', in certain restricted and elevated functions, especially the recitation of myths (usually with linguists or anthropologists present), but use English for everyday communication. A second group, comprised of people in their 50s, use what is called 'broken Wasco', mainly with children and pets, and very occasionally with their peers outside the home. There is, says Moore, 'a delicate pattern' of inter-generational avoidance, manifested linguistically in the fact that all generationally 'vertical' communication, to use Schmidt's term, is in English, and Moore describes no use of Wasco among people under the age of 50. Philips (1983) provides additional contextualization for this generational split: She observes that at Warm Springs one sees an exaggerated differentiation between 'verbal' elders and 'physical' youth, whose energies are directed towards skill in such athletic pursuits as bronc-riding and calf-roping, not toward verbal performance.

Moore's work is especially concerned with the indigenous characterization of 'broken Wasco', the local term for the usage of semi-speakers in their 50s. Moore finds their speech to be differentiated from 'real Wasco' in ways that develop upon indigenous tendencies. Historical study has shown that Wasco has often developed new lexicon through the lexicalization of combinations of derivational prefixes (called 'postpositions' in the verb construction) and verb roots to form new stems. Speakers of 'broken Wasco' exaggerate this tendency, even using fully inflected verbs as the basis for further (sometimes redundant) inflection. In order to avoid points of difficulty in manipulating the head-marked oblique arguments, they construct dependent-marked formations with Wasco independent pronouns prefixed to Sahaptin postpositions, which are not part of the verb. Note that Sahaptin borrowings are chosen, rather than English prepositions, because Sahaptin is 'Indian'. (In the 1950s, French (1961) noted borrowing of English into Wasco, with English roots inflected with Wasco affixes, but Moore does not note such usages.)

Moore found Wasco speakers to be very articulate about what they believe to be the problem with 'broken Wasco': that people 'forget' lexical items, especially verb roots and stems. In fact, the lexical impoverishment of 'broken Wasco' is an indirect result of an over-generalized application of existing derivational principles; people often, in Moore's view, 'know' a verb, but can use it only in a frozen form with a new layer of inflection. The strategies they use are conservative ones; Moore gives examples of apparent nonce forms uttered by semi-speakers that turned out to occur also in field notes elicited from fluent speakers 30 years ago. Yet Wasco speakers seem unaware that these usages have any past, and are also unconscious of the fact that the real confusion is about derivation, not about 'remembering' roots.

Moore argues that the focus on 'forgetting words' is part of a larger and very conservative linguistic ideology among Wasco speakers. In a well-known study, Hymes (1966) exemplified this with an analysis of three important speech events from the pre-reservation period: the singing of the song given by a guardian spirit, the uttering of a name, and the recitation of myths. The song could be sung only on a person's death-bed. Names were uttered only at the moment when they were given as titles during an elaborate ceremony, and used to address their bearers only by those specially authorized in the ceremony to do so. Myths were recited only in the winter. All of these events were 'world-creating', constituting significant aspects of the Wasco–Wishram universe. Names were unanalyzable and were not even meaningful in a referential sense: To call them out in bestowal placed their bearer with other bearers in a hierarchy of titles that constituted the real social order, through which living people simply passed. Silverstein (1984) has described two locutionary verbs found in myths, which encode a fundamental Chinookan distinction between serious, world-creating speech uttered by authorized personnel ($-u-\sqrt{xam}$), and expressive verbal self-display ($-k+kim$). Philips (1983) has suggested that the pattern is manifested even in English by a certain extreme deliberateness of speech and avoidance of idle chatter and speculation.

Moore gives numerous examples which suggest that the entire

Wasco language and all words considered to be part of it have been elevated into the realm of the most contextually restricted and powerful traditional speech acts. To speak Wasco today constitutes a presentation of 'valuables', and is hedged round with restrictions. Thus, his consultants have stated that they cannot utter words for birds or animals unless the referent is present; should this happen, they will suddenly 'remember' and call out the term, which has become like a 'name' or title. Speakers frequently frame elicited expressions with 'Grandma would say', adopting an ideology that permitted out-of-context speech when it was 'quoted' from the name ceremony or the myth cycle (in the case of the guardian spirit song, 'quotation' took the form of wearing paraphernalia associated with the spirit at the winter dances). Moore observes that 'all words that are 'rememberable' according to the local ideology are by definition words that implicate a deceased relative as speaker or addressor' (Moore, 1988:466). Moore finds that the inability of younger speakers to manage Wasco derivational morphology elevates words to an unanalyzable 'name-like' character. One of Moore's consultants has decided that all connected Wasco speech is like myth recitation, and during elicitation sessions in the summer often refuses to utter more than single words, since to say a sentence might 'bring on bad weather'. (Moore attends to the possibility that fieldwork sessions may be constructed by speakers as an opportunity for the display of 'valuables,' more than for the exploration of grammar.) Moore concludes that this 'objectualization' of words as things of value 'poses a set of cultural problems for contemporary survivors and descendants who have some command of the language, and forms the cultural background to the linguistic 'production problems' of today's speakers and semi-speakers' (Moore, 1988:467).

DISCUSSION

An important theme in common between all three speech communities, Jambun, Malinche, and Warm Springs, is a deep anxiety about what we may loosely call 'boundaries', about how to construct some kind of identity where a community is seen as 'different', but where this difference is viewed by outsiders as merely pathological, rather than as having some recognized function in the larger scheme of things. In every case there is reason to be anxious about boundaries, even beyond the oppression of community members that is so obvious. Jambun is a new community, built out of fragments, including speakers of two dialects in a situation where dialect differences were important differentiators between local groups. The economic base of the community is precarious, and the new pattern of avoiding whites, which seems to date from the founding of Jambun, suggests something of the intensity of anxiety about autonomy and identity.

On the Malinche, the intricate minutiae of internal status differentiation among communities of peasant cultivators are radically challenged by the universal availability of wage labour, such that a man's well-being no longer rests in an obvious way in making common cause with his neighbours to assure that the human and sacred worlds are coherently aligned. A man's work for wages, in fact, may make it impossible for him to participate in this system, which may lead to the questioning of his identity from within the community. The fervent purism and egalitarianism of workers seem designed to ward off this sort of challenge. Further, it is likely that wage labour is, in the long run, a burden on the communities, since very low wages and minimal fringe benefits for workers constitute a case of 'superexploitation', where the costs of reproduction of the labour force are borne largely by the indigenous community itself, at the same time that the labour of its most productive members is turned to the benefit of outsiders.

French (1961) described the traditional Wasco as traders, open to interchange with all comers, relatively unconcerned about boundaries, and assimilating well to membership in the multi-ethnic Warm Springs Confederation. Yet he reports routines that seem to attest to a certain anxiety about 'being Wasco'. Wasco people would discuss a stereotyped continuum of 'civilization', with whites at one end, themselves in the middle, and Sahaptins at the most 'Indian' end, even when only a handful of people were 'pure Wasco' after generations of intermarriage. Wasco people were concerned to be recognized as people who made status distinctions, in contrast to the egalitarian Sahaptin, and nearly all Wasco would assert chiefly ancestry. The pattern reported by Moore, of displaying Wasco words as 'valuables', fits nicely into this routine. In summary, in all three communities boundaries and identities that were apparently at one time relatively unselfconscious and taken for granted have become the focus of anxiety and concern. This anxiety translates into an anxiety about the forms of talk that come to 'stand for' the fragile identity.

Dressler (1982) has also urged that we attend to the practices and feelings of speakers, and suggested that a significant moment in language death occurs when speakers convert the subordination of their community into an unfavourable evaluation of the language of the community. I believe Dressler's claim requires modification. First, as I have emphasized, the notion 'language of the community' must be seen as problematic. The Mexicano case is evidence of this: Stigmatization of Spanish loan words apparently begins only in the 1950s, when Van Zantwijk (1965) first documented purism in Central Mexico. Note that one of Dressler's 'markers' for impending language obsolescence is that the community stops giving indigenous names to its children. Every Mexicano child has been *José* or *María* since at least 1540. While certain nationalist intellectuals in the capital have given children Nahuatl names since the 1920s, only in the last 10 years have children's names become an issue on the Malinche. (In 1985, I was told the story of a young couple in the most conservative Malinche town who wanted to name their daughter 'Xochitl' (flower). The priest objected, so they waited until he was out of town and had an unwary substitute conduct the baptism.)

Second, I have shown that 'evaluation' of 'the language of the community' is not universally unfavourable, in spite of stigmatization by the dominant group. Indeed, in the three cases I have discussed, precisely the most moribund 'language of the community' – 'traditional Dyirbal', *legítimo mexicano*, 'real Wasco' – is viewed in a highly favourable light – paradoxically, a light so favourable that speech that at one time apparently passed unnoticed, and that might constitute 'normal variation' in many bilingual communities, becomes highly noticeable and accessible to challenge.

I share with Dressler, though, the view that the evaluation of the language by its speakers, not by outsiders, is a pivotal locus of reproductive practice. Unfavourable evaluation of one's speech sufficient to make a speaker avoid using the community's language even within the community must occur, not in response to the opinions of outsiders, however powerful, but to those of other insiders, people who are part of the primary social systems of kinship and friendship.

While negotiations over the worth of speech can play out deep anxieties about community identity, such negotiation can serve another function as well: the construction of local lines of cleavage. Generational differences are an obvious locus of differentiation in all three cases. Socialization techniques will be responsive to such generational splits. While Dressler has suggested that parents who see their language in an 'unfavourable light' may be less than vigilant in the language socialization of their children,[7] socialization processes in these communities in general do not show this. In Dyirbal, elders censure young people quite directly, and the language tests administered to young speakers by Malinche purists are positively terrifying. The man who assisted us on the Malinche as a teenager still remembers, 15 years later, how miserable he was made to feel on these occasions. Even though he was objectively far more fluent than his attackers, he did not control purist routines.

Other lines of cleavage are apparent also. In Mexicano, cleavage between traditional cultivators and 'workers' overlaps to some degree with generational cleavage but is not identical with it. Middle-aged 'worker' men function as the 'talk police'; their attitudes heighten linguistic self-consciousness in the communities. Workers tend to be younger than cultivators in any given community, and their egalitarian usage amplifies the generational cleavage by convincing cultivators that 'young people' lack 'respect'. The Wasco case invites exploration of the role of Wasco language in the display of ethnic differentiation.

The contexts of intimacy to which unconfident speakers seem to retreat in all these cases may be relatively impenetrable to the influence of conservative or purist vigilance, and may, in fact, be fundamentally opposed to its semiotic tendencies. The obscene language of resistance, whether among Malinche youth patrolling the roads or among Dyirbal children on the playground, certainly exemplifies this type, but teasing, joking, and 'field chatter' constitute less extreme cases of the same tendency. Focusing in dense closed networks is well known, and seems to be often the domain of 'covert prestige' and 'counter-hegemonic' usage. In Dyirbal, focusing within the in-group, driven by the fact that network solidarity is a higher value than good usage, has precisely the effect of exacerbating the division between the usage of the young and that of the old.

Thus, while political economy is articulated with functional attrition by the code-defending practices of speakers, the second articulation, between functional attrition and structural attrition in the language itself, almost certainly occurs through speaker practice in the new restricted domains to which the substratum code retreats. Contexts where the construction of intimacy is at stake, the very contexts into which exaggerated code-defining and contextualizing negotiations tend to drive a subordinate language among young speakers, are likely to exhibit what I have called 'solidarity coding' (Hill, 1989a). There is not time in this paper to develop the detailed semiotic arguments (I have made some of them in Hill, 1989a), but solidarity coding is a communicative hothouse for the kind of linguistic phenomena that have been included under the rubrics of simplification, rule generalization, and the like. The lowest-common-denominator effect that Schmidt observed in Dyirbal may be quite general to network-based focusing, especially where 'defensive' solidarity is at stake, as among groups of adolescents *vis-à-vis* adults, or in exclusionary teasing and joking when non-speakers are present. The structural impact of solidarity coding in language shift is exacerbated by two additional features. The dominance of the superstrate language favours convergence phenomena (although, if solidarity coding is 'defensive' *vis-à-vis* speakers of the dominant language, these may occur only at levels below the 'limits of awareness' (Silverstein, 1981)). The breaking of links of 'vertical' communication, or other communication with non-intimates that favours rule complication, hypercorrections in the traditional sense, and other coding phenomena that yield a tendency toward relative homeostasis in the 'normal' indigenous language system also heightens the impact of solidarity coding among intimates.

The lines of cleavage along which negotiations over code validation are likely to be conducted are related to the subordinate status of the communities, providing us with another point where political economy and language articulate. A shrinking base of local resources results directly from community subordination and economic peripheralization. The Mexicano usage of Malinche-area workers attempts to validate their claim to scarce resources that are distributed through the ritual sector internal to the communities. In the case of the Wasco, their domination of high tribal office and executive position in tribal businesses is hardly trivial, and depends to some degree on their claim of 'superiority' *vis-à-vis* Sahaptins, manifested by control of 'valuables' that are partly linguistic. Schmidt does not provide much information about what might be at stake for Dyirbal; in another aboriginal community, however, McConvell (1988) has documented code-switching among men butchering beef as part of the negotiation of claims of intimacy and consequent rights to desirable cuts of meat.

How does the retreat of language use into a very limited range of registers, either ritual registers from which young people are excluded, or, especially, the registers of in-group intimacy, translate into sudden 'tip' in language shift? Here I can only speculate about what may happen in families, since only Don Kulick (in this volume) has carefully explored socialization processes in language obsolescence. But it seems likely that the phenomenon involves, essentially, three groups of people – often, three generations. The first, threatened by increasingly acute oppression, develops a repertoire of identity-defending practices oriented toward code definition and contextualization. These are radical enough to discourage communication among non-intimates by those whose usage they attack. This second group retreats in the face of the attack to the contexts of solidarity coding. Young parents from this group, especially those who control no other registers, will use these strategies within the family; occasions which are inappropriate to such strategies, including all the more formal and elevated contexts within family interaction, will be conducted in the superstrate language, as I have seen happen often in Mexicano families. The well-known use of a substrate code as a 'secret language' that permits parental plotting against children is certainly a logical extension of such a system. Their children, then, hear a considerably impoverished input in the indigenous language. Even if children are exposed to elevated contexts (taken to ceremonies, say), they have no 'bridge' to the level of usage in which these are conducted: In Vygotskian terms, it is beyond the 'zone of proximal development' even for solidarity-coding young adults, let alone children. In this context, children are more likely to expand the domain of the superstrate language than they are to 'creolize' the limited resources of the parental substrate code. If this account is correct, the critical period in language death may often be only about twenty years long.

IMPLICATIONS

The claim here is thus that culturally conservative language ideologies can be shaped toward exaggerated boundary-marking activities within a community, practised in the context of intense anxiety about the defence of threatened identities and intense competition for a restricted base of resources. While these practices may reflect a very positive view of the linguistic practices that they attempt to defend, they may become such a formidable barrier that young speakers restrict speech in the defended language to contexts where they are 'safe' among peers and intimates. These contexts yield solidarity codes exhibiting simplification and convergence. Speakers who use only this coding strategy in the substratum language provide inadequate input for children, who shift entirely to the superstrate language. This system of feedback thus yields language shift 'tip'.

The proposals I have made here suggest that research on language shift must combine ethnographic and linguistic skills and methods. Investigation of language shift must include close attention to what actually happens (and does not happen) in natural communicative contexts in a community. Attention to a wide range of cultural and social factors, ranging from the close study of language ideologies to attention to the local political economy, is also necessary. However, at the same time we must understand the nature of speaker competencies and how these are distributed in the community, so we must use the range of elicitation devices that will reveal these, including both quantitative socio-linguistic and more standard field-linguistic techniques. Research programmes that have only an ethnographic, or only a linguistic, dimension will not permit advances in our understanding of the articulations between structure and practice in language shift.

These proposals also have implications for the design and conduct of language maintenance programmes. One reason that the feedback loop works to drive out the dying language is that insecure speakers have an escape route: They can use superstrate languages in contexts other than those of peer-group intimacy. Customs of generational priority often restrict the right to speak in the most elevated registers to elders. Yet for language maintenance programmes to intervene in the vernacular peer-group contexts where the indigenous code may persist is something of a contradiction in terms. Language maintenance programmes should therefore focus particularly on 'bridge' registers. These are coding contexts that are somewhat decontextualized, in that they may target interlocutors who are not necessarily intimates, and which enhance code elaboration and enrichment in a positive way, appropriate to youth. These may be best attached to domains that linguists and schoolteachers aren't especially comfortable with, making an excellent opportunity for young people themselves to be deeply involved in shaping language maintenance. For instance, a programme might encourage young people to compose popular songs in the indigenous language in whatever genre they're most enthusiastic about ('rap' is quite popular with some Native American youth), and to make music videos of these. It might encourage composition in popular forms such as comic books or the type of biography of popular singers that is found in fan magazines. In most language maintenance programmes that I'm familiar with the available 'bridge' materials are relentlessly uplifting, providing little that young people find fun or interesting. The heavy emphasis on 'traditional culture' characteristic of many language maintenance programmes may enhance pride in this culture, but may fail in language maintenance. This occurs if the programme exposes young people mainly to registers of the language that they can't really use because it's inappropriate for their age group (such exposure may also yield extreme concern on the part of elders that ritual knowledge is being discussed inappropriately, by unqualified people in profane contexts), or to kinds of knowledge, like the traditional uses of plant materials, that have little relationship to contemporary life and are unlikely to be retained beyond the classroom.

While it's very important for teachers to have positive attitudes about the indigenous language, language maintenance programmes located entirely in schools do nothing about the feedback loops operating between young people and language socializers outside the classroom. Such programmes will only be effective if they include heavy involvement of families, and encourage and facilitate opportunities for 'vertical' communication in the indigenous language. Oral history projects conducted by students, for instance, provide an excellent opportunity for vertical communication, may be of considerable value to the community (as when data thus gained are used in land-claim cases), and can be enhanced with high-tech paraphernalia, like tape recording, video filming, and computerized database management, that are both interesting and skill-enhancing for youth. Further, language maintenance programmes must involve traditional opinion-makers in key positions. This has been a serious problem in school-based programmes in the United States. Even where there is an adequate cadre of teachers who speak the indigenous language, they usually come from a generation in which usage is perceived locally as already deteriorating. Teachers may be acutely conscious of this, yet rigid standards for credentialization make it impossible for them to involve elders in other than very low-paid or even unpaid volunteer roles, as classroom aides or occasional visitors. Any serious effort toward language maintenance must attack this problem of credentialization, and make it possible for the most knowledgeable people in a community, regardless of their education in the dominant system, to be employed and paid fairly as leaders in language-maintenance programmes. In the United States the Native American Languages Act, signed by President George Bush in November 1990, addresses the problem of credentialization by urging that alternative sets of standards be developed that will recognize traditional knowledge. Currently, though, it is very common for elders to be on the outside spreading doubt about language-maintenance programmes in the community by attacking their (often very real) inadequacies and the competence of those involved in them. While it is impossible to completely insulate language maintenance programmes from community politics, it is important to design and implement them in such a way that they interrupt rather than exacerbate the lines of cleavage constructed by negotiation over language.

I hope that the present analysis does not constitute a case of 'blaming the victim'. Unquestionably, direct prohibitions on the use of dying languages and economic subordination and stigmatization, violently enforced, are major factors in every case of language obsolescence discussed here. The maintenance of the linguistic wealth of the human race cannot be accomplished without ending such injustice. Yet I believe that in order for a language to die, injustice and oppression must be mediated precisely by the culturally appropriate practices that oppressed people adopt in order to defend threatened identities. In the context of severe undermining of traditional systems of socialization, over which indigenous people have little control, these practices may have effects that actors do not desire and can not foresee, and cannot interrupt without help. The problem is to build on the positive, tradition-honouring, identity-enhancing aspects of such practices, exploiting these in the cause of language maintenance, and to minimize the negative, factionalizing side that yields language extinction.

NOTES

1 An account of the issue in the history of the discipline and major discussion by current theorists can be found in Ortner (1984).

2 Let me hasten to add that by emphasizing 'practice' I do not mean to say that community members operate without constraint, or that all structure is simply the illusory trace of action. It seems very likely that some aspects of both interpretation and production are constrained by properties of human perception and cognition that are genetically transmitted and universal to human beings.

3 I use the word 'men' advisedly; while some of the features of male speakers described here are found in the speech of women, women often have somewhat different usages and attitudes from men. This question is considered in Hill (1987b) and Hill (1992).

4 Communities exhibiting Mexicano only in the function of 'remembering' were not found in the Malinche region itself.

5 At the time of my fieldwork so few Malinche students went to schools outside their communities (secondary and preparatory schools) that it is unlikely that there would have been opportunities for boundary marking by Mexicano teasing in a Spanish-dominated schoolyard. I never observed it and nobody ever mentioned it.

6 'Wasco' is named for the Indian town of Wasqu at The Dalles. Speakers of Upper Chinookan at Warm Springs come not only from there, but from other communities as far west as the Willamette River at Portland. The pre-contact indigenous community also included the people now known as 'Wishram,' who live mainly on the Yakima Reservation in the state of Washington.

7 Dorian (1977) also thought that communities might relax their standards; speakers of East Sutherland Gaelic seemed unaware of production problems experienced by semi-speakers of the languages.

REFERENCES

Bakhtin, M. ((1929) 1973), *Problems of Dostoevsky's poetics*. Ann Arbor, Mich.: Ardis.

((1935) 1980), *The dialogic imagination*. Austin, Tex.: University of Texas Press.

Brandt, E. A. (1988), Applied linguistic anthropology and American Indian language renewal. *Human Organization*, 47, 322–9.

Dixon, R. M. W. (1972), *The Dyirbal language of North Queensland*. Cambridge: Cambridge University Press.

Dorian, N. (1977), The problem of the semispeaker in language death. *International Journal of the Sociology of Language*, 12, 23–32.

(1986), Abrupt transmission failure in obsolescing languages: How sudden the 'tip' to the dominant language in communities and families? In Nikiforidu, V., Van Clay, M., Niepokuj, M. and Feder, D. (eds.). *Proceedings of the twelfth annual meeting of the Berkeley Linguistic Society*, pp. 72–83. Berkeley, Calif.: Berkeley Linguistics Society.

Dressler, W. U. (1982), Acceleration, retardation, and reversal in language decay? In Cooper, R. L. (ed.), *Language spread*, pp. 321–36. Bloomington, Ind.: Indiana University Press.

French, D. (1961), Wasco-Wishram. In Spicer, E. H. (ed.) *Perspectives in American Indian culture change*, pp. 337–430. Chicago: University of Chicago Press.

Hill, J. H. (1987a), Spanish as a pronominal argument language: The Spanish interlanguage of Mexicano speakers. In Saka, P. (ed.), *Coyote Papers*, 6, 68–90.

(1987b), Women's speech in modern Mexicano. In Philips, S. U., S. Steele, and Tanz, C. (eds.), *Language, sex, and gender in comparative perspective*, pp. 121–60. Cambridge: Cambridge University Press.

(1988), Language, genuine and spurious. In Kroskrity, P. V. (ed.), *On the ethnography of communication: The legacy of Sapir*, pp. 9–54. (*Other Realities* Volume 8), Los Angeles, Calif.: University of California at Los Angeles, Department of Anthropology.

(1989a), Relativization in obsolescent and non-obsolescent languages. In Dorian, N. (ed.), *Investigating obsolescence*, pp. 149–164. Cambridge: Cambridge University Press.

(1989b), The cultural (?) context of narrative involvement. In B. Music et al. (eds.), *Papers from the 25th Annual Regional Meeting of the Chicago Linguistic Society*, pp. 138–56. Chicago: Chicago Linguistic Society.

(1992), 'Today there is no respect': Nostalgia, 'respect', and oppositional discourse in Mexicano (Nahuatl) language ideology. *Pragmatics*, 2, 263–80.

Hill, J. H. and Hill, K. C. (1986), *Speaking Mexicano*. Tucson, Ariz.: University of Arizona Press.

Hymes, D. H. (1966), Two types of linguistic relativity. In Bright, W. (ed.), *Sociolinguistics*, pp. 114–65. The Hague: Mouton.

McConvell, P. (1988), MIX-IM-UP: Aboriginal codeswitching, old and new. In Heller, M. (ed.), *Codeswitching*, pp. 97–150. Berlin: Mouton de Gruyter.

Mohan, P. and Zador, P. (1986), Discontinuity in a life cycle: The death of Trinidad Bhojpuri. *Language*, 62, 291–320.

Moore, R. E. (1988), Lexicalization versus loss in Wasco-Wishram language obsolescence. *International Journal of American Linguistics*, 54, 453–68.

Philips, S. U. (1983), *The invisible culture*. New York: Longman, Inc.

Ortner, S. B. (1984), Theory in anthropology since the sixties. *Comparative Studies in Society and History*, 26, 126–66.

Sahlins, M. (1985), *Islands of history*. Chicago: University of Chicago Press.

Schmidt, A. (1985), *Young people's Dyirbal*. Cambridge: Cambridge University Press.

Silverstein, M. (1981), The limits of awareness. *Sociolinguistic Working Papers*, 84. Austin, Tex.: Southwest Educational Development Laboratory.

(1984), The culture of language in Chinookan narrative texts; or, On saying that ... in Chinook. In Nichols, J. and Woodbury, A. C. (eds.), *Grammar inside and outside the clause*, pp. 132–71. Cambridge: Cambridge University Press.

Van Zantwijk, R. (1965), La tendencia purista en el náhuatl del centro de México. *Estudios de Cultural Náhuatl*, 5, 129–42.

4 · Growing up monolingual in a multilingual community: how language socialization patterns are leading to language shift in Gapun (Papua New Guinea)

DON KULICK

This paper summarizes some of the results of a study that has dealt with language shift in a rural Papua New Guinean village called Gapun. Gapun is a small village with a population which in 1986–7 fluctuated between 90–110 people. It is located about ten kilometres from the northern coast of Papua New Guinea, roughly midway between the lower Sepik and Ramu rivers. Gapun is an isolated village. It is surrounded on all sides by rain-forest and sago swamps, and is connected to other villages (the nearest of which is about a two hour journey away) and to the outside world only by narrow, choked waterways and slim bush paths subject to flooding. Between March 1986–July 1987, I spent 15 months in Gapun conducting anthropological fieldwork, trying to discover why this isolated jungle community, far away from urban centres and experiencing none of the oft-cited pressures of industrialization, market-economy penetration, out-migration, or influx of non-vernacular speakers, was abandoning its vernacular language.

Most villagers in Gapun speak a language which they call *Taiap mɛr* (Taiap language).[1] The language exists only in Gapun, and was, in 1987, spoken actively and fluently by exactly eighty-nine people. Even by the somewhat extreme standards of Papua New Guinea, where over 700 languages are spoken, many of them by fewer than 1,000 people, this is a small language. Since the late 1970s, however, the number of people who speak Taiap has been getting even smaller, despite the fact that the village population is the largest within memory. As of 1987, no village child under 10 actively used this village vernacular in verbal interactions. These children either speak, or, in the case of the 1 to 3-year-olds, are clearly on their way to acquiring, Tok Pisin, a creole language that arose in Melanesia in the mid–late 1800s (see Mühlhäusler, this volume). Today, Tok Pisin is Papua New Guinea's most important language in terms of communicative expediency. Tok Pisin entered Gapun shortly after the First World War, when two village men, who had been away working on a copra plantation on a faraway island, returned to the village. Since that time, Tok Pisin has become an integral part of the communicative repertoires of virtually everybody living in the village.

The aspect of language shift in Gapun that I found most intriguing, and that I want to use as a frame for this paper, was that the adult villagers were at a loss to understand why their children suddenly are no longer learning the vernacular. Knowledge of the vernacular Taiap is seen as a self-evident attribute of all villagers. Taiap is the language of the ancestors, and it has strong associations with the land on which the villagers live. It is what most strikingly sets one apart from one's neighbours. Several people described it as 'sweet'. Taiap, others explained, has a foundation, a deep-rooted-ness (*i gat as bilong em*), and the capacity for nuance and subtlety (*i gatol liklik liklik mining*) that Tok Pisin lacks. Every villager wants his or her child to learn the vernacular. There has been no conscious effort on anyone's behalf not to teach their children Taiap.

So to what do villagers attribute the shift? Their children. 'It's them, these little kids', one woman explained, as she indicated her suckling 14-month-old baby with a sharp jab of her chin. This woman expressed the consensus opinion of the villagers when she described babies like her own as '*bikhed*' [big-headed, strong-willed]. 'They don't want to know our village language', this woman continued, 'They just want to speak Tok Pisin all the time'.

This situation is the backdrop for the points I wish to raise in this paper. My point of departure is that, in order to understand the reasons why the vernacular language is no longer being acquired by children in Gapun, it is necessary to take seriously the statements of adults that pre-verbal children are responsible for the language shift in the village. What can be the basis of this parental allocation of blame? What are the underlying assumptions about the nature of children, of learning, and of language which make it seem reasonable for the villagers to blame their babies for the demise of the village vernacular?

What I hope to demonstrate here is that, in allocating blame for language shift in the way they do, village parents are not being disingenuous or evasive. The people of Gapun impute intentionality and strong wills to their children from a very early age, and, given this, it is not surprising that they can believe babies capable of rejecting one language in favour of another. From the perspective of an outsider, however, it is clear that children would undoubtedly learn to speak the vernacular as they always have in the past, if there was sufficient input and need to communicate in it. The fact that children are no longer growing up speaking Taiap indicates that this input and need are now lacking. But since parents in the village do not see themselves as having altered their linguistic interactions with children, what an outsider can do is look closely at the language socialization patterns in the village to determine if there is anything in the very structure of caregiver–child interactional patterns that is now favouring Tok Pisin without caregivers being aware of it. If this should be the case, such a finding would be of theoretical interest not just for an understanding of the process of language shift, but also – if one follows Susan Gal (1979:4) in viewing shift as a 'special instance of linguistic change' – for an understanding of the processes behind linguistic change generally.

Before going on to discuss the specifics of Gapun, however, it may be helpful to orient the analysis to be presented here in the context of work currently being done on language shift. Since the late 1970s, a number of detailed and sophisticated studies on language shift have been produced by sociolinguists and anthropological linguists, some of whom appear as contributors to this volume. A characteristic of the overwhelming majority of studies on shift to which I would like to draw attention here, however, is that they tend to concentrate almost exclusively on the analysis of the speech of adults to one another. This focus on the speech of adults has predominated in the study of shift largely because it is through adult speech that researchers can establish that the different languages used within a community have different connotations of solidarity and prestige. In language shift situations it is thus common, for example, for speakers to switch consistently from their vernacular to Spanish or English or some other national language in order to lend more weight to their arguments (Gal, 1979:177; Hill and Hill, 1986:104) and/or as a way to appeal to prestigious values or lifestyles (Sankoff, 1971; Blom and Gumperz, 1972; Scotton, 1979).

But while close attention to the speech of adults does indeed allow researchers to establish the kind of associations that are linked to each language used in a community, it leaves uninvestigated the question of exactly how those value–language complexes become transmitted to children in such a way that the latter do not learn the vernacular of their parents. This issue of transmission is at the very heart of language shift, since languages cannot be said to be shifting until it can be established that children are no longer learning them. By the time the first generation of non-vernacular speaking children has been raised, the boundary between language shift and incipient language death has in most cases quite intractably been traversed.

In spite of the importance of understanding exactly how and why the transmission of a vernacular language simply comes to cease within a community, studies have not focused on the socialization of the first generation of non-vernacular speaking children. Work on language shift has instead concentrated heavily on examining the end result of shift. The process of shift has been documented most extensively in its advanced stages, and much of the research on language shift, especially by linguists, focuses on languages in their final death throes (e.g. Elmendorf, 1981; Cooley, 1979). For non-linguists not concentrating on structural decay in dying languages, this emphasis on the terminal stages of shift is sometimes uninten-tional; while recognizing the value of observing earlier phases, most investigators simply 'arrived too late' (Dorian, 1981:53) to document them.

But another reason for the lack of detailed attention to the process of language transmission in situations of shift has been that researchers have not seemed to think it necessary. Throughout the literature, parents are portrayed either as having consciously and explicitly decided not to teach their children their own vernacular, or, phrased more passively, parents are reported to decide not to encourage their children to learn the vernacular, even if they continue to use it among themselves. Usually the reasons underlying such a decision are said to have to do with parental opinions about the relative prestige of the vernacular in relation to a language of wider currency; i.e. parents consider that their children 'don't need' to learn the vernacular to get by in society, or they are concerned that the child's school language might suffer if s/he speaks the vernacular, etc. (e.g. Hill and Hill, 1986:112–13; Gal, 1979:164; Schmidt, 1985:24; Denison, 1977:21; articles in Schach, 1980; Giles, 1977). This widely held view that parents consciously decide not to pass on their vernacular to their children, and that this is the 'direct cause' of shift (Denison, 1977:22) has led some scholars to wonder whether language shift in most cases should not perhaps be more accurately referred to as 'language suicide' (Denison, 1977; Dutton, 1978; Edwards, 1985:51–3).

A major difficulty with such terminology and the assumptions which underlie it is that it is not in fact always clear to what extent a parental decision not to pass on their vernacular is a 'direct cause' of shift, and to what extent this decision is a consequence and recognition of shift already underway. When thinking about what language(s) children in bilingual environments end up speaking, it is important to keep in mind that a child's language acquisition is influenced by many factors other than parental decisions and wishes. For example, a number of scholars working on language shift have stressed that the role that older siblings play in the language socialization of their younger brothers and sisters has great significance for whether these children become bilingual, semi-speakers (i.e. markedly imperfect speakers of the vernacular) or monolingual in the majority language (Dorian, 1981:107, 1980; Schmidt, 1985:25–26; Hill and Hill, 1977:60, 1986:112–13). Other sociolinguistic and anthropological studies have documented the influence that peers have on a child's language (Goodwin and Goodwin, 1987; Heath, 1983). And research on children in bilingual households has highlighted a wide variety of factors, including type of input and parental reactions to their children's responses, that influence what language(s) these children acquire (Arnberg, 1981; Döpke, 1986; Lanza, 1988; Fantini, 1985). In general, recent studies on child language acquisition have been increasingly moving away from a view of socialization that sees it as 'something done to novices by members' (Wentworth, 1980:64; Ochs, 1988; Schieffelin, 1990), to a framework stressing the interactional nature of language socialization.

What emerges very clearly from the literature in these fields is that parental decisions and wishes regarding their children's language are only one factor of many that influence which language a child learns. Once this is fully appreciated, the issue of why a particular generation of children in a bilingual community suddenly grows up not speaking the vernacular becomes more complicated than parental wishes and more problematic than the lack of attention accorded the process in the literature would seem to indicate.

One way of approaching the question of the non-transmission of particular languages in a community is to pay close attention to the precise ways in which language is used as part of the child socialization process. The conceptual and methodological framework with which to undertake such an investigation has been under development for a number of years now, by scholars working with what have come to be known as 'language socialization' studies. Language socialization is a relatively new area of inquiry that attempts to synthesize the study of child language acquisition and the study of socialization. This synthesis highlights a new area of research which takes as its focus the documentation of 'both socialization through the use of language and socialization to use language' (Schieffelin and Ochs, 1986:163). The goal of such a focus is to understand the ways in which 'children and other novices in society acquire tacit knowledge of principles of social order and systems of beliefs (ethnotheories) through exposure to and participation in language-mediated interactions' (Ochs, 1986:2).

In practice, the study of language socialization patterns is done by carefully analyzing caregiver–child interactions, showing how the structure and content of these interactions is organized by and expressive of wider cultural patterns of thought and interaction. This is the approach which I now intend to take as I move on to discuss some characteristic examples of caregiver–child interactions from Gapun village, based on my detailed observations of caregiver–child interactions and on thirty-seven hours of transcribed tapes focusing on those interactions. My goal here, once again, is to arrive at a culturally informed explanation of why children in the village are no longer learning the village vernacular, even though their parents want them to.

CODE-SWITCHING WITH CHILDREN

Let us begin with an extended example of speech by a mother to her 25-month-old daughter, in order to both exemplify speech patterns in the village and to identify particular features of those speech patterns that are contributing to children's not learning the village vernacular. In this example, a little girl named Masito has been crying insistently for several minutes. Her mother Sopak has been trying to distract her and quiet her by offering her a breast, her favourite butcher knife, and a big red wad of betel nut that Sopak had been chewing. Despite all these offers, Masito won't stop crying. Her temper growing short, Sopak finally swoops the child off the floor and tries once again to silence her with a breast:

(4.1)
> Drink it, drink it [the breast]. Drink it and swallow. Sss. Quiet.
> Quiet, Quiet now, Eye, her eye is hurting. Enough, Kama [Masito's
> 6 year old sister] that sago head [Kama's nickname] just left again.
> Enough! Baso! [Masito's 16 year old brother] Baso, Baso, Sia [an
> 5   exclamation] I haven't washed, her dirty skin [Masito's] is gonna
> mess me up. Drink the breast. Tsk. Oh Kama died. Ah! I'm gonna

box your ears now! Why are you doing this? Your tears are gonna
block your eyes now. Drink the breast. Drink the breast. Ding bes.
[baby talk] Eh. Uh. Father's child [exclamation of exasperation].

10   *Asapoi* [kin term meaning nonkin] I call out to their kids
and they're *bikhet* [Sopak means here that she calls to her
Mother's Sister's children to come and amuse Masito
but they treat her like nonkin and don't listen to her].

Look at the pig! Yo the pig died.
15   Look at it.
Look Obriwa's gonna spear a chicken.
Look. Obriwa's gonna spear a chicken now. Ah. [Masito stops
crying]
Priest. Priest. Priest here.
20   The priest is coming.
Nurse. Mariana [the nurse's name] here.
Mariana is coming.
Priest. Father Pita is coming.
Over there, he's sitting in Kruni's men's house. [Masito begins to
25   whine]
We're gonna go see him. [Masito stops]
The priest is going with the nurse. The nurse is coming.
Oh a couple of these hermits crabs [in a bag on the floor] are
crawling away. Yesterday they went to get hermit crabs, but there
30   were none at all. [Masito starts to whine]
Enough.
Uncle's baby is gonna fall down and die. She's sleeping in the
house and everyone's gone. Yapa [the baby's older sister] went
somewhere.
35   Michael's-eh-Ngom's chicken here.
I haven't seen Basama's. [Masito whines louder]
There. Ngom's chicken.

Ngom's chicken. There.
It has a nice color. [Masito stops whining]

The most important feature of this monologue is the way in which
Sopak oscillates between the village vernacular, Taiap, and Tok
Pisin. (This is signalled in the transcription through underlining –

underlined text was spoken in Taiap; non-underlined text was spoken in Tok Pisin).

This oscillation between these two languages is a characteristic feature of virtually all verbal interactions between villagers – they always occur in both Taiap and Tok Pisin, with some villagers who command other vernacular languages sometimes mixing them in as well.[2] Villagers can keep the two languages separated, and they do so when they talk to people from outside the village. But whenever they converse among themselves, villagers see no reason to separate the two (Kulick and Stroud, 1990; Stroud, 1992). This same pattern of continual code-switching is carried over to adult interactions with children, as can be seen in Example 4.1. There is, however, one significant difference between talk between adults and talk by adults to children.

Sopak begins speaking in the vernacular and continues this way throughout the first half of the monologue, switching only briefly to Tok Pisin to startle Masito with a loud shout of 'Enough!' (line 4); to frighten her by telling her that her sister Kama is dead (line 6); and to comment on the tears blocking her eyes (lines 7–8). Throughout this part of the speech, Masito remains crying. She stops only after Sopak initiates a specific and extremely common type of distracting routine, one that is signalled by the high rise-fall intonation on her utterance 'yo, the pig died' and by a switch to Tok Pisin (line 14). Once Sopak successfully captures Masito's attention with a series of urgently enunciated directives in both languages (*rarεtukun/ lukim* = look at it; lines 14–17), Masito actually stops crying. When this happens, Sopak, in her continuing talk to Masito, *switches exclusively to Tok Pisin*, except when she voices observations about the hermit crabs (lines 28–30) and about her daughter Basama's chicken (line 36). The other vernacular utterance here directed to Masito is 'Ngom's chicken' (line 37), but this is immediately translated into Tok Pisin (see Kulick, 1992: ch. 2).

In choosing to use Tok Pisin in talk addressed directly to Masito, Sopak is displaying a pattern of speech common to all village parents. Although villagers speak their usual mixture of vernacular languages and Tok Pisin in the presence of their children and in their talk to children, there is an overwhelming tendency for caregivers to switch to Tok Pisin when they especially want a child to attend to their talk, and when they see that they have the child's attention, as Sopak does here (lines 19ff.). This tendency is so strong that even those village women who rarely speak Tok Pisin to anyone else tend to switch to this language when they directly address their children.

One reason why caregivers switch to Tok Pisin in this manner when speaking to children is because of their beliefs about the relative difficulty of Tok Pisin and Taiap. The Taiap language has a reputation throughout the entire lower Sepik area as being composed of two separate languages – a man's and a woman's. This reputation arose, and is maintained, because Taiap appears to be the only language in that region that marks gender on the second person singular forms of imperative intransitive verbs, in the following manner.

	said to a man	said to a woman
you come!	wɛ-tɛt	wɛ-tak
you go!	ɔ-tɛt	ɔ-tak
you talk!	nam-tɛt	nam-tak
you sit!	tutɔ-tɛt	tutɔ-tak

This system is very straightforward and uncomplicated. Men and women from other villages who hear these commands being given, however, observe that, whereas they in their own vernaculars use only one imperative form for both sexes, Taiap speakers have to know two different forms to say exactly the same thing. This confounds and appalls them, and in this way, a 'two language' myth about Taiap gets perpetuated throughout the lower Sepik. And because the language really is 'two languages' Taiap is held by its neighbours to be an exceptionally 'hard' language, one that is 'broken in two'.

Gapuners hear the evaluation of their vernacular by others and they know that everybody else considers Taiap to be an unusually 'hard' language. This characterization of their vernacular has influenced the villagers' perceptions of their own vernacular, and they themselves will admit to one another that Taiap is in fact 'a little bit hard' (*i hat liklik*). By contrast, no one ever suggests that Tok Pisin is a difficult language, and the fact that everyone in Gapun and all surrounding villages has learned Tok Pisin as a second language underscores its straightforwardness and accessibility. Only *ol buskanaka* (country bumpkins) and *ol longlong man* (idiots) do not know Tok Pisin.

This perception of the vernacular as difficult is coupled with an adult appreciation of the limited processing and productive capabilities of young children. Villagers observe and comment on the fact that children have difficulty pronouncing certain sounds and that they often don't listen to, or understand, adult conversations. This observation is in turn tied to a strong ethic of linguistic accommodation that exists in Gapun. That is to say, villagers try very hard to accommodate others in terms of the topics they discuss, the opinions they express, and the language they speak in. This ethic of linguistic accommodation results in villagers sometimes modifying their speech to children, in the same way that adults strive to modify their speech and choice of language in conversation with others so as to accommodate them verbally. In the case of adult talk to children, this accommodation takes the form of adults speaking to children in Tok Pisin, which villagers see as the simpler language.

SIBLING CAREGIVERS

That adults tend to switch to Tok Pisin when speaking directly to young children means that from an early age, the linguistic input that these children receive is unbalanced. Children hear both Taiap and Tok Pisin spoken around them constantly and the vernacular is often used when speaking to them, as is clear from Sopak's talk to her daughter Masito in Example 4.1. But the great bulk of the talk that gets addressed directly to children and to which the children are expected to attend is in Tok Pisin.

This input in Tok Pisin is augmented by the kind of talk that a child hears from his or her older siblings and their friends. These older children are a major source of linguistic input for a child, because caregiving responsibilities in the village are not confined to mothers, but are distributed among all female relatives in the household.

Villagers consider that a mother should never stray far enough from her nursing baby that she cannot be on hand to feed the child should it begin crying incessantly. Beyond this responsibility, however, mothers are free to delegate caregiving tasks to others. Since a school was built in a neighbouring village in the late 1960s, girls between the ages of 8 and 14 are away from Gapun going to school for much of the time. This means that caregiving responsibilities in Gapun have come to fall heavily on a woman's preschool daughters. These daughters are expected to be constantly on hand to hold the baby when a mother is preparing meals, to amuse it while the mother is leaching sago pith in the forest, or to simply take it off the mother's hands and away when she is tired or in a bad mood.

Sharing caregiving responsibilities in this way results in babies and young children spending as much time (and in some cases more time) in the company of their preschool sisters and their playmates as they do together with their mothers. And on the backs and in the laps of these girls, infants and young children are the objects of extensive physical and verbal play. Preschool girls can amuse themselves and their infant charges for up to twenty minutes at a time with songs and word play. In the following example, Bonika (6 yrs) is sitting alone with her little sister Armambwira (7 months) on the porch of their house.

(4.2)
Bonika: [bouncing Armambwira up and down on her lap]

. . . bús mangi bús mangi	búsh kid búsh kid
bús mangi	búsh kid
bús bús músh músh búsh	búsh búsh músh músh búsh
yu bús mangi bús mangi yu	you búsh kid búsh kid you
bús mangi músh músh	búsh kid músh músh
bús mangi músh músh	búsh kid músh músh

[seeing their seven year old sister Yapa emerging from the forest, Bonika slaps Armambwira lightly on the face and points to Yapa]

Yapa ia Yapa ia   There's Yapa there's Yapa

em ia em ia em ia   there there there

Yapa tata ia   there's older sibling Yapa

lukim tata Yapa   look at older sibling Yapa

apa apa apa   apa apa apa

em ia Yapa Bapa ba pa   there Yapa Bapa ba pa

pa pa pa   pa pa pa

[Bonika suddenly puts Armambwira belly down on the floor and spanks her bottom to the rhythm of:]

yu sindáun   you sit dówn

sindáun   sit dówn

sindáun   sit dówn

sindáun   sit dówn

[Bonika lifts Armambwira up and lays her across her lap]

Nau bai yu slip.   Now you're gonna sleep

Sip sip bebi.   Seep seep baby.

Bebi! Sip sip sip.   Baby! Seep seep seep.

Bebi! Bobi bobi   Baby! Bobi bobi

bebu bebu   bebu bebu

wo wo wo wo wo wo...   wo wo wo wo wo wo...

This interaction lasted for fifteen minutes, and engaged Armambwira both physically and verbally in ways which do not occur between adults and children. Although Armambwira remained silent for most of this interaction, the babbling sounds of babies and young children are frequently incorporated into such play, providing a framework for the older children's rhymes and songs. This type of word play often consists for the most part of isolated syllables and nonsense words. But whenever language does occur, that language is always Tok Pisin. Like adults, older siblings talk to their young charges in Tok Pisin. But unlike adults and those children who have cared for infants in the past, the use of Tok Pisin by the present generation of child caregivers is no longer based on choice. The current generation of children who assist their mothers in the care of new babies does not actively command Taiap. This ensures that all of those babies now growing up in the village hear only Tok Pisin spoken to them by their sibling caregivers in all verbal interactions.

INTERPRETING CHILDREN'S SPEECH

In addition to the adult tendency to switch to Tok Pisin when directly addressing young children, and the amount and kind of input in Tok Pisin that children receive from their pre-school sisters, there is a further factor in village communicational patterns which weights the language acquisition process in favour of Tok Pisin. This is the way in which caregivers interpret infant vocalizations.

In order to understand the way in which caregivers interpret infant vocalizations, it is necessary at this point to first say a few words about how villagers view children.

Children in Gapun are considered to embody a dimension of the self known as *hed* (*kɔkɨr*, in the vernacular). *Hed* means head. Each individual, the villagers believe, 'has *hed*'. Each individual, they mean by this, has a basic and volatile sense of personal will and autonomy. The concept of *hed* in Gapun signifies egoism, anti-social thoughts and behaviour, selfishness and maverick individualism. So babies, who embody this characteristic, are thought of as fundamentally asocial, aggressive, stubborn, and strong-willed. This conception of children is reflected, among other ways, in the first words which villagers attribute to children.

In Gapun, a child's very first word is generally held to be <u>ɔki</u>. This is a Taiap word meaning approximately, 'I'm getting out of here'. Attributed to infants as young as two months, this word encapsulates the adult belief that babies will 'do what they want' (*bihainim laik bilong ol yet*) and go where they will, regardless of the wishes of others. The two words that villagers consider rapidly follow <u>ɔki</u> also underscore the notion of a baby as a gruff, independent individualist with a 'strong' *hed*. These words are the Taiap *mnda* (I'm sick of this) and *aiata* (stop it).

After caregivers note that their babies have uttered these first three declarations of general dissatisfaction, there is a long period where they do not attribute linguistic meaning to a child's vocalizations; for a long time a child's babbling is either ignored or dismissed as incomprehensible 'rubbish talk' (*rabis tok*), 'nothing calls' (*ŋgar sindɛr*), or 'bird talk' (*tok bilong ol pisin/tamma nam*).

Only at about 18 months do some mothers begin once again to interpret their child's vocalizations as words. But now, without exception, these words are no longer interpreted as Taiap. From this point, all a child's 'talk' is considered to be in Tok Pisin. When one mother heard her 20 month old daughter utter to herself in private speech [*ta'tai*], for example, she turned to the child's older sister and said, 'That's it. She said to you: "Older sibling is leaving (*tata i go*)".' Using the same interpretive strategy, Sopak, the mother in Example 4.1, when she saw her daughter Kama giving Masito (18 months) a betel nut and heard Masito murmur '*mama ka* (inaudible babble)' announced 'She's talking about betel nut': 'Kama has chewed betel nut' (*Kama i kaikai buai pinis*).

This point at which caregivers once again begin attributing linguistic meaning to their children's vocalizations is a significant one, because it is the point in the villagers' ethno-theory of development at which knowledge (*save*) is beginning to 'break open' inside the child. Like the concept of *hed*, this notion of *save* is a central concept in Gapun villager's thoughts about what people are. *Save* is a fundamental aspect of self which all people have and which constitutes the very possibility of social life. In its most basic sense, *save* means knowledge: the knowledge of facts and being able to learn from experience and through doing. But this concept of *save* also signifies social knowledge; the knowledge about appropriate behaviour and speech, awareness of social obligations and roles, and cognizance that one must co-operate with others and accommodate them in order to be able to live together at all. A basic expectation of all parents is that their children will come to understand as they mature that they must 'suppress' their *hed*, their egoistic individualism, and constantly show their *save*, their sociability and co-operativeness.

Villagers believe, however, that *save* itself is not taught; *save* exists inside each human being, and it 'breaks open' (*bruk/krarara ɔ-*) inside children, like an egg. What is interesting and significant in this context is that the eruption of *save* in children coincides with, and is concretely manifested through, the attribution of Tok Pisin in the child's speech.

Villagers see a link between the 'breaking open' of *save* and Tok Pisin because *save*, the expression of social knowledge, has increasingly come to be associated with Christianity, white people, and the modern world. The reasons behind this shift in the meaning of *save* from social knowledge embedded in traditional knowledge systems to social knowledge displayed through expressions of familiarity with Christianity and the ways of white people have been documented in a previous work (Kulick, 1992) and are far too convoluted to attempt to summarize here. For the purposes of this chapter it is enough to know that, for a variety of reasons, villagers nowadays consider that social cognizance and awareness are best expressed through Tok Pisin. The significance of this fact for language socialization patterns is this: Because *save* is nowadays believed to be expressed primarily through Tok Pisin, and because caregivers consider that children begin showing *save* at about 18 months, when they observe the children increasingly using vocalizations to get attention or to engage others in interaction, a child's vocalizations are consistently interpreted by caregivers as being in Tok Pisin. It is important to appreciate that although some of what children say at this age is Tok Pisin, the vast majority of their vocalizations are not clearly Tok Pisin at all. Often they are babbles, whines, and moans. The point is, however, that from about 18 months caregivers begin treating children as though they speak Tok Pisin.

At the same time that children are considered to be showing *save* through their vocalizations in Tok Pisin, they have also begun to walk. This physical independence allows caregivers to test the child's emerging *save* and put it to use; and at this stage, the nature of caregiver talk to children changes. Although distraction sequences like those used by Sopak when talking to her daughter Masito in Example 4.1 remain common when the child starts to cry, caregivers now begin increasingly to use directives in their talk to children. These directives function to involve children in social life. Rather than just tell a child 'Sleep, sleep' or 'Drink the breast', caregivers now begin to command toddlers to give betel nut to their visiting mother's brother, to pass an ember to their grandmother so that she can dry her tobacco leaf, to fetch a carving knife from across the room from an older sibling. By successfully carrying out a command to fetch betel nut, tobacco leaves, embers, knives or tongs, children demonstrate their *save*; at the same time that they for the first time become active participants in the social interactions occurring around them.

The increased amount of talk to children at this stage in their development, in the form of directives, is in effect an increased amount of input in Tok Pisin. Because they are believed to be producing it, parents now assume that children understand Tok Pisin, but not Taiap. This belief gets reinforced each time a child correctly carries out an order in Tok Pisin. And because adults continue to switch to Tok Pisin whenever they speak directly to their children, the bulk of the directives to children is in that language.

Once children begin responding to and carrying out directives, parents begin to become aware that children tend to react much more frequently and readily to speech in Tok Pisin than they do to directives in Taiap. This results not only in even more Tok Pisin being used in speech to children, but also in Taiap utterances being increasingly systematically translated into Tok Pisin whenever the speaker wants to elicit a response from the child. This translating will be done by either the speaker her- or himself, by one of the child's older siblings, or, especially in the several village households in which mothers speak a great deal of Taiap, by the child's father,

whenever he is present. Example 4.3 is an example of translation
from Taiap to Tok Pisin being done by a child's older sibling:

(4.3)
Ermina, and Giang's older sister Gut (10 yrs) want Giang (3;8) to come away
from the cake of sago he is playing with and sit down near them, but for
several minutes he has ignored their calls to 'come.' Now Giang's mother
Ermina flicks at her head in the direction of the visiting anthropologist:

Ermina:	_Wɛtɛt. Munjɛ tutɔtɛt._	E:	Come. The man is sitting
	Ariɔ.		there. He's gonna get you.
Gut:	_Giang em bai ronim yu ia._	G:	Giang he's gonna come after
	Giang kam.		you. Giang come.
Ermina:	_Ŋi nda ɔrunɛtana indɛ._	E:	He's gonna shoot you now.
	Kɛmbatik aŋgudɛ.		There's his bow.
Gut:	_Giang kembatik bilong em ia._	G:	Giang there's his bow. He's
	Em bai sutim yu nau.		gonna shoot you now.
Ermina:	_Kam. Wɛtɛt._	E:	Come. Come.
Gut:	_Em bai sutim yu nau._	G:	He's gonna shoot you now.

[Giang runs over to Ermina and Gut laughing]

Another way in which Tok Pisin also frequently gets
foregrounded in caregiver–child interactions at this stage is through
the increased use of Tok Pisin verbs in vernacular utterances:

(4.4)
David 3;3 holds up a bit of string to his mother Paso and whines:

Paso: _Katim ah?_   P: Cut it ah?
    [David whines]

Paso: _Anakŋa katim-kru?_   P: Cut it where?
    [David whines]

Paso: _Anakŋa katim-kru?_   P: Cut it where?
    [David whines]

Paso: _Katim em ah?_   P: Cut this ah?
    [David whines]

Paso: _Ambukəni katim-kru?_ P: Cut it how?
    [David whines]

Paso: _Orait, yu ŋgɔ_   P: OK you let it go then.
 lusim-tukun.

[Paso cuts the string and David stops whining]

That caregivers are so willing to translate their vernacular utterances into Tok Pisin or use Tok Pisin verbs in their talk means that children come to understand that whatever is said to them in Taiap will be repeated in Tok Pisin, sooner or later. They learn that they can influence and even determine the surface forms of caregiver utterances by not responding, by whining (as Masito does when Sopak speaks to her in Taiap towards the end of her monologue in Example 4.1, and as David in Example 4.4 does in order to get Paso to cut his string), or by responding with 'Ah?'

The types of communication patterns described above combine continually in caregiver–child interactions in Gapun, and they work together to result in a language rich in Tok Pisin, but relatively poor in Taiap.

STARTING TO TALK

This mass of input in Tok Pisin that children receive during their early years occurs against the background of the villagers' understanding of the nature of children. A central tenet of Gapun culture, and one that seems prevalent throughout much of Melanesia, is that one does not infringe on the personal autonomy, the *hed*, of other people. This anxiety about infringing on others applies to all relationships in the society, even those between parents and their children. Among other ways, concern not to infringe on others manifests itself in a dispreference for making a child do anything against his or her will, including talk. So adults and older siblings speak *to* young children in the village, but they neither encourage or expect the children to talk back. At no point in her long monologue with Masito (Example 4.1), for example, does Sopak try to elicit any type of verbal reaction from the child.

Caregivers sometimes tell young children to call out the name of a relative, and they may ask 'what?' (*wanem/ambin*) if the child vocalizes especially loudly. But if the child doesn't call out the relative's name or respond to the 'what?' after two or three prompts, then the matter will invariably be dropped. By the age of about 2, as was mentioned above, children have been observed to have said a few words, and, as adults comment that their *save* has begun to 'break open', they are increasingly prompted to respond to directives by carrying them out. Children of this age are not, however, expected to be actively using language to communicate. Until they are 6 or 7, and sometimes even older, parents asking children questions or giving them directives accept either no verbal response at all, or extremely minimal responses such as the grunts and moans which David uses to get Paso to cut his string in Example 4.4. Like the Athabaskan children described by Scollon and Scollon (1981), children in Gapun are not expected to really begin talking until they are 5 or 6 years old. If a child is especially verbal at a young age, this will be encouraged by adults and older children, who will engage the child in short exchanges and try to get him or her to answer information questions. A talkative child is somewhat unexpected, however, and whereas no one would remark on a 4-year-old who said very little and who still relied heavily on whines and groans to communicate with his mother, villagers notice, and occasionally express surprise at, and annoyance with, a loquatious child. Bapong was a very talkative 4-year-old who frequently talked and sang to himself, sometimes loudly, in adult company. More than once on these occasions he was suddenly shushed in half serious tones with the cry: 'Sia! *Liklik man na maus tasol i bikpela olgeta!'* (Sia! Little man the only thing big on you is your mouth!)

Partly because they are not encouraged or expected to talk, and partly because the bulk of linguistic input addressed directly to them is in Tok Pisin, by the time village children do begin to use language in their interactions, at about 1;6–2;3 years, the language they produce is Tok Pisin.

Children begin speaking by picking up and repeating parts of words and phrases they hear in conversations around them. This repeating is not normally noticed or commented upon by caregivers. A 23-month-old boy named Bini demonstrated this kind of early speech, as his mother Tambong recounted for a group of listeners her reaction when she, staying in Wongan, heard the slit gong drum signalling the death of a Gapun woman. Bini was laying across his mother's lap during this interaction, and nobody noticed his repetitions.

(4.5)

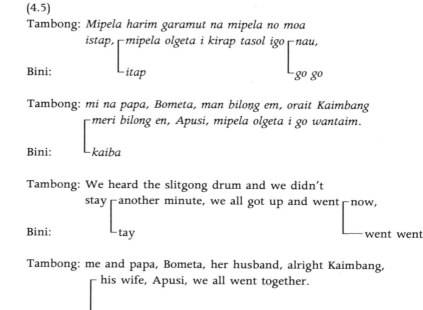

Tambong: *Mipela harim garamut na mipela no moa*
         istap, ⌐*mipela olgeta i kirap tasol igo* ⌐*nau,*

Bini: └*itap*   └*go go*

Tambong: *mi na papa, Bometa, man bilong em, orait Kaimbang*
         ⌐*meri bilong en, Apusi, mipela olgeta i go wantaim.*

Bini: └*kaiba*

Tambong: We heard the slitgong drum and we didn't
         stay ⌐another minute, we all got up and went ⌐now,

Bini: └tay   └──went went

Tambong: me and papa, Bometa, her husband, alright Kaimbang,
         ⌐ his wife, Apusi, we all went together.

Bini: └ kaiba

An interesting aspect of these early repetitions is that children do not appear to spontaneously repeat or produce the vernacular in this way. When adult conversations or narratives like this occur primarily in Taiap or some other vernacular language, children most often simply remain silent. If they do repeat to themselves during such talk, they do so with sounds that do not have their source in the adult talk.

The most common linguistic situation for village children to find themselves in, however, is one in which both the vernacular and Tok Pisin are used in the course of the same interaction. In these cases, even these young children who have hardly begun to talk show themselves to be adept at focusing on those elements in the conversation which are either Tok Pisin or are Taiap nominals habitually used in Tok Pisin speech (such as the vernacular words for betel nut, sago, coconut, chicken, tobacco, and other common objects). It is always these elements, to the exclusion of all others, that the children repeat and incorporate into their own private monologues. That is to say that even though these children live in a multilingual community where Taiap and Tok Pisin continually are interspersed in the speech of all adults, they do not seem to go through a period of mixing languages in the way that studies of bilingual children have shown to be common (Taeschner, 1983; Volterra and Taeschner, 1978; Vihman, 1985; Pye, 1986). Instead, by the time they begin using language, children in Gapun appear to have already managed to separate the two linguistic systems from one another. And they use only Tok Pisin.

Once children begin using Tok Pisin themselves, the village convention of accommodating other speakers in their own choice of language becomes activated continually, with the result that parents switch to Tok Pisin even more systematically when they talk to their children. It is at this stage in the child's language development that parents may realize that their children do not, in fact, speak the vernacular. Although parents at this point begin explicitly blaming their children for being *bikhed* (stubborn) and refusing to speak Taiap, the association between children and Tok Pisin is so strong that adults will address children in that language even if a child should actually happen to answer in the vernacular.

(4.6)
Kapiru, from inside her house, calls to her daughter Mbup (7 yrs), who is playing with Kama (6 yrs) in Kama's house

Kapiru: *Mbup!*	K: Mbup!
Kama: *Aŋɔdɛ.*	Ka: Here.
Kapiru: *Yu ambin nirkwankuk?*	K: What are you doing?
Kama: *ŋgu ɔmrariakuk* [laughs]	Ka: She's playing [laughs]
Kapiru: *Go kisim sampela buai moa.*	K: Go fetch some more betel nut.

This association between children and Tok Pisin feeds back on itself so that it influences how parents talk to even very small children. And also, as it now becomes clear to caregivers that their children only speak Tok Pisin, the vernacular begins to assume the character of a secret code which caregivers use to talk about the children in their presence. The vernacular also increasingly comes to be associated with reprimand and scolding (cf. Metraux, 1965; Redlinger, 1978).

Between the ages of 3–5, boys begin spending less and less time in the company of their mothers and older sisters, and more time together with their older preschool brothers or cousins, whose play takes the boys out into the jungle for much of the day. Girls of this age also form playgroups, but, burdened by the toddlers that have been left in their care by mothers who are off leaching sago pith or hunting with their husbands, they usually remain closer to the village. In these peer groups, children of both sexes practise and develop their language skills as they play, recount stories, argue with one another, and explore their environment. But, because they are now speaking Tok Pisin, and because their older pre-school siblings and friends are not active bilinguals, the language skills which get developed during this period continue to be language skills in Tok Pisin.

CONCLUSION

The most basic point about language socialization and language shift in Gapun that I have wanted to stress throughout this chapter is that language socialization patterns in the village structure, and are structured through, a number of culturally specific ideas that villagers have concerning the nature of language, children, and self. The most important of these ideas, and the one that encompasses all the others, is the belief that people are composed of two fundamentally conflicting dimensions, which the villagers call *hed* and *save*.

A central aspect of *save* in Gapun is seen to be accommodation. Speakers should accommodate their listeners in certain ways, such as their choice of language. This idea of listener accommodation results in adults biasing their speech to children towards Tok Pisin, because that language is held to be simpler than Taiap, and therefore more appropriate for children.

But accommodation for this reason is not the only reason why adult speech to children is biased towards Tok Pisin. Because the villagers now see *save* as most appropriately expressed through Tok Pisin, speech to children in Tok Pisin is not only simple accommodation. The basic expectation of all parents in Gapun has always been that their children will come to understand as they grow older that they must 'suppress' their *hed* and show their *save*. What has happened over the course of the past 50 years is that *save* has come to be seen by the villagers as tied to the ways of white people and to the language of white people, which, according to the villagers (who have only lately begun to understand the importance of English in the white man's world) is Tok Pisin. The other dimension of self, *hed*, has, at the same time, come to be seen by the villagers as tied to the ancestors and the language of the ancestors, i.e. the village vernacular Taiap. Because of this shift in the way *save* and *hed* are perceived by the villagers, the parental expectation that their children will 'suppress' their *hed* and show their *save* is resulting in the subtle, but definite, suppression of the Taiap language and the continual display of Tok Pisin, as manifested, for example, in the way that caregivers consistently interpret all vocalizations by children over 1 year of age as Tok Pisin, and never Taiap.

The dynamics of this process of language shift are exceedingly subtle and complex, and this complexity is the reason why adult villagers do not understand why their children are no longer learning Taiap. Adults are doing nothing new, as far as they can see, when they raise their children. They accommodate the child's aggressive *hed* as they have always done, by speaking to it in a simpler language, and by not imposing on it and making it talk if it doesn't want to. And, once parents notice that a child's *save* is beginning to 'break open', they treat the child much as their parents treated them. They gently encourage their children to show their *save* by directing them to do things like give betel nut to visitors. Parents do not appreciate that the bulk of their direct speech to children is not in the vernacular. Because they code-switch as much as they do in all their talk, adults are not aware that their code-switching patterns to children are systematically biased towards Tok Pisin. And even if they could somehow be made aware of this, their conceptions of knowledge as something which 'breaks open' inside a child preclude adults from taking an active role in teaching their children language. Children learn what they want to learn, regardless of what anyone else has to say about it. So adults are genuinely surprised when they notice that their children only speak Tok Pisin, and their own explanation that their children are strongly autonomous, stubborn, and simply unwilling to speak Taiap is logical and quite in line with their understandings of *hed*, of knowledge, and of the nature of children.

NOTES

1 Taiap is a non-Austronesian language which has been classified by Laycock and Z'graggen (1975) as a sub-phylum level isolate within the Sepik-Ramu Phylum (they call the language 'Gapun'). The structure of Taiap is outlined in Kulick and Stroud (1992).

2 Even though this paper concentrates on only two of the villagers' languages (Taiap and Tok Pisin), Gapun is a multilingual community, as I indicate in the title. In addition to Taiap, two other vernacular languages (called Kopar and Adjora in the linguistic literature) are regularly heard and spoken in the village. In addition to speaking Taiap and Tok Pisin, most villagers over 14 have a passive command of at least one other vernacular (usually Kopar). Most men over 40 and women over 35 speak one or two vernacular languages in addition to Taiap (and Tok Pisin). And some men over 50, in addition to speaking Taiap, Tok Pisin, and two additional vernaculars, also understand one or two more.

REFERENCES

Arnberg, L. (1981), *The effects of bilingualism on development during early childhood: a survey of the literature.* (Linköping Studies in Education Reports No. 5.) Linköping, Sweden: Linköping University.

Blom, J. P. and Gumperz, J. (1972), Social meaning in linguistic structure: code-switching in Norway. In J. Gumperz and D. Hymes (eds.), *Directions in sociolinguistics*. New York: Holt, Rinehart and Winston.

Cooley, R. (1979), Variation in Delaware: a dying language. Paper read at the Conference on non-English language variation, University of Louisville, Louisville, Kentucky, 12 October 1979.

Denison, N. (1977), Language death or language suicide? *International Journal of the Sociology of Language*. 12, 13–22.

Döpke, S. (1986), Discourse structures in bilingual families. *Journal of Multilingual and Multicultural Development*. 7:6, 493–507.

Dorian, N. (1980), Linguistic lag as an ethnic marker. *Language in Society*. 9, 33–42.

   (1981), *Language death: the life cycle of a Scottish Gaelic dialect*. Philadelphia: Univesity of Philadelphia Press.

Dutton, T. (1978), The 'Melanesian problem' and language change and disappearance in southeastern Papua New Guinea. MS.

Edwards, J. (1985), *Language, society and identity*. Oxford: Blackwell.

Elmendorf, W. (1981), Last speakers and language change: two California cases. *Anthropological Linguistics*. 1, 36–49.

Fantini, A. (1985), *Language acquisition of a bilingual child: a sociolinguistic perspective*. Avon: Multilingual Matters.

Gal, S. (1979), *Language shift: social determinants of linguistic change in bilingual Austria*. New York: Academic Press.

Giles, H. (ed.) (1977), *Language, ethnicity and intergroup relations*. London: Academic Press.

Goodwin, M. and Goodwin, C. (1987), Children's arguing. In S. Philips, S. Steele, and C. Tanz (eds.), *Language, gender and sex in comparative perspective*. Cambridge: Cambridge University Press.

Heath, S. B. (1983), *Ways with words: language, life and work in communities and classrooms*. Cambridge: Cambridge University Press.

Hill, J. and Hill, K. (1977), Language death and relexification in Tlaxcalan Nahuatl. *International Journal of the Sociology of Language*. 12, 55–67.

Hill, J. and Hill, K. (1986), *Speaking Mexicano: dynamics of syncretic language in Central Mexico*. Tuscon: University of Arizona Press.

Kulick, D. (1992), *Language shift and cultural reproduction: Socialization, – self, and syncretism in a Papua New Guinean village*. New York: Cambridge University Press.

Kulick, D. and Stroud, C. (1990), Code-switching in Gapun: social and linguistic aspects of language use in a language shifting community. In Verhaar, J. (ed.), *Melanesian Pidgin and Tok Pisin*. Amsterdam: John Benjamins.

(1992), The structure of the Taiap (Gapun) language. In Dutton, T., Ross, M. and Tryon, D. T. (eds.), *The language game: papers in memory of Donald C. Laycock*. Canberra: Pacific Linguistics, C–110.

Lanza, E. (1988), Conversations with bilingual two year olds. Paper read at Eleventh Annual Meeting of the American Association for Applied Linguistics, New Orleans, 17–29 December 1988.

Laycock, D. and Z'graggen, J. (1975), The Sepik-Ramu Phylum. In Wurm S. (ed.), *New Guinea area languages and language study. Vol. 1: Papuan languages and the New Guinea linguistic scene*. Canberra: Pacific Linguistics C-38.

Metraux, R. (1965), A study of bilingualism among children of U.S.-French parents. *French Review*. 38, 650–65.

Ochs, E. (1986), Introduction. In B. Schieffelin and E. Ochs (eds.), *Language socialization across cultures*. New York: Cambridge University Press.

(1988), *Culture and language development: language acquisition and language socialization in a Samoan village*. New York: Cambridge University Press.

Pye, C. (1986), One lexicon or two? An alternative interpretation of early bilingual speech. *Journal of Child Language*. 13, 591–3.

Redlinger, W. (1978), Mother's speech to children in bilingual Mexican–American homes. *International Journal of the Sociology of Language*. 17, 73–82.

Sankoff, G. (1971), Language use in multilingual societies: some alternate approaches. In G. Sankoff 1980.

(1980), *The social life of language*. Philadelphia: University of

Pennsylvania Press.

Schach, P. (ed.) (1980), *Languages in conflict*. Lincoln: University of Nebraska Press.

Schieffelin, B. (1990), *The give and take of everyday life: language socialization of Kaluli children*. New York: Cambridge University Press.

Schieffelin, B. and Ochs, E. (1986), Language socialization. *Annual Review of Anthropology*. 15, 163–91.

Schmidt, A. (1985), *Young people's Dyribal: an example of language death from Australia*. Cambridge: University Press.

Scollon, R. and Scollon, S. (1981), *Narrative, literacy and face in interethnic communication*. Norwood, N.J.: Ablex.

Scotton, C. M. (1979), Code-switching as a 'safe choice' in choosing a lingua franca. In McCormack, W. and Wurm, S. (eds.), *Language and society: anthropological issues*. The Hague: Mouton.

Stroud, C. (1992), The problem of intention and meaning in code-switching. *Text*, 12, 127–55.

Taeschner, T. (1983), *The sun is feminine: a study on language acquisition in bilingual children*. Berlin: Springer-Verlag.

Vihman, M. (1985), Language differentiation in the bilingual infant. *Journal of Child Language*. 12, 297–324.

Volterra, V. and Taeschner, T. (1978), The acquisition and development of language by bilingual children. *Journal of Child Language*. 5, 311–26.

Wentworth, W. (1980), *Context and understanding: an inquiry into socialization theory*. New York: Elsevier North-Holland.

5 · Language change in a creole continuum: decreolization?[1]

CHARLENE J. SATO

INTRODUCTION

Decreolization is typically viewed as the process through which a creole language gradually merges with its lexifier language, i.e., the standard language of the community, as a result of creole speakers' increased access to, and 'targeting' of, the latter (Andersen, 1983; Bickerton, 1975; DeCamp, 1971; Rickford, 1983). The study of this process, largely motivated over the last 20 years by questions about the consequences of language contact and the nature of language change, has made less mysterious the extensive linguistic variation observed in contemporary creole communities. Specifically, the proposal that synchronic variation reflects diachronic change in systematic ways (Weinreich, Labov and Herzog, 1968) has received considerable support in cross-sectional investigations (see, e.g., Bickerton, 1973 and 1975; DeCamp, 1971; Rickford, 1979). Perhaps because these studies have yielded significant insights into the systematicity of variation in creole settings, it has been assumed, rather than demonstrated, that their findings reflect how decreolization actually occurs in real time. Yet, as researchers (e.g., Meisel, Clahsen and Pienemann, 1981) in the field of second language acquisition have convincingly shown, important aspects of interlanguage development can be distorted or inadequately described in cross-sectional studies. Among creolists, Rickford (1983) has discussed this problem most extensively, and emphasized the need for longitudinal studies to document actual patterns and rates of change.

The present paper reports on such a study of Hawai'i's creole continuum, focusing on (1) the decreolization rates of different linguistic and discoursal features; (2) the proposal that substantial decreolization occurs, not over the lifetimes of individuals (as in the case of 'normal' second language acquisition), but across generations of speakers (Rickford 1983); and (3) the role of political and socio-psychological factors in decreolization. The first and second issues will be addressed through quantitative analysis of longitudinal data from four Hawai'i Creole English (HCE) speakers.[2] The third will draw upon this writer's analysis, based on participant-observation, of recent public controversies involving HCE.

While cross-sectional studies as early as DeCamp's (1971) on the Jamaican continuum have examined a wide range of linguistic variables (e.g., pronouns, tense–modality–aspect markers, and negative constructions), few have directly addressed the question of differential patterns of decreolization. The most explicit finding comes from work by Escure (1981) in Belize, who reported that morphosyntactic, but not phonological, variables were decreolizing extensively. More recently, Mühlhäusler (1986) has called for greater attention to 'global', rather than 'local', phenomena in decreolizing systems, in light of clear evidence that changes in one linguistic domain, e.g., the lexicon, have repercussions in other domains, e.g., phonology. Such multilevel interactions have already been detailed in interlanguage development (e.g., Sato, 1986 and 1990), thereby strengthening the motivation for examining them more closely in decreolization. Confirmation of the (admittedly limited) cross-sectional findings is viewed here as the next step in determining, ultimately, the causes of variability in decreolization rates.

The question of rate must also be considered in terms of the link between societal and individual characterizations of decreolization. Rickford (1983:302) has convincingly argued for a 'quantitative model which indicates that the primary impact of decreolization might be in the declining proportion of people who speak the creole or basilectal variety, rather than in any decline in the "purity" of that variety itself'. In other words, decreolization as a group phenomenon involves the gradual loss of varieties, beginning at the basilectal end of the continuum and continuing with mesolectal varieties, due to a historical decline in the number of speakers using these varieties.

At the level of the individual, this societal pattern could result primarily from substantial numbers of speakers shifting toward the acrolect within their lifetimes, or it could be due to the appearance of new generations of speakers who acquire mesolectal and acrolectal rather than basilectal varieties. Cross-sectional work on Guyanese Creole by Rickford (1983) indicates that the latter, in fact, contributes more significantly to the societal pattern. Rickford (1983) reports substantive differences across generations of speakers, i.e., between basilectal parents and their children, rather than in the same speaker at different times. Here, then, is another cross-sectional finding that warrants confirmation with longitudinal data from basilectal speakers.

The third issue treated in this paper continues to be debated by creolists, with one perspective limiting the domain of inquiry to language-internal mechanisms of change (Bickerton, 1975, 1977, 1980) and another arguing that social and psychological factors in creole communities affect the process of decreolization in crucial (and currently poorly understood) ways (e.g., LePage and Tabouret-Keller, 1985; Mühlhäusler, 1986; Rickford, 1983 and 1987; Romaine, 1988). Support for the latter view will be provided in this paper through an analysis of recent public controversies involving Hawai'i Creole English (HCE), whose purpose is to illustrate how critical institutional events perceived by creole speakers as attacks on their personal and social identity may actually serve to decelerate decreolization.

HAWAI'I'S ETHNOLINGUISTIC DIVERSITY

Hawai'i's population of a little over a million is unique among the 50 US states in that no single ethnic group comprises a majority. Most islanders are of Asian and Pacific island, rather than European or African, origin. The population is approximately 27% Caucasian, 23% Japanese, and 11% Filipino. Pure native Hawaiians amount to about 0.7%, although part-Hawaiians amount to almost 17%. The remainder of the population includes a sizeable group of non-Hawaiian persons of mixed ancestry (11%), as well as much smaller numbers of Chinese, Africans, Koreans, Puerto Ricans, Samoans, and others (Schmitt, 1982).

This cultural mix is largely the result of massive labour importation during the late nineteenth and early twentieth centuries. In this period, thousands of Chinese, Portuguese, Japanese, and Filipinos (among others) were brought by north Americans to work on their sugar plantations. Sugar rapidly became 'king' (Fuchs, 1961; Kent, 1983) in what had originally been a native Hawaiian kingdom with a subsistence agricultural economy. This economic takeover was soon followed by the islands' formal incorporation into the US, with the overthrow of Hawaiian monarchy in 1893, annexation in 1898, and statehood in 1959.

The plantations also brought a new social order. The native Hawaiian population was physically and culturally decimated (Trask, 1984/1985). By the end of the nineteenth century, they amounted to only one-fifth of the population (Reinecke, 1935/1969) and were outnumbered by the major immigrant labour groups. All lived and worked within the ethnically stratified plantation society controlled by Caucasian owners.

Sugar dominated Hawai'i's economy until the mid-1950s. Since then tourism and, to a lesser extent, the US military and civil service bureaucracies have taken its place. Significantly, the plantation social hierarchy now has its counterpart in the ethnic stratification of workers in the tourist industry, aptly characterized as 'a new kind of sugar' (Kent, 1974). Today, Hawai'i's middle class is primarily Caucasian and Asian, while the working class is largely composed of native Hawaiians, Filipinos, and recent Asian and Pacific island immigrants (Kent, 1983).

Extended contact among Hawai'i's native and immigrant peoples produced, first, a pidginized Hawaiian by the end of the nineteenth century, then a pidginized English during the early 1900s, and a flourishing creole by the 1920s (for detailed discussion, see Bickerton and Odo, 1976; Bickerton and Wilson, 1987; Day, 1987;

Reinecke, 1935/69; and Sato, 1985). Over the last half-century, industrialization, mass education, and urbanization have substantially increased the HCE-speaking population's exposure to American English, thereby setting the stage for widespread decreolization among HCE speakers. There is, after several years of research (see, e.g., Bickerton, 1977 and 1981; Day, 1972; Neff, 1978; Odo, 1975; Peet, 1978; Perlman, 1973; Purcell, 1984; Sato, 1978), abundant synchronic evidence of decreolization at the societal level. On the basis of the socio-economic and linguistic evidence, one might reasonably expect to find most HCE speakers moving steadily toward the acrolect in Hawai'i's creole continuum. In fact, this process has been attenuated in some speakers, as will now be shown.

DECREOLIZATION IN INDIVIDUALS: A LONGITUDINAL STUDY

In the larger study from which the present data are taken, six male speakers of HCE were contacted and interviewed by a male HCE-speaking researcher. All had participated in Bickerton's major survey of pidgin and creole English in Hawai'i roughly 15 years earlier (see Bickerton, 1977; Bickerton and Odo, 1976) and were selected for the follow-up study on the basis of their basilectal HCE. A preliminary analysis of conversational data from 4 of the 6 subjects, listed in Table 5.1, will be reported here.

At the end of the data collection session, each subject was asked by the interviewer for biographical information, and was questioned about his work history and changes in his social networks over the last 15 years. All of the speakers indicated increased and sustained contact with standard English (SE) speakers, in their workplaces and/or in the community, during this period. A more detailed description of the nature of their exposure to SE would, of course, be required for any specific connection between social profiles and linguistic behaviour to be drawn, but this is not the present objective. It is sufficient to point out here that these speakers have

Table 5.1. *Subjects*

JA	Filipino, 61, Big Island (Hawai'i)
	Foreman for shipyard, former welder
	High school education
	Residence for the past 10 years: Maui
GN	Japanese, 45, Big Island
	Coffee farmer in Kona
	$1\frac{1}{2}$ years of university
VV	Filipino, 56, Kaua'i
	Sugar plantation machine operator
	Completed 1 year of high school
	13 children
HK	Part-Hawaiian, 51, Kaua'i
	Welder, musician, former lifeguard

not been hermits or otherwise avoided contact with SE in any way. Rather, they appear to have lived in circumstances conducive to decreolization.

Although the total corpus of HCE interviews consists of approximately three hours of tape per subject, the present analysis is limited to a phonetically transcribed half-hour excerpt (the first half-hour of the session) for each subject, in which the following features are examined: (1) post-vocalic *r*, (2) indefinite reference as encoded in articles, and (3) past time reference for non-stative verbs. In each case, an increase in the percentage of SE surface forms from Time 1 to Time 2 is viewed as evidence of decreolization.

The finding for post-vocalic *r*, as in the words 'aboard' (abawd/ abord) and 'here' (hia/hir), is that little decreolization has occurred in the four speakers (see Table 5.2).[3] No one uses substantially more post-vocalic *r* at Time 2 than at Time 1, and the highest percentage of *r*-fulness at Time 2 is only 6% (for GN and VV). Moreover, even generally *r*-ful lexical items exhibited some variability.

Results for the analysis of past time reference with nonstative verbs reveal even more variation across the speakers. The variants of interest here are the following:

Table 5.2. *Post-vocalic* r

Subject	ϕ		r		Total
	no.	%	no.	%	no.
JA-T1[a]	248	100	0	0	248
JA-T2[a]	194	97	6	3	200
GN-T1	434	99	5	1	439
GN-T2	224	93	18	7	242
VV-T1	198	95	11	5	209
VV-T2	300	89	37	11	337
HK-T1	255	90	27	10	282
HK-T2	93	89	12	11	105

Note:
[a]T1 = Time 1 (1973), T2 = Time 2 (1986, 1988 or 1989)

ϕ ai kawl__ wan taim
       'I called once'

bin   aen hi *bin* bulshet mi
       'and he bullshitted me'

wen   so wen da wahinez *wen* kam intavyu mi
       'so when the women came to interview me'

haed   e mai sista *haed* krai yu no
       'hey, my sister cried, you know'

neva   kawz ai *nea* laik haeng aut oa dea
       'because I didn't want to hang out over there'
Strong past and weak past tense verbs, e.g., 'caught,' 'wanted'

Two of the speakers, GN and VV, show a preference for SE
variants at Time 2, whereas there is no appreciable increase for JA
and a 20% *decrease* in SE forms for HK. In other words, only 2 of the
4 can be said to have decreolized with respect to the marking of past
time on non-stative verbs. As has been widely reported in the SLA

Table 5.3. *Indefinite reference*

Subject	HCE		SE		Total
	no.	%	no.	%	no.
JA-T1	11	35	20	65	31
JA-T2	37	73	14	27	51
GN-T1	33	75	11	25	44
GN-T2	22	49	23	51	45
VV-T1	14	78	4	22	18
VV-T2	17	44	22	56	39
HK-T1	52	73	19	27	71
HK-T2	17	58	12	41	29

literature (e.g., Sato 1986) the verbs marked for SE past tense tend to be strong/irregular verbs rather than weak/regular verbs.

It is also worth noting what appears to be non-decreolizing change in two speakers' use of HCE past time auxiliaries. First, VV seems to have shifted from *bin* to the Kaua'i variant *haed* (which HK also uses) between Time 1 and Time 2. VV attributes this shift to the influence of his children. Second, JA, one of the Big Island speakers, also decreases his use of *bin* at Time 2, but in favour of *wen*, which is the most widely used variant across the islands.

The analysis of indefinite reference involves the HCE ϕ-article, *wan*, and SE *a*, as in this example: *no kaen meik* $\left\{ \begin{array}{c} \phi \\ wan \\ a \end{array} \right\}$ *gaden* ('you can't make a garden'). Table 5.3 shows that 3 of the 4 speakers appear to have decreolized to some extent; that is, GN, VV, and HK show an increase of 26%, 34%, and 14%, respectively, in their use of the SE variant. JA, however, shows a 38% *decrease* in SE *a* from Time 1 to Time 2.

As with past time reference, increased use of SE *a* parallels a pattern commonly observed in 'normal' SLA; that is to say, *a* tends to appear first and frequently in formulaic expressions such as 'give a

Table 5.4. *Past time reference (nonstatives)*

Subject	HCE		SE		Total
	no.	%	no.	%	no.
JA-T1	82	65	45	35	127
JA-T2	49	64	28	36	77
GN-T1	35	48	38	52	73
GN-T2	28	32	59	68	87
VV-T1	57	79	15	21	72
VV-T2	51	54	43	46	94
HK-T1	13	50	13	50	26
HK-T2	52	70	22	30	74

damn'. Analysis of two other features, existential predication and *aeh*-tags, is still in progress, but some tentative observations can be offered. In the case of existential predication, encoded in utterance-initial *get* or SE expletive *there* (e.g., aen den *get* faiv aen a haef eikaz oa hea, 'and *there are* five and a half acres over here'), all 4 speakers strongly prefer the HCE variant at Time 2; only 2 speakers produced the expletive *there*, once each.

What can be said about *aeh*-tags is even more tentative. In HCE conversation these tags function mainly as confirmation checks roughly equivalent to SE utterance-final 'you know' or 'you see,' as in

yae bikawz ai chro frt aeh?
'Yeah, because I throw fertilizer [i.e., fertilize sugar cane], you know?'
no, waz-waz lo taid aeh, aeswai
'no, because it was low tide, you see'

Speakers use *aeh*, in other words, to keep the listener engaged, often during narrative sequences in conversation. This feature behaves differently from the others thus far examined in that only 2 (VV and JA) of the 4 speakers appear to use it frequently, and neither of them seems to be giving it up.

Table 5.5. *Relative rates of decreolization of three features*

Post-voc. *r*	Past Time Ref.	Indef. Ref.
− <	DECREOLIZATION	> +

Returning to the three features for which quantitative results are available, the picture for decreolization appears to be the one sketched in Table 5.5, with Post-vocalic *r* at the least decreolized end of the scale, indefinite reference at the other end, and past time reference in between. This result coincides with Escure's (1981) observation for Belize, that decreolization was more prominent in morphosyntactic than phonological features.

The variable results across speakers is also notable. JA appears to have decreolized the least among the 4, showing a mere 3% increase for post-vocalic *r* insertion, no movement towards SE past time marking, and a preference for HCE variants in marking indefinite reference. In HK's data, movement toward the acrolect is discernable for past time reference, but not for indefinite reference of post-vocalic *r* use. The other two speakers show a shift toward the acrolect in all three domains.

In sum, while there is some evidence of decreolization in these data, it is not much of a change over a 15-year period, and it seems plausible to conclude, following Rickford (1983), that extensive decreolization is not manifested in individuals during their lifetime. The claim here, of course, is that the speakers examined in this study are not unrepresentative of the basilectal HCE-speaking population. If this claim is correct, what accounts for the cross-sectional evidence of community-wide decreolization? Perhaps this is largely due to the behaviour of mesolectal speakers, who may decreolize more rapidly and extensively than basilectal speakers do, owing to a 'starting' point closer to the acrolect. Or, as Rickford (*ibid.*) claims, it is in fact the generation following that of the speakers examined here to whom the mesolectal to acrolectal shift should be attributed. Such questions will need to be addressed in future work. What will be taken up now is a related question: how the course of decreolization is affected by language-external factors in creole communities.

THE SOCIOPOLITICAL CONTEXT OF DECREOLIZATION

Throughout its history as a marker of ethnic (actually, non-white) identity during the plantation era, and of working-class identity subsequently, HCE was heavily stigmatized (Reinecke, 1935/1969; Sato, 1985). Creole speakers have typically been ashamed of their speech, referring to it as 'broken' or 'bad' English, a bad habit that must be overcome in order to 'succeed' in life. Studies of language attitudes in Hawai'i have repeatedly reported predominantly negative attitudes towards HCE on the part of creole and non-creole speakers alike (e.g., Day, 1980; McCreary, 1986; Yamamoto, 1982; see Sato, 1991 for review). Only in its more recent crystallization as a marker of a pan-ethnic, 'local' (vs. the mainland US) identity has HCE acquired overt prestige, at least among some segments of the community. Moreover, as the following account of public controversies will illustrate, a somewhat militant stance against the replacement of HCE by SE in public domains has emerged. This is a remarkable trend, if one considers the extensive socialization toward all things American that islanders have actively colluded in, or had imposed on them, for several generations.

In the autumn of 1987 a major debate about the status of HCE was provoked by the state Board of Education's (BOE)[4] attempt to implement a SE-only policy in the schools, and by a civil rights discrimination lawsuit brought against the US National Weather Service by two local meteorological technicians. Only a brief sketch of these events follows, since the main point here is simply to illustrate how social forces can dramatically problematize language use in a decreolizing community (for more detailed discussion, see Sato, 1989, 1991 and in preparation; Watson-Gegeo, 1990).

The language policy originally proposed by a sub-committee of the BOE stated:

Standard English will be the mode of oral communication for students and staff in the classroom setting and all other school related settings except when the objectives cover native Hawaiian or foreign language instruction and practice. (Hawai'i Board of Education memorandum, August 1987)

Board members apparently thought their action would be favourably received by the community.[5] Much to their consternation, reaction came immediately from several quarters, including parents, teachers, university faculty, native Hawaiian and other community activists, and even some elements of the mass media. The proposed policy was perceived as discriminatory, i.e., as an unfair attack on HCE, on local culture and on the educational rights of local people. Researchers, mainly from the University of Hawai'i's Department of English as a Second Language, criticized the Board's unprofessional rejection of research in creole languages, second language acquisition, and language teaching, which uniformly discredited the assumptions and directives of the policy (Sato, 1989). All of these objections were raised at what proved to be a historic four-hour evening meeting held by the board to receive public testimony.

The meeting was packed with over 100 people, a well as news crews from the three major TV stations and various newspapers. All but a few who offered testimony on the policy vigorously opposed it, some through academic argument, others through HCE poetry recitation, and still others through political oratory. All of the 'opposition' speakers received rousing applause and cheers from the audience. Never before in Hawai'i's history had such a diversity of voices been raised, in a formal institutional setting, in defence of Hawai'i Creole English. Taken aback by this extraordinary display of feeling against the policy, the Board eventually adopted a much weaker version which simply 'encouraged' the modelling of SE by teachers and staff members in the Department of Education.

The publicity generated by this event was unprecedented. Letters flooded the newspapers, and radio talk shows and TV news programmes covered the controversy every day for a week in September. One of the two major daily newspapers commissioned a special week-long series on HCE, which proved informative and generally quite supportive of HCE as a marker of local identity (see Brislin, 1987; Hartwell, 1987; Hollis, 1987; Keir, 1987; Matsunaga, 1987; Reyes, 1987a–g).

The language policy debate coincided with what was perhaps a more critical event concerning the civil rights of HCE speakers: A lawsuit (Kahakua et al. v. Hallgren) against the National Weather Service which went to trial during the same week the BOE language policy was debated. The NWS was charged with, among other things, race and national origin discrimination. US civil rights legislation prohibits discrimination in federal employment on the basis of race or national origin, the latter including not only an individual's or his or her ancestor's place of origin, but also physical, cultural or linguistic characteristics of an individual which are attributable to a national origin group (appellants' Opening Brief, Kahakua et al. v. Friday, 1988).

The plaintiffs were two male meteorological technicians, a part-Hawaiian American and a Japanese–American (hereafter referred to as J and G, respectively), who had been born and raised in Hawai'i, and who had worked for the NWS for several years. J and G applied for vacancies, one in April 1985 and another in October 1986, in the Public Service Unit of the NWS's Honolulu office. On both occasions, they were required to submit (contrary to established NWS hiring procedures) an audiotaped weather forecast as part of their applications, and on each occasion, a young Caucasian far less qualified than either J or G, and with a mainland American English accent, was hired. In the suit, J and G claimed that their candidacies were downgraded because of their HCE accents and in spite of their superior qualifications and exemplary employment records with the NWS. The NWS countered that the Caucasians had been selected because they 'sounded better' than J and G.

Newspaper headlines about the case, such as 'suit says men rejected because of "pidgin" use' (Oshiro, 1987) and 'complaints about "pidgin" told in job bias trial' (Wiles, 1987), gave the impression that J and G spoke basilectal, i.e., unintelligible to mainland US ears, creole. Expert witness testimony by the present writer countered this view on the basis of phonetic analysis of taped weather forecasts by J and G, such as those they had submitted to the NWS (Sato, 1987). The following HCE features were observed in their speech, given here in decreasing order of their frequency in the transcripts examined:

1 Full vowels where many mainland varieties of English reduce vowels: e.g., /u/ rather than /ə/ in 'today;'
2 /d/ where many mainland varieties of English have /ð/, as in 'with;'
3 Monophthongs where many mainland varieties of English have diphthongs: e.g., /o/ rather than /oṳ/ in 'low;' and
4 φ where many mainland varieties of English have a sulcal /r/, as in 'afternoon'.

Whereas (1) and (2) were frequent for both J and G, (3) and (4) were rare, i.e., the SE variants were usually produced. These results, along with an analysis of conversational speech from both men, showed that they were far from basilectal in the data examined. It was entirely possible, of course, that J and G were capable of basilectal HCE. However, the crucial point was that, in performing their professional duties, they used standard Hawai'i English of the sort spoken by the majority of highly educated, locally born professionals, including the state's part-Hawaiian Governor and Filipino Lieutenant Governor.

At the end of three-and-a-half days of testimony, the judge, brought in from California for the trial, announced his ruling: The NWS had not discriminated against G and J. He even suggested that the men put more effort into improving their speech. The suddenness of his ruling, immediately following closing arguments, surprised everyone, as it is common practice for decisions to be issued several weeks following trial. G and J subsequently filed an appeal in the US Court of Appeals for the Ninth Circuit (in San Francisco, California), but in 1989 the original ruling was upheld. They have since decided not to pursue matters any further, an understandable decision in the face of a legal climate that is overwhelmingly hostile to language diversity and challenges to the sociolinguistic status quo.

Although the discrimination case received far less publicity than did the BOE language policy, and newspaper accounts tended to present the crux of the case as a matter of 'good' vs. 'bad' English, a surprising degree of public support for J and G's position became evident. Listeners who heard G interviewed on the radio called in to comment on how well he in fact spoke and asked 'what all the fuss was about anyway'. Several of this writer's friends, family members, and colleagues at the university had similar reactions upon watching G perform a weather forecast on TV. Perhaps the most troubling aspect of the case was keenly felt by local professionals (e.g., teachers, lawyers, news reporters) who speak like J and G: That they, whatever their substantive qualifications, were vulnerable to discrimination simply because of an HCE accent.

While no large-scale survey data can be offered as yet on public reaction to this case or the BOE language policy, it is clear that these events have at least raised the community's awareness of what is at stake in retaining HCE. While some HCE speakers may strive even harder to acquire a mainland US accent, others appear prepared to publicly defend and maintain, not only a creole accent, but other features of HCE as well. In Milroy's (1982) terms, a solidarity ideology has emerged in Hawai'i, partly, it is argued here, as a result of a political crisis. After a half-century of decreolization, it seems that those who might otherwise subscribe to a status-based interpretation of linguistic diversity in Hawai'i, i.e., one which assigns prestige exclusively to SE, have been moved to reject it in favour of one which more accurately reflects the social and political reality of their lives.

Hawai'i may have entered a phase described by Rickford (1983) as an intermediate stage of decreolization which may be maintained for generations because of sociopsychological factors favouring creole maintenance, even by speakers who have added an acrolectal variety to their repertoire. If the events described above have in fact politicized a sizeable number of individuals, stylistic shifting may be significantly restructured in public domains. More than ever before, intraspeaker variation along Hawai'i's continuum will be describable as 'acts of identity' by creole speakers (LePage and Tabouret-Keller, 1985), who are subject throughout their lives to the tensions inherent in post-colonial capitalist societies.

Hypotheses about the future course of decreolization can be derived, at least in general terms, from recent governmental projections about Hawai'i's economy and plans to ensure its continued 'growth'. Tourism, Hawai'i's primary industry, 'is predicted to grow $2\frac{1}{2}$ times faster than the labor force, in a state already experiencing labor shortages in 1990' (Watson-Gegeo, 1990:18). Workers will be needed to fill jobs in expanded trade and service sectors, jobs which will not, by the government's own admission, pay well (Pai, 1990). Since local workers could not survive on the low wages to be offered, the industry will resort to a familiar solution: Massive labour importation.

Demographic effects by the year 2010 are predicted to include a 23% population increase in Honolulu and, more notably, an 81% increase in the neighbouring islands, precisely the areas in which 'HCE is the most widespread and least decreolized' (Watson-Gegeo, 1990:19). At least 25% of the immigrants are expected to come from Southeast Asia and various Pacific islands. Most of these will not speak English and, depending on circumstances surrounding their arrival, are likely to acquire HCE or participate in its repidginization.

Perhaps as important to the course of decreolization as labour importation will be the maintenance of socio-economic stratification by the tourist industry. Class lines will be more sharply drawn than they have been over the last quarter of a century, and it would be surprising for HCE *not* to have a unifying influence among the multi-ethnic workforce, just as it did a century ago on the sugar plantations.

CONCLUSION

In the decades to come, the process of decreolization in Hawai'i will be subject to a new configuration of influences, both linguistic and non-linguistic. It is the interaction of the influences, rather than the dominance of one or the other, that requires attention in future work in this area. Hopefully, this paper has succeeded in demonstrating the value of real-time studies of this process, not as a substitute for cross-sectional studies, but as a means of revealing patterns and rates of change that cross-sectional studies cannot easily capture. It should be uncontroversial to suggest at this point that ecologically valid accounts of language change in creole continua must go beyond strictly linguistic constraints on decreolization. Ideally, they should examine how these constraints are neutralized, if they are, by the social marking of HCE features or particular types of features (e.g., prosodic as opposed to morphological). How best to accommodate the social-psychological dimensions of linguistic variation to the study of decreolization remains a problem, of course, but not an insurmountable one. It may be a reasonable starting point to think of decreolization as only one direction of change in a creole community.

NOTES

1 Grateful acknowledgement is made to the US National Science Foundation for funding the research reported in this paper (NSF grant no. BNS-8710928) and to Don Topping, Director of the University of Hawai'i Social Science Research Institute, for his generous support of this project. I would also like to thank Kent Sakoda for his invaluable help in collecting the data.

2 These data come from the larger corpus collected for the NSF Project, 'A longitudinal study of decreolization' (NSF grant no. BNS-8710928).

3 All HCE examples in this paper are written in an orthography developed for the Nonstandard Hawaiian English Project (Bickerton, 1977; Bickerton and Odo, 1976) by Dr. Carol Odo.

4 The Board of Education, an elected body of thirteen members, controls the educational policy and finances of Hawai'i's centralized public school system. It appoints the Superintendent of the Department of Education, who implements the Board's policies and administers the school system.

5 In a September 18, 1987 memo, the BOE Curriculum Committee advised

the Chair of the Board as follows: 'Although no field input was obtained, major arguments against the [English only] policy are not anticipated inasmuch as there appears to be general public recognition of the problem.'

REFERENCES

Andersen, R. (1983), Introduction: A language acquisition interpretation of pidginization and creolization. In Andersen, R. (ed.), *Pidginization and creolization as language acquisition*. Rowley, Mass.: Newbury House.

Bickerton, D. (1973), The nature of a creole continuum. *Language*, 49, 641–69.

(1975), *Dynamics of a creole system*. Cambridge: Cambridge University Press.

(1977), Change and variation in Hawaiian English, II: Creole syntax. (Final Report on National Science Foundation Project No. GS-39748).

(1980), Decreolisation and the creole continuum. In Valdman, A. and Highfield, A. (eds.), *Theoretical orientations in creole studies*. New York: Academic Press.

(1981). *Roots of language*, Ann Arbor: Karoma Publishers.

Bickerton, D. and Odo, C. (1976), Change and variation in Hawaiian English, Volume I: General phonology and pidgin syntax. (Final Report on National Science Foundation Project No. GS-39748).

Bickerton, D. and Wilson, W. (1987), Pidgin Hawaiian. In Gilbert, G. (ed.), *Pidgin and creole languages: Essays in memory of John E. Reinecke*. Honolulu: University of Hawai'i Press.

Brislin, T. (1987), 'Pidgin Laureate' praises both tongues. *The Honolulu Advertiser*, 27 September, pp. A6–7.

Day, R. R. (1972), Patterns of variation in copula and tense in the Hawaiian post-creole continuum. Unpublished Ph.D. thesis, University of Hawai'i.

(1980), The development of linguistic attitudes and preferences. *TESOL Quarterly*, 14, 27–37.

(1987), Early pidginization in Hawaii. In Gilbert, G. (ed.), *Pidgin and creole languages: Essays in memory of John E. Reinecke*. Honolulu: University of Hawai'i Press.

DeCamp, D. (1971), Toward a generative analysis of a post-creole speech continuum. In Hymes, D. (ed.), *Pidginization and creolization of languages*. London: Cambridge University Press.

Escure, G. (1981), Decreolization in a creole continuum: Belize. In Highfield, A. and Valdman, A. (eds.), *Historicity and variation in creole studies*. Ann Arbor: Karoma Publishers.

Fuchs, L. (1961), *Hawaii Pono: A social history*. New York: Harcourt, Brace and World.

Hartwell, J. (1987), Pidgin was invented by Hawaiians, traders. *The Honolulu Advertiser*, 27 September, p. A6.

Hollis, R. (1987), Pidgin called too deeply rooted to die out. *The Honolulu Advertiser*, 30 September, pp. A1, A12.

Kahakua, et al. v. Hallgren, Civil No. 86-0434, US District Court, Honolulu, Hawai'i (1987).

Keir, J. (1987), The great expectations on English in schools. *The Honolulu Advertiser*, 28 September, p. A5.

Kent, N. (1974), A new kind of sugar. In Finney, B. and Watson, K. A. (eds.), *A new kind of sugar: Tourism in the Pacific*. Honolulu: The East–West Center.

   (1983), *Hawaii: Islands under the influence*. New York: Monthly Review Press.

Le Page, R. and Tabouret-Keller, A. (1985), *Acts of identity*. Cambridge: Cambridge University Press.

Matsunaga, M. (1987), Most officials don't talk li' dat these days. *The Honolulu Advertiser*, 29 September, pp. A1, A4.

McCreary, J. (1986), Attitudes of non-native speakers of English to language variation in Hawai'i. Unpublished MA thesis, University of Hawai'i.

Meisel, J., Clahsen, H. and Pienemann, M. (1981), On determining developmental stages in natural second language acquisition. *Studies in Second Language Acquisition*, 3, 109–35.

Milroy, L. (1982). Language and group identity. *Journal of Multilingual and Multicultural Development*, 3, 207–16.

Mühlhäusler, P. (1986), *Pidgin and creole linguistics*. Oxford: Basil Blackwell.

Neff, K. (1977), Theories of the syntax of aspect. Unpublished Ph.D. thesis, University of Hawai'i.

Odo, C. (1975), Phonological processes in the English dialect of Hawai'i. Unpub. Ph.D. diss., University of Hawai'i.

Oshiro, S. (1987), Suit says men rejected because of 'pidgin' use. *The Honolulu Advertiser*, 16 September, p. A3.

Pai, G. (1990), The dynamics of global change and post-secondary education in Hawaii. Presented to the University of Hawai'i Professional Assembly's Faculty Representative Forum, 10 February, Honolulu.

Peet, W. (1978), Relativization in a creole continuum. Unpublished Ph.D. thesis, University of Hawai'i.

Perlman, A. (1973), Grammatical structure and style shift in Hawaiian pidgin and creole. Unpublished Ph.D. thesis, University of Chicago.

Purcell, A. (1984), Code-shifting Hawaiian style: Children's accommodation along a decreolizing continuum. *International Journal of the Sociology of Language*, 46, 71–86.

Reinecke, J. E. (1935/1969), *Language and dialect in Hawaii*. Honolulu: University of Hawai'i Press.

Reyes, D. (1987a), Panel wants pidgin kept out of schools. *The Honolulu Advertiser*, 2 September, pp. A1, A5.

(1987b), Panel urges pidgin ban in schools. *The Honolulu Advertiser*, 16 September, p. A1.

(1987c), Board votes 7–4 to keep pidgin out of classroom. *The Honolulu Advertiser*, 18 September, pp. A1, A4.

(1987d), Pidgin use in schools clarified. *The Honolulu Advertiser*, 19 September, pp. A1, A12.

(1987e), Pidgin: Teachers – and children – face a dilemma. *The Honolulu Advertiser*, 27 September, pp. A1, A6.

(1987f), Pidgin: School board, other educators have their say on its place in the schools. *The Honolulu Advertiser*, 28 September, p. A5.

(1987g), Switch to English may mean talking pidgin. *The Honolulu Advertiser*, 28 September, pp. A1, A4.

Rickford, J. (1979), Variation in a creole continuum: Quantitative and implicational approaches. Ph.D. Thesis, University of Pennsylvania.

(1983), What happens in decreolization. In Andersen, R. (ed.),

Pidginization and creolization as language acquisition. Rowley, Mass.: Newbury House.

(1987), *Dimensions of a creole continuum.* Stanford: Stanford University Press.

Romaine, S. (1988), *Pidgin and creole languages.* London: Longman Group.

Sato, C. J. (1978), Variation in Hawaiian Pidgin and Creole English: *go* plus verb constructions. Unpublished MA thesis, University of Hawai'i.

(1985), Linguistic inequality in Hawaii: The post-creole dilemma. In Wolfson, N. and Manes, J. (eds.) *Language of inequality.* Berlin: Mouton Publishers.

(1986), Conversation and interlanguage development: Rethinking the connection. In Day, R. (ed.), *Talking to learn.* Rowley, Mass.: Newbury House.

(1987), Technical description of plaintiffs' speech. Unpublished MS., Honolulu, Hawai'i.

(1989), A nonstandard approach to standard English. *TESOL Quarterly,* 22, 259–82.

(1990), *The syntax of conversation in interlanguage development.* Tübingen: Gunter Narr.

(1991), Sociolinguistic variation and language attitudes in Hawaii. In J. Cheshire (ed.), *English around the world: Sociolinguistic perspectives.* Cambridge: Cambridge University Press.

(In preparation). Language politics and applied sociolinguistics: Hawai'i Creole English on trial.

Schmitt, R. (1982), Hawai'i's social rating. *Social Process in Hawai'i,* 29, 151–7.

Trask, H.-K. (1984/1985), Hawaiians, American colonization, and the quest for independence. *Social Process in Hawaii,* 31, 101–36.

Watson-Gegeo, K. (1990), Language and education in Hawai'i: Sociopolitical and economic implications of Hawai'i Creole English. Paper presented at the conference on 'The social significance of creole language situation', 2–3 March, Pomona College, Pomona, California, USA.

Weinreich, U., Labov, W. and Herzog, M. (1968). Empirical foundations for a theory of language change. In Lehmann, ʻW.

(ed.), *Proceedings of the Texas conference on historical linguistics*. Austin: University of Texas Press.

Wiles, G. (1987). Complaints about 'pidgin' told in job bias trial. *The Honolulu Advertiser*, 17 September.

Yamamoto, J. (1982). The perception and stereotyping of speech varieties in Hawaii. *University of Hawaii Working Papers in Linguistics*, 14:2, 75–88.

Psycho- and neurolinguistic aspects

6 · Neurolinguistic aspects of first language acquisition and loss[1]

JEAN BERKO GLEASON

This paper will begin with a discussion of normal language acquisition by children, and a consideration of the neurolinguistic concomitants of both normal and atypical language development. The major perspective here is a social interactionist one: That is, it seems clear now that children acquire language both by virtue of the inherent neuropsychological endowments that are unique to humans, and by the nature of their early interactions with (not just exposure to) older speakers.

After the basic evidence related to acquisition has been presented, the paper will discuss briefly the loss or regression of a first language both in children and adults: Here, the major view is that when some condition such as brain damage causes language regression, the patterns of loss that occur in children are not the same as those that result when adults lose their language under similar conditions—childhood aphasia is qualitatively different from adulthood aphasia. Finally, when adults lose their language through neurological damage, the order of loss is not a mirror image of language acquisition in childhood, although this claim is often made (Jakobson, 1968). The assumption throughout this chapter is that bilingualism and second language development are best understood in the context of our knowledge about monolingual or first language development.

THEORETICAL APPROACHES TO THE STUDY OF LANGUAGE ACQUISITION

Although there is general agreement in the research world about *what* is entailed in the course of language acquisition by children, there is considerable controversy among theorists about *how* language development takes place. Recently, information processing models and theories have appeared which are useful for the elucidation of how particular syntactic structures such as plurals or past tenses may be acquired (McClellan, Rumelhart and PDP Group, 1986). More general theories which attempt to account for all facets of linguistic development are based on at least four major theoretical perspectives:

Behavioural theory

Learning theorists (e.g., Skinner, 1957) claim basically that language is a learned behaviour, like any other learned behaviour. Behaviourists see language development as a result of adults' reinforcement and gradual shaping of infants' babbling, and apply the general principles of learning to later developments. No special language mechanisms are postulated, since external behaviour rather than mental activity is the object of study. Learning theorists do not deny that there may be neuropsychological mechanisms that underlie language, but they deny the usefulness of mentalistic approaches.

Linguistic/innatist theory

Linguistic theorists rely heavily on theories of mind, and on special abstract mechanisms, such as a postulated LAD or Language Acquisition Device (Chomsky, 1965, 1972). In contrast to learning theorists, they believe that the basic principles of language are innate, and that language unfolds once the human infant has been exposed to language. Language is a hard-wired bioprogramme that will develop once the infant is exposed to language. The language that infants hear provides data for their (infants') grammatical hypotheses. Infants may be innately endowed with linguistic switches or parameters that they set once they hear the adult language around them; for instance, they may note that English is a subject/verb/object language (Hyams, 1986). Language is seen as a separate, autonomous faculty, and infants are believed to be innately driven to acquire it. There may be a critical or sensitive period during which the Language Acquisition Device and parameter setting can optimally function, according to this view.

Cognitive theory

Cognitive theorists believe that language is one aspect of human cognition (Piaget, 1926; Sinclair-deZwart, 1973). According to this view, infants must learn about the world around them, which they do through active experimentation and 'construction'. For instance, the infant crawls around the floor, observes objects from all angles, and slowly develops an understanding of the space in which she lives. Primitive notions of time and causality develop, as well as an understanding that people and objects continue to exist, even when they are out of sight. According to a Piagetian perspective, language is mapped on to an individual's set of prior cognitions, and the principles of language are no different from other cognitive principles.

Social interactionist theory

Social interactionists (e.g. Snow, 1981) are rather eclectic. They do not deny the existence of special neuropsychological endowments, but they also hold that biological factors, while necessary, are not sufficient to ensure that language will develop. There is less reliance on postulated hard-wired and time-limited neural structures (such as the Language Acquisition Device) for which there is no anatomical evidence. Nor is language development seen as simply one aspect of

SPEAKING A HEARD WORD

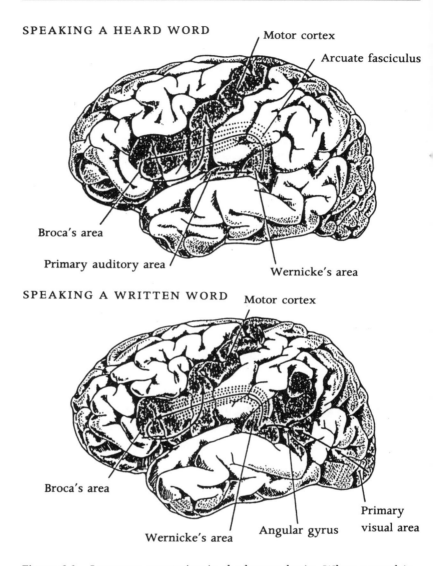

Figure 6.1   Language processing in the human brain. When a word is heard (*upper diagram*), the sensation from the ears is received by the primary auditory cortex, but the word cannot be understood until the signal has been processed in Wernicke's area nearby. If the word is to be spoken, some representation of it is thought to be transmitted from

cognitive development. Instead, social interactionists view language as a facet of communicative behaviour which develops through interaction with other human beings. This paper will take this basic perspective in explaining how biological and social factors interact during the course of language development in children.

FIRST LANGUAGE ACQUISITION: 'NORMAL' DEVELOPMENT

Biological bases

Research over the last 30 years has provided us with a large database as well as evidence of universal, neuropsychologically based, processes in language development. Linguistic capacity relies upon, among other things, neuroanatomical structures that are unique to our species.

Left hemisphere specialization for language appears to be innate; cerebral asymmetries have been noted as early as the 18th week of gestation (Witelson, 1977). In particular, the *planum temporale* (temporal plane) of the left hemisphere is larger than its homologue

Caption for fig.6.1 (*cont.*)
Wernicke's area to Broca's area, through a bundle of nerve fibres called the arcuate fasciculus. In Broca's area the word evokes a detailed program for articulation, which is supplied to the face area of the motor cortex. The motor cortex in turn drives the muscles of the lips, the tongue, the larynx and so on. When a written word is read (*lower diagram*), the sensation is first registered by the primary visual cortex. It is then thought to be relayed to the angular gyrus, which associates the visual form of the word with the corresponding auditory pattern in Wernicke's area. Speaking the word then draws on the same systems of neurons as before. Adapted from "Specializations of the Human Brain" by N. Geschwind. Copyright © 1979 Scientific American, Inc. All rights reserved. Reprinted by permission.)

on the right; ultimately, the left temporal plane develops into Wernicke's area (in the medial and superior left temporal lobe; see Fig. 6.1). Wernicke's area is known to be involved in the processing of incoming speech, and damage to Wernicke's area in an adult speaker results in a typical language deficit, Wernicke's aphasia. Other areas of the brain are also known to be intimately involved with language. These include Broca's area in the posterior inferior left frontal lobe, and the arcuate fasciculus, which is a band of subcortical fibres that connects Wernicke's area to Broca's area. In a simplified neurolinguistic model, repetition of a word such as *cat* that one has heard would entail the following: first the individual hears the spoken word. After processing in the auditory association area, the word is transmitted to Wernicke's area, which aids in comprehension. From Wernicke's area, it is transmitted to Broca's area, where it is programmed for speech production, after which the individual repeats the word 'cat'. This model is displayed in Figure 6.1, along with a schema that details how one may speak a word after reading it.

Much of the evidence for this neuroanatomical specialization derives from the aphasiological literature. We know, for instance, that damage to Broca's area results in a problem with producing speech, that damage to Wernicke's area leads to problems with comprehension, and that damage to the arcuate fasciculus results in an inability to repeat words that one has heard. A discussion of other cortical and subcortical regions that subserve language processing is beyond the scope of this chapter, but it should be noted that there are other areas, such as the cerebellum and basal ganglia, as well as cortical areas such as Heschl's gyrus and the angular gyrus that underlie the human ability to understand language and to speak, as well as to read and write. Left hemisphere specialization is the rule, although in some small percentage of individuals language appears to be represented in the right hemisphere. There is also evidence that there is sufficient plasticity of function in the human brain that if there is damage or loss of the left hemisphere before language is acquired the right hemisphere in large measure takes over. Work with children who have had the left hemisphere removed in order to alleviate the symptoms of intractable epilepsy reveals that they acquire language normally, although careful testing reveals that they have some syntactic deficits (Dennis and Kohn, 1975).

Thus, human infants are born with neuropsychological endowments in place that make ultimate perception, comprehension, and production of language in all its forms possible. There is no evidence that any other creatures have this kind of linguistic capacity, not even our close relatives the chimpanzees.

Assuming an intact neurological system, infants' cognitive and affective propensities lead them to acquire language relatively rapidly during the first few years of life, and with remarkable similarity across languages. It is important to emphasize, however, that affective factors are as important as cognitive capacity if language development is to take place (Gleason, Hay, and Cain, 1989). It is widely recognized that there are some cognitive prerequisites to language, or at least some cognitive milestones associated with the various stages of language development; but the acquisition of language is not simply an intellectual exercise engaged in by infants, and language acquisition is not simply an example of a young intellect's 'cracking the code' for its own sake, as many researchers in child language development have believed. Before infants begin to speak, they must develop an attachment to the important people around them, and in many ways the early use of language can be seen as the exercise of attachment behaviours. Interpretation of the same data varies with the theoretical stance of the researcher. How, for instance do we interpret the actions of a child just learning to talk, who points at the family cat and says 'kitty'? According to learning theory, the child has been rewarded in the past for speaking, and has been reinforced for producing successive approximations of the word *kitty* in the presence of the cat. This behaviour is explained by cognitive theorists and linguist/innatists as an example of the child's exercise of cognitive and linguistic proclivities: The child is seen as driven to categorize and name her experience. A social interactionist theorist sees this behaviour as socially and emotionally motivated as well: The child uses language to get and hold the attention and affection of another person. This is not to deny cognitive activity, or the fact that the child is learning to categorize the world and acquire the lexical system of English, but the act of saying 'kitty' is also an interactional phenomenon, and is a behaviour that is extraordinarily successful in capturing the notice of parents and others. Like other attachment behaviours (smiling, following the parent, crying when the parent leaves) early language serves the social and affective needs of both infants and their parents. Like language itself, attachment is a universal phenomenon and is biologically based (Bowlby, 1969).

The course of language development

As children grow older there is increasing individual variation in their linguistic development; the earliest stages of communicative development are therefore the most predictable and consistent across individuals. This phenomenon is consonant with what is seen in other biologically based development: Evidence from embryology, for instance, indicates that prenatally individuals are very similar at each stage – it is possible to make an embryological atlas that describes quite accurately the appearance and developmental status of most, if not all, zygotes or embryos at seven days or seven weeks post conception. By seven days or seven weeks after birth, there is obvious variation in individuals. This differentiation continues throughout the lifespan. Four-year-olds, for instance, are a great deal more predictable and less varied in their thoughts, behaviour, appearance, and language than 40-year-olds. Because of the relative uniformity of early development we can talk about the 'course of language development', even though there are stylistic differences among children as well as differences in adult interaction with language learning children.

The typical course of early communicative development that has emerged from studies of the past 30 years reveals a significant neuropsychologically based, and maturationally determined, sequence of events. The infant acquires language as part of a complex process of communicative development that begins essentially at birth – the process of attachment alluded to earlier may actually begin before birth, since studies of neonates have indicated that they prefer to hear their own mothers' voices – perhaps having become familiar with them while still *in utero* (DeCasper and Fifer, 1980).

Earlier theorists, (e.g. Chomsky, 1965) spoke of the infant as having a Language Acquisition Device that processes the ambient language and derives hypotheses about the way the language is structured. Increasingly, we see the infant not as an individual working out the rules, but as part of a communicative system: The parent, typically the mother, serves as an interface device as Silber (1990) notes, both in presenting linguistic data to the child, and in interpreting the infant's signs and utterances to herself or to others. This notion of parent as interface is a useful one, since it specifies the role rather than the behaviour of the parent, and can be generalized to cover many different kinds of societies, where infants may be treated in quite different ways. Since language acquisition takes place universally, it is clear that it is a robust system that can develop in a very broad range of social contexts. The only way to insure that it will *not* develop in a normal infant is to prevent the infant from interacting with older speakers.

Prelinguistic development

The course of early communicative development has been summarized by Sachs (1993), who notes many of the following hallmarks:

Speech to infants is specially modified. Speech to infants has special characteristics – in our society it is marked by slow rate, exaggerated intonation, high fundamental frequency, many repetitions, simple syntax, etc. These features make it easier for the infant to decode the language. The work of Fernald (1985) has shown that mothers use very typical intonation patterns in speaking to infants, and that it is the prosodic envelope that carries information about such things as approval or disapproval in the early weeks. Fernald's work in several language communities has shown that mothers use quite similar patterns to tell their children 'no' or to encourage them.

Child directed speech (CDS) or babytalk (BT) exists in one form or another in all societies that have been studied. But it is not uniform from society to society; rather, it is culturally determined. CDS is one of a number of linguistic codes or registers available to speakers of a language; and, although it has features that are determined by the needs and proclivities of the infant hearer, it varies from society to society. For instance, high fundamental frequency appears to be a feature to which infants attend preferentially, and it is frequently a feature of CDS, but there are some languages such as Quiche Mayan (Bernstein Ratner and Pye, 1984) in which high fundamental frequency is reserved for other purposes. In Quiche Mayan the babytalk register is characterized by *low* fundamental frequency, and high fundamental frequency is used in speech to social superiors.

Adults hold conversations with prelinguistic infants. Adults impute meaning to infants' early utterances, and engage them in 'conversations' long before babies have any recognizable language. For instance, the adult may assume that the baby's burp is a conversational turn, and respond to it:

MOTHER: There's a nice little smile
INFANT: (burps)
MOTHER: What a nice wind as well!
          Yes, that's better, isn't it?
          (Snow, 1977)

As infants begin to acquire language, adults become more demanding and more rigorous in what they will accept as a conversational turn. The overall effect of these early conversations is to increase infants' vocalizations and to teach them conversational turn-taking. From a learning theory perspective, the fact that adults accompany nurturing with speech implies that the sound of language, and language itself, will take on positive value for infants.

Any even casual observation of infants and adults reveals that language begins in an interactive and social context.

Prelinguistic infants show evidence of the intention to communicate. Infants' intentions, like their conversational turns, are originally in the eyes of their beholders. Not only do parents assume that burps are conversational turns, they also assume that infants have intentions even before the intentions are actually there. For instance, they may say of a two-month old, 'He wants to go for a ride in the car'. By the time they are eight or nine months old infants express their intentions in a variety of prelinguistic ways: They may make consistent word-like sounds, they gesture or point at what they want, use their eyes expressively, and become persistent when misunderstood. It is difficult, of course, to know in detail what an infant may be trying to express, but researchers have concluded that these early attempts at communication include both protodeclaratives (language about something) and protoimperatives (requests that something be done for or given to the infant) (Bates, 1979).

Infants have special abilities to perceive speech sounds. In addition to their cognitive, social, and affective proclivities and the specialized brain structures mentioned earlier, infants have a number of special abilities that make ultimate language acquisition possible. One of these neuropsychological capacities is that of speech perception. In the first weeks of life infants are able to make fine distinctions among speech sounds, to distinguish, for instance between voiced and unvoiced phonemes such as /p/ and /b/ in English. In fact, infants are able to make distinctions that adults cannot: Janet Werker (1984) and her colleagues have shown that Canadian babies can distinguish Czech /ř/ from /ž/, although Canadian adults are unable to hear the difference between these sounds (the first is a combination of [r] and [ž], as in the composer's name *Dvořak*, and the second is the sound [ž], as in the word *azure*. Thus, Werker and her colleagues have shown that infants from eight to ten months of age have the ability to discriminate phonemes that are not in the local language, whereas the adults in the community cannot. This ability begins to disappear by the end of the first year.

This loss of the ability to make phonemic distinctions is some of the strongest evidence we have of anything like a critical period for language development. (But see Michael Long's chapter, this volume, for a discussion of the critical period.)

Maturation guides the production of speech sounds. Early vocalization is probably also highly determined by underlying neuropsychological development. Babbling appears on a fairly predictable timetable in the human species. For instance, Stark (1979) has described some developmental stages of vocal behaviour: In a typical infant, until about the age of two months, sounds made are mostly either reflexive (i.e. non-modulated) crying or vegetative sounds. Beginning when they are about 2 months old, babies begin to coo and laugh. At five or six months they begin to engage in the sort of vocal play with sounds and syllables that is usually recognized as babbling. Around the first birthday the babbling contains many reduplicated syllables such as *mama* and *dada*. Many babies also begin to say their first words around this time (either because they have intentionally used one of these forms referentially, or, perhaps because the adults around them have imputed meaning to the reduplicated babble: e.g. the baby babbles *dada* and the adults excitedly decide that she has called for her father). In many babies there is a later stage of babbling that may overlap with the use of some actual words. This kind of babbling, called 'jargon' babbling, may have sentential intonation patterns, and may be produced with such fluency that adults feel that the child is surely speaking, however incomprehensibly. Jargon babbling may last well into the second year and overlap with actual speech. On the other hand, some babies never engage in jargon babbling, and seem to prefer to produce one careful word at a time. Thus there is individual variation, more than one learning style, even in the acquisition of one's native language.

The social and affective bases of prelinguistic communication

As the previous sections have noted, during the first year of life children progress through some typical early communicative stages, and much of this development is maturational or determined by neuropsychological development.

Linguists who are not also psychologists familiar with the immense research literature in developmental psychology tend to think that during a baby's first year she is best described as merely 'prelinguistic', as if the main task of that period were to lie about engaged in phoneme discrimination, learning to babble, etc. But it is important to emphasize that during the period of infancy children are also developing socially and emotionally. These social and affective characteristics may actually cause changes in the neuro-psychological mechanisms that undergird language and make language development possible.

Babies' innate social and affective dispositions lead them to be intensely interested in other human beings, and to seek and maintain social contact with them. For example, there is much research which indicates that babies are more interested in people than in objects. They are especially interested in the normal human face, which they prefer to look at when given a choice of various stimuli. They prefer an undistorted human face to a rather Picasso-like 'face' with scrambled features, and they prefer the scrambled-feature face to a similarly complex, but inanimate, picture (Fantz, 1961; Sherrod, 1981). Infants' ability to hear fine auditory distinctions was noted earlier. Their preference for the human voice also appears very early on; in fact, it seems quite likely that infants are innately predisposed to attend preferentially to human speech versus other sounds (Gibson and Spelke, 1981). Even more impressive is the finding of DeCasper and Fifer (1980) that new-born infants prefer to hear their own mothers' voices. In the research paradigm, the infants were given the opportunity to suck a blind nipple in order to evoke either the voice of the mother or that of a stranger. In this study 8 out of 10 new-borns adjusted the pauses in their sucking in such a way as to hear their mother's voice. When given further choices, they showed a preference for their own mother's voice over that of another woman, and preferred the voice of a strange woman to that of a man. The possibility that children become attached to their own mother's voice while still *in utero* thus presents itself.

Infants have many other innate neuropsychological capacities that may underlie ultimate language acquisition; for instance, they are able to imitate others from a very early age. Meltzoff and Moore (1977) found that infants less than a week old can distinguish among happy, sad, and surprised adult facial expressions. They appear to imitate those expressions as well. When looking at surprised faces, for instance, the infants produced an open mouth and wide eyes themselves. This research, while controversial, shows that infants are capable of both emotional sensitivity and responsiveness even at the earliest ages. Language development is one facet of psychological development, and it is dependent on much more than cognitive attainment – it is predicated on a complex base of social and emotional development as well, and it arises in an intensely interactive arena.

Early language

Early language, as we are aware, exhibits some fairly universal characteristics that are undoubtedly tied to underlying neuro-psychological mechanisms and limited by the child's processing capacity. Typically – but not always – communicative ability co-ordinates with other developments, including the attainment of cognitive milestones. A general cognitive prerequisite for the establishment of intentional communication, for instance, is that the infant must first develop a primitive understanding of cause and effect. The attainment of object permanence typically precedes the use of words such as 'all gone' (Gopnik and Meltzoff, 1987). We cannot prove, however, that any particular cognitive level must be reached before an individual has language, and the literature contains fascinating examples of children with marked dissociations between their linguistic and cognitive development (Curtiss, 1982; Yamada, 1990).

Once language development is under way, researchers have noted universal characteristics in the ways young children ʻprogress toward full adult competence. The work of Brown and his colleagues

(Brown, 1972; deVilliers and deVilliers, 1973; Slobin, 1985) has revealed that children's early utterances in a great variety of languages around the world are very similar. At the earliest stage, children produce one meaningful word at a time, and that word is inevitably a concrete word (such as *kitty* or *mommy*, but certainly not *of* or *the* or *truth*). Early words are embedded in the child's environment. After children have about 50 of these early words in their vocabularies, they begin to put them together into rudimentary two-word sentences. The words that were previously uttered singly now appear in combinations like *nice kitty* and *more cookie*. The sentences are limited in meaning (for instance they are not generally about events in the past or future) and are produced without function words or inflections. Early sentences the world around have similar characteristics, regardless of the language children are learning. Once children learning a particular language begin to acquire grammatical markers they all do so in basically the same order within that language; for instance, in English children learn the prepositions *in* and *on* before other prepositions, and they acquire the progressive ending -*ing* before other verb markers.

The universal characteristics that have been documented in early language are powerful evidence for innate linguistic capacity, as well as for neuropsychological constraints on the form and content of early language. The fact that there is also individual variation in children's language acquisition in no way contradicts or detracts from these findings. There appear to be at least several different styles of language acquisition by children. For instance, Nelson (1973) described children as being either expressive or referential in their early language. Expressive children are more interested in social interaction and have more social/interactive words (like *hi* or *whoops-a-daisy*) in their early vocabularies. Referential children, as compared with expressive children, have a higher ratio of nouns and are seemingly more interested in naming the aspects of their environment. Of course, a child who chooses a referential style may still be using language for social purposes. Actually saying *kitty* may be motivated more by wanting the attention of a proud parent rather than by a basic drive to name things out loud. If we looked only at the speech of children, as was common in the early days of child language research, we might conclude that language development is an autonomous process that unfolds essentially by itself, driven by a robust bioprogramme. This is only partially true: If children are programmed to acquire language, adults are also predisposed to interact with them in ways that facilitate, or make possible, that acquisition.

Pervasive effects of child directed speech

Parents' speech to children learning language has effects that go well beyond making the structure of the language more obvious. Parent speech contains both direct and indirect socialization messages in addition to its language lessons. For instance, children's gender roles are subtly shaped by parent speech, a careful examination of which reveals that what we have thought of as innate differences between males and females may actually be the result of differential socialization – linguistic and otherwise – on the part of parents. For example, women are thought to be more emotionally sensitive than men, and more likely to engage in 'emotional' language (discussing their own and others' feelings.) This may be true, and there may be innate gender differences in emotional responsivity; but it is difficult to know what is innate, since infants are treated differently based on their sex from the moment they are born. Recent research has shown that mothers of infant girls are much more likely to use emotion words speaking to them than are mothers of comparable aged sons speaking to their children, and, by the time the children are 2 years old, girls use reliably more inner-state words than boys (Dunn, Bretherton, and Munn, 1987). Mothers of boys are also more likely to use direct prohibitives with them, to tell them *No* whereas mothers of infant girls in the same situation, and in response to the same kinds of actions, are more likely to attempt to distract their children from prohibited activities (Perlmann and Gleason, 1990). Even warm and affectionate language, for instance the use of diminutives, is used differently with infant girls and boys. In a recent study of the use of diminutives we found, for instance, that diminutives (words ending primarily in *-ie* or *-y* in English, such as *duckie* or *mommy*) are used more pervasively in speech to girls. The words made diminutive carry a message about the parent's world view (we only make diminutive that which we like: *dog > doggie*, but not *roach > roachie*) and the use of diminutives conveys warmth and affection to the addressee (Gleason, Perlmann, Ely, and Evans, in press). Thus, language development proceeds in an interactive fashion; the infant's innate capacities are nurtured, amplified, and actually shaped by the adults around her.

Parents' use of language to affect children's language is not always subtle, moreover, and in some instances is clearly didactic in nature. It has become almost axiomatic in the child language literature that children do not receive 'negative evidence' about the ill-formedness of their sentences (Pinker, 1989). This is certainly arguable: Anyone who has listened to a young child and adult converse has heard the adult ask for clarification, and that evidence of misunderstanding is surely negative evidence, despite the fact that the child may be unable to tell just what is wrong with her utterance (whether the problem was perhaps phonetic rather than syntactic, or lexical).

Even if the argument that syntactic information is not readily available to children were persuasive, there are, particularly within the pragmatic realm, quite unarguable instances in which the parent makes very clear indeed just what the child should be saying. The explicit teaching of politeness is one such arena (Snow, Perlmann, and Gleason, 1990). Here, for instance, is a conversation recorded between a mother and her 4-year-old daughter:

CHILD: Mommy, I want more milk.
MOTHER: Is that the way to ask?
CHILD: Please.
MOTHER: Please what?
CHILD: Please gimme milky.
MOTHER: No.
CHILD: Please gimme milk.

MOTHER: No.
  CHILD: Please...
MOTHER: Please, may I have more milk?
  CHILD: Please, may I have more milk?

                              (Gleason, Perlmann and Greif, 1984:500–1)

In this example the child begins with a simple demand (*I want milk*), and is then led through a series of approximations to politeness by the parent, until, ultimately she produces the adult polite request: *Please, may I have more milk?* It is a dramatic example of explicit teaching.

The foregoing has meant to be a brief review of some of the evidence for the interactive nature of language development; it does not deny our biological heritage nor the possibility that individual differences may be innate, but it makes clear that even if that is so, if, for instance, females are innately more disposed toward emotional sensitivity than males, our society provides social and interactional enhancements of those possibly very slight inborn differences.

Parents' speech to children carries many covert messages, and it also provides them with models and lessons in language acquisition and overt linguistic behaviour.

A TYPICAL LANGUAGE DEVELOPMENT

Language does not always develop in the ways that have been described above. Atypical development occurs under varying circumstances – either as an isolated phenomenon present in an otherwise 'normal' individual, or as part of a larger constellation of atypical characteristics, as, for instance, in individuals with Down syndrome or with autism; there are different neuropsychological implications to be drawn from these varying syndromes.

In discussing atypical development, it is especially important to maintain the traditional distinction between *language* and *speech*. *Language* refers to the abstract capacity that individuals have to the vast internalized linguistic system that they have acquired. *Speech* is performance: It is what we hear. An individual may have total linguistic competence, but may none the less have impaired speech. Persons with cerebral palsy, for instance, very frequently have severe articulatory problems, or they may be unable to speak at all because of damage to those parts of their brains that control the motor system. Yet they may have superior intelligence and unaffected linguistic competence. The Irish novelist and poet Christy Nolan (1987), for example, though unable to talk, has produced prize-winning work one letter at a time on an electric typewriter. The cerebral mechanisms that support speech production are well mapped, and in cases of disordered speech the presence of a known lesion can often be demonstrated. For instance, a lesion in the motor strip, or in the cerebellum, or even agenesis (failure to develop) of the cerebellum may be associated with dysarthria or a typical pattern of difficulty in producing speech at the motor level, even though the actual mental representation of language, including the entire phonological system, may be unaffected.

Atypical language development takes different patterns in individuals with varying diagnoses. Those differing syndromes are strong evidence for the existence of separate, and perhaps 'modular', linguistic subsystems. Some of the typical features of language in atypical populations have been described by Bernstein Ratner (1993).

Deafness

Children with hearing losses of about 90 decibels are considered deaf, and they cannot acquire spoken language naturally. Even with optimal intervention, severely deaf children who acquire spoken language are liable to have articulatory problems, and to have atypical syntactic and semantic systems. The problems with language are also persistent: deaf college students with high performance IQs still have reading and writing difficulties with the standard language.

There are many aetiological factors involved in deafness. These may include sensorineural damage, middle-ear disease or malformation, and conditions leading to conductive hearing loss. In general, the earlier the child becomes deaf, and the greater the hearing loss, the greater will be the degree of linguistic impairment. Deafness by itself, however, does not really affect linguistic *capacity*. The language problems appear to stem rather from interactional and input deficits. Most deaf children are born to hearing parents who are unable to communicate with them in any complex way. By contrast, the few deaf children who are born to deaf parents and who learn American Sign Language (ASL) as their first language, begin to sign at an early age and pass linguistic milestones in ASL that are comparable to what has been observed in the development of children acquiring spoken language (Klima and Bellugi, 1979). Recent research reveals that ASL is a rich and complex language. There is a growing controversy among scholars in and out of the deaf community in the US about whether deaf individuals should be made to acquire English as a second language, or if they should continue their educations and lives using ASL as the primary means of communication (Lucas, 1989).

Mental retardation

Mental retardation is a generic term that is applied to individuals with a range of conditions; some mentally retarded people are at the low end of the normal intelligence curve and have no obvious neurological or physiological problems, while others have mental retardation along with other problems as a result of pre- or post-natal accidents, or inherited conditions. Fragile X syndrome and Down syndrome are two of the commonest congenital forms of retardation. Children with mental retardation tend to acquire language in roughly the same stages as normally developing children, but at a slower rate. Interestingly, not all linguistic subsystems are equally at a disadvantage in retardation: children with Down syndrome are less impaired pragmatically than syntactically. They tend to have poor morphological skills, but their vocabularies are often quite good. If a retarded child has an IQ of about 50, language is liable to develop.

The nature of the neurological problem in Down syndrome is not well understood, but ultimately individuals with this condition develop the sorts of cortical neurofibrillary plaques and tangles that are also seen in Alzheimer's disease.

Autism

Children with autism are very different from typical mentally retarded children, although many autistic children are also retarded. Some autistic people are generally retarded, but have remarkable abilities to calculate sums, compute the days on which dates may fall many years distant, memorize information, or even play the piano. During the prelinguistic period, infants who will ultimately become autistic display aberrant interactional behaviour – for instance they do not seem to have the same interests in the human face that were described earlier, or in other humans, for that matter. The emotional, affective base on which much of language is predicated is not established. Their language development does not follow the course of typical development, even at a slower pace; rather it is characterized by echolalia (repeating all or part of what is said to them) and by inappropriateness. Some researchers (Rutter, 1983) feel that autistic children are unable to extract social meaning from situations. Ultimately, their language deficits are primarily in the pragmatic and social realm. It is generally agreed that autistic individuals have some underlying neurological mis-organization, but no lesions have been reliably reported. Many autistic people, however, exhibit neurological 'soft signs' such as exceptional clumsiness and perceptual deficits.

Specific language impairment (SLI)

As the term implies, specific language impairment refers to language problems in the absence of any other known atypical condition. Children with SLI were previously labelled 'developmentally dysphasic' or 'developmentally aphasic', but it is necessary to distinguish between SLI and true childhood aphasia, which results from a stroke or other accident. Children with SLI may be very delayed in beginning to talk as infants, and exhibit a variety of problems with language as system. They frequently have some degree of anomia (inability to name), and may have extremely long latencies when successful in retrieving names (Wolf and Goodglass, 1986). Some researchers (e.g. Tallal, 1987) have suggested that SLI children are unable to process language at the requisite speed. We do not know what causes SLI, but infer neurological atypicalities or minimal brain damage (mbd) in such individuals. In general, SLI children cannot be expected to catch up with the normally developing population without intervention, and it is likely that SLI in its later manifestations becomes the sort of learning disability (LD) that characterizes children who have problems learning to read in the early school years.

Thus, we postulate some sort of neuropsychological disturbance in most individuals who exhibit atypical language development. Deaf children are an interesting case, because they may be neurologically intact, except for the deafness, but the deafness leads them to have an impoverished linguistic environment when they are raised among speaking adults. If they are raised among ASL users they develop sign language at an early age and in stages similar to those observed in speaking children. Children who are neurologically intact may also fail to develop language in a typical way if they are kept in extreme social isolation. These cases are rare, but have occurred, for instance when psychotic parents have kept their child isolated from human interaction (Curtiss, 1982) or even when deaf parents of hearing children have not given them the opportunity to interact with speakers of the language. These rare cases are none the less strong evidence for the dual bases – biological and social-interaction – on which language development is predicated.

LANGUAGE REGRESSION OR LOSS

Loss, or regression of first language skills can occur for a variety of 'environmental' reasons or through a change in the neurolinguistic underpinnings of language; in the first instance, loss occurs through attrition in an individual who remains healthy, whereas in the second the loss may be one of the sequelae of a stroke, an accident, dementia, or other condition that causes a neuropsychological malfunction. In the case of attrition, language is frequently lost over a period of time when an individual moves to an area where another language is dominant; when a child who is a member of an ethnolinguistic minority enters school and begins schooling in the societal language; when a second language is no longer studied or needed; or even when a language drops out of use and 'dies', as in the case of e.g. Scottish Gaelic, (Dorian, 1983) and the speakers adopt the dominant language. These examples are all types of language skill attrition, and there is a relatively new literature devoted to this topic (Lambert and Freed, 1982; Pan and Gleason, 1986; other papers, this volume). Language loss through attrition is certainly a more common occurrence than aphasia or other language loss through brain damage, but the literature on aphasia is far more extensive.

Aphasia in adults and children

Aphasia in adults takes many typical forms, depending on the site of the lesion. Lesions can be caused by trauma – for instance gunshot wounds or motor-cycle accidents, or by cardiovascular accidents (CVAs) such as strokes, emboli, aneurysms, etc. Earlier, we described three kinds of aphasia, each the result of a localized lesion, and the relevant areas are pictured in Figure 6.1:

Broca's aphasia is associated with lesions to Broca's area, in the left frontal lobe. Broca's area is at the foot of the motor strip, adjacent to areas that control the tongue and other articulatory organs. Patients with Broca's aphasia have laboured, difficult articulation, and usually produce very short utterances, which are quite nonfluent. Their speech is often agrammatic (lacking tenses, articles, and inflections), and tends to consist mainly of content words, often nouns and proper nouns. For instance, in response to the question 'What are you planning to do on Saturday?' one of our patients replied 'Uh, Saturday. Boston College. Football'.

Conduction aphasia. Patients with conduction aphasia are unable to repeat what they have heard. They have lesions to the arcuate fasciculus, or to other structures deep within the brain. Their comprehension of language is essentially normal, and their production is fluent. The inability to repeat is striking, by contrast, and likely evidence of some disconnection between the posterior and anterior language processing areas.

Wernicke's aphasia. These patients have lesions to Wernicke's area in the temporal lobe. Wernicke's aphasics produce fluent speech, but it is often empty and incomprehensible. They may produce meaningless jargon words, which they themselves will not recognize on later presentation, and their comprehension is poor. In attempting to describe a series of pictures showing a tall man taking a suitcase down from an overhead rack on a train and handing it to a shorter man, one of our Wernicke's patients said, 'He's tryin' to get this. He had this in his hand, right? And he took it down and he gave it to this guy...' (Gleason, Goodglass, Obler, Green, Hyde, and Weintraub, 1980).

These examples are of some major syndromes of aphasia, and, of course, they are not exhaustive. They are also what one sees in a patient who has had a single stroke, rather than a series of CVA's, since multiple accidents produce much more diffuse brain damage, and the resulting aphasia is liable to be of a mixed nature. Perhaps half of aphasic patients have a relatively pure aphasia of one of the types described.

Childhood 'developmental aphasia,' now called SLI, bears little relation to these aphasias. Children who have already acquired language normally, however, are also subject to language loss through trauma or stroke. What can be said of the consequences of sudden brain damage in children? The classic description of true childhood aphasia was made by Guttman in 1942; he examined a number of cases of children who had suffered various accidents and consequently become aphasic. Perhaps the most telling point in this research is that, *regardless* of the site of the lesion, children display the same typical pattern of aphasia: the child may be mute temporarily, and then gradually regain language. There are essentially no attested cases in the literature of a Wernicke's aphasia in anyone younger than about 14 years. Although recovery from childhood aphasia may not be perfect (the young subject may have a persistent anomia), the kinds of auditory comprehension difficulty seen in older subjects with posterior lesions also does not occur. In sum, the young brain reorganizes itself. Identical brain damage in children and adults produces quite different neurolinguistic results.

Patterns of acquisition and loss

A patient with Broca's aphasia may be agrammatic; he may omit tenses, particles, and function words from his utterances. In response to the question, 'The baby has a toy. I take the toy away. What happens?' The relatively severely impaired Broca's aphasic is liable to reply 'Baby cry.' This response may sound very like the speech of a young child just learning language; young children also omit articles and inflections, and appear to operate primarily with content words. They are often called 'telegraphic' rather than 'agrammatic', but there are at least some superficial parallels in the speech of aphasic and very young speakers. Similarities of this sort have led researchers to postulate that there is a mirror-image regression that take place when language is lost, that patients lose language in inverse order to the way it is acquired by children.

The very term *regression* was first used by Freud to refer to this presumed linguistic phenomenon in his 1891 work *On aphasia*; only later did regression become a psychiatric event. Roman Jakobson, one of the leaders of the Prague School of linguistics, made similar claims about the acquisition of the phonological system when he wrote that dissolution of language reproduces in inverse order the pattern of acquisition (1968). Jakobson had noted that the Czech /ř/, which is acquired last by Czech children (for good reason!) is also lost early by Czech aphasics. A more detailed comparison of the speech of aphasic patients however, reveals that the similarities between child language and aphasic language are fairly superficial.

At the metalinguistic level, young children are incognizant of their language, but aphasic persons, especially those with frontal lesions, may be keenly aware of their imperfect linguistic performance: we tested one patient, for instance, who was so dissatisfied with his *Baby cry* response (instead of *The baby cries*) that he attempted, and failed, to do it correctly seventeen times.

At the lexical level, very young children acquire a quite predictable set of early words. There is considerable overlap among the first fifty words acquired by children in a given language community: These are liable to be a restricted set of frequent nouns, action words, modifiers, and personal/social words (Nelson and Lucariello, 1985). A baby's first words are liable to be *kitty, daddy, juice, up, no*, etc. In cases of language dissolution, we cannot predict what few words might be left in a subject's lexicon, but they might well be unprintable in a proper publication; it is not unusual for swear words, or for formulaic expressions including politeness routines to be the only words left to a severely aphasic adult.

Comparable observations about the dissimiliarities between child and adult aphasic morphological and syntactic systems can be made. For instance the fourteen grammatical morphemes acquired first by English-speaking children, do not follow a reverse pattern of loss in aphasia (deVilliers, 1978). Aphasic patients are operating linguistically with what remains of their prior language, and their linguistic knowledge is variably available to them. They may be limited in what they can say, but, unlike children, they may have sophisticated understanding of language, and relatively intact cognitive ability. Their brain damage has not rendered them children, linguistically or in any other respect.

CONCLUSION

This chapter has attempted to show that there are some neurologically based and socially facilitated universals in language acquisition, and that there are different kinds of atypical language development associated with different developmental syndromes. If children and adults lose their language they do not do so in the same ways, and aphasic adults do not lose language in the mirror-image of the way children acquire it. While we may talk of these broad general truths, it is also the case that general statements do not cover all individuals, and that individual variation in language acquisition and loss is a biologically based and pervasive factor. In the case of children learning language, their neuropsychological integrity is vital, but they also acquire language in an interactive environment; and their motivations for acquiring language are social and affective, as well as cognitive and intellectual. Parents and older speakers provide specialized input that socializes children to their roles, conveys a world view, and provides both subtle and explicit information about the linguistic system.

NOTE

1 Preparation of this paper was supported by the National Institutes of Child Health and Human Development through grant no. HD-23388.

REFERENCES

Bates, E. (1979), *The emergence of symbols: cognition and communication in infancy.* New York: Academic Press.

Bernstein Ratner, N. (1993), Atypical language development. In Gleason, J. Berko (ed.), *The development of language.* 3rd edition. New York: Macmillan.

Bernstein Ratner, N. and Pye, C. (1984), Higher pitch in babytalk is *not* universal: Acoustic evidence from Quiche Mayan. *Journal of Child Language,* 11, 515–22.

Bowlby, J. (1969), *Attachment and loss. Vol. 1.* New York: Basic Books.

Brown, R. *A first language.* Cambridge, Mass.: Harvard University Press.

Chomsky, N. (1965), *Aspects of a theory of syntax.* Cambridge, Mass.: MIT Press.

(1972), *Language and mind.* New York: Harcourt Brace Jovanovich.

Curtiss, S. (1982), Developmental dissociations of language and cognition. In Obler, L. and Menn, L. (eds.) *Exceptional language and linguistics*. New York: Academic Press.

DeCasper, A. J. and Fifer, W. P. (1980), Of human bonding: Newborns prefer their mother's voice. *Science*, 208, 1174–6.

Dennis, M., and Kohn, B. (1975), Comprehension of syntax in infantile hemiplegics after cerebral hemidecortication: Left hemisphere superiority. *Brain and Language*, 2, 472–82.

deVilliers, J. G. (1978), Fourteen grammatical morphemes in acquisition and aphasia. In Caramazza, A. and Zurif, E. (eds.), *Language acquisition and language breakdown*. Baltimore: Johns Hopkins.

deVilliers, J. G. and deVilliers, P. A. (1973), A cross sectional study of the acquisition of grammatical morphemes in child speech. *Journal of Psycholinguistic Research*, 2, 267–78.

Dorian, N. C. (1983), Natural second language acquisition from the perspective of the study of language death. In Andersen, R. (ed.), *Pidginization and creolization as language acquisition*. Rowley, Mass.: Newbury House.

Dunn, J., Bretherton, I. and Munn, P. (1987), Conversations about feeling states between mothers and their young children. *Developmental Psychology*, 23, 132–9.

Fantz, R. L. (1961), The origin of form perception. *Scientific American*, 204, 66–72.

Fernald, A. (1985), Four-month-old infants prefer to listen to motherese. *Infant Behavior and Development*, 8, 181–95.

Freud, S. (1953), *On aphasia*. Translated by E. Stengel. New York: International Universities Press. (First published in German in 1891.)

Gibson, E. J. and Spelke, E. S. (1983), The development of perception. In Flavell, J. H. and Markman, E. M. (eds.), *Handbook of child psychology: Cognitive development. Vol. 3*. New York: John Wiley and Sons.

Gleason, J. Berko, Goodglass, H., Obler, L., Green, E., Hyde, M. R., and Weintraub, S. (1980), Narrative strategies of aphasic and normal-speaking subjects. *Journal of speech and hearing research*, 23, 370–82.

Gleason, J. Berko, Hay, D., and Cain, L. (1989), Social and affective determinants of language acquisition. In Rice, M. L. and

Schiefelbusch, R. L. (eds.), *The teachability of language*. Baltimore: Paul H. Brookes.

Gleason, J. Berko, Perlmann, R. Y., Ely, D., and Evans, D. (In press) Aspects of babytalk: Parents' use of diminutives in speech to infants and children. In Sokolov, J. L. and Snow, C. E. (eds.), *Handbook of research in language development using CHILDES*. New York: Lawrence Erlbaum Associates.

Gleason, J. Berko, Perlmann, R. Y. and Greif, E. B. (1984), What's the magic word? *Discourse Processes*, 7, 493–502.

Gopnik, A., and Meltzoff, A. N. (1987), Early semantic developments and their relationship to object permanence, means-end understanding, and categorization. In Nelson, K. E. and van Kleeck, A. (eds.), *Children's language, Volume 6*. Hillsdale, N.J.: Lawrence Earlbaum Associates.

Guttman, E. (1942), Aphasia in children. *Brain*, 65, 205–19.

Hyams, N. (1986), *Language acquisition and the theory of parameters*. Dordrecht: Reidel.

Jakobson, R. (1968), *Child language, aphasia, and phonological universals*. Translated by A. R. Keiler. The Hague: Mouton.

Klima, E. and Bellugi, U. (1979), *The signs of language*. Cambridge, Mass.: Harvard University Press.

Lambert, R. D. and Freed, B. F. (eds.) (1982), *The loss of language skills*. Rowley Mass.: Newbury House.

Lucas, C. (ed.) (1989), *The sociolinguistics of the deaf community*. New York: Academic Press.

McClelland, J., Rumelhart, D., and PDP Research Group. (1986), *Parallel distributed processing: Explorations in the microstructure of cognition*. Cambridge, Mass.: Bradford Books.

Meltzoff, A. and Moore, W. (1977), Imitation of facial and manual gestures by human neonates. *Science*, 198, 75–8.

Nelson, K. (1973), Structure and strategy in learning to talk. *Monographs of the society for research in child development*, 38.

Nelson, K. and Lucariello, J. (1985), The development of meaning in first words. In Barrett, M. (ed.), *Children's single word speech*. Chichester, England: Wiley.

Nolan, C. (1987), *Under the eye of the clock: The life story of Christopher Nolan*. New York: St. Martin's Press.

Pan, B. A. and Gleason, J. B. (1986), The study of language loss;

Models and hypotheses for an emerging discipline. *Applied Psycholinguistics*, 7, 193–206.

Perlmann, R. Y. and Gleason, J. Berko (1990), Patterns of prohibition in mothers' speech to children. Paper presented at the congress of the International Association for the Study of Child Language, Budapest.

Piaget, J. (1926), *The language and thought of the child*. New York: Harcourt Brace Jovanovich.

Pinker, S. (1989), *Learnability and cognition*. Cambridge, Mass.: MIT Press.

Rutter, M. (ed.) (1983), *Developmental neuropsychiatry*. New York: Guilford.

Sachs, J. (1993), Communication development in infancy. In Gleason, J. Berko (ed.) *The development of language*. 3rd edition. New York: Macmillan.

Sherrod, L. R. (1981), Issues in cognitive-perceptual development: The special case of social stimuli. In Lamb, M. E. and Sherrod, L. R. (eds.), *Infant social cognition: Empirical and theoretical approaches*. Hillsdale, N.J.: Lawrence Earlbaum Associates.

Silber, R. (1990), Child directed input and information processing in word learning. Unpublished MS. Program in applied linguistics, Boston University.

Sinclair-deZwart, H. (1973), Language acquisition and cognitive development. In Moore, T. (ed.), *Cognitive development and the acquisition of language*. New York: Academic Press.

Skinner, B. F. (1957), *Verbal behavior*. Englewood Cliffs, N.J.: Prentice-Hall.

Slobin, D. I. (ed.) (1985), *A cross linguistic study of language acquisition*. Hillsdale, N.J.: Erlbaum.

Snow, C. E. (1977), The development of conversation between mothers and babies. *Journal of Child Language*, 4, 1–22.

(1981), Social interaction and language acquisition. In Dale, P. and Ingram, D. (eds.), *Child language: An international perspective*. Baltimore: University Park Press.

Snow, C. E., Perlmann, R. Y. and Gleason, J. Berko (1990), Developmental perspectives on politeness: Sources of children's knowledge. *Journal of Pragmatics*, 14, 289–305.

Stark, R. (1979), Prespeech segmental features in development. In Fletcher, P. and Garman, M. (eds.) *Language acquisition: Studies in first language development*. Cambridge: Cambridge University Press.

Tallal, P. (1987), Developmental language disorders. In *Learning disabilities: A report to the US Congress*. Washington, D.C.: Interagency Committee on Learning Disabilities.

Werker, J., and Tees, R. C. (1984), Cross-language speech perception: Evidence for perceptual reorganization during the first year of life. *Infant Behavior and Development*, 7, 49–64.

Witelson, S. F. (1977), Early hemispheric specialization and interhemispheric plasticity: An empirical and theoretical review. In Segalowitz, S. J. and Gruber, F. A. (eds.), *Language development and neurological theory*. London: Academic Press.

Wolf, M. and Goodglass, H. (1986), Dyslexia, dysnomia, and lexical retrieval: A longitudinal investigation. *Brain and Language*, 28, 154–68.

Yamada, J. (1990), *Laura: A case for the modularity of language*. Cambridge, Mass.: MIT Press.

7 · Neurolinguistic aspects of second language development and attrition

LORAINE K. OBLER

INTRODUCTION

Neurolinguistics itself is a relatively young discipline, with no single overarching theory, and no governing paradigm guiding our study of the ways in which language is organized and processed in the brain. With respect to the neurolinguistics of second languge organization and processing, then, our knowledge must necessarily be limited. However there are pockets of accepted knowledge in neurolinguistics generally, and a sizeable number of accepted techniques that have yielded this knowledge. This paper is structured to discuss, first, that knowledge we appear to have concerning the neurolinguistics of second language acquisition and processing, and second, the phenomena of second language acquisition and processing that should eventually be accountable for by neurolinguistic techniques. It will be seen that, even in the areas where we have some knowledge, there is still a certain degree of controversy.

EXISTING KNOWLEDGE

Lateral dominance for language in the bilingual or second language learner

While knowledge of lateral dominance in monolinguals appears settled (left hemisphere dominance for language in 98% of right handers; about an equal split between left dominance, right dominance, and bilateral organization among left handers) the knowledge about lateral organization in second language acquirers and bilinguals remains disputed. One set of findings has purported to show no difference in lateral organization, either between monolinguals and bilinguals, for L2, or for each of the two languages of the bilingual. The more compelling evidence, by my analysis, comes from the literature which demonstrates greater right hemisphere involvement, particularly in the earlier stages of second language acquisition, than in monolinguals of an equivalent age. In her review of this literature, Vaid (1983) concludes that left hemisphere processing appears to be more likely in more advanced stages of second language acquisition. Silverberg, Bentin, Gaziel, Obler, and Albert (1979) had previously demonstrated a shift from primarily right hemisphere responsibilities in early stages of second language acquisition to primarily left hemisphere dominance in later stages. These findings concord neatly with the general belief among neurolinguists that materials which may be treated in 'Gestalt' fashion in the early stages, can come to be treated analytically in later stages, as these are the two gross characterizations of the ways of processing attributed to the right and left hemispheres respectively.

Curiously enough, it is the more modern techniques for neurolinguistic study that yield the above findings. That is to say, it is studies of tachistoscopic presentations of visual materials and dichotic studies of auditory materials that suggest subtle right hemisphere involvement in the early stages of second language acquisition. Cruder, older, methods lead rather to the conclusion that it is the left hemisphere that is dominant for both L1 and L2 in the bilingual person. The traditional measure of laterality in neurolinguistics is the study of aphasia as it relates to the hemisphere of lesion. As Broca (1865) and many others following him noted, the vast majority of aphasics are right-handed individuals who have had left hemisphere damage. With respect to the literature on bilingual and polyglot aphasics, it is the case that for most individuals, a single left hemisphere lesion results in language disturbance, and *indeed* similar types of language disturbance, across both or all languages

(Charlton, 1964). Moreover, we find virtually no instance in the case-study literature of brain damage to the right hemisphere resulting in aphasia to the second or later languages, and no damage to the first-learned language. (Paradis and Goldblum, 1983, is the apparent exception to this, although the language disturbance of their subject is more stuttering rather than a true aphasia.)

In early analyses (e.g. Gloning and Gloning, 1965) it appeared that there was a higher incidence of crossed aphasia (i.e., aphasia in which the brain damage resulting in aphasia occurred to the right hemisphere, despite the fact that the subject is right-handed) among bilingual aphasics (10%) than among monolingual aphasics (under 3%). It has been pointed out (Albert and Obler, 1978) that cases of crossed aphasia are much more likely to be reported than cases with standard lesions, and indeed in the several studies of consecutively tested bilingual patients with aphasia, no such tendency was seen (Charlton 1964, April and Han, 1980). In addition, the sodium amytal procedures performed on bilingual patients in Montreal have not evidenced differential impairment of the two languages, in so far as I can tell (Milner, personal communication).

We suspect (Obler and Mahecha, 1991), rather, that pre-language brain organization influences lateral organization for language in the bilingual as in the monolingual. In our review of factors predicting first language loss in the bilingual and polyglot aphasic, one of the few factors to stand out was handedness, our best measure, in this population, of lateral dominance for language (left-handers were markedly more likely to lose their L1). This suggested that they acquired L1, and perhaps L2, differently from their right-handed peers. Thus we have an apparent paradox, whereby one set of respected techiques indicates more right hemisphere involvement in the early stages of second language acquisition, while the other appears to indicate equal left dominance for both first and second languages. One way to resolve the paradox is to note that very few of the aphasic patients seen, or perhaps the sodium amytal patients seen as well, are in the early stages of second language acquisition.

Thus it makes sense that for them language organization is virtually altogether left-dominant.

Vaid (1983) also maintains, based on her review of the bilingual laterality literature, that left hemisphere dominance is more likely the 'earlier the second language is acquired relative to the first and the more formal the exposure'. Yet many of the aphasics in the literature on bilingual aphasia were immigrants who experienced late and informal L2 acquisition. Vaid concludes that the laterality data demonstrate that 'bilinguals are more likely to show a comparable pattern of hemispheric involvement across their two languages the more similar the language acquisition conditions are'; clearly many of the aphasics had dissimilar language acquisition conditions.

A third possible resolution to this apparent contradiction is that traditional modern laterality techniques employed with normal subjects evidence language *processing* more, while studies of aphasia and sodium amytal techniques evidence language *organization* more. Although it runs contrary to standard neurolinguistic tenets, perhaps we should consider two different forms of lateral dominance, one for storage and one for processing. In the bilingual, then, or even in the monolingual, these would be differently lateralized.

Organization of the bilinguals' two languages
within the left hemisphere

Our data on this topic come from two papers which report on the evidence of cortical stimulation in a small group of subjects. Cortical stimulation involves a surgeon baring the subject's cortex and placing micro-electrodes at sites within a broad area that should include the language area. As small electric pulses are passed to a given location, subjects are asked to read the words on a card which says, 'this is an "x"' or 'that is a "y"', and then has a picture which the subject must name. Evidence for language organization has been inferred from those instances in which the subject has no difficulty reading the card but has difficulty naming the object, since confrontational naming abilities have been determined, on the basis of the aphasia literature, to obtain with damage, even minimal damage, anywhere in the language area.

In the first study of bilinguals (Ojemann and Whitaker, 1978), the authors reported on the results of stimulation of the left cortex of a Dutch–English bilingual and the right cortext of an English–Spanish bilingual. One subject had learned the second language at a relatively late age (25); he was 37 when tested. The second, a left-hander, had learned both her languages from infancy, and was tested at age 20. Both subjects continued to use both languages at the time of testing. Nevertheless the pattern was the same for both subjects; both showed certain core areas within what we would term the traditional language area in which both languages were affected by electric pulses, and micro-areas elsewhere where one or the other language was more affected.

In the study by Rapport, Tan, and Whitaker (1983), 3 bilingual speakers were tested via cortical stimulation. All spoke and read English and spoke one or more Chinese dialects. In these three cases, as in the two studied previously by Ojemann and Whitaker, certain areas were seen to cause problems to primarily one language or the other. For these three patients, the dominant language seemed more strongly concentrated around the Sylvian fissure.

One final study must be mentioned, that of Berthier, Starkstein, Lylyk and Leiguarda (1990). While the authors interpreted their findings to support the findings of Ojemann and Whitaker, in fact, as Paradis (1990) points out, they contradict them in that sodium amytal anesthetization in their Spanish L1/English L2 subject suggested fewer peripheral areas involved in processing English.

While these data do not speak of subcortical participation in a second language, nor right hemisphere participation in second language processing, all but the Berthier, et al. (1990) study do suggest that within the core left hemisphere language area the two languages are both tightly interwoven and differentiated to a certain degree.

The language switch and language monitor

Reviews such as that of Paradis (1977) which have looked at polyglot aphasics in whom the switch would seem to be impaired (in particular, they can speak with difficulty in one language, but simply cannot access the other, at least for production) are few; however, the evidence on where the damage was in these patients shows no overlap, suggesting there is no single locale serving the switch. Recent work on the behaviours of patients with Alzheimer's dementia is suggestive, however. While virtually none of the individuals studied violate the linguistic rules determining the points within sentences at which it is appropriate to switch, a number of patients have difficulties choosing the correct language in which to address an interlocutor. This is particularly evident when the interlocutor is monolingual and the demented patient is addressing him or her in a language the interlocutor does not know at all (Hyltenstam and Stroud, 1985, 1989, this volume; de Santi, Obler, Sabo-Abramson, and Goldberger, 1990).

Since the primary cellular degeneration in Alzheimer's dementia, that relatively common dementia from which the subjects studied have suffered, is in frontal and parietal areas of the brain, it would appear that either frontal and/or parietal lobes are responsible for this difficulty in activating the switch which assures we speak the language appropriate to our interlocutor. We must grant, however, that cellular damage is diffuse in Alzheimer's dementia, and not all bilingual patients with the disease studied manifest the phenomenon of problems with language choice, so it remains possible that other more specific areas are involved in making this decision. The frontal lobes are a particularly plausible site for the switch, as the task of language choice is similar to that involved in deciding in what register to speak depending on our interlocutor, or other such executive decisions that the frontal lobes have traditionally been held responsible for.

There is virtually no study of the brain bases underlying the perceptual counterpart of the switch, namely the monitor which scans incoming speech in order to determine whether to process in language A or language B. There have been no studies, to our knowledge, of aphasics or demented patients who have difficulty processing language that includes code-switching, nor have there been studies such as PET scan or blood-flow studies, which might show activation of one or another area of the brain during this process. Thus it is virtually impossible to go beyond speculations that the frontal lobe would be an appropriate site for participating in such behaviour, based on our general neuropsychological knowledge.

The critical period

The classic evidence for critical and sensitive periods in communication comes from the study of hemisphericity in birds. In humans, until the past 5 years, discussion of critical periods centred only on development of cerebral dominance. Although cerebral dominance starts in intrauterine life and may develop over childhood, it is unclear when it ceases. Less is known about the development of the language centre within the left hemisphere, but intrahemispheric organization is likely crucial to the critical period question as well.

Evidence for critical periods in monolingual acquisition comes from studies of childhood aphasia, hemispherectomies, and feral children. All suggest that a certain plasticity is maintained throughout childhood, but lost around puberty.

The behavioural linguistic evidence does suggest a critical period in L2 acquisition, at least for accent. Evidence against a critical period for second language acquisition comes from studies of cerebral dominance (see Vaid, 1983, for a review). To test whether age of L2 acquisition influences eventual processing, one would need to employ dynamic techniques such as PET scanning, evoked potential studies, or cerebral blood-flow techniques. It is certainly conceivable that, as Bever has discovered left-handers and right-handers process syntax differently, early and late L2 acquirers process language differently, even if the resulting 'performance' is the same. (See Obler and McNamara, 1991 for an elaborated argument on critical period in second language acquisition.)

Talent in second language acquisition

A small percentage of individuals appear to escape the generalization that after puberty it is difficult for individuals to learn a second language and speak it as if they were native speakers. Studies such as those of Schneiderman and Desmarais (1988) and Novoa, Fein, and Obler (1988) suggest that these particular talents in second language acquisition may be related to brain organization for language. The neuroimmunoendocrinological theory of Geschwind and Galaburda (1985) considered mathematical and artistic talent to be brain-based. This same theory would appear to account for talented second language acquisition, on the basis of the case studies of unusually talented post-pubertal second language acquirers that have been published. In particular, it is to be noted that there is what appears to be a high incidence of the factors Geschwind and Galaburda pointed to among these subjects: left-handedness, twinning, and homosexuality in the Novoa et al. case. Until norms are developed, however, for all the phenomena Geschwind and Galaburda have implicated (so far only handedness has been studied) it is hard to make an evaluation of the extent to which these subjects exceed the norm.

The data with respect to particularly untalented language acquisition are somewhat more dubious. The 43-year-old I reported on (1989a,b), although a very intelligent individual with a Master's degree and great professional success, was unable to learn a second language that he desired and needed to learn. Nevertheless, contrary to the predictions of the Geschwind and Galaburda hypothesis, which in its strong form would have placed particularly poor second language learners, like particularly good second language learners, in the families with clusters of shared neurological, immunological, and endocrinological factors, few such factors could be found in this individual or his family, apart from the important fact that he was dyslexic and a stutterer in his first language as a child.

The study of Humes-Bartlo (1989) only found a high incidence of the Geschwind–Galaburda factors in the single most exceptional second language learning child. Few in the population of Spanish-speaking learners of English who were two standard deviations above the norm in their performance, or two standard deviations below the norm, evidenced *familial* Geschwind factors. It must be noted, however, that the proportion of subjects for whom question-naires on the Geschwind and Galaburda phenomena were returned was only 77% and returned questionnaires were not always complete.

PHENOMENA REMAINING TO BE ACCOUNTED FOR

Two phenomena of second language acquisition, and several of second language attrition have not yet been studied from a neurolinguistic perspective, but may nevertheless be speculatively linked to our neurolinguistic and neuropsychological knowledge of language processing and organization.

Simultaneous acquisition of two languages

We do not know how the brain goes about apparently simultaneous-ly acquiring two languages when the healthy child is exposed to them. Schlyter argues elsewhere in this volume that the apparent simultaneous acquisition is in fact somewhat staggered, which would accord with the findings from the cortical stimulation literature, of an intertwined, but at some points distinguishable, organization of the two languages. Nevertheless, case studies strongly suggest that in the earliest stages the brain acquires bilingual language by simply assuming a single language exists (e.g. Leopold, 1939–49). By about age 3, the child can, and does, produce one or the other language appropriately according to interlocutor, and can talk about the bilingual situation, and thus by this time one might expect the beginnings of subtle differentiation within the brain bases underlying language.

The ability to distinguish the two languages

This early ability to distinguish the two languages, presumably for input as well as for output, must itself have a basis in the brain. I suspect that the same Language Acquisition Device that is acquiring two languages quickly picks up a given language's distinctions in order to produce more adult-like forms, and thus is attuned to the differences it hears. Since adults in the child's environment are likely to be discussing the bilingual situation, and children as young as 2 have the ability to talk about words as such, it would appear that either it requires little sophistication to make this distinction, or else the child's brain is particularly attuned to discover and elaborate on it by age 2.

Attrition of highly specific words

The phenomenon reported by Olshtain and Barzilay (1991) whereby well-educated bilinguals may lose access to highly specific words in their first language when that language is no longer clearly the dominantly used one, must have its explanation in the brain substrate. Of course this phenomenon offers a particularly nice example of the Jakobsonian regression hypothesis, since these same highly specific words are likely to be later learned by L1 acquirers. It is hard to dissociate specificity from frequency, and the neurolinguistic literature on frequency (some studies of aphasics, in particular) suggests that these less-frequent words are likely to be harder to access. It would appear that some automatic routes are set up for accessing more frequently used words, and words that go unused for any length of time become harder to access, although this may only be evident in the instance of aphasia.

Specific versus global attrition

The findings reported in Weltens (1987), Weltens and Van Els (1986) and Weltens, Van Els, and Schils (1989) likewise documented a differential loss whereby some receptive language skills (such as performance on a multiple-choice cloze test and performance scores on a listening comprehension test) remained unimpaired following 4 to 6 years of training in a second language. However, specific lexical and grammatical skills were seen to decline during the course of the 4 years subsequent to formal study. These findings can be accounted for in part by some combination of the redundancy in natural language (which could explain the listening comprehension results) and the choice of distractors on the cloze test (these did not result in ceiling performance, but nevertheless may have simply provided unlikely distractors for specific items). However, it is certainly possible that a dissociation obtains between receptive and production abilities, since the 'hard-wiring' of the two abilities is demonstrably independent in normals, as evidenced by the fact that limited brain damage may affect only one or the other ability.

Interlanguage interference in some aspects of attrition

This same phenomenon, of apparent hard-wiring of much-used or automatic forms, may be hypothesized to underlie the findings of Berman and Olshtain (1983) whereby certain formulaic utterances, much used in daily discourse, were retained in subjects who otherwise were losing access to their second language, (specifically they were losing less-frequent aspects of the lexicon and irregular verb structure).

As Bahrick (1984) pointed out, most markedly in the first 6 years after learning stops, attrition can be seen in certain language abilities (in particular grammar recognition, word order, reading comprehension, and vocabulary recall). However, for other aspects, (in particular idiom recall, grammar recall, and vocabulary recognition) no decline was seen. This dissociation was seen in the oldest subjects in his study, that is, subjects who were tested 50 years after they stopped learning the second language, as compared to the youngest subjects. Not only are specific language behaviours relatively lost or spared, as Cohen (1986) points out, certain aspects of vocabulary items may be particularly spared or impaired. (By aspects he means form, grammatical patterns and collocations appropriate for the word, function, and its meanings – both concepts and associations.) These findings of relative sparing or impairment of subaspects of the linguistic system come as no surprise to the neurolinguist, since the literature on aphasia has long documented differential organization under conditions of frank brain damage suggesting differential organization premorbidly. That the same phenomena should show up with attrition, then, appears most likely.

Jakobson's regression hypothesis

Overall in the neurolinguistic literature it appears that Jakobson's (1941; 1968) regression hypothesis (that what is first learned is last lost, and what is last learned is first forgotten) cannot be maintained in detail (Caramazza and Zurif, 1978). However, certain subaspects of it seem to hold true with respect to first language attrition. Cohen (1975) reported that in schoolchildren learning a second language the regression seen over the course of the summer was evident in that vocabulary items that had been learned closest to the end of the school year were those most forgotten upon testing at the beginning of the next school year. One might argue, however, that it is because these late-learned items had been used less, rather than that they were learned late, that they appeared to have been forgotten first. Olshtain also (1986) reports that for her subjects, although the lexicon itself did not evidence such a pattern, irregular verb morphology appears to have. To the extent the regression hypothesis holds, we may argue that overlearned items are stored in some more automatic core which facilitates access. Alternately, we may argue that recent access has primed the relevant items for recall. In exactly what neuroanatomic or neurochemical behaviours this priming consists remains to be discovered.

The possibility of no language attrition in the elderly bilingual as compared to the monolingual

de Bot and Clyne (1989) returned to the population on which Clyne had reported some evidence of decline in elderly bilinguals, particularly in their L1, to demonstrate that, while such decline occurred in certain subjects, it did not occur in all. Moreover, those who had acquired a higher peak proficiency were the ones who showed no decline. Such a phenomenon may enter into Pietilä's (1989) results on L2 attrition. Obler, Albert and Lozowick (1986) likewise studied a group of eleven elderly English-dominant bilingual subjects whose average age was 74, and compared them to 32 monolinguals of a similar age on a broad battery of language tests in the second language. On certain aspects of performance the bilinguals were significantly better than the monolinguals (word fluency, and the Stroop colour word task in the congruent condition); on two verbal tasks the monolinguals were better than the bilinguals (on automatic speech, such as reciting the alphabet, and on the proverbs task). However, on the vast majority of the tests given there were no group differences seen, neither on a noun-naming test, nor a verb-naming test, nor on a test of naming famous faces, nor on a word-fluency task (generating words beginning with certain letters), nor in generating antonyms or reciting months forward and backward, responding to a number facts test, performance on the incongruent condition of the Stroop colour word test, performance on the Speech Perception in Noise (SPIN) comprehension test, or performance on idiom interpretation. All these bilinguals had learned English before the age of 6, and although some had continued to use their L1 to some degree, their second language showed virtually no attrition relative to that of monolinguals.

By my way of thinking, Pietilä's (1989) results may be interpreted to suggest that older bilinguals show attrition in their L2 abilities, but, as she acknowledges, due to differing circumstances of cohorts in immigration, she was not able to balance such factors as initial level of English upon immigration, socioeconomic status, and occupation, which may have resulted in a lesser proficiency acquired before ageing among her older subjects than will have occurred among her younger adults. While these factors were statistically demonstrated not to have an effect on the language factors she measured, the effect may have been a subtle one. In any event, if we compare her study and ours, we may conclude that bilinguals do not *necessarily* suffer in late adulthood any more language attrition than do monolinguals. Neurolinguistic research that delineates the mechanisms of language decline in monolinguals, then, should contribute further to our understanding of the first or second language attrition of bilinguals when it occurs.

RESEARCH TO BE DONE

In addition to studies replicating and expanding on those discussed above, it would be of particular interest to use the dynamic brain imaging techniques such as PET scan and blood-flow studies to demonstrate the dynamics of bilingual language processing by the brains of bilingual individuals. Then, once neurochemists have had the opportunity to develop their science so that we know how learning takes place in the brain of a human at the cellular level (for now all we know is how it takes place in lower animals such as the snail), it will be of great interest to study how second languages are acquired biochemically.

ACKNOWLEDGEMENTS

Patrick McNamara is to be thanked for the discussions on critical and sensitive periods that led to our joint paper presented at the AAAS meetings (February 1991). Thanks also to Andrew Cohen for sharing his extensive library on language attrition with me.

REFERENCES

Albert, M. and Obler, L. K. (1978), *The bilingual brain: Neuropsychological and neurolinguistic aspects of bilingualism.* New York: Academic Press.
April, R., and Han, M. (1980), Crossed aphasia in a right-handed bilingual Chinese man. *Archives of Neurology,* 37, 342–5.
Bahrick, H. (1984), Semantic memory content in permastore: Fifty

years of memory for Spanish learned in school. *Journal of Experimental Psychology: General*, 113, 1–29.

Berman, R., and Olshtain, E. (1983), Features of first-language transfer in second-language attrition. *Applied Linguistics*, 4, 222–33.

Berthier, M., Starkstein, S., Lylyk, P. & Leiguarda, R. (1990), Differential recovery of language in a bilingual patient. *Brain and Language*, 38, 449–53.

Broca, P. (1865) Sur la faculté du langage articulé, Bulletin de la Société d'anthropologie, Paris 6, 337–93.

Caramazza, A., and Zurif, E. (eds.) (1978), *Language acquisition and language breakdown*. Baltimore: Johns Hopkins University Press.

Charlton, M. (1964), Aphasia in bilingual and polyglot patients. *JSHD*, 29, 307–11.

Clyne, M. (1977), Bilingualism of the elderly. *Talanya*, 4, 45–56.

Cohen, A. (1975), Forgetting a second language. *Language Learning*, 25, 127–38.

(1986) Forgetting foreign-language vocabulary. In Weltens, B., de Bot, K., and van Els, T. (eds.) (1986), *Language attrition in progress*, 143–58. Dordrecht: Foris.

de Bot, K., and Clyne, M. (1989), Language reversion revisited. *SSLA*, 11, 167–77.

Geschwind, N. and Galaburda, A. (1985), Cerebral lateralization: Biological mechanisms, associations and pathology. *Archives of Neurology*, 42, 428–59, 521–52, and 634–54.

Gloning, J. and Gloning, K. (1965), Aphasien bei Polyglotten. Wiener Zeitschrift für Nervenheilkunde, 22, 362–97.

Humes-Bartlo, M. (1989), Variation in children's ability to learn second languages. In Hyltenstam, K. and Obler, L. K. (eds.), *Bilingualism across the lifespan: Aspects of acquisition, maturity, and loss*, pp. 41–54. Cambridge: Cambridge University Press.

Hyltenstam, K. and Stroud, C. (1985), The psycholinguistics of language choice and code-switching in Alzheimer's dementia: Some hypotheses. *Scandinavian Working Papers on Bilingualism*, 4, 26–44.

(1989), Bilingualism in Alzheimer's dementia: Two case studies. In

Hyltenstam, K., and Obler, L. K. (eds.) *Bilingualism across the lifespan: Aspects of acquisition, maturity and loss.* Cambridge: Cambridge University Press.

Jakobson, R. (1941), *Kindersprache, Aphasie und allgemeine Lautgesetze.* Uppsala: Almquist and Wiksell. English Translation, 1968.

Johnson, J., and Newport, E. (1989), Critical period effects in second-language learning: The influence of maturational state on the acquisition of English as a second language. *Cognitive Psychology,* 21, 60–99.

Krashen, S. (1973), Lateralization, language learning, and the critical period: some new evidence. *Language Learning,* 23, 63–74.

Leopold, W. (1939–49), *Speech development of a bilingual child.* 4 vols. Evanston, Ill.: Northwestern Press.

Newport, E. (1990), Maturational constraints on language learning. *Cognitive Science,* 14, 11–28.

Novoa, L. D., Fein, D., and Obler, L. K. (1989), Talent in foreign languages: A case study. In Obler, L. K. and Fein, D. (eds.), *The exceptional brain: Neuropsychology of talent and special abilities,* pp. 294–302. New York: Guilford.

Obler, L. K. (1989a), Exceptional second-language learners. In Gass, S., Madden, C., Preston, D., and Selinker, L. (eds.), *Variation in second-language acquisition, Vol. II: Psycholinguistic issues.* Clevedon: Multilingual Matters.

(1989b), Talented and untalented L2 acquisition. SLRF Plenary, Los Angeles: February 1989.

Obler, L. K., Albert, M., and Lozowick, S. (1986), The aging bilingual. In Vaid, J. (ed.), *Language processing in bilinguals: Psycholinguistic and neuropsychological perspectives.* Hillsdale, N.J.: Erlbaum.

Obler, L. K., and Mahecha, N. (1991), First language loss in bilinguals with brain damage. In Seliger, H., and Vago, R. (eds.), *First language attrition: Structural and theoretical perspectives.* Cambridge: Cambridge University Press.

Obler, L. K. and McNamara, P. (1991), Neurological evidence concerning a critical period for second language acquisition. Presented at AAAS meetings, Washington D.C., February.

Ojemann, N., and Whitaker, H. (1978), The bilingual brain. *Archives of Neurology*, 35, 409–12.

Olshtain, E. (1986), The attrition of English as a second language with speakers of Hebrew. In Weltens, B., de Bot, K., and van Els, T. (eds.), *Language attrition in progress*, pp. 185–204. Dordrecht: Foris.

Olshtain, E., and Barzilay, M. (1991), Lexical retrieval difficulties in adult language attrition. In Seliger, H., and Vago, R. *First language attrition: Structural and theoretical perspectives*. Cambridge: Cambridge University Press.

Paradis, M. (1977), Bilingualism and aphasia. In Whitaker, H., and Whitaker, H. (eds.), *Studies in Neurolinguistics*, 3, 65–121. New York: Academic Press.

(1990), Differential recovery of languages in a bilingual patient following selective amytal injection: A comment to Berthier et al. (1990). *Brain and Language*, 39, 469–70.

Paradis, M. and Goldblum (1988), Selected crossed aphasia followed by reciprocal antagonism in a trilingual patient. *Brain and Language*, 36, 62–75.

Pietilä, P. (1989), *The English of Finnish–Americans with reference to social and psychological background factors and with special reference to age*. Turku: Turun Yliopisto.

Rapport, R. L., Tan, C. T., and Whitaker, H. A. (1983), Language function and dysfunction among Chinese- and English-speaking polyglots: Cortical stimulation, Wada testing, and clinical studies. *Brain and Language*, 18, 342–66.

de Santi, S., Obler, L. K., Sabo-Abramson, H., and Goldberger, J. (1990), Discourse Abilities and Deficits in Multilingual Dementia. In Joanette, T. and Brownell, H. (eds.), *Discourse ability in brain damage*. New York: Springer Verlag.

Schneiderman, E. and Desmarais, C. (1988), A neuropsychological substrate for talent in second-language acquisition. In Obler, L. K. and Fein, D. (eds.), *The exceptional brain: Neuropsychology of talent and special abilities*, pp. 103–26. New York: Guilford Press.

Silverberg, R., Bentin, S., Gaziel, T., Obler, L. K., and Albert, M. L. (1979), Shift of visual-field preference for English words in native Hebrew speakers. *Brain and Language*, 8, 184–90.

Vaid, J. (1983), Bilingualism and brain lateralization. In Segalowitz, S. (ed.), *Language functions and brain organization*, 315–39. New York: Academic Press.

Weltens, B. and Van Els, T. (1986), The attrition of French as a foreign language: Interim results. In Weltens, B., de Bot, K., and van Els, T. (eds.), *Language attrition in progress*. Dordrecht: Foris.

Weltens, B., Van Els, T., Schils, E. (1989), The long-term retention of French by Dutch students. *SSLA*, 11, 205–16.

8 · Second language acquisition as a function of age: research findings and methodological issues

MICHAEL H. LONG

The possibility that language acquisition, like so many aspects of human development, is at least partly a function of biological programming has long intrigued students of first and second language acquisition and loss. Demonstrating the existence of maturational constraints, specifically, one or more sensitive periods for language development, would have ramifications both for language acquisition theory and language teaching practice. Language learning after the close of the period(s) identified might be a qualitatively different process, and a theory would have to account for that. The existence of sensitive periods would hold implications for first and second language teaching programmes of various kinds. The type and timing of instruction − either in or through a new language − for abnormal first language, and normal child and adult second language, populations would be influenced, for example, by a finding that native-like abilities in one or more linguistic domains could only be achieved by learners first exposed to a language before a certain age.

A sensitive period, following Oyama (1979), is best conceived as a time of heightened responsiveness to certain kinds of environmental stimuli, bounded on both sides by states of lesser responsiveness, with abrupt *or gradual* increases or decreases in learning ability expected and sufficient to support the claim. It is recognized, after all, that even some of the clearest cases of sensitive periods in the animal world, such as imprinting, are often not 'developmentally fixed' (genetically determined and impervious to environmental influence), and so can be variable.

As Johnson and Newport (1989) have pointed out, two possible versions of Lenneberg's (1967) critical period hypothesis are open to test. The first version, the so-called *exercise hypothesis*, holds that, early in life, humans have a superior language learning capacity. If not exercised during this time, it will disappear or decline with maturation; if exercised, i.e. used for normal L1 acquisition, it will remain permanently intact for later SLA. The second version, the so-called *maturational state hypothesis*, holds that, early in life, humans have a superior language learning capacity. The capacity disappears or declines with maturation, i.e. even when it is used normally for L1 acquisition. Thus, both the exercise hypothesis and the maturational state hypothesis predict that children will do better than adults in first language learning. In SLA, however, whereas the exercise hypothesis predicts that children will do no differently from adults, the maturational state hypothesis predicts that children will be better. Data on SLA, therefore, are crucial for distinguishing between the two.

RESEARCH FINDINGS

While the issue remains controversial (see, e.g. Genesee, 1988; Snow, 1987), a review of first and second language research findings (Long, 1990) produced considerable evidence that the age at which learners are initially exposed to a language (age of onset, or AO) is a robust predictor of their long-term success in that language, particularly as to whether or not they can reach native-like abilities in a L2. The relationship between age and ultimate attainment is not simply an inverse linear one, however. An AO of 0–6 appeared to be sufficient for subjects to reach native-like proficiency (given sufficient opportunity) in all linguistic domains. Those who began SLA after age 6, on the other hand, showed decreasing levels of ultimate attainment, with increasing AO affecting long-term achievement not just in phonology, but in different linguistic domains cumulatively.

Thus, the likelihood of achieving native-like suprasegmental and segmental phonology apparently declined rapidly with starting ages later than 6, whereas native-like morphosyntax seemed possible for some learners whose first exposure was as late as age 15. Achievement in all linguistic domains among those whose first exposure occurred after the mid-teens was less predictable on the basis of age alone, with many other variables playing a part.

The extensive literature on *rate of development* as a function of AO has been reviewed elsewhere (see, e.g. Scovel, 1988; Long, 1990) and will not be dealt with in any detail here. Krashen, Long and Scarcella (1979/1982) suggested that if short-term (rate) and long-term (ultimate attainment) studies are distinguished, then results support three generalizations:

1 adults proceed through early stages of morphological and syntactic development faster than children,
2 older children acquire faster than younger children,
3 child starters outperform adult starters in the long run.

(1) and (2) refer to rate, only. Research findings which have appeared since the Krashen et al. review are consistent with (1) and (2) (see, e.g. Morris and Gerstman, 1986). The exceptions, some laboratory studies using elicitation tasks for phonology with children (e.g. Snow and Hoefnagel-Hohle, 1977; Tahta, Wood, and Lowenthal, 1981a, 1981b; Yamada, Takatsuka, Kotake, and Kurusu, 1980) appear to be artifacts of the tasks and/or procedures utilized (for detailed discussion, see Long, 1990). (3) refers to ultimate attainment, but is neutral as to the absolute abilities achievable by children and adults. Subsequent findings, including those of Adiv (1980), Harley (1982, 1986), Johnson and Newport (1989), and Patkowski (1980a, 1980b), have again been consistent with this generalization.

The most critical data are those on *long-term ultimate attainment*, in particular, the absolute abilities (native-like or not) achievable by learners with different starting ages. Five especially important studies are those of the acquisition of American Sign Language (ASL) by Newport (1984, 1990); of second language and second dialect phonology by Oyama (1976) and Payne (1980), respectively; and of SL morphosyntax by Patkowski (1982, 1990) and Johnson and Newport (1989).

Newport examined the command of ASL after 10 years of use of three groups of learners first exposed to ASL (as a first language) at different ages, and reached the following conclusions:

1   Native/early learners, exposed to ASL from birth until about age 6, reach native standards, and show very uniform error types, especially errors of omission and sequentialization (producing the component morphemes sequentially rather than simultaneously), suggesting they are learning ASL via morphological analysis, even when from older non-native or late acquirers who provide them with poor (morphologically unanalyzed or erratic) input.

2   Learners first exposed after age 7 make some errors in closed class items (grammatical morphology) after 10 years of use, and show progressively more evidence of holistic (unanalyzed) learning the later they start.

3   Late/adult learners, first exposed after age 12, stop far short of native standards, and show much greater individual variation in error types, generally making few omission or sequentialization errors, but many arising from their use of frozen forms (signs holistically related to their meanings, not constructed from their component morphemes), with much of their production either monomorphemic or of unanalyzed chunks containing 2+ morphemes, suggesting holistic rote learning.

Similar findings involving non-native-like morphology and syntax have been reported from case studies of 'Chelsea' and other hearing-impaired adult starters (for review, see Curtiss, 1988).

In a major early study of the maturational constraints issue, Oyama (1976) showed a main effect for age of arrival (range 6–20) in the United States on the pronunciation ability of 60 Italian immigrants, and no effect for either length of residence (LOR, a rough measure of amount of exposure, range 5–18 years) or motivation, once the effect for AO was partialled out. Child arrivals performed in the range of native speaker (NS) controls, arrivals older than 12 did not, and (importantly) accents were also evident in some who arrived earlier than 12. In a second dialect study of the acquisition of the King of Prussia, Philadelphia, accent by people who had relocated to Philadelphia from other parts of the US, Payne (1980) found that the predictable, regularly conditioned vowel phonemes of the second dialect were acquired by all children, but that unmotivated exceptions were learned only by children who arrived before age 6 and who had at least one locally born parent. (See, also, Shanta, 1985.)

As was the case with the ASL work, two second language studies show that maturational constraints are not limited to phonology, but affect morphosyntax, too. Patkowski (1982, 1990) conducted oral interviews with 67 immigrants to the US, each with a minimum LOR of 5 years and differing AO, and 15 NS controls. The interviews were then transcribed, thereby removing any aural clues. The transcripts of five-minute samples from all 82 interviews were presented in random order to two trained judges, whose job it was to assign proficiency ratings using a 10-point scale similar to that employed in the US Foreign Service Institute oral interview procedure. Patkowski found a strong main effect for age of arrival, no effect for any other variables (LOR, informal SL exposure, and formal SL instruction), and no interaction effects. Thirty-two of 33 immigrants in the sample who had arrived in the US before puberty received near-perfect $(4+, n = 10)$ or perfect $(5, n = 22)$ 'native speaker' ratings on the 10-point, 0 to 5 scale. Conversely, of the 34 immigrants who had arrived after puberty, only 5 received such high ratings (4 near-perfect and 1 perfect). The shapes of the distributions for pre- and post-puberty arrivals were markedly different. The distribution for the pre-puberty group was heavily positively skewed, whereas that for the post-puberty group was normally distributed, suggesting that the subjects represented not 1, but 2 (slightly overlapping) samples distinguished by AO, with early to mid-teens implicated as the close of a sensitive period for native-like acquisition of a SL morphosyntax.

Additional evidence of a relationship between AO and ultimate attainment in SL morphosyntax has been provided by Johnson and Newport (1989). Whereas proficiency ratings in Patkowski's study were assigned on the basis of subjects' production abilities using spontaneous speech samples, Johnson and Newport studied non-native recognition abilities, using data from the performance on a grammaticality judgment test probing a wide range of English structures, of 46 NSs of Korean and Chinese. AO in the US ranged from 3 to 39, and LOR from 3 to 26 years at the time of testing. A strong advantage was found on all structures tested for early over late arrivals. Most important, however, test scores were linearly related to AO up to puberty, but after that, while low, were very variable and unrelated to AO, suggesting (consistent with Patkowski's results) a sensitive period, not simply a general age-effect, for SL morphology and syntax. As has often been the case in such studies, there was no effect for LOR, motivation, self-consciousness or American identification.

There is no evidence that the deteriorating prognosis with increasing AO is a function of a decline in general cognitive abilities, any more than that children's initial language learning abilities are limited by their otherwise relatively poor problem-solving skills. These facts, coupled with the inability of social, affective, or input factors to account for the data (see Long, 1990, for discussion), suggest the existence of maturationally constrained language-specific biology and, specifically, of one or more sensitive periods for both first and second language developoment by children and adults. In sum, support exists for the following claims:

1   Initial learning rate and ultimate attainment are partly a function of AO.
2   Language development is governed by sensitive periods, during which the acquisition of different linguistic abilities is successful, and after which it is irregular and incomplete.
3   The loss in learning capacity is not limited to phonology. Nor is it a catastrophic one-time event, but cumulative, affecting first one linguistic domain and then another.

4   The deterioration begins as early as age 6 in some individuals, not at puberty, as if often claimed.
5   These findings disconfirm the exercise hypothesis and are consistent with the maturational state hypothesis.

Since completion of the review cited, at least one other major investigation relevant to the sensitive periods issue has been conducted, involving a study by the Stockholm University's Centre for Research on Bilingualism of the acquisition of Swedish as a SL by native speakers of Spanish and Finnish (see Hyltenstam, 1988, 1992; Hyltenstam and Stroud, to appear; Stroud, 1988). Hyltenstam (1992) provides evidence which suggests that an AO of 0–6 may not just be crucial for phonology, but for lexis and morphosyntax, too.

The Stockholm study involved 24 highly proficient 17–18-year-old bilinguals, all with Swedish L2, selected by their teachers as not immediately identifiable as NNs in their everyday spoken Swedish. Twelve were NSs of Spanish, 12 of Finnish. Twelve monolingual NSs of Swedish served as controls. The 3 groups were matched for age, average grades and tracks at school, and parental socio-economic status. The 24 bilinguals included 16 with AO below 6, and 8 with AO later than 7. The full study involved oral and written data, the former consisting of retellings of 4 prepared texts, the latter of unspeeded compositions based on part of the Charlie Chaplin film, *Modern Times*.

Hyltenstam (1992) reports quantitative and qualitative analyses of lexical and grammatical errors in the speech data. Error frequencies for the 36 subjects are shown in Figure 8.1. The error distributions of the 12 NSs and the 16 learners with AO less than 6 overlap to a considerable extent. While six members of the latter group do less well, with from 12 to 23 errors each, the other 10 early starters perform on a par with the NSs, with from 1 to 10 errors each. That is, the distributions of these 2 groups overlap to some extent. In contrast, the third group, the 8 learners with AO greater than 7, clearly represent a separate population, the *best* of the late starters committing 13 errors, the worst 26.

Table 8.1. *Distribution of errors among 24 second language learners of Swedish with AO < age 6 (♯) and > age 7 (*), respectively, compared to 12 first language learners (o) (Hyltenstam, 1992)*

Total number of errors

1	2	3	4	5	6	7	8	9	10	11	12	13	14	15	16	17	18	19	20	21	22	23	24	25
♯	o	♯	o	♯	♯	♯	o	o	♯		♯	♯	♯	*	♯				*	♯		♯	*	*
o	♯		♯	♯	o	o	o							*		*			*					
o	♯			o	o									*										
o																								

Based on the qualitative analysis, Hyltenstam reports that there were two main kinds of lexical errors. First, there were several *close approximations* to the Swedish target form in the bilinguals' data, e.g. **mellan chefen ser det* for *medan chefen ser det* ('*between* the boss sees it' for '*while* the boss sees it'), and **majskorv* ('corn-sausage') for *majskolv* ('corn-cob'), with both the intended and supplied item sometimes involving frequent L2 vocabulary items.[1] The Swedish controls also made this type of error, but less often (Finnish 59, Spanish 70, Swedish 21), and never with frequent, everyday words, e.g. **demostrera* for *demonstrera* ('demonstrate'), although frequency is, of course, relative. There were also *contaminations*, where elements of two or more Swedish forms were combined to produce a non-existent one, e.g. **man beräknar med att* from '*räknar med*' and '*beräknar*' ('one reckons on that' from 'counts on' and 'reckons'). All 3 groups made contamination errors equally.

Grammatical errors among the bilinguals, while infrequent, included problems with quite basic points, such as gender agreement on definite and indefinite articles, *den* for *det* ('the') and *ett* for *en* ('a'), choice of reflexive and non-reflexive pronouns, violation of the verb second constraint in Swedish, and adverb placement, e.g. **han troligen blir bortförd* for *blir troligen* ('he gets probably taken away'). Monolinguals made some errors like these (e.g. an article deletion and a reflexive pronoun error), but they were very rare and usually clearly performance slips.[2]

Hyltenstam notes that the differences between the NS and bilingual subjects in the frequencies (not types) of lexical errors (especially approximation errors on high frequency lexical items), and in both the frequency and (in this corpus) type of grammatical errors (e.g. word order and verb tense forms), support the claim that sensitive periods exist for areas other than phonology. He points out, however, that these areas seem to be affected earlier than hypothesized by Long (1990), possibly again by age 6.

The work of Hyltenstam and Stroud raises the possibility that, just as earlier placement of the upper bounds of a sensitive period for phonology at puberty (e.g. Scovel, 1988) may have been due to studies having used insufficiently sensitive measures and/or inadequate corpora to detect L2 accents, research on late acquirers' abilities in other linguistic domains may have led to an overly optimistic prognosis there, too. Accordingly, we now turn to a brief discussion of these and other methodological issues. What are some of the design features that might strengthen future studies of maturational constraints on second language acquisition?

METHODOLOGICAL ISSUES

Subject selection – non-native speakers

NNS subjects in future ultimate attainment studies need to be very advanced and to have had sufficient opportunity to acquire the L2. There is no value in studying obviously non-native-like individuals intensively in order to declare them non-native-like. Hence, screening subjects into studies is important.

One approach to screening is to recruit an initial subject pool via 'friends of friends' networking (Milroy, 1987a, 1987b), word-of-mouth, or public announcements which include non-technical descriptions of the kind of proficiency levels of interest. Once such an initial subject pool has been obtained, follow-up screening interviews (e.g. Neufeld, 1978) can help identify potentially interesting individuals more precisely. Self-evaluations alone, on the other hand, are inadequate, for, while asking people to respond to public requests for subjects implies the procedure has some validity, it is also clear that far more people rate themselves as native-like than really are. In a study by Seliger, Krashen, and Ladefoged (1975), for example, fully 47% of 100 adults who had emigrated to the US and Israel between the ages of 10 and 15 rated themselves as having a native-like accent in their second language, as did 6.9% of 173 informants who had emigrated at 16 and over, whereas objective laboratory tests of SL phonology have yet to produce a single late starter with such abilities. Word-of-mouth recommendations from people who know the individuals well and can attest to their 'lack of an obvious non-native accent' or some similar criterion, as used by Hyltenstam and Stroud, seems to work better. Using general proficiency test scores is another possibility, but only if the test concerned, e.g. the FSI Oral Interview Procedure, demands genuinely high standards for its 'advanced' proficiency ratings and maintains rigorous, reliable administration procedures.

Subject selection − native speakers

To serve as legitimate controls and to provide valid baseline data on NS competence in the target variety, NS subjects clearly need to be more comparable to NNS comparison groups than has sometimes been the case in the SLA literature in the past. The most crucial requirement, that NSs speak the L2 variety or second dialect that was the acquisition target for the NNSs, is discussed below. In addition, NS controls should be comparable in age, sex, education, and social class, and in any other way known to be sociolinguistically relevant in the language or dialect concerned. Ideally, they should also be monolinguals, since there is increasing experimental and anecdotal evidence that learning additional languages can sometimes affect first language abilities in as yet poorly understood ways, and might influence NSs' judgements of the grammaticality or acceptability of potential test items.[3]

The L2 target

It is desirable that the target variety be relatively homogeneous, as this will facilitate the establishment of unambiguous NS base-line data. Where a target variety is very heterogenous, as in cities with a heavy and varied immigrant population and also in creole speech communities, it is difficult to find pronunciation norms and even quite simple test items, let alone items involving subtle grammar points, for which uniform NS judgements (of grammaticality, acceptability, nativeness, etc.) can be obtained.[4]

The particular variety of the L2 to which subjects have been exposed and which has been their acquisition target should be the same variety as that spoken by the NS controls. If different varieties of an L2 are represented in a study, two threats to internal validity may exist. NNSs may be judged non-native-like simply because they speak a different variety of the L2, and/or they may be judged native-like because interlingual (or inter-dialectal) forms or uses are wrongly assumed to reflect natural target language variation.

The mere physical presence of the NNSs in the town or region where the NS control variety is standard may not be enough to guarantee that this variety was the NNS subjects' acquisition target. The potential subjects may recently have moved to that area and have learned a different variety and/or received formal instruction in a different variety there or elsewhere. A 'standard' dialect may prevail because of the political and economic power of the elites who speak it, but the potential subjects for a study may have had higher personal exposure to, and learned, a different, 'non-standard' variety, e.g. Hawai'i Creole English in the case of some Korean immigrant children in Hawai'i (Klein, 1981), and Black English in the case of some Hispanic teenage boys in New York (Goldstein, 1987). Alternatively, they may indeed have been long-time residents of the area where the variety of interest is spoken and/or have been primarily exposed to it elsewhere (e.g. through a spouse), but have resisted it as an acquisition target in favour of another variety perceived as having higher prestige. Bio-data on language use will be necessary, with interviews, rather than questionnaires, usually required to ensure reliability.

Operationalization of independent and moderator variables

The measurement of such commonly assessed variables in sensitive period studies as amount and type of language exposure and use, motivation, integrative orientation, and attitude to the target language or dialect, is notoriously difficult, especially cross-culturally, and has been insufficiently addressed in SLA research in general, not just in age research (see, however, Oller, 1981; Skehan, 1989; Crookes and Schmidt, 1991). Where age studies are concerned, even the measurement of seemingly easily ascertained AO and LOR (or some other index of exposure), warrants closer scrutiny than it has typically been accorded. Subjects (and researchers) need to be clear just what is of interest when AO is (self) reported. The crucial issue is the age at which the subject was first exposed to the second language or dialect. This may or may not be the time the individual first took up residence in a community where that variety is spoken, although it is often (one suspects, too often) assumed to be the same in some studies. It needs to be clearly established whether subjects had prior exposure at an earlier age, e.g. through caretakers or grandparents who spoke the L2 in the home, short visits to the L2 environment, or formal instruction. Failure to identify such exposure inflates AO in a study and seriously threatens tests of supposed sensitive periods for language learning. The reverse possibility also needs to be considered. Arrival in the L2 environment may not initially entail exposure to the L2, as shown by the experience of many working-class immigrants and young children, whose domestic and work situations or age can sometimes mean that they spend considerable periods living in an L1 linguistic ghetto before first contact with the L2 is made.

Assessment of first language or dialect maintenance

While higher native language competence before initial L2 exposure appears beneficial for both first and second language eventual attainment in sequential child SLA (Cummins, 1980, 1981), there is also evidence that L2 proficiency in adults can be negatively associated with L1 maintenance – the so-called 'displacement effect' (Palij, 1990), most obviously in cases of complete L1 loss. Whether this relationship reflects varying communicative needs in the two languages, differential opportunities for their use, or some underlying cognitive, neurolinguistic or social–psychological constraints on the human capacity to control two languages at native-like levels, as some have suggested (Buckley, 1988; Guiora and Schonberger, 1989), is unclear. Meanwhile, it will strengthen the interpretability of a study's results if researchers collect data on their L2 subjects' L1 proficiency and use, despite the extra work this will inevitably involve.

Task types and language samples

It is of interest to know what late starters in a second language or dialect can do on various free production tasks. Where the assessment of native-like abilities is concerned, however, studies have shown the need to probe areas of difficulty, i.e. what learners cannot do, as well, and that this requires careful attention to the modality, tasks, and items involved in collecting performance samples, and an emphasis on narrowly targeted comprehension tasks rather than free production. With regard to modality, studies by Scovel (1981) and Ioup (1984), for example, show that raters may not be able to distinguish NSs and NNSs, and NNSs of different L1 backgrounds, on free-writing tasks, yet be able to do so when presented with speech samples from the same subjects.[5]

Another reason for employing forced production (e.g. elicited imitation) and/or comprehension (e.g. grammaticality judgement) tasks, in addition to, or instead of, free production tasks is the need with very proficient learners to probe knowledge of low frequency and/or easily (and grammatically) avoided items. An example might be subject–auxiliary inversion in English statements after certain 'negative' adverbials (Seldom had she heard . . . Only on a clear day can you see . . .). Such items might never occur in free speech or free writing samples, yet it would be unwarranted to assume either (a) lack of knowledge on the basis of non-use, or (b) that error-free performance on what the learner did say or write can be interpreted as native-like competence in all unobserved domains, as well. Three issues affecting the construction and use of such tasks/tests remain largely unexplored in the literature: content (motivation for the choice of items or features to include in test items), item difficulty, and the reliability and validity of various test and task types and formats.

Test content

With respect to content, with the exception of those working within a UG framework, most researchers appear to have chosen to sample a miscellany of linguistic items on the basis of their intuitions as to what might be difficult for highly proficient NNSs, perhaps supplemented by contrastive analyses of the contact languages and/or the results of error analyses. All of these undoubtedly constitute useful sources of potential test items. Another option for future work is predictions derivable from theoretical linguistics, e.g. structures which are marked either in the typological sense (especially structures which are more marked than the equivalent item in the learner's L1) or as determined *a priori* by Chomskyan theory, especially language-specific, peripheral features and unmarked or less marked values of parameter settings where the learner's L1 setting is marked or less conservative and where learning from positive evidence alone will be impossible (e.g. Johnson and Newport, 1991). These would often correspond to the target items in studies of L2 stabilization, fossilization, and learnability (from positive evidence alone), such as Schachter's (1990) work on relative clauses. Language-specific, optional rules and distinctions are also generally promising candidates. Finally, a hitherto untapped source of guidance may be advanced learners themselves. Highly proficient NNSs have usually been willing and easily capable of providing the writer with impromptu lists of linguistic features and domains that 'always cause me problems', as well as specific examples of lexical items, collocations, and word stress assignment they are 'never sure of' or 'just guess at'. Again, these have often been low frequency items on which the informants had usually not been heard to make the errors concerned, and some of which would not have been obvious as candidates for inclusion in a test.

Item difficulty

Where difficulty is concerned, some studies would seem to employ overly simple tests, thereby risking the design equivalent of a type 2 statistical error, i.e. concluding that no difference exists between (NS and NNS) groups when that is not the case. For example, a grammaticality judgement test used by Johnson and Newport (1989) with Korean and Chinese students at a US university included (among many others) such items as 'The woman paints' versus 'Paints the woman', and 'Yesterday the hunter shot the deer' versus 'Yesterday the hunter shoots the deer', grammatical points mastered at quite early stages of development. While inclusion of some items of this kind may be important for statistical and other reasons, it would clearly be undesirable to conclude that subjects able to score 100% on a test pitched wholly at this difficulty level were native-like. Less obviously, samples of free speech obtained under certain circumstances, e.g. a relaxed conversation on a familiar topic, may be equally unsuitable as a measure of what a learner cannot do, even in the phonological domain, since evidence exists that task familiarity and other psycholinguistic dimensions of performance are critical sources of interlanguage variation (Sato, 1985, 1990; Selinker and Douglas, 1985; Hulstijn, 1989).

Issues of task type, content, and format occasionally interact in especially problematic ways, as became clear during the development by the writer and two graduate students of a battery of six tasks to be used in a study of maturational constraints on the acquisition of Hawai'i Creole English (HCE) by speakers of other English dialects (Buckley, 1987; Hurley, 1987). First, while variation in NS grammaticality judgements due to sociological and educational differences is to be expected (Birdsong, 1989), the especially high degree of variation common in creole speech communities (see Bickerton, 1977a, 1977b; Rickford, 1987; Sato, 1978, 1991) prevailed in the NS cohorts from whom judgements of grammaticality were sought during the process in which an initially large pool of potential test items was refined for inclusion in the final tasks. The variation led to numerous items having to be rejected because, while acceptable to many NSs of HCE, they were rejected by others. Second, the fact that HCE, like many so-called 'non-standard' varieties, is rarely written, and, when written, rarely read by many of its speakers,[6] resulted in some HCE NSs rejecting some clearly grammatical sentences as ungrammatical because the modified spelling being used in the research (understandably) looked strange to them. Such judgements also reflected misunderstandings of the task, of course, and the difficulty found in explaining a (written or spoken) grammaticality judgement task to some (cooperative) informants. Indeed, it was often difficult to establish an understanding of the grammaticality concept itself, despite avoiding technical terms, and even when a training task was employed for the purpose. These issues were not made easier, thirdly, by the fact that some of the best speakers of basilectal varieties of HCE are in their 70s, poorly educated and test-naive. Similar problems may affect studies using learners who are illiterate in their native language and/or the L2. Needless to say, it will be especially important to establish the reliability and validity of tasks with populations of these kinds.

Reliability and validity

With some notable exceptions (e.g. Oyama, 1976; Patkowski, 1980; Flege and Fletcher, to appear), the reliability and validity of language measures and ratings of (non)nativeness in age studies are rarely reported, and so, presumably, rarely assessed before data collected with those measures are used for hypothesis-testing. This is clearly undesirable, as researchers in the field would be the first to agree; one suspects the present state of affairs reflects short-cuts taken due to the lack of financial support for most SLA research. Procedures for assessing both the reliability and validity of language measures are well known and standardized, and so will not be treated here (see, e.g. Henning, 1987; Bachman, 1989; Chaudron, Crookes, and Long, 1989; Groot, 1990; Chaudron, 1991).

The age research that has reported reliability and validity data suggests that future work will have to take such matters seriously, as the outcome of studies can sometimes be determined by the methodology employed rather than the variables supposedly being studied. To illustrate, Coppieters (1987) has documented the ability of a very proficient group of NNSs to respond to grammaticality judgement items correctly, but also how a follow-up interview can nevertheless reveal substantial differences between the underlying rule systems the NNSs access to make the judgements and the tacit knowledge available to NS controls. This was the case even with fairly 'low level' grammatical and semantic items in the L2 (French), including rules governing *imparfait/passé composé* tense choices, article use, and *il/elle* vs. *ce* meaning differences. (For an important methodological critique of Coppieters' study, and a replication with rather different findings, see Birdsong, 1992.) Grammaticality judgement tasks in particular are in need of scrutiny in SL research, and when used, are more reliably and validly employed in conjunction with a scalar, rather than a nominal, conception of grammaticality (Chaudron, 1983; Birdsong, 1989).

Native speaker ratings of L2 performance can also be affected by task, task format, and various rater characteristics, although findings are sometimes mixed and not yet fully understood. To illustrate, Flege (1981) reported that non-native accents could be identified equally well on the basis of spontaneous speech or a phrase-reading task. Thomson (1984, 1991) found that sentences 'seeded' with difficult sounds (for Russian learners of ESL) were rated as more accented than spontaneous speech about their daily routine by the same subjects. Flege and Fletcher (to appear) showed that the inclusion of a higher proportion of native or near-native speech samples elicited more strongly negative accentedness ratings of the non-native speakers.

Where raters are concerned, Calloway (1980) showed that linguistically experienced raters performed comparably with linguistically naive raters (although somewhat more reliably) when assessing the intelligibility, acceptability, and nativeness of non-native pronunciation samples. Thompson (1984, 1991) found that a group of linguistically naive raters, and a linguistically sophisticated group who had also had frequent contact with Russian speakers, were equally accurate at detecting non-native accents, but that the former group were less 'tolerant', giving lower ratings to the non-natives than the latter. Flege (1984) reported that phonetically trained undergraduates correctly identified non-native speech samples more accurately (90% correct) than did untrained undergraduates (77% correct) with comparable experience with foreign languages and listening to accented speech. Finally, in a series of by far the most sophisticated studies of these issues to date, Flege and Fletcher (to appear) obtained encouragingly high inter-rater reliability coefficients for the ability of groups of NS judges to assess quite small variations in degree of both native and non-native accent. While not as high, inter- and intra-rater reliability was also acceptable for separate sets of judgements on a relatively homogensous set of strongly accented sentences. Flege and Fletcher suggest that the lower reliability coefficients here were a product of the groups of raters concerned being untrained, inexperienced with speech research, and having to make assessments on the basis of a small sample (a single sentence) occupying a narrow range of foreign accentedness.

CONCLUSION

Research on age-related issues in second language and second dialect acquisition has passed the descriptive, ground-breaking stage. A number of interesting, sometimes conflicting, but testable claims and hypotheses have been advanced. The stage is set for a series of carefully designed experimental studies, and it is hoped that the discussion of methodological issues will be helpful in such work. While sometimes onerous, greater rigour and precision in future research must be worthwhile, given the importance of the findings for SLA theory construction, public policy, and educational practice.

NOTES

1 To the writer, a non-speaker of Swedish, it is not always clear that the examples Hyltenstam provides of close approximations are pure lexical, as opposed to phonological, errors.

2 Supplementary follow-up probes, e.g. grammaticality judgements and/ or a debriefing interview (Coppieters, 1987; Birdsong, 1992), would be desirable to determine whether such deviations are truly non-systematic. On this issue, see, also, Hyltenstam's (1992) discussion of competence and control errors.

3 Buckley (1988) provides experimental evidence of the retroactive influence of L2 phonology on the L1 pronunciation of French–English bilinguals in Montreal. Expatriate language teachers frequently report diminishing abilities to make confident judgements of even quite low level grammatical phenomena, such as English prepositions, after lengthy exposure to non-native student errors in those areas.

4 For vivid examples of the difficulties of obtaining reliable NS base-line judgements, and some solutions, see Bickerton, 1977b; Rickford, 1987; and the HCE case described below.

5 Apparent modality differences may really be reflections of task differences in some studies. For example, it will generally be much easier to avoid linguistic problems, co-plan, monitor, attend to form, and edit during an unspeeded writing task than in a speeded speaking task, which may allow 'accented' non-natives to pass undetected on the former but not the latter.

6 There is a growing modern literature, especially poetry, plays, and short stories, written in HCE (see, e.g. Sumida, 1991; *Bamboo Ridge, the*

Hawai'i Writers' Quarterly and publications of Bamboo Ridge Press), as well as a developing pride in HCE among younger speakers (Sato, 1991). The number of people exposed to HCE literature at school or university remains depressingly small, however, and few older creole speakers had any such opportunities during their school-days.

REFERENCES

Adiv, E. (1980), An analysis of second language performance in two types of immersion programs. Unpublished Ph.D. thesis. Montreal: McGill University.

Bachman, L. (1989), *Fundamental considerations in language testing*. Oxford: Oxford University Press.

Bickerton, D. (1977a), Change and variation in Hawaiian English, II: Creole syntax. (Final Report on National Science Foundation Project No. GS-39748).

(1977b), Some problems in the acceptability and grammaticality in pidgins and creoles. In Greenbaum, S. (ed.), *Acceptability in language*, pp. 27–37. The Hague: Mouton.

Birdsong, D. (1989), *Metalinguistic performance and interlinguistic competence*. New York: Springer-Verlag.

(1992), Ultimate attainment in second language acquisition. *Language*, 68, 706–55.

Buckley, D. (1987), Methodological considerations for acquisition of a second dialect studies. Term paper, ESL 360 (pidgin and creole English in Hawai'i), University of Hawai'i at Manoa.

(1988), First language attrition in additive bilinguals. MA thesis. Honolulu: Department of English as a Second Language, University of Hawai'i at Manoa.

Calloway, D. R. (1980), Accent and evaluation of ESL oral proficiency. In Oller, J. W., and Perkins, K. (eds.), *Research in language testing*, pp. 102–15. Rowley, Mass.: Newbury House.

Chaudron, C. (1983), Research on metalinguistic judgements: a review of theory, method and results. *Language Learning*, 33:3, 343–77.

(1991), Validation in second language classroom research: The role of observation. In Phillipson, R., Kellerman, E., Selinker, L., Sharwood-Smith, M., and Swain, M. (eds.), *Foreign/Second language pedagogy research*, pp. 187–96. Clevedon, Avon: Multilingual Matters.

Chaudron, C., Crookes, G., and Long, M. H. (1988), Reliability and validity in second language classroom research. Technical Report No. 8. Honolulu: Center for Second Language Classroom Research, Social Science Research Institute, University of Hawai'i at Manoa.

Coppieters, R. (1987), Competence differences between native and fluent non-native speakers. *Language*, 63, 544–73.

Crookes, G., and Schmidt, R. W. (1991), Motivation: reopening the research agenda. *Language Learning*, 41, 469–512.

Cummins, J. (1980), The cross-lingual dimensions of language proficiency: implications for bilingual education and the optimal age issue. *TESOL Quarterly*, 14, 175–88.

(1981), The role of primary language development in promoting educational success for language minority students. In *Schooling and language minority students: A theoretical framework*, pp. 3–49. National Evaluation, Dissemination and Assessment Center, California State University.

Curtiss, S. R. (1988), Abnormal language acquisition and the modularity of language. In Newmeyer, F. J. (ed.), *Linguistics: The Cambridge survey. II Linguistic theory: Extensions and implications*, pp. 96–116. Cambridge: Cambridge University Press.

Flege, J. E. (1984), The detection of French accent by American listeners. *Journal of the Acoustical Society of America*, 76, 692–707.

Flege, J. E., and Fletcher, K. L. (to appear), Talker and listener effects on degree of perceived foreign accent. *Journal of the Acoustical Society of America*.

Genesee, F. (1988), Neuropsychology and second language acquisition. In Beebe, L. M. (ed.), *Issues in second language acquisition: Multiple perspectives*, pp. 81–112. Cambridge, Mass.: Newbury House.

Goldstein, L. M. (1987), Standard English: The only target for nonnative speakers of English? *TESOL Quarterly* 21:3, 417–36.

Groot, P. J. M. (1990), Language testing in research and education: The need for standards. In De Jong, J. H. A. L. (ed.), *Standardization in language testing*, pp. 9–23. Amsterdam: AILA Review 7.

Guiora, A., and Schonberger, R. (1989), Native pronunciation of bilinguals. Paper presented at the first annual JAAL conference, Tokyo: Aoyama Gakuin University, 13–14 May.

Harley, B. (1982), Age-related differences in the acquisition of the French verb system by anglophone students in French immersion programs. Unpublished Ph.D. thesis. Toronto: University of Toronto.

Harley, B. (1986), *Age in second language acquisition*. Clevedon, Avon: Multilingual Matters.

Henning, G. (1987), *A guide to language testing. Development, evaluation, research*. Cambridge, Mass.: Newbury House.

Hulstijn, J. (1989), A cognitive view on interlanguage variability. In Eisenstein, M. (ed.), *The dynamic interlanguage*, pp. 17–31. New York; Plenum Press.

Hurley, D. (1987), Methodological problems in second dialect acquisition research. Term paper, ESL 650, University of Hawai'i at Manoa.

Hyltenstam, K. (1988), Lexical characteristics of near-native second-language learners of Swedish. *Journal of Multilingual and Multicultural development* 9:1 and 2, 67–84.

(1992), Non-native features of near-native speakers. In Harris, R. J. (ed.), *Cognitive processing in bilinguals*. Amsterdam: Elsevier.

Hyltenstam, K., and Stroud, C. (to appear), Tvåspråkiga gymnasie-elevers svenska. Stockholm: Centre for Research on Bilingualism, Stockholm University.

Ioup, G. (1984), Is there a structural foreign accent? A comparison of syntactic and phonological errors in second language acquisition. *Language Learning*, 34:2, 1–17.

Johnson, J. S., and Newport, E. L. (1989), Critical period effects in second language learning: the influence of maturational state on the acquisition of English as a second language. *Cognitive Psychology*, 21, 60–99.

Johnson, J. S., and Newport, E. L. (1991), Critical period effects on universal properties of language: The status of subjacency in the acquisition of a second language. *Cognition*, 39, 215–58.

Klein, E. F. (1981), The acquisition of English by Korean adolescent immigrants: A longitudinal study of verbal auxiliary development. Unpublished Ph.D. thesis. Honolulu: University of Hawai'i at Manoa.

Krashen, S. D., Long, M. H., and Scarcella, R. C. (1979), Age, rate, and eventual attainment in second language acquisition. *TESOL Quarterly*, 13, 573–82.

Krashen, S. D., Scarcella, R. C., and Long, M. H. (eds.) (1982), *Child-adult differences in second language acquisition*. Rowley, Mass.: Newbury House.

Lenneberg, E. H. (1967), *Biological foundations of language*. New York: Wiley.

Long, M. H. (1990), Maturational constraints on language development. *Studies in Second language Acquisition* 12:3, 251–85.

Milroy, L. (1987a), *Language and social networks*. 2nd edition. Oxford: Basil Blackwell.

(1987b), *Observing and analysing natural language*. Oxford: Basil Blackwell.

Morris, B. S. K., and Gerstman, L. J. (1986), Age contrasts in the learning of language-relevant materials: some challenges to critical period hypotheses. *Language Learning*, 36:3, 311–52.

Neufeld, G. (1978), On the acquisition of prosodic and articulatory features in adult language learning. *Canadian Modern Language Review*, 34:2, 163–74.

Newport, E. (1984), Constraints on learning: studies in the acquisition of American sign language. *Papers and reports on Child Language Development*, 23, 1–22.

(1990), Maturational constraints on language learning. *Cognitive Science* 14, 11–28.

Oller, J. W. Jr. (1981), Research on the measurement of affective variables: some remaining questions. In Andersen, R. W. (ed.), *New dimensions in second language acquisition research*, pp. 14–27. Rowley, Mass.: Newbury House.

Oyama, S. C. (1976), A sensitive period for the acquisition of a nonnative phonological system. *Journal of Psycholinguistic Research*, 5:3, 261–83.

(1979), The concept of the sensitive period in developmental studies. *Merrill-Palmer Quarterly*, 25:2, 83–103.

Palij, M. (1990), Acquiring English at different ages: The English displacement effect and other findings. *Journal of Psycholinguistic Research*, 19:1, 57–70.

Patkowski, M. (1980a), The sensitive period for the acquisition of syntax in a secondary language. Unpublished Ph.D. thesis. New York: New York University.

(1980b), The sensitive period for the acquisition of syntax in a second language. *Language Learning*, 30:2, 449–72.

(1982), The sensitive period for the acquisition of syntax in a second language. In Krashen, S. D., Scarcella, R. C., and Long, M. H. (eds.), *Child-adult differences in second language acquisition*, pp. 52–63. Rowley, Mass.: Newbury House.

(1990), Age and accent in a second language: a reply to James Emil Flege. *Applied Linguistics*, 11, 73–89.

Payne, A. (1980), Factors controlling the acquisition of the Philadelphia dialect by out-of-state children. In Labov, W. (ed.), *Locating language in time and space*, pp. 143–78. New York: Academic Press.

Rickford, J. R. (1987), The haves and have nots: Sociolinguistic surveys and the assessment of speaker competence. *Language and Society*, 16, 149–78.

Sato, C. J. (1978), Variation in Hawaiian pidgin and creole English: *go* plus verb constructions. MA thesis, Department of Linguistics, University of Hawaii at Manoa.

(1985), Task variation in interlanguage phonology. In Gass, S., and Madden, C. (eds.), *Input in second language acquisition*, pp. 181–96. Rowley, Mass.: Newbury House.

(1990), *The syntax of conversation in interlanguage development*. Tübingen: Gunter Narr.

(1991), Sociolinguistic variation and language attitudes in Hawaii. In Cheshire, J. (ed.), *English around the world*, pp. 647–63. Cambridge: Cambridge University Press.

Schachter, J., (1990), On the issue of completeness in second language acquisition. *Second Language Research*, 6, 93–124.

Scovel, T. (1981), The recognition of foreign accents in English and its implications for psycholinguistic theories of language acquisition. In Savard, J-G., and Laforge, L. (eds.), *Proceedings of the 5th Congress of AILA*, pp. 389–401. Laval: University of Laval Press.

(1988), *A time to speak. A psycholinguistic inquiry into the critical period for human speech*. Cambridge, Mass.: Newbury House.

Seliger, H., Krashen, S. and Ladefoged, P. (1975), Maturational constraints on the acquisition of second languages. *Language Sciences*, 38, 20–2.

Selinker, L., and Douglas, D. (1985), Wrestling with 'context' in interlanguage theory. *Applied Linguistics*, 6:1, 190–204.

Shanta, D. (1985), The acquisition of the phonological features of a second dialect. Unpublished MA thesis. Raleigh, South Carolina: Department of Linguistics.

Skehan, P. (1989), *Individual differences in second-language learning*. London: Edward Arnold.

Snow, C. E. (1987), Relevance of the notion of a critical period to language acquisition. In Bernstein, M. (ed.), *Sensitive periods in development: An interdisciplinary perspective*, pp. 183–209. Hillsdale, N.J.: Lawrence Erlbaum Associates.

Snow, C. E., and Hoefnagel-Hohle, M. (1977), Age differences and the pronunciation of foreign sounds. *Language and Speech*, 20, 357–65.

Stroud, C. (1988), Literacy in a second language: A study of text construction in near-native speakers of Swedish. In Jorgensen, J. N., Hansen, E., Holmen, A., and Gimbel, J. (eds.), *Bilingualism and the individual*, pp. 235–51. Clevedon, Avon: Multilingual Matters.

Sumida, S. H. (1991), *And the view from the shore. Literary tradition of Hawai'i*. Seattle: University of Washington Press.

Tahta, S., Wood, M., and Lowenthal, K. (1981a), Foreign accents: factors relating to transfer of accent from the first language to a second language. *Language and Speech*, 24, 265–72.

(1981b), Age changes in the ability to replicate foreign pronunciation and intonation. *Language and Speech*, 24:4, 363–72.

Thompson, I. (1984), Experimental study of foreign accents. Ph.D. thesis, George Washington University.
   (1991), Foreign accents revisited: The English pronunciation of Russian immigrants. *Language Learning*, 41:2, 177–204.
Yamada, J., Takatsuka, S., Kotabe, N., and Kurusu, J. (1980), On the optimum age for teaching foreign vocabulary to children. *International Review of Applied Linguistics*, 28:3, 245–7.

9 · Second language regression in Alzheimer's dementia

KENNETH HYLTENSTAM
AND CHRISTOPHER STROUD

INTRODUCTION

The bulk of research on language attrition has dealt with monolingual speakers and has traditionally focused on individuals suffering from aphasia (Goodglass and Kaplan, 1972). More recently, non-pathological cases of language attrition and normal language changes in late phases of the lifespan have attracted a greater share of research interest (cf. e.g. articles in Seliger and Vago, 1991), but it is only during the last two decades that language regression related to dementia has become a topic of focused research (see Obler, 1983; Bayles and Kaszniak, 1987). Work on dementia has been especially concerned with Alzheimer's disease, where the successive nature of the deterioration provides possibilities for a longitudinal investigation of language regression, something that is excluded in the case of aphasia with its abrupt onset. Furthermore, the degree of uniformity between cases is seemingly large enough to allow a determination of stages of linguistic regression (Obler and Albert, 1984).

Research in the area of language loss in bilinguals is no exception to the generalizations presented above. Bilingual aphasia has long been the preferred field of study (see, for example, Paradis, 1977, 1983; Albert and Obler, 1978), and this research has been of the utmost importance for the understanding of the psycho- and neurolinguistics of bilingualism. While studies of second and foreign language attrition have more recently also begun to play a greater role in research (see articles in Lambert and Freed, 1982, and Weltens, de Bot and van Els, 1986, and the overview in Weltens, 1987), bilingual dementia has still hardly begun to be addressed at all – excepting a handful of recent studies in the field.

In this article, we are going to present a study of one very typical linguistic characteristic observed in bilinguals suffering from Alzheimer's dementia, namely the difficulties they exhibit throughout a conversation in choosing and upholding the appropriate language in relation to their interlocutor. The fact that demented speakers may address an interlocutor in a language this person does not understand naturally has devastating practical consequences for Alzheimer patients' communicative interaction and social integration. This alone is reason enough for studying linguistic manifestations of the pathology, as a more thorough understanding of the communicative implications of dementia may suggest ways in which interactive breakdowns can be alleviated. At the same time, the nature of the linguistic problems displayed in dementia promises to provide valuable theoretical insights into what neuro- and psycholinguistic mechanisms are implicated in the human ability to choose an appropriate language, or more generally, an appropriate speech variety.

As a background to the present study, we will first sketch some linguistic and communicative characteristics of monolingual and bilingual Alzheimer's dementia. Following a presentation of how the patients in the present study cope with language separation and language choice, we will conclude the article with a theoretical discussion and interpretation of the data, relating our findings to a model of language production conceptualized within the vocabulary of human information processing.

GENERAL REMARKS ON THE LANGUAGE AND COMMUNICATION IN ALZHEIMER'S DEMENTIA

Knowledge of the linguistic and communicative behaviour of Alzheimer's patients is derived from research based on both experimental and more naturalistic language data. On the basis of various linguistic and pragmatic criteria that can be argued to be indicative of different degrees of linguistic deterioration, Obler and Albert (1984) suggest a six-stage model of linguistic regression. For the purposes of this presentation, we can summarize these stages as early, middle, and late phases of deterioration:

In *early phases* (I-II), the patients characteristically exhibit:

· digressions in discourse
· mild word finding problems accompanied by pre-lexical hesitation pauses, some verbal paraphasias and circumlocutions
· some inadequate answers to questions, where the patient focuses on key words to guide his answer
· egocentric speech which is somewhat repetitious and vague
· awareness of communicative and linguistic difficulties
· omissions of items in automatic sequences.

In *middle phases* (III-IV) many of these characteristics are exacerbated, and new problems are added. Typically we find:

· very severe digressions
· many uncorrected verbal paraphasias
· 'incorrect' answers to yes/no-questions and questions that require morphosyntactic processing
· many deictic expressions, indefinite terms and pronouns without antecedents, an abundance of stereotyped expressions ('empty speech')
· aberrant use of conjunctions
· no awareness of communicative and linguistic difficulties
· task initiating difficulties with automatic speech and non-completion of series
· relatively unaffected turn-taking, gesture and mimicry.

In *late phases* (V-VI), the predominant characteristics are

· echolalia, palilalia, muteness or logorrhea.

Notable in this list is a predominance of problems associated with linguistic specificity. Throughout the progression of the disease, the patient exhibits increasing difficulties in providing semantically (especially lexically) and pragmatically specific information for the interlocutor. Another typical, and interesting, characteristic of the language of dementia is the comparative dearth of noticeable syntactic and phonological problems.

As to whether the problems exhibited by Alzheimer patients are caused by the inaccessibility of an intact linguistic system, mediated by processing difficulties, or the unavailability of a once mature and intact language capability, through destruction and loss, there is evidence from different studies suggesting that both factors may in fact be implicated. Case studies of lexical problems, for example, show that lexical access is unquestionably affected, i.e. processing mechanisms are impaired, in early stages of dementia. However, as the disease progresses, the semantic specification of lexical items seems to become blurred, making distinctions between minimally contrasting items impossible. In a study by Schwartz, Marin, and Saffran (1979) it was shown that one patient was unable to distinguish dogs from cats, but never failed in distinguishing these animals from birds. In other words, it would appear as though process-level difficulties characterize early stages of dementia, and that these are successively replaced by problems on the knowledge level at more advanced stages of the disease.

BILINGUAL DEMENTIA

To date, only a small number of studies have been published on the linguisitic behaviour of bilinguals suffering from Alzheimer's dementia. These studies all ascertain that the same kind of phenomena that have been observed in monolinguals are also manifested in each of a bilingual's 2 languages. In one study of a multilingual demented patient speaking, among other languages, L1 Dutch and L2 English, Dronkers, Koss, Friedland, and Wertz (1986) noted on the basis of an assessment of the patient's language ability that both languages were equally affected by the dementia. Despite this, the patient resorted increasingly to Dutch, even when speaking with non-Dutch speakers. Santi, Obler, Sabo-Abramson, and Goldberger (1989), on the other hand, studying 4 cases of English–Yiddish bilingual Alzheimer's patients found that the nature of the linguistic problems exhibited by the patients differed in each language. In a study of two subjects (Hyltenstam and Stroud, 1989), we found that one of them, a German–Swedish bilingual who had acquired Swedish as a second language at middle-age, fared better in interaction with a speaker of his first language, German, than with a speaker of Swedish on measures of topic treatment, lexical availability, and so called automatic speech, as well as in the quality of the communicative strategies he employed. The other patient, a Swedish–Finnish bilingual who had acquired her second language, Finnish, at pre-school age, and who was thus bilingual from childhood, exhibited no such preference for any one of her languages.

In addition to the studies that compare the impact of dementia on a bilingual's 2 languages, research on bilingual demented patients has also focused on phenomena that are salient and specific to bilinguals, namely language mixing, comprising language choice, language separation, code-switching and borrowing.[1] Both Santi et al. (1989) and Hyltenstam and Stroud (1989) investigating bilingual patients' ability to choose the appropriate language found that, although more severely demented patients generally could be said to show greater impairment in this aspect of bilingual ability than less severely demented individuals, there was, interestingly enough, a substantial individual variation in how patients at similar levels of regression managed language choice and separation.

Unintentional code-switching, that is switching to a language the interlocutor does not know,[2] was noted in two of Santi et al.'s patients. In our own study, the German–Swedish subject code-switched in conversation with the Swedish interlocutor, who had some (quite limited) knowledge of German, but did not code-switch at all with the German interlocutor who was a bilingual with more or less balanced proficiency in German and Swedish.

Although some of the switching noted in these studies is thus pragmatically inappropriate, both studies emphasize that it is grammatically adequate, following the grammatical constraints that healthy bilingual speakers have been observed to follow in their strategic use of 2 languages in bilingual conversations (Poplack, 1980; Clyne, 1987).

PRESENT STUDY

The issue which is of specific interest in this study concerns demented speakers' language choice and language separation behaviour in contexts where the use of their second language is required. What we specifically intend to focus on here is the question of how to account for why some patients seem to retain their bilingual abilities at late stages of regression, while others lose the capacity to correctly choose and uphold the appropriate language in very early phases of the disease. A straightforward hypothesis that we had, in fact, initially entertained in the present research, and that others have also suggested and found certain support for (see Santi et al., 1989), is that language choice and language separation problems would become more severe as the patient's linguistic and other cognitive abilities deteriorate generally. In other words, we had expected that more severely demented bilinguals would have more problems with the appropriate choice of language than the less severely demented. What we have seen from previous studies, and what we will see from the present data, is that this hypothesis cannot be upheld. Obviously, other factors must be implicated than mere level of linguistic regression.

Subjects

We base our presentation on results from six subjects. All six had Finnish as their first language and had acquired Swedish as a second language in adult life. They had all used Swedish on a regular basis prior to the onset of dementia symptoms. All were women in the age-range of 73 to 94 years. On a comprehensive medical examination undertaken by a bilingual physician they were diagnosed as suffering from dementia of the Alzheimer type (DAT) (see Ekman, Robins Wahlin, Viitanen, Norberg, and Winblad, in press).

Data

Both spontaneous speech and formally elicited data were gathered from each patient in a monolingual interaction with a native speaker of each language, as well as in a 'bilingual' interaction, where both a native speaker of Swedish and a native speaker of Finnish were simultaneously present. For the spontaneous interaction a number of predetermined topics dealing with aspects of day-to-day life had been prepared, but the patients were also quite free to initiate and develop topics of their own choosing.

The formal instruments were either adopted and modified from existing materials or specifically constructed for the present study. The instruments tapped the subjects' ability to name pictured objects and actions, repeat stimulus sentences with varying syntactic and lexical complexity, produce so-called automatic sequences, translate between the languages, and handle metalinguistic tasks in both languages. In this chapter, only data from the monolingual Swedish interaction where the subjects are required to interact in their second language will be considered. The analysis is based on data from the spontaneous speech, and the interaction around pictures.

Data on the patients' linguistic background were gathered from close relatives using an extensive and detailed sociolinguistic questionnaire prepared in the project. The instrument contained, among other things, questions on the role of each language over the lifespan, the conditions surrounding the acquisition of Swedish as a second language, and estimated oral and written proficiency. Here, a five-grade scale was used, where 5 implied near-native, and 1 very limited, proficiency. The actual score for oral proficiency was obtained by averaging the scores for listening and comprehension ability, fluency, pronunciation, and grammatical correctness. Written proficiency was calculated on the basis of scores from reading comprehension and writing ability. A central batch of questions dealt with whether the patient had mixed languages to any extent prior to the onset of dementia.

Procedure

The collection of data was spread over a number of elicitation sessions, and the time-limit for each session was constrained by whether the patient showed signs of fatigue or distress. Some of the patients were unable to complete all subparts of the elicitation procedure because of the severity of their dementia. Each monolingual and bilingual interaction was carried out on separate days.

RESULTS AND INTERPRETATIONS

Degree of deterioration

The assessment of the patients' degree of linguistic regression was based on an analysis of free conversational data and the results of a naming task and a repetition task. In the conversational data, a 300-word sample of the patients' speech was quantified for (1) the proportion of content words, (2) the amount of deictic expressions without clear reference and other indefinite terms, and (3) aberrant use of conjunctions. In addition, a qualitative judgement was made of the pragmatic interaction with the interlocutor, i.e. whether the patient typically made digressions and gave inappropriate answers to questions. In the naming task, the number of correct noun identifications (irrespective of what language these were produced in) was calculated for each patient (maximum number 26), and the occurrence of perseverative speech, paraphasias, and neologisms was noted. The analysis of the repetition task used a progressive weighting based on frequency of lexical content and clause length

Table 9.1. *Assessment of the patients' degree of linguistic regression. Conversational data.*

Subject	% content words	N unspec. reference	N aberrant conjunctions	aberrant pragmatics
MA	27	3	0	−
JE	29	1	0	+
VH	25	16	2	+
AKJ	26	20	2	+
RA	17	29	2	+ +
KJ	18	43	11	+ + +

Note:

− = no

+ = some

+ + = substantial

+ + + = abundant

Table 9.2. *Assessment of the patients' degree of linguistic regression. Naming task and repetition task.*

Subject	N correct naming	neologisms etc.	repetition	metalinguistic negotiation
MA	13	+	25,5	yes
JE	25	+ + +	na	minimal
VH	19	+ +	5,5	minimal
AKJ	9	+ +	2,5	no
RA	0	+	4,5	no
KJ	4	+	na	no

Note:

na = not applicable

(with a maximum score of 44). For details of this analysis, see Hyltenstam and Stroud (in preparation).

The result of this assessment is presented in Tables 9.1 and 9.2. On the basis of these assessments, we arrived at the following ranking of the patients in terms of phases of regression:

Early phases: MA
                       JE

Early middle phases: VH
                       AKJ

Late middle phases: RA
                       KJ

Although it might not appear motivated at first glance to order MA before JE (especially considering the higher scores for JE on the naming task, measures of content words and amount of unspecified reference), factors other than score results *per se* have contributed to our ranking. MA's pragmatic behaviour is generally more appropriate, her performance on the naming task contains no neologisms and perseverations, and she displays easy access to the lexical items she produces. Even though JE can superficially be seen to cope better on the naming task, her responses are, in fact, the (admittedly successful) result of a laborious use of a variety of phonological and semantic search strategies. She produces substantially more neologistic speech than MA, and is not as interactive or metalinguistically negotiative around the tasks.

LANGUAGE CHOICE AND LANGUAGE SEPARATION PROBLEMS

The most striking aspect of the present material is that some of the subjects respond in the language unknown to the interlocutor. Looking more closely at the amount each language is used in the interaction with the Swedish-speaking interlocutor, we can see that the patients range from having an almost appropriate use of only one language over alternating between the two languages to the categorical use of the non-appropriate language (see Table 9.3). The extent to which the subjects use Finnish in their conversation with the non-Finnish-speaking interviewer is, thus, quite varied. We can see in the table that subjects MA and RA use Swedish appropriately in almost 100% of their utterances, while JE, VH,

Table 9.3. *Proportion and number (in parentheses) of utterances in interaction with the Swedish interlocutor produced completely in Swedish (S), mixed in Swedish and Finnish (M), and completely in Finnish (F).*

Subject	S		M		F		Total	
MA	96%	(386)	2%	(7)	2%	(9)	100%	(401)
JE	14%	(38)	18%	(49)	69%	(192)	100%	(279)
VH	8%	(52)	11%	(75)	82%	(561)	100%	(688)
AKJ	56%	(271)	7%	(35)	37%	(178)	100%	(484)
RA	99%	(275)	1%	(2)	0%	(1)	100%	(277)
KJ	15%	(86)	13%	(74)	73%	(429)	100%	(589)

and KJ use predominantly Finnish. The more mixed case is AKJ, who has a slight dominance for Swedish, but who also produces a large amount of Finnish. All the subjects except MA and RA thus have clear problems with either choosing and/or keeping to Swedish, frequently lapsing into their first language. The proportion of monolingual Swedish utterances produced by each subject is displayed in Figure 9.1. Although we do not consider the analysis of the monolingual Finnish interaction in detail here, a short comment on the nature of these data may still be of interest.[3] Briefly, the observations on language choice and language separation are as follows: Only one of the subjects, MA, mixes in Swedish elements in her Finnish to any significant extent. Three of the subjects, JE, VH, and AKJ, do not show any sign of Swedish in their Finnish whatsoever, while two, RA and KJ, have single such elements. Here, one should keep in mind that the Finnish interactant was also a speaker of Swedish. This means that the Finnish interaction could quite reasonably be interpreted as a bilingual speech situation, which is hardly true of the Swedish one. Thus, for the majority of the patients, there is a clear difference in the severity of the problems in language choice and language separation when the subjects interact with speakers of their first and second language respectively.

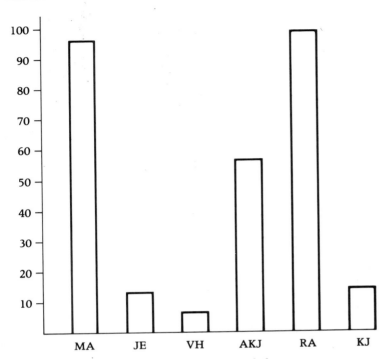

Figure 9.1   Proportion of monolingual Swedish utterances

Interestingly, although the patients exhibit problems in separating the languages in production we find, to the extent it is possible to judge, that they are able to follow the Swedish interlocutor's contributions and tailor the content of their own contributions in a reasonably appropriate way, given the limits placed on their ability by their level of regression. At least in the earlier phases, they therefore appear to be able to process Swedish receptively, even if their responses happen to be in the non-appropriate language, as illustrated in Example 9.1.

Example 9.1

I: Tycker du det är svårt att   'Do you think it is difficult
     förstå mig när jag talar   to understand me when I
     svenska?   speak Swedish?'

P: *No kyllä minä en oikein aina*   *'Well I don't even quite*
    ymmärrä ite omaa   *understand what I say myself*
    puhettanikaan sitä vähemmin   *even less so when someone*
    sitten vieraitten.   *else is talking.'*

In actual fact it would appear as though many of the patients are unaware of the fact that they are not using the same language as the interlocutor.

In conclusion, MA, as an exception, is less affected by the other language when speaking Swedish than when speaking her first language, Finnish. RA is the one who is most appropriate in her language choice and language separation behaviour with a total of only four in-mixed elements from the other language in both the Finnish and Swedish interactions. Again, this is the more remarkable, as she is one of the patients who show the greatest degree of overall linguistic regression. The other four seem to operate in Finnish most of the time – one might say that they choose Finnish as the base language in both interactions – even though their larger proportions of Swedish elements, when speaking with a Swedish interlocutor, lead us to conclude that they may be sensitive to the situational demands for language choice to some extent.

How can we account for this variation between subjects? Our results clearly do not give direct support for the hypothesis we had previously entertained, viz. that level of regression would correlate with increasing difficulties in language choice and language separation. As we have seen, both early and later-phase patients had the ability to choose and uphold the appropriate language, and both earlier- and later-phase patients also exhibited problems in this respect. The present data, then, points to a more complicated situation. One direction in which we have sought an explanation for this fact is to see if there is any connection between the subjects' premorbid degree of second language proficiency and their ability to choose and keep to the correct language. We know from studies of second language acquisition that the production and comprehension of a second language, even at advanced levels, require comparatively

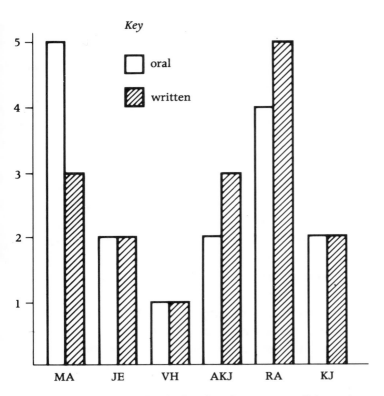

Figure 9.2   Premorbid level of oral and written proficiency in
L2 Swedish

more processing capacity than a first language (McLaughlin,
Rossman, and McLeod, 1983). It would therefore seem reasonable to
explore the interaction of attained L2 proficiency for these subjects
with their degree of dementia. Consequently, in the present study we
attempted to relate language choice and language separation
problems to the severity of the patients' overall level of language
regression, on the one hand, and to their premorbidly attained level of
second language proficiency on the other.

In Figure 9.2 the subjects' estimated maximal premorbid level of
oral and written proficiency in Swedish is displayed. It can be seen
that the subjects range from an estimated, almost native, proficiency

Table 9.4. *Swedish (S), mixed (M), and Finnish (F) utterances produced by RA at 3 different time periods.*

	S	M		F		Total	
January–April							
1988	99% (275)	1%	(2)	0%	(1)	100%	(277)
March 1989	94% (272)	4%	(10)	3%	(7)	100%	(289)
September 1989	64% (103)	5%	(5)	31%	(32)	100%	(140)

in Swedish, such as MA and RA, to a very limited level of proficiency as in the case of VH. The others had a below-average level of proficiency. If we compare Figures 9.1 and 9.2, we find a suggestive pattern of parallelism. In particular, the two subjects who had the greatest proficiency in Swedish premorbidly, are also the ones who succeed in separating the 2 languages, in RA's case, even at an advanced stage of regression.

Is it then the case that some subjects do not lose their language choice and language separation ability at all? The most reasonable interpretation, in our view, is that there is an interaction between degree of dementia and premorbid level of proficiency. Patients who have attained a higher level of L2 proficiency would retain their ability to choose and uphold the appropriate language in later phases of dementia than those individuals who have had lower levels of L2 competence. We find some evidence for this interpretation from subject RA. When we saw her at two different occasions, 12 months and 18 months later respectively, she was at a later stage of language regression and had also, in fact, increased problems in keeping Finnish elements out of the interaction with the monolingual Swedish speaker. The differences can be seen in Table 9.4.

DISCUSSION

A number of the current psycho- and neurolinguistic models of bilingual processing have been developed on the basis of data from aphasic patients (Obler, 1984; Paradis, 1985; Green 1986). While, of course, also aiming to account for normal bilingual behaviour, these models specifically cover the various patterns of language loss and language recovery observed in bilingual aphasia. In doing so, they work with the assumption that 'the temporarily or permanently inaccessible language is not destroyed, but inhibited' (Paradis, 1989: 134). A similar case could be made, at least to some extent, for demented bilingual speakers. Our observation that subjects may still understand a language they can hardly produce is one piece of evidence that can be used in such reasoning.

As Paradis (1989) points out, most of the models proposed are not incompatible with each other, but are either terminological alternatives or complementary accounts. The general idea common to them all is that certain items and subsystems in a language are more available to the speaker than others. Researchers differ in the vocabulary they use to speak about such variation in availability. According to the so called subsystem hypothesis (Paradis, 1985) of how two languages are organized in the brain, each of the bilingual's languages is seen as a subsystem within a unitary language system in the same way as different registers can be seen as subsystems within the same language. Obler refers to the potency of a subsystem or a unit, Paradis assumes that the more available item has a stronger trace or a lower threshold of activation, and Green says that it requires less resources for its control. Availability, in this framework, is considered to be a function of frequency and recency of the item's activation.

A system of inhibition and disinhibition or activation is involved in the selection of items or subsystems. The language processing system is thought to operate in such a way that the selection of an item or subsystem, either in production or comprehension involves the inhibition of alternatives, in Paradis' terms raising the threshold of activation for these alternatives, and disinhibiting the item or language to be executed, or lowering its threshold of activation. This inhibition and disinhibition consumes processing resources. It is proposed that more resources are needed to produce or self-activate an item than to understand or recognize it.

Green (1986) proposes three different levels of activation to account for the fact that bilinguals in certain situations can keep their languages separate when speaking, and in other cases alternate between the two. Items or subsystems can be either selected, activated, or dormant. Paradis talks of different levels of inhibition, and claims that the unselected language is not totally inhibited. Thus, the idea that the non-selected language may not be totally out of the picture accounts for the fact that the bilingual also has access to this language in production and comprehension.

Applying models of this type to our data, one could say that many of the patients lack resources to control or to inhibit their first language, and therefore produce structures from this language instead of the competing alternatives from the second language. For those subjects who predominantly speak in Finnish, one could claim that this subsystem is generally more potent or has a lower threshold of activation than the Swedish subsystem. This implies that less resources are needed to select and activate it. As we mentioned above, the patients' ability to understand Swedish is greater than their ability to produce the language. This fact is also compatible with the model in that it assumes that the non-selected language is activated and available for comprehension, although at a higher threshold level.

As demented subjects progressively deteriorate and loose processing capacities, it would be natural to claim, within the framework of these models, that the patients' ability to separate their two languages in production would become successively impaired. In fact, this assumption has been the point of departure for our initial hypothesis on progressive deterioration mentioned above. However, in the present data there is clearly no simple relation between the degree of dementia and the patients' problems in separating languages.

We would like to suggest that one solution to this paradox is related to the question of how to define the notion of availability. We mentioned earlier that availability is seen as a function of frequency and recency of use. However, more specific conditions need to be given. The fact that a second language is less available and requires more processing capacity than a first language is partly an effect of the lower degree of automatization in a second language, and partly a consequence of the different structuring of this language system. As language acquisition involves both automatization and restructuring (McLaughlin, Rossman, and McLeod, 1983), it is feasible to hypothesize that an incompletely acquired language has a lower degree of automatization and/or a less appropriate structuring, and relies more on controlled processing. (For a similar interpretation of variability in language attrition in healthy, elderly subjects, see de Bot and Clyne, 1989.) This would account for the differential patterns of language separation problems we have found among the patients. Those subjects who have not premorbidly acquired their L2 to a sufficient level require more processing capacity for the use of this language. This means that they do not have the requisite recourses to inhibit their L1 and activate their L2, even at early stages of dementia, while subjects who have a high premorbid proficiency need comparatively less processing capacity to control the selection and execution of their L2.

ACKNOWLEDGEMENTS

This research was supported by grants no. F 635/87, F 502/88, and F 541/89 from the Swedish Council for Research in the Humanities and Social Sciences (HSFR). We thank Matti Viitanen for his medical diagnoses of the patients, and Sirkka-Liisa Ekman for helping to localize relevant patients for this investigation. We owe special thanks to Eija Kuyumcu for her co-operation in this project.

NOTES

1 Language mixing is used here as a generic term to cover various types of language contact phenomena such as *language choice*, *language separation*, *code-switching*, and *borrowing*. Language choice refers to a bilingual speaker's choice of one of his/her languages, with or without in-mixing

of the other, for a specific discourse (cf. Grosjean, 1982). Language separation is used 'to designate the bilingual speaker's ability to keep two languages apart *in production* when speaking in a monolingual mode' (Hyltenstam and Stroud, 1989). Code-switching is the 'alternate use of two languages within the same discourse' (Poplack, 1980), and borrowing is the use of a lexical element from language A which has been morphologically and syntactically, but not necessarily phonologically, integrated into language B when speaking language B, or *vice versa*.

2 Such unintentional code-switching is observed to occur also in healthy, but momentarily inattentive, speakers, typically under conditions of fatigue, stress, affect, or under the influence of drugs such as alcohol. Hasselmo (1961), in discussing code-switching, uses the term 'derailment' to distinguish this type of switching from 'functional switching', which is thus the speaker's intentional use of 2 languages within the same discourse. Derailment is often observed to be triggered by the use of a name or loan-word from the language not spoken, or in Clyne's (1967) notion of trigger, by an item that has ambiguous affiliation due to similarity in phonological form in both languages. With Clyne (1987:740) one might characterize this type of unintentional switching as psycholinguistically conditioned in contrast to normal sociolinguistically conditioned switching.

3 The subjects' language choice and languge separation behaviour in their monolingual Finnish interactions is not the foci of this chapter. This has been reported on briefly elsewhere (Hyltenstam, Kuyumcu, and Stroud, 1990), and is given a more detailed treatment in Kuyumcu (in preparation).

REFERENCES

Albert, M., and Obler, L. K. (1978), *The bilingual brain. Neuropsychological and neurolinguistic aspects of bilingualism*. New York: Academic Press.

Bayles, K. A., and Kaszniak, A. W. (1987), *Communication and cognition in normal aging and dementia*. London: Taylor and Francis.

Clyne, M. (1967), *Transference and triggering*. The Hague: Nijhoff.
(1987), Constraints on code switching: how universal are they? *Linguistics*, 25, 739–64.

de Bot, K., and Clyne, M. (1989), Language reversion revisited. *Studies in Second Language Acquisition*, 11, 167–77.

Dronkers, N. F., Koss, E., Friedland, R. P., and Wertz, R. T. (1986), 'Differential' language impairment and language mixing in a polyglot with probable Alzheimer's disease. Paper presented at the International Neuropsychological Society meetings.

Ekman, S.-L., Robins Wahlin, T.-B.,Viitanen, M., Norberg, A. and Winblad, B. (in press), Preconditions for communication in the care of bilingual demented persons. *International Psychogenatrics*.

Goodglass, H., and Kaplan, E. (1972), *Assessment of aphasia and related disorders*. Philadelphia: Lea and Febiger.

Green, D. W. (1986), Control, activation, and resource: A framework and a model for the control of speech in bilinguals. *Brain and Language*, 27, 210–23.

Grosjean, F. (1982), *Life with two languages*. Cambridge, Mass: Harvard University Press.

Hasselmo, N. (1961), *American Swedish*. Unpublished Ph.D. thesis. Harvard University.

Hyltenstam, K., Kuyumcu, E., and Stroud, C. (1990), Svenska som andraspråk hos äldre dementa. In: Tingbjörn, G. (ed.), *Andra symposiet om svenska som andraspråk i Göteborg 1989*. Stockholm: Scriptor.

Hyltenstam, K., and Stroud, C. (1989), Bilingualism in Alzheimer's dementia: two case studies. In: Hyltenstam, K., and Obler, L. K. (eds.), *Bilingualism across the lifespan. Aspects of acquisition, maturity, and loss*. Cambridge: Cambridge University Press.

Hyltenstam, K., and Stroud, C. (in preparation) Linguistic indices of bilingual dementia.

Jakobson, R. (1941), *Kindersprache, Aphasie und allgemeine Lautgesetze*. Uppsala: Almqvist and Wiksell.

Kuyumcu, E. (in preparation), Language choice and code-switching in demented Finnish–Swedish bilingual speakers' interaction with a Finnish interlocutor.

Obler, L. K. (1983), Language and brain dysfunction in dementia. In Segalowitz, S. (ed.), *Language functions and brain organization*. New York: Academic Press.

Obler, L. K. (1984), The neuropsychology of bilingualism. In Caplan, D., Lecours, A. R., and Smith, A. (eds.), *Biological perspectives on language*. Cambridge, Mass.: The MIT Press.

Obler, L. K., and Albert, M. (1984), Language in aging. In Albert, M. (ed.), *Clinical neurology of aging*. New York: Oxford Press.

Paradis, M. (1977), Bilingualism and aphasia. In Whitaker, H., and Whitaker, H. A. (eds.) *Studies in neurolinguistics, Vol. 3*. New York: Academic Press.

Paradis, M. (ed.) (1983), *Readings in aphasia in bilinguals and polyglots*. Montreal: Marcel Didier.

(1985), On the representation of two languages in one brain. *Language Sciences*, 7, 1–39.

(1989). Bilingual and polyglot aphasia. In Boller, F., and Grafman, J. (eds.), *Handbook of neuropsychology, Vol. 2*. Elsevier Science Publishers.

Poplack, S. (1980), Sometimes I'll start a sentence in Spanish Y TERMINO EN ESPAÑOL: Toward a typology of code-switching. *Linguistics*, 18, 581–618.

Santi, S. de, Obler, L. K., Sabo-Abramson, H., and Goldberger, J. (1989), Discourse abilities and deficits in multilingual dementia. In Joanette, Y., and Brownell, H. (eds.), *Discourse abilities and brain damage: Theoretical and empirical perspectives*. New York: Springer Verlag.

Schwartz, M., Marin, O., and Saffran, E. (1979), Dissociation of language function in dementia: A case study. *Brain and Language*, 7, 277–306.

Weltens, B. (1987), The attrition of foreign-language skills: A literature review. *Applied Linguistics*, 8, 22–38.

Weltens, B., de Bot, K., and van Els, T. (1986), *Language attrition in progress*. Dordrecht: Foris.

The linguistic perspective 1:

· Discourse, grammar, and lexis ·

10 · Crosslinguistic perspectives on native language acquisition

RUTH A. BERMAN

Current crosslinguistic acquisition research reflects varied motivations. Three of these are analyzed as background to a developmental perspective on acquisition across and within languages.[1] Each of the three orientations discussed below has a rather different focus: on mechanisms of acquisition, on endstate grammars, and on linguistic functions and the development of discourse respectively. These concerns are clearly not mutually exclusive, either in principle or practice, but it proves useful to distinguish between them for purposes of exposition.

MECHANISMS AND PRINCIPLES GUIDING ACQUISITION: A CONFLUENCE OF CUES

One major thrust in current research is concerned with psycholinguistic factors underlying the *process* of acquisition, what have been called 'mechanisms of language acquisition' (MacWhinney, 1987). Such mechanisms include 'the competition model' (Bates and MacWhinney, 1987; MacWhinney, 1989);[2] a concern with various kinds of 'bootstrapping' (Naigles, Gleitman and Gleitman, in press; Pinker, 1984, 1987; Shatz, 1986);[3] as well as extensions of earlier work on acquisitional strategies and principles for relating forms to meanings, such as Eve Clark's (1987, 1988) 'principle of contrast' and, most particularly, Slobin's (1973, 1985b) 'operating principles'. Researchers differ in how committed they are to nativism – i.e. the

245

weight they assign to innate principles and categories compared with the importance of environmental factors such as input, on the one hand, and learner-internal 'constructivist' factors, on the other. They also differ in their commitment to modularity – i.e. the extent to which they view language – particularly the syntactic component – as a self-contained or encapsulated domain of knowledge or as bound up with other cognitive domains.

All agree, however, that the principles and mechanisms governing language acquisition are universal, shared across children and across languages. And the burden for crosslinguistic research, then, is to specify how the acquisition process is affected by interaction with the specific database of particular languages. My view is that no single mechanism can account for all facets of the acquisition process. Rather, language acquisition is achieved by various routes, through multiple sources of bootstrapping. These include: (i) *perceptual factors* as discussed by Slobin (1973, 1985) and by Gleitman, Gleitman, Landau, and Wanner (1988); (ii) *semantic categorizations*, such as those considered from different perspectives by Bowerman (1990), Pinker (1984, 1989), Schlesinger (1988), Talmy (1985), and Van Valin (1990b); (iii) *syntactic information* – including reliance on structural categories such as grammatical relations and form–class membership, rules governing the application of structural devices such as word order and other distributional factors, or inflectional and adpositional markings of grammatical agreement, of case-relations, and so on, as well as principles underlying processes of anaphora, on the one hand, or verb–argument structure on the other; and (iv) *typological bias*, by which I mean sensitivity to the particular target language – including recognition of its most favoured devices (e.g. syntactic and/or morphological marking of transitivity), and sensitivity to constructions or categories which have a particular status in the native grammar (e.g. clitics in a language like French, verb-morphology and noun-gender in Hebrew, auxiliaries in English). In other words, rather than relying on one single, unitary mechanism in acquisition, children have recourse to a 'confluence of cues' – both in gaining initial entry into and subsequently in achieving mastery of the various subsystems of their native tongue (Berman 1989, in press).

ENDSTATE LINGUISTIC THEORY: ACQUISITION OF GRAMMAR OR OF LANGUAGE

A second motivation for crosslinguistic acquisition research is more strictly 'endstate' in orientation, and typically derives from a well-articulated model of the adult grammar. Such research is primarily concerned with the individual's acquisition of the 'core grammar' or the computational components of language, most particularly syntax, which is construed as autonomous. This applies to studies conducted within the framework of a current model of generative grammar – particularly Government-Binding Theory and, to some extent, also Lexical-Functional Grammar (e.g. Pinker, 1984). Such studies aim to show how young children attend to formal, structure-dependent principles of syntax, which are assumed to be innate. Between-language variation is explained through the theory of parameter-setting, according to which children 'set parameters' (e.g. whether the language allows null subjects, or where modifiers are positioned with respect to heads) on the basis of minimal data from the native language(s) to which they are exposed. An excellent example of this type of crosslinguistic motivation is provided by Hyams (1986) and the research it has since generated, mainly, but not only, in English, concerning the so-called 'null subject parameter' (e.g Valian, 1990; Weissenborn, 1992). Other domains investigated within this paradigm include directionality (reviewed in Lust and Mazuka, 1989); negation (Weissenborn and Verrips, 1989); verb placement (Clahsen, 1988); inflection (Meisel, 1990); and the general issue of 'functional categories' (Meisel, 1992; Radford, 1990).

A major advantage of such research is that it is driven, and constrained, by a clearly formulated model of grammar. By focusing on the endstate of the acquisition process, such research aims to provide a fully explicit account of *what* it is the child must acquire, first and foremost by stipulating the formal rule and principles which govern syntactic constructions in universal grammar. This enables the researcher to make well-articulated predictions, and to test specific hypotheses, about the possible forms of grammar and hence of grammar acquisition. Such models thus avoid the theoretically unsatisfying need to confine research to *post hoc* explanations at best, and to *ad hoc* descriptive statements at worst. Besides, as noted, they have generated a large amount of research on different syntactic topics in an increasing number of languages.

Clearly, the study of language acquisition should feed on the best currently available theory of language. But such a theory need not in principle entail either pure nativism (and hence a totally continuous view of development), nor the isolation of syntax as autonomous. This is argued by Van Valin (1990), in his attempt to relate acquisition to the semantically motivated 'functional' model termed Role and Reference Grammar (and see also Rispoli, in press).[4] Clearly, also, specification of crosslinguistic universals is critical for defining the constraints operating on language acquisition, and these are likely to be innate, rather than learned. But these constraints need not be only formal principles which specify the possible form of grammatical rules and constructions. There are also constraints on possible linguistic *content* and possible *devices* – that is, what the available meanings are, and how they can be expressed in languages. Whatever language a child acquires, there is a restricted set of shared target categories to which he may or must attend. These include: (i) the categories which can occupy semantic space in such areas as space, time, manner, and causation (Talmy, 1985, 1987, 1988); (ii) the kind of form classes – closed class items and open class lexical items – available across languages (Berman, 1988a; Talmy, 1985); (iii) possible subcategorizations of lexical classes – e.g. gender or classifier systems for nouns; and (iv) the range of formal devices which can be used to express these and other systems – word order, affixes, clitics, particles. That is, children do not start out to acquire a given native language with a *tabula rasa* plus a general, non-modular set of perceptual, cognitive, and/or social predispositions. They are severely constrained, and their learning load is considerably lightened by universal grammar, where this means the constraints which define not only the form of possible grammars, but also the content of possible languages.

Research which is strongly endstate focused suffers from other, quite severe, even if self-imposed, limitations. For one thing, this perspective lacks a motivated account of language *development*, and hence is not capable of, and/or is not interested in, characterizing the interim processes *en route* from the initial to endstate of grammar acquisition.[5] It largely disregards interim grammars or other transitional states of the sort defined as 'interlanguages' in second language acquisition research. This implication of a one-leap progression from entry to endstate is consistent with the nativist view of language acquisition, and its concomitant claims of continuity. And it necessarily avoids concern with 'stages' in language development or with reconstructive processes of the kind which has informed the important work of Karmiloff-Smith (1986, 1992). My position is that language acquisition theory must account for developmental changes and reorganizations across time. There is not simply a direct line between initial knowledge (however staggered across different components of the grammar) and endstate mastery. Rather, the route from entry to exit involves complex patterns of re-analysis and reorganization, as knowledge of particular systems become consolidated and reintegrated with acquisition of other systems (Berman, 1986b, 1987).

A second limitation of views which focus on endstate linguistic theory follows from the insistence on the autonomy, and the priority, of syntax. This divorces the study of language acquisition from the classic issue of how meaning is related to form, and how children learn to relate conceptual content to linguistic form. Besides, preoccupation with 'grammar' entails focusing on the sentence as the prime unit of analysis. Thus grammatical forms and constructions are dealt with in isolation, rather than as deployed in connected discourse. Yet an adequate model of language acquisition needs to embed the acquisition of grammar within a broader frame of the acquisition and development of *language use* (see Berman, 1985, 1986b, and the discussion below).

LINGUISTIC FUNCTIONS: BECOMING NATIVE SPEAKERS AND USERS[6]

A third perspective is represented by adherents of various types of 'functionalism'. This term is employed by many people in many senses.[7] Here, it is taken to mean concern not only for the particular formal devices that children use at different phases of development, but also how linguistic forms are deployed in discourse. This is the orientation which has motivated the work on early language development and on children's narratives conducted by students of Slobin (e.g. Budwig, 1989; Gee-Gerhardt and Savasir, 1985, and Bamberg, 1987; Dasinger, 1990, respectively); and it underlies a study of mine on the use of the coordinator 'and' in early narratives (Berman, 1990b). A major thrust of such work has been to show how, with development, a given form will acquire an increasing variety of functions. A more difficult enterprise is to demonstrate how, across time, a particular linguistic function is expressed by a more varied range of forms – where a 'function' refers, for instance, to temporal notions like iterativity or simultaneity, or to discourse-bound parameters such as object-specification, perspective-taking, or maintaining reference.

A broadly functional motivation underlies much of the crosslinguistic analysis of narrative development undertaken by Dan Slobin and myself in recent years (Berman, 1988b; Berman and Slobin, in press; Slobin, 1989, 1990, 1991; Slobin and Bocaz, 1988). We compared the way children aged 3, 5, and 9 years as well as adults – native speakers of English, German, Hebrew, Spanish, and Turkish – give verbal expression to the contents of the same series of events, as depicted in a picture-book story about the adventures of a boy and a dog in search of their missing frog. One very important set of results concerns the relation between language and thought, which Slobin has formulated in neo-Whorfian terms of 'thinking for speaking' (Slobin, 1987). He analyzed how children of different language backgrounds describe specific scenes in the story in terms of tense/aspect markings and locative trajectories, as well as use of passive voice, relative clauses, and markers of connectivity. Slobin concludes that, from an early age, languages shape the way people *speak* about events, even if not necessarily how they perceive them nor even how they think about them. In a recent talk on this subject, he ends by noting that 'in sum, we can only talk and understand one another in terms of a particular language. The language or languages that we learn in childhood are not neutral coding systems of an objective reality. Rather, each one is a subjective orientation to the world of human experience, and this orientation affects the way in which we think while we are speaking' (Slobin, 1991).

Several other findings have emerged from our study of narrative development. First of all, it became clear that languages cannot be compared *in toto*, across the board, when acquisition is viewed from a functional perspective. Rather, subsystems of their grammars are differently deployed by speakers, and so are acquired differently by children. For instance, the following 'clusters' or pairings emerge for 4 of the languages in our data-base:

(1) Form–function relations in crosslinguistic narratives:
   (a) Grammatical aspect (durativity) – Eng, Span ˜ Heb, Gm

       Locative trajectories   – Eng, Gm   ˜ Heb, Span

   (b) Passive voice   – Eng, Heb ˜ Span, Gm

       Relative clauses   – Eng, Gm ˜ Heb, Span

The first row reflects the fact that both English and Spanish encode durativity of events through grammatical aspect – progressive in English, imperfective as well as progressive in Spanish, so that these two languages make distinctions which are not formally available in the inflectional systems of either Hebrew or German. The second line reflects the fact that locative trajectories are typically marked by adverbial particles such as those meaning *out* or *down* in English and German, whereas Hebrew and Spanish verbs encode directionality directly in the lexical form of verbs like those meaning *exit* (cf. *go out*) or *descend* (cf. *go down*); and speakers of these two languages typically dispense with any further reference to the path taken by an actor or an object.[8] We found that the availability of a grammatical form makes it accessible to children as young as 3 years old. Where the grammar lacks such a device, it typically remains unexpressed. This represents another major finding of our study: Where a language lacks a grammatical device for marking a certain distinction, such as durativity or locative path, speakers *can* talk about these notions, but they typically choose not to. We found almost no evidence for the mechanism of *compensation* – seeking to express a distinction which may be readily available in the grammar of some other language(s), but which would require some form of circumlocution in one's native tongue. This makes first language acquisition critically different from second language acquisition, where it seems only natural for speakers to seek some parallel device to express distinctions obligatorily marked by the grammar of their native tongue.

The examples in (1b) demonstrate a rather different finding: All four languages in question have grammatical devices for expressing passive as compared with active voice, and also for constructing relative clauses to meet similar discourse functions (e.g., of introducing new participants into the discourse, of identifying or locating referents, or of continuing the narrative). But these devices display different patterns of *use* in the languages: In order to present a patient-perspective on a scene, English and Hebrew speakers typically use passive forms – either pure syntactic passives or something like 'get' passives in English, unaccusative or adjectival-passive morphology in Hebrew. For example, they might say 'the dog got stuck in the jar' or 'the boy got caught in the deer's antlers' – but the Spanish and German narrators rarely use the corresponding constructions in their languages in describing these same scenes. The reason is that the languages differ not only in formal typology, but also in the 'typology of use' (Slobin, 1989) and the relative functionality of formally parallel constructions like passives or relatives (Berman, 1986a, Berman, 1990b). Similar considerations also explain why, for instance, passive constructions emerge, and consolidate, quite early in Mayan Quiche (Pye and Poz, 1988) and in Sesotho (Demuth, 1989), and so do relative clauses in Hebrew and Sesotho by comparison with English and other European languages. These findings cannot be accounted for simply on the grounds of relative formal complexity. A critical factor is how particular grammatical constructions interact with other means for expressing similar functions in a given language. In other words, structural availability of a given construction in the grammar does not suffice to explain 'productivity of use'. How widely a form will be used, and how soon it will be acquired, depends on how favoured it is as an option for expressing a given function in the target language (Clark and Berman, 1984).

Our functionally oriented narrative study also yielded important developmental findings. Each group of children in our study was both amazingly alike and distinctly different from every other group. Along the one dimension, of crosslinguistic comparison, 3-year old Hebrew speakers were telling a Hebrew type of story, distinct from that of the English, German, or Spanish children. The Israelis used morphology to mark gender and number, and distinctions between past and present tense in verbs, without any aspectual markings at all; the American children, in contrast, used a rich array of particles to describe paths in space, and progressive *ing* to mark activities as ongoing. And they did so from the earliest age investigated, around age 3. But the narratives of these children were very different from those of 5 or 9-year olds, and these in turn differed from the adults' (as discussed at length in Berman 1988b, and see also Bamberg 1987). The implications of these developmental trends are considered next.

AN INTEGRATED VIEW OF LANGUAGE ACQUISITION AND LANGUAGE DEVELOPMENT

An adequate developmental model will apply across children and across languages. A schematic representation of a possible subset of such progressions is set out in (2.1) to (2.6). This scheme delineates an acquisitional path for both language structure and language use, and it integrates factors relating to syntax, morphology, semantics, and connected discourse within a single developmental frame.

(2.1) Construction:
Utterance 〉 Clause 〉 Coordination 〉 Subordination 〉 Nominalization

(2.2) Syntactic markings / Deformation of simple clause structure:

Sbj–Vb Agr	May change	Anaphora or elision	No agreement
Case marking	Sbj elision	Arg elision	Neutralized
Tense/Aspect	No change	Sequence of tenses	Loss of tense
Basic Wd Order	No change	May change	May change

(2.3) Semantic content (S = sentence, P = proposition):

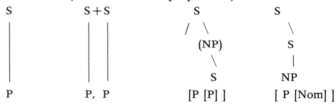

```
     S              S + S           S               S
     |              |  |           / \               \
     |              |  |          (NP)                S
     |              |  |            \                 |
     |              |  |             S                NP
     P              P, P         [P [P] ]         [ P [Nom] ]
```

(2.4) Scope of application:
Lone Clause 〉 Combining Adjacent Clauses 〉 Extended Discourse

(2.5) Thematic discourse structure:
Associative connectivity 〉 Chaining 〉 Local embedding 〉 Global coherence

(2.6) Developmental phase:
Pregrammar 〉 Linguistic Structures and Relations 〉 Thematically Organized Discourse

The progression set out in (2.1) to (2.6) involves the following claims. First, as shown in (2.1) there is an evolution in *construction types*. Language acquisition starts out with *utterances*, which constitute the initial scope for expressing the relation between linguistic content and linguistic form. In contrast to syntactic units such as clauses or sentences, utterances are not 'structure-dependent': they do not make reference to grammatical relations such as Subject or

Direct Object, nor are they constructed out of structural units such as NP or VP. Early utterances are single lexical items or strings of words. These lexical units are then combined, and clause-structure emerges, manifested by morpho-syntactic markings, as in the first list in (2,2); these express structure-dependent knowledge in domains such as subject–verb agreement and case-marking. Next, adjacent clauses are combined, first by co-ordination, subsequently by various kinds of subordinate constructions, ending with derived nominalizations. An example of the progression outlined in (2.2) is given in (3) below starting with the word 'tower' – a word commonly used by young Israeli children when playing with building blocks.

(3) a single words, e.g. *tower*
　　 b combining words, e.g. *build tower; here tower*
　　 c *long clauses*, e.g. *I building tower; It('s) my tower*
　　 d conjoining, e.g. *It my tower, not yours; I building tower and I take blocks*
　　 e subordination, e.g. *I'm building a tower cos I want to; I can tell you how to build a tower*
　　 f nominalizations, e.g. *building towers is easy; He's in charge of the building of towers*

　　The progression in (2.2) shows a decrease in degree of *transparency* of how form-meaning relations are marked: Simple clauses typically contain the most clear, overt marking of grammatical relations, gender and case-marking, tense–aspect assignment, etc. The more complex syntactic constructions manifest increasing deformation of the basic structure of the simple clause (e.g. Subject–Aux inversion in single-clause questions compared with embedded questions in English; the difference in verb position in main compared with subordinate clauses in German; or the fact that 3rd person verbs allow subject pro-drop in complement but not main clauses in Hebrew).

　　The schematic path in (2.3) suggests that in *semantic* terms, there is a universal progression from non-propositional utterances to single-propositions, then to the combining of two equi-valent propositions by conjoining or juxtaposition, followed by subordination of one proposition as dependent on or background to another, until finally, under nominalization, one proposition becomes so 'submerged' as to lose its clausal properties almost entirely.

Concurrently, as shown in (2.4) and (2.5), there is also a progression in the construction of *discourse*: To start with, children's language lacks structure-dependent connectivity, and the way they juxtapose utterances is motivated by non-text based associations; subsequently, children learn to 'chain' – first utterances and then clauses; and this is followed by local embedding of adjacent clauses connected by grammatical subordination. Only at a later stage of development, when command of grammar is well established, will children have reached the phase where they can embed whole sets of utterances within the larger chunks of discourse, organized coherently around a single discourse theme.

The claims set out in (2.1) to (2.5) are tentative, but they are supported by evidence on acquisition of Hebrew in both early pre-school grammatical development (Berman, in press a) and in extended narratives of children from age 3 to 12 (Berman, 1988b). Such ideas need to be further tested, for different children and different discourse contexts in a single language, as well as across languages. Quite radical revision might be required to adjust details of the scheme to other language types, e.g. verb-final languages and/or a language like Turkish, in which subordination and nominalization are closely interwoven. This in no way invalidates the overall view presented here, which aims to provide a broad framework for generalizing about the path of language progression across languages; across domains of linguistic structure; across language structure, language content, and language use; and across children at different stages of development.

THE DEVELOPMENT FROM LANGUAGE TO NATIVE LANGUAGE

The progressions set out in (2) are consistent with a more general model of language development which I have proposed (Berman,

1986a, 1986b, 1987). At first, language is very close to non-linguistic interaction, at the level of the single utterance or speech act; it then becomes bound by grammar, in the form of structure-dependent phrase-structure, conjunction, and clause-embedding; and finally this structure-bound knowledge is reintegrated within a broader discourse frame, constrained by factors of text cohesiveness, thematic coherence, and usage conventions.

It follows that *language-particular factors* come to play an increasing role as development progresses. As shown in (2.6) and repeated in (4.1) below, children start out with a shared repertoire of linguistic notions, neutral to any particular grammar. Language development proceeds from pre-grammatical foundations, at a stage where the child's construals are not yet structure-dependent, to structurally constrained knowledge, and on to appropriate deployment of these devices and constructions to meet the needs of extended discourse and conventions of use. Moreover, as indicated in (4.2), this route proceeds in an increasingly particularistic direction in terms of linguistic typology, thus:

(4.1) Phase:

   Pre-grammatical – Structure-dependent – Conventions of use

(4.2) Scope:

   Any language – Native language-type(s) – Native language(s) – Only native language

Initially, children could be speaking *any* language, subsequently they become attuned to a particular *type* of language, eventually they are confined to only their highly specific mother tongue or subdialect of the mother tongue. This progressive broadening *and* narrowing of options applies in different areas of linguistic structure: phonology, syntax, and the lexicon. For example, in the domain of *phonology*, the sounds produced by infants are not strictly speech-like at all – they include crying and vegetative fussing, followed by more speech-like cooing; when babies move into babbling, the sounds they produce become more and more speech-like in form; subsequently, by late in the first year, they produce sounds which are closer to the repertoire of what will be their native tongue, as they move into the 'typological' phase: They are able to distinguish native-like prosodies, whether intonational or tone-based; with time, they come to sound more and more distinctly English or Hebrew or Sesotho-speaking; and, eventually, this set of sounds, and this sound system, takes over so thoroughly that it will impinge on (or 'interfere with') the sounds used in any other language to which the speaker is exposed.

An example from the domain of syntax is that of *question-formation*. Initially children query merely by intonation, in much the same way across the world; then they distinguish in a language-like way between the universal categories of yes/no questions compared with questions of information; next they move into the typology of their language as one which, say, puts wh-question words at the front, or leaves them *in situ*; finally they construct questions as specified by the grammar of their language; and at some point, they will have a hard time learning how to construct questions in a language which deploys a different mechanism (e.g. word order changes such as Subject-Aux or Subject-Verb inversion) for this purpose. Again, children move further and further away from the shared universal base of acquisition across the path of development.

Finally, in the domain of *word-formation*, children start out by using both conventional and non-conventional lexical items ('nursery terms' and the like); subsequently they are able to innovate items to fill gaps in the conventional lexicon in both their spontaneous speech output (from as young as age 2 years) and in structured elicitation tasks. When children first start doing this, they pay attention to the *kind* of devices favoured by their type of language. For instance, English children will innovate by adding suffixes to word-stems, e.g. 'jammy' or 'caker,' by zero derivation, or by noun compounding, whereas Hebrew children will use affixation of morphological patterns to consonantal roots in creating new verbs and even nouns (Clark and Berman, 1984; Berman, 1987).[9] Eventually, children's use of words manifests increasing attention to *convention*, as they gain more knowledge both of grammatical structure and of the established lexicon, and their innovations become more and more like endstate, adult usage. In this respect, too, as command of the mother tongue expands, the linguistic options accessible to learners narrow down to the confines of their particular native language, ruling out whatever lies beyond its range.

Similar progressions can be assumed for other aspects of language knowledge and language use. During the sensitive period for language acquisition, learners become better and better knowers, and users of their native tongue. But concurrently, they become more and more constrained by its particularities, and hence, perhaps, also worse and worse learners of any other language.

NOTES

This is a revised version of a position paper entitled 'Crosslinguistic aspects of first language acquisition' presented to the Conference on Progression and Regression in Language, Botkyrka, Stockholm, 13–16 August 1990. I am grateful to Kenneth Hyltenstam and Åke Viberg of the University of Stockholm for inviting me to participate, and to members of the conference for helpful comments and discussions.

1 More detailed overviews of crosslinguistic L1 research are provided in two earlier papers, relating the endeavour to second language acquisition (Berman, 1984) and to a more general model of language development (Berman, 1986a). Other relevant studies which I did not have access to at that time include: Bates and MacWhinney (1989), Bowerman (1985), Maratsos (1988), Rispoli (1990), Slobin (1985, 1990, 1991), and Van Valin (1990a). The database on acquisition of ten different oral languages and of ASL has been greatly enriched by the collection in Slobin (1985), reviewed by Weist (1989). I have also seen prepublication versions of chapters on three of the other languages to be covered in volumes 3 and 4 of the same series: Mayan Quiche – by Clifton Pye, Sesotho – by Katherine Demuth, and Walpiri – by Edith Bavin.

2 The basic idea of this model is that 'forms grow in strength with each

correct presentation (MacWhinney, 1989:63). Thus, the model assigns a major role to cues from *input*, and it focuses on expectations set up by access to specific lexical items in specific contexts in the on-line processing of language material. In crosslinguistic terms, languages are noted to 'differ markedly in the strengths they assign to basic grammatical cues' (1989:72) such as word order, inflectional markers of agreement, or noun animacy.

3 The term 'bootstrapping' was originally used by Pinker (1984) as a metaphor for describing the semantic underpinnings of syntactic acquisition. In general, it refers to the mechanism that enables children to break into linguistic systems, so as to be able to relate to them in the abstract, structure-dependent terms required both by UG and by the grammar of their particular mother tongue.

4 Van Valin presents a 'constructivist' view of language acquisition, as a process, in which the child constructs a particular grammar on the basis of shared language universals. (And see, also, Slobin's (1985) preference for the term 'language-making capacity' over the Chomskian 'language acquisition device'.) Van Valin thus objects to the 'adaptionist' view of acquisition which he associates with Chomsky and Pinker alike, since both view the child as merely adapting UG to the particular target language to which he or she happens to be exposed, rather than as actively constructing the grammar on the basis of the input.

5 Recent retreats from Chomsky's original construal of language acquisition as 'instantaneous' in terms of a maturational schedule (particularly Borer and Wexler, 1987) are concerned only with accounting for why entry is later for some systems compared with others. Irrespective of whether one adopts a strong or weaker version of the maturational hypothesis (Clahsen, 1992), acquisition is still viewed as all-or-nothing, hence as basically instantaneous, for any given parameter or principle of the grammar. Moreover, these accounts are confined to strictly grammar-internal factors, and do not relate to any more general theory of development, whether linguistic, cognitive, interactive, or all three together.

6 This heading deliberately echoes part of the title of a paper by Slobin (1987).

7 For reviews and references, see Berman, in press b; MacWhinney, 1989:64.

8 This can be predicted for children acquiring other languages which share similar typologies with respect to the type of semantic information

necessarily or optionally encoded within the verb, as described by Talmy (1985).

9 Another example that applies to the phonological, lexical, and grammatical domains of acquisition is the special attention to consonantal elements which develops in children acquiring a Semitic language whose grammar entails rule-bound vowel alternation and whose lexicon is based on discontinuous consonantal roots (Berman, 1990a; Clark and Berman, 1984).

REFERENCES

Bamberg, Michael. (1987), *The acquisition of narratives: Learning to use language*. Berlin: Mouton de Gruyter.

Bates, E., and MacWhinney, B. (1987), Competition, variation, and language learning. In MacWhinney, B. (ed.), *Mechanisms of language acquisition*.

Berman, Ruth A. (1984), Cross-linguistic first language perspectives on second language acquisition research. In Andersen, R. (ed.), *Second languages: a cross-linguistic perspective*, pp. 13–38. Rowley: Newbury House.

(1986a), The acquisition of morphology/syntax: A cross-linguistic perspective. In Fletcher, P., and Garman, M. (eds.), *Language acquisition*. 2nd edition, pp. 429–47. Cambridge University Press.

(1986b), A step-by-step model of language development. In Levin, I. (ed.), *Stage and structure: Reopening the debate*, pp. 191–226.

(1987), A developmental route: Learning about the form and use of complex nominals. *Linguistics*, 27, 1057–85.

(1988a), Word-class distinctions in developing grammars. In Levy, Y., Schlesinger, I. M., and Braine, M. D. S. (eds.), *Categories and processes in language acquisition*. Erlbaum, 45–72.

(1988b), On the ability to relate events in narratives. *Discourse Processes*, 11, 469–97.

(1989), Multiple bootstrapping: A confluence of cues for acquired zero subjects in Hebrew. Paper given at the Kolloquium in Schwerpunkt 'Spracherwerb,' Hamburg, June 1989.

(1990a), New-root formation in Modern Hebrew. Paper given at

Israel Association for Theoretical Linguistics Workshop on Hebrew Grammar, Hebrew University, Jerusalem, February 1990.

(1990b), Acquisition of an (S)VO language: Subjectless sentences in children's Hebrew. *Linguistics*, 28, 1135–66.

(In press a), Developmental perspectives on transitivity: A confluence of cues. In Levy, Y. (ed.), *Other children, other languages: Issues in the theory of Language acquisition*. Hillsdale, N. J.: Lawrence Erlbaum.

(In press b), Form and function in developing narrative abilities. In Slobin, D. I., Gerhardt, J., Kyratzis, A., and Guo, J. (eds.), *Social interaction, social context, and language: Essays in honor of Susan Ervin-Tripp*. Hillsdale, N. J.: Lawrence Erlbaum.

Berman, Ruth and Slobin, Dan I. (in press), *Different ways of relating events in narrative: A crosslinguistic developmental study*. Hillsdale, N. J.: Lawrence Erlbaum.

Borer, Hagit and Wexler, Kenneth (1987), The maturation of syntax. In Roeper, T., and Williams, E., (eds.), *Parameter Setting*, pp. 123–72.

Bowerman, Melissa, (1985), What shapes children's grammars? In Slobin, D. I. (ed.), *The crosslinguistic study of language acquisition, Vol.. 2*, Erlbaum.

Bowerman, Melissa and Choi, Soonja (1990), The origins of children's semantic categories of spatial relations: A crosslinguistic study of English and Korean. Presented at the International Congress on Study of Child Language, Budapest, July 1990.

Budwig, Nancy (1989), The linguistic marking of agentivity and control in child language. *Journal of Child Language*, 16, 263–84.

Clahsen, Harald. (1988), Parameterized grammatical theory and language acquisition: A study of the acquisition of verb placement and inflection. In Flynn, S. and O'Neill, W., (eds.), *Linguistic theory in second language acquisition*. Kluwer Press.

(in press), Learnability theory and the problem of development. In Weissenborn, J., Goodluck, H., and Roeper, T. (eds.), *Theoretical issues in language acquisition: Continuity and change in development*. Hillside, N.J.: Erlbaum.

Clark, Eve V. (1987), The principle of contrast: A constraint on language acquisition. In MacWhinney, B. (ed.), *Mechanisms of language acquisition*.

(1988), On the logic of contrast. *Journal of Child Language*, 15, 317–38.

Clark, Eve V., and Ruth A. Berman. (1984), Structure and use in the acquisition of word-formation. *Language*, 60, 542–90.

Dasinger, Lise. (1990), Towards a functional approach to the acquisition of language: A crosslinguistic study of the development of the functions of relative clauses. Unpublished MS. University of California, Berkeley.

Demuth, Katherine. (1989), Maturation and the acquisition of the Sesotho passive. *Language*, 65, 56–80.

Gee-Gerhardt, J. G., and Savasir, I. (1985), On the use of *will* and *gonna*. *Discourse Processes*, 8, 143–75.

Gleitman, Lila R., Gleitman, Henry, Landau, Barbara, and Wanner, Eric (1988), Where learning begins: initial representations for language learning. In Newmayer, F. (ed.), *Linguistics: The Cambridge survey: Vol. III*, pp. 150–93.

Hyams, Nina. (1986), *Language acquisition and the theory of parameters*. Reidel.

Karmiloff-Smith, Annette. (1986), Stage/structure versus phase/process in modelling linguistic and cognitive structure. In Levin, I. (ed.), *Stage and structure: Reopening the debate*, pp. 164–90.

(1991), Beyond modularity: Innate constraints and developmental change. In Carey, Susan and Gelman, Rochel (eds.), *Epigenesis of the mind: Essays in biology and knowledge*. Erlbaum.

Levin, Iris (ed.) (1986), *Stage and structure: Re-opening the debate*. Ablex.

Lust, Barbara and Reiko, Mazuka (1989), Cross-linguistic studies of directionality in first language acquisition: the Japanese data. *J. Child Language*, 16, 665–84.

MacWhinney, Brian (ed.) (1987), *Mechanisms of language acquisition*. Erlbaum.

(1989), Competition and teachability. In Rice, M., and Schiefelbusch, R. L. (eds.), *The teachability of language*, pp. 63–104. Paul Brookes.

MacWhinney, Brian and Bates, E. (eds.) (1989), *The crosslinguistic study of language processing*. Cambridge: Cambridge University Press.

Maratsos, Michael (1988), Crosslinguistic analysis, universals, and language acquisition. In Kessel, F. S. (ed.), *The development of language and language researchers: Essays in honor of Roger Brown*, pp. 121–52. Erlbaum.

Meisel, Jürgen (1992), Inflection: Subjects and subject-verb agreement in early child language. In Meisel, J. (ed.), *The acquisition of verb placement: Functional categories and V2 phenomena in language acquisition*. Dordrecht: Kluwer.

Naigles, L. G., Gleitman, H., and Gleitman, L. (in press), Syntactic bootstrapping in verb acquisition: evidence from comprehension. In Dromi, E. (ed.), *Language and cognition: A developmental perspective*. Albex.

Pinker, Steven (1984), *Language learnability and language development*. Harvard University Press.

(1987), The bootstrapping problem in language acquisition. In MacWhinney, B. (ed.), *Mechanisms of language acquisition*.

(1989), *Learnability and cognition: The acquisition of argument structure*. MIT Press.

Platzack, Christer (1990), A grammar without functional categories: A syntactic study of early Swedish child language. Paper presented at the Congress for the Study of Child Language, Budapest, July 1990.

Pye, Clifton, and Quixtan Poz, Pedro (1988), Precocious passives (and antipassives) in Quiche Mayan. *Papers and Reports in Child Language Development*, 27.

Radford, Andrew (1990), *Syntactic theory and the acquisition of English syntax*. Cambridge: Cambridge University Press.

Rispoli, Matthew (in press), The mosaic acquisition of grammatical relations. In Levy, Y. (ed.), *Other children, other languages: Issues in the theory of language acquisition*. Hillsdale, N. J.: Lawrence Erlbaum.

Schlesinger, Izchak M. (1988), The origin of relational categories. In Levy, Y. Schlesinger, I. M., and Braine, M. D. S. (eds.), *Categories and processes in language acquisition*, pp. 121–78. Erlbaum.

Shatz, Marilyn (1987), Bootstrapping operations in child language.

In Nelson, K. E., and von Kleech, A. (eds.), *Children's language,*
Vol. 6. Erlbaum.

Slobin, Dan I. (1973), Cognitive prerequisites for the development of
grammar. In Ferguson, C., and Slobin, D. I. (eds.), *Studies in*
child language development. Holt, Rinehart, and Winston.

(1985a), Why study acquisition crosslinguistically? Introduction
to *The crosslinguistic study of language acquisition, Vol. 1,*
pp. 3–26. Erlbaum.

(1985b), Crosslinguistic evidence for the language-making capacity. *The Crosslinguistic Study of Language Acquisition, Vol. 2.*

(1987), Thinking for speaking. Proceedings of the 13th Annual
Meetings of the Berkeley Linguistic Society, *BLS,* 13.

(1989), Factors of language typology in the crosslinguistic study of
acquisition. Paper presented at the symposium on Crosslinguistic Study of Child Language, Int'l Society for the Study of
Behavioral Development, Jyväskylä, Finland, July 1989.

(1990), The development from child speaker to native speaker. In
Stigler, J. W., Schweder, R. A., and Herdt, G. (eds.), *Cultural*
Psychology, pp. 233–56. Cambridge: Cambridge University
Press.

(1991), Learning to think for speaking: Native language, cognition, and rhetorical style. *Pragmatics,* 1, 7–26.

Slobin, Dan I., and Bocaz, A. (1988), Learning to talk about
movement through time and space: The development of
narrative abilities in English and Spanish. *Lenguas Modernas*
(Universidad de Chile), 15, 5–24.

Talmy, Leonard (1985), Lexicalization patterns: Semantic structure
in lexical forms. In Shopen, T. (ed.), *Language typology and*
syntactic description, III. Cambridge: Cambridge University
Press.

Talmy, Leonard (1987), The relation of grammar to cognition. In
Rudzka-Ostyn, B. (ed.), *Topics in cognitive linguistics.* John
Benjamins.

(1988), Force dynamics in language and cognition. *Cognitive*
Science, 12, 1.

Valian, Virginia (1990), Null subjects: A problem for parameter-
setting models of language acquisition. *Cognition,* 35, 105–22.

Van Valin, Robert (1991), Functionalist linguistic theory and language acquisition. *First Language*, 10, 7–40.

(1990b), A synopsis of role and reference grammar. In Van Valin, R. (ed.), *Advances in role and reference grammar*. John Benjamins.

Weissenborn, Juergen (1992), Null subjects in early grammars: Implications for parameter-setting theories. In Weissenborn, J., Goodluck, H., and Roeper, T. (eds.), *Theoretical issues in language acquisition: Continuity and change in development*. Hillsdale, N. J.: Lawrence Erlbaum.

Weissenborn, Juergen and Verrips, Maaike (1989), Negation as a window to the structure of early child language. Paper presented to Boston University Conference on Language Development. Boston, October 1989.

Weist, Richard M. et al. (1989), Review of Slobin, D. I. (ed.), *The Crosslinguistic study of language acquisition*, I and II. *Journal of Child Language*, 16, 429–626.

11 · Syntactic development in Danish L2

ANNE HOLMEN

This chapter reports on a longitudinal study of the acquisition of Danish syntax by young immigrants to Denmark (Holmen, 1988, 1990). The study deals with the early syntactic development, in formal, as well as functional, terms, of six adolescent speakers of Albanian, English, and Vietnamese.

In a way the study is a traditional interlanguage (IL) study in which a number of learners of a target language is followed for a certain period of time with the purpose of establishing similarities and differences in their learning process. On the other hand the study is more influenced by functional grammar and by interactional approaches to language than most interlanguage studies – or at least more than the early ones. Today functional analyses seem to be gaining support in this area (Sato, 1990; Huebner, 1983) in much the same way as in child language research (e.g. Berman, this volume).

The present study was designed when performance analysis (Færch, 1979), variability in IL (Hyltenstam, 1978; Tarone 1982), and discourse analysis (Hatch, 1978; Larsen-Freeman, 1980) were the focus of second language researchers' attention. More than anything else the study was inspired by Evelyn Hatch's claim that 'one learns how to do conversations, one learns how to interact verbally, and out of this interaction syntactic structures develop' (1978:404). However, the study did not really take shape till the analysis of IL data was combined with the functional approach, which was emerging as a new paradigm within linguistics (e.g. Givón, 1979, 1985; Dik, 1978, 1989).

A basic point in functional grammar is the insistence on the interdependence of different linguistic levels. In the case of syntax, this means that morphological, semantic, and pragmatic aspects should be included in the analysis. Related to this is the view that 'languages should be taken seriously' (Dik, 1989), i.e. linguistic forms and distinctions are basically seen as motivated by communicative and coding purposes. To take this as the starting point of linguistic analyses fits well with the IL-approach to language acquisition by which learner language is considered highly dynamic, yet systematic at any given point in time (i.e. governed by rules that are internally consistent, Tarone, 1982). Thus a functional approach makes it possible to look at IL-development as a whole, through a focus on the coding relationship between what is communicated by the learner (in semantic and pragmatic terms) and the way this is being expressed (in phonetic, lexical, and grammatical terms).

IL DEVELOPMENT

The present study focuses on the process of second language acquisition, i.e. on *how* language learning is brought about, rather than on *what* is being learnt or *why* learning takes place. Early IL development is characterized by rapid and continuous change, and the process may best be viewed as a movement along a continuum. The crucial question is what the nature of that continuum is: what does it look like, which processes and principles determine the changes in the IL, and what is the role of the mother tongue?

Pit Corder (1978) has suggested a distinction between a restructuring continuum in which rules and elements of the mother tongue are gradually replaced by those of the target language with the same level of complexity, and a developmental continuum in which the IL 'grows' in complexity as it approaches the target norm. In the latter the mother tongue plays little or no role.

Originally the two continua represented two theoretical frameworks with each of the two processes considered responsible for the general process of language development. Since then the role of the mother tongue has been somewhat redefined, and today the two processes are not considered incompatible, although they seem to be active at different linguistic levels (Corder, 1983) and at different points in the learning process (Schachter, 1983).

SYNTACTICIZATION

Talmy Givón (1979, 1985) has proposed a developmental continuum for languages in general. The process of change, which Givón calls syntacticization, is found to apply to first and second language acquisition, creolization, and diachronic development. Furthermore it applies to shifts between variants within the adult register (e.g. in terms of planned versus unplanned speech). In all these languages Givón has observed a tendency for 'loose, paratactic, "pragmatic" discourse structures [to] develop – over time – into tight, "grammaticalized" syntactic structures' (Givon, 1979: 208).

The extreme points of Givón's developmental continuum are described as 2 communicative modes, a paratactic/pragmatic/presyntactic mode and a syntactic mode:

	Pre-syntactic mode	Syntactic mode
(a)	topic–comment structure	subject–predicate structure
(b)	loose coordination	tight subordination
(c)	slow rate of delivery	fast rate of delivery
(d)	small chunks under one intonation contour	large chunks under one intonation contour
(e)	lower noun/verb ratio in discourse, with more simple verbs	higher noun/verb ratio in discourse, with more complex verbs
(f)	no use of grammatical morphology	extensive use of grammatical morphology
		(Givón, 1985:1018)

According to Givón early IL is characterized by the features of the pre-syntactic mode. As it gradually becomes syntacticized, it also becomes more complex (with variants within the register). By

complex syntax Givón refers to 'the use of the three coding devices –
word order, morphology, and intonation – to create various
structural variations from the neutral/canonical clause type' (1985:
1010). These structural variations (e.g. embedding, negatives,
passives) express a number of discourse-pragmatic and semantic
functions: they code different speech acts, different ways of
introducing, modifying, and connecting information etc.

SIMPLIFICATION

The logical counterpart of the fully developed, complex IL is a basic,
simplified version of the same language or of a universal grammar,
and it is a well-observed fact that simple forms and structures are
characteristic of early IL. However, the process of simplification has
been one of the most debated issues in second language research, the
crucial question being how learners can simplify rules they have not
yet acquired (Færch and Kasper, 1983). One answer would be to
distinguish consistently between the IL-product and the processes
involved in the learning and production of the IL, and only use
simplification about the latter. Thus it makes sense to simplify the
burden of learning a new language through 'employing what is
already known' (McLaughlin, 1978) and to minimize the processing
pressures through expressing only the new information or the most
salient semantic elements. Both kinds of simplification (as a learning
process and as a production strategy) may result in a formally
simplified language product.

Ellis (1982) has suggested that semantic simplification (rather than
formal simplification) is the process most characteristic of the early
IL. The second language learner is obviously more mature intellec-
tually and socially than the child who is acquiring his mother
tongue. Besides a more developed knowledge of the world in
general, he is aware of the communicative functions of language –
i.e. he knows how to refer to people, concepts, events etc., and how
to express semantic and pragmatic relations. He has learnt how to

use language to refer to absent people and events or how to express modality. When faced with the task of communicating in the second language the learner tries to express these more complex relations. However, he is kept back by his limited, non-automatized linguistic resources, e.g. in the vocabulary, and therefore he must rely on the situational context to supply the missing elements.

From this early stage Ellis sees the IL development as a process of semantic and formal complexification made possible through auto-matization of rules and elements.

THE PRESENT STUDY

The combination of IL theory with the perspective of functional grammar makes the following questions relevant at every stage of the developmental process: what do the learners express through their limited proficiency in Danish, how do they manage to do this, and what is the role played by syntax?

In order to trace the development over time and discover variations within the acquisitional process the study is longitudinal. However, functional-syntactic analyses of free speech require plenty of data, which studied thoroughly are very time-consuming to work with. Therefore the project only covers a fairly small number of learners (see below), selected according to their linguistic and social background.

The six learners are compared in order to answer the following research questions: does the acquisition of Danish syntax follow a pattern, or do the learners differ not only in rate of learning, but also in the developmental route they take? Is Ellis (1985) right in maintaining that learners basically go through the same sequence of development with respect to functional (semantic) terms, but through different orders of development, as regarding formal and language specific terms (influenced by the target language and the mother tongue among other factors)? If this is the case for the acquisition of Danish L2, does the common sequence of development resemble Givón's syntacticization continuum? To what extent are the early stages of the IL characterized by simplification, and in what sense of the term?

Learners

Data have been collected from six adolescent learners of Danish who had moved to Denmark a few months before the data collection started.

In the following they are referred to by a letter indicating their mother tongue (A = Albanian, E = English, V = Vietnamese) and a number:

A1 – Yugoslavian boy who came to Denmark as the son of a migrant worker. He was 15 years old when the data collection started. He lived with his parents in the inner city of Copenhagen where he attended a reception class for migrant children. During the year he left school for shorter periods of time to work (e.g. dishwashing at restaurants). The family is Muslim.

A2 – same background, school etc. as A1 though 2 years older and living with his father and an older brother.

V1 – Vietnamese girl who came to Denmark as the daughter of a political refugee; 15 years old. She lived with her family (parents, 4 sisters, and 1 brother) in a suburb of Copenhagen where she attended a reception class. The family is Catholic.

V2 – older sister of V1 (17). Same school.

E1 – American boy who came to Denmark as an exchange student at the age of 18. He lived with a Danish family in a northern suburb of Copenhagen where he attended the local high school.

E2 – American girl, 17 years old. Same description as E1 except that her Danish host family lived in a town west of Copenhagen.

Clearly, the learners differ not only in linguistic, but also in cultural and socio-economic background, and in social conditions in

Denmark. It is most likely that this will affect the quality and degree of their exposure to Danish as well as their opportunity and motivation to use the language.

Data

Data consist of audiotaped face-to-face conversations between the learners and a native speaker of Danish collected regularly during the first 3–15 months of the learners' stay in Denmark (from A2 only during the first 3–9 months). The learners take part in 4–8 conversations each. The conversations are semi-structured drawing on pictures and school events as starting points, and they include small-talk, picture description, and narratives. Each conversation was audiotaped in its full length and then transcribed in ordinary orthography.

The analysis of the data falls in two parts: an in-depth analysis of all the conversations with A1 and V1 (a total of 15 conversations, 20–40 minutes each) and a comparison of extracts from four conversations per learner (only three with A2, a total of 23 extracts, 10 minutes each). The purpose of the former is to identify linguistic features that seem to change with the acquisitional process, i.e. to find relevant points of comparison for the latter. This includes a number of interactional and grammatical aspects (semantic, syntactic, and pragmatic), some of which are easily quantified, whereas other aspects have to be dealt with in a more interpretative way.

RESULTS

Quantitative measures

It is hardly surprising that the quantitative analyses show a general increase in the learners' performance over time. Not only do they gradually take longer turns and produce longer utterances, but they also use more verbs, noun phrases, and adverbs, more morphological

Table 11.1. *Proportion of learner words per extract (in %)*

learner/conversation	I	II	III	IV
A1	23	51	56	66
A2	28	39	49	–
V1	39	52	69	76
V2	34	46	55	61
E1	47	65	67	66
E2	41	67	76	84

coding and grammatical words, more subordination and co-ordination etc. Space permits only a few examples here (see Holmen, 1990, for the full description).

At the interactional level the learners seem to be getting more control over the situation. At first the native speaker nominates all topics and initiates all exchanges, but gradually the learners take more initiatives. At the same time shifts to the metalinguistic level (due to problems of production or comprehension) become less frequent.

Over time the learners also get more of the floor in terms of words produced in the conversation. See Table 11.1, e.g. A1 producing 23% of the words in the first extract and 66% in the fourth (the native speaker producing 77% and 33% respectively). It is hardly surprising that the number of back channel cues ('mm,' 'yes' etc.) shows the reverse pattern, i.e. going down for the learners and up for the native speaker.

The analyses of information structure and of simple and complex syntax are carried out at utterance level (and not at sentence level) as the most relevant unit of speech production. The number of utterances produced by the learners within the 10 minutes varies between 53 and 174 with a general, but not stable, increase. So much clearer is the steady development of learner words per utterance (see Table 11.2, e.g. A1's mean of 3.55 words per utterance in the first conversation and 5.88 in the last).

Table 11.2. *Mean number of words per utterance produced by the learner / number of utterances*

learner/conversation	I	II	III	IV
A1	3.55/53	4.91/102	5.78/130	5.88/166
A2	2.17/78	5.15/78	4.74/114	–
V1	3.65/101	5.08/79	5.53/155	6.74/174
V2	3.59/86	5.66/65	6.37/78	6.78/99
E1	5.48/84	8.42/98	7.42/115	7.93/110
E2	6.17/53	8.69/100	6.52/169	9.86/148

Number of words per utterance may be regarded as a crude measure of the amount of information expressed by the learners. As such it is also a measure of linguistic complexity (cf. MLU in child language research). However, it needs to be combined with a study of the kind of information that is being expressed at different stages of development and of the way the information is being organized within the utterances. An outline of this study will follow below. At this point it should be mentioned that the tendency towards growing complexity seen in Table 11.2 is supported by other complexity measures applied to the same data, e.g. number of verbs or noun phrases per utterance and number of modality markers (modality according to Fillmore, 1968).

Degree of subordination is often considered a measure of complexity. However, in the present study this does not give the same clear picture of development. Whereas subordinate clauses gradually become more frequent in the data produced by V1, V2, E1, and E2 – though at a different rate – A1 and A2 never really get started (Table 11.3).

Changes in the information structure

Among other functions, the information structure concerns two basic distinctions which must be made in all languages (including

Table 11.3. *Proportion of utterances with subordination (in %) / number of subordinate clauses*

learner/conversation	I	II	III	IV
A1	0	0	8/10	4/8
A2	3/2	1/1	4/5	–
V1	0	5/4	10/16	14/24
V2	0	9/6	5/4	17/17
E1	2/2	13/11	18/21	27/30
E2	15/5	35/35	32/54	58/86

the early IL) if communication is to succeed. It must be clear which parts of the utterance carry the semantic roles of agent and patient in connection with the verb. At the same time the information expressed through the utterance must be organized so that it is clear what is given and what is new information (Chafe, 1976). Altogether, the speaker must find linguistic ways of bringing about referent identification and textual coherence while expressing non-redundant information (Givón, 1984).

Through an analysis of the changing information structure in the learner data a pattern of development emerges. This consists of 4 stages, which the learners seem to go through in the same order (only 3 of them reach stage 4):

1 only one piece of information introduced at a time,
2 background information added,
3 breaking up complex information into chains of utterances,
4 embedding of complex information.

The stages are characterized through descriptions of the functional focus of the learner and of the formal features. The elements and structures that are being described at each stage, appear with a certain frequency during that particular period of time, but there is no way of knowing whether they are yet acquired by the learner.

Stage 1: only one piece of information introduced at a time

During the first stage it is clearly difficult for the learners to produce Danish utterances at all. However, in several cases they manage to stay in the conversation by using one-word utterances or by repeating (parts of) the utterances produced by the native speaker (NS) (Example (1)):

(The examples are given in Danish orthography with an English word-by-word translation – when necessary an interpretation is added in brackets.)

(1) NS: er der kommet en ny dreng i jeres klasse

         has there come a new boy in your class (is there . . .)

     A1: ja kommer ny

         yes comes new

     NS: taler han albansk

         speaks he Albanian (does he speak Albanian)

     A1: ja taler

         yes speaks

In Example (1) A1 repeats only some of the words from NS's utterances as he affirms the information given there. He does not add any new information. The learners produce a considerable number of affirmatives and negatives at this early stage, in which they tend to leave out one or two words that are obligatory in Danish. This is not the case with utterances that contain new information. These are often 'created' by the learners who seem to prefer two particular sentence structures which both contain the obligatory elements of Danish sentences (subject and verb): 'det er NP' (it is NP) to introduce new referents, and S V (O/Adv) to add new information to a referent given by the NS and repeated here. (S, V, O, and Adv are used to refer to the elements which correspond to subject, verb, object, and adverb in the fully developed language. It is possible that they do not have that function in the early IL.) In Example (2), which follows the question: 'do you have a bicycle?', there are two utterances each containing new information at the end:

(2)   V2: jeg har en i Vietnam det er fem cykel

I have one in Vietnam it is five bicycle

(= I/my family had five bicycles in Vietnam)

The same pattern of S V + new information may be seen in Example (3), which follows the question: 'where do you work?':

(3)   A2: jeg arbejd hospital

I work hospital

Only on a few occasions do the learners need to introduce a referent and at the same time apply a comment. This they do by combining the two structures, as in Example (4) (neither V2's brother nor the activity of drum-playing have been mentioned before):

(4)   V1: det er min lillebror han spiller trommer

it is my little brother he plays (the) drums

Almost all utterances are simple (i.e. containing only one (or no) verb). In complex utterances the verbs are linked by being listed in order of real-time occurrence (Example (5) in which V1 explains about a water tap):

(5)   V1: den åbner kommer vand luk

it opens come water close

V1 and V2 each produce a few sentences which resemble topic–comment structures, i.e. in the beginning of the utterance the frame is given, followed by a comment, which is also new information, without any syntactic ties (Example (6) in which the two girls have been asked what a certain spoon is used for):

(6) V2: det er spise øh spise aftensmad

      it is eat er eat supper (= for when you eat supper)

   V1: eller drikke kaffe sukker

      or drink coffee sugar (= or for sugar when you have coffee)

Topic–comment structures only occur when V1 and V2 try to include background information (e.g. time or place) in relation to a verb.

In general, the learners manage to communicate in very short utterances which are organized according to the two sentence structures, and which follow the principle of one piece of new information per utterance (typically an agent or a verb). The word orders enable the learners to make the basic semantic distinction between agent–verb–patient as well as the pragmatic distinction between new and old information. Most utterances express fairly simple matters, and this might be one reason for their apparent success. In a few cases, the learners try to put slightly more complex matters into words with the result that the sentence structures break down, and the utterances are organized solely according to pragmatic principles (cf. Givón above).

Stage 2: background information added

During the second stage the learners use the same basic sentence structures, but often add an adverb or an adverbial phrase which gives some background information (e.g. indicating time as in Example (7)):

(7) A1: på Jugoslavien jeg forstår avis Dan' jeg ikke forstår

      in Yugoslavia I understand newspaper Den' I not (don't) understand

The adverb is pre- or postposed and does usually not affect the propositional string of agent – verb – patient. However, as Example

(7) also shows, the negation is often placed in the string, often before the verb. At the earlier stage anaphoric or external negation is more frequent.

Occasionally, the learners try to express more complex information through paratactic structures (Examples (8) and (9)):

(8) NS: kan du forstå Helle når hun taler

     do you understand Helle when she speaks

     V1: ja Helle måske Helle hun taler jeg forstår meget godt

     yes Helle maybe Helle she speaks I understand very well (= yes maybe/sometimes when Helle speaks I understand her/Danish very well)

(9) A1: min mor er lille øh har skole koran skole nu ikke har koran skole i Jugoslavien

     my mum is little er have school Koran school now not have Koran school in Yugoslavia (= when my mum was little there were/they had Koran schools in Yugoslavia now they don't . . .)

Examples (8) and (9) may also be used to point to a difference between the learners during the second stage. Whereas E1, E2, V1, and V2 consistently use the two sentence structures, and therefore include most obligatory subjects, A1 and A2 show more variation in word order. They frequently leave out anaphoric pronouns (as in Example (9)) and make self-repairs. Besides, it is possible that their word order at this stage follows a principle of transitivity rather than the pragmatic principle of information structure. In Example (10) A1 changes the order of S and V. He has been asked whether he attends a sports club together with a class-mate called Ibrahim:

(10) A1: ikke kommer Ibrahim – min kammerat Jugoslavien kommer på min familie

     not comes Ibrahim – my friend Yugoslavia comes on my family (= Ibrahim does not come – my friend from Y. visits my family)

With the other learners there are also certain traces of a

redefinition of the (pragmatic) word order principle. In Example (11) V1 changes the order of the nouns according to their semantic role (agent/recipient or patient) and not only to their pragmatic value:

(11) NS: hvorfor ser hunden på kongen

      why looks the dog at the king

   V1: det er måske konge han kan lide hund – eller hund elsker konge

      it is maybe king he likes dog – or dog loves king

Stage 3: breaking up complex information into chains of utterances

Based on the development from stage 1 till stage 2 one might expect further additions to the SVO-string at stage 3 resulting in longer and more complex utterances with some embedding. However, this development does not take place until the following stage. Instead there is a period in which the learners produce long sequences consisting of simple utterances. In that way they manage to express fairly complex information, but by breaking it up into chains of utterances they are able to speak faster. To attain fluency in speech production seems important to them at this stage.

The clearest sign is a remarkable amount of utterances starting with 'det/der er...' (it/there is...), not only used to introduce referents (as in Example (12)), but also predicates (as in Example (13)):

(12) V1: det er hver uge det er om lørdag der er min moster og (hans) mand og min mormor og min anden moster de de kommer og besøger min far og min mor og jeg familien

      it is every week it is on Saturday there are my aunt and (his) husband and my grandma and my other aunt they come and visit my dad and my mum and I the family

(13) A1: det er operation her i Danmark – det er hun – sådan – det er ikke færdig det er operation det er ikke færdig med den

it is operation here in Denmark – it is she – so – it is not finished it is operation it is not finished with that (my mother, who was operated in Denmark earlier, is to be operated again now)

Another important development during this stage is the placing of adverbials within the propositional string (and not before or after), e.g. 'også' in Example (14) (but not the initial time indication):

(14) E1: de drikker kaffe og på fredag og lørdag øh de drikker også whisky

    they drink coffee and on Friday and Saturday er they drink also whisky

Thus the basic sentence structures are replaced by variable word order, and at the same time by a certain conformity in the production of longer sequences (through 'det er . . .'). Finally, nominal morphology begins to appear at this stage.

Stage 4: embedding of complex information

Not only embedding, but also verbal morphology emerge at stage 4. Both have to do with the linking of information across utterances, which makes it possible to express different semantic relations (spatial, temporal, causal etc.) and to include utterances within other utterances (e.g. reported speech):

(15) V2: fordi Helle hun sagde til mig hvis jeg går til højskole det er godt nok

    because Helle said to me if I go to (folk) high school that is all right

The development of verbal morphology covers tense and aspect, e.g. expressed through the first serial verbs:

(16) E1: så pludselig de begyndte at snakke rigtig meget dansk

    then suddenly they started to speak Danish quite a lot

With the two English speakers there is a further development after this stage. In the last conversation they seem to have acquired (or are in the process of acquiring) some of the more advanced grammatical and pragmatic rules of spoken Danish. This covers inversion after a preposed object or adverb (second clause in Example (17)), the inclusion of dummy subjects ('der' in Example (18)), the preverbal negation in subordinate clauses, passive and cleft sentences (first clause in Example (17)):

(17) E2: det må godt være ham der købte tipsen og så fik forældrene pengene i stedet for

it could be him who bought the lot and then got the parents the money instead (= maybe he was the one to bet his money on the football pools, but his parents got the money)

(18) E2: fordi jeg kunne ikke finde ud af hvad der står i billedet

because I could not make out what there say in the picture (. . . what it says in the picture)

The above-mentioned grammatical and pragmatic rules are important in a well-developed language system, but it is likely that they have little or no function at the earlier stages. In other words, it takes a language of a certain 'size' and complexity to develop means of linking larger chunks of information or of using the information structure more creatively. It seems that the learners do not reach this point until they control the basic rules of embedding and morphology. Therefore a separate stage (5) is introduced to cover this development.

ONE DEVELOPMENTAL LINE FOR THE ACQUISITION OF DANISH

In spite of differences in language background and in learning environment the six learners show remarkably similar IL development. This is best described as a growth and change of the information expressed by the learners' utterances and by the syntactic and morphological changes that accompany the changes in information structure. This common line of development is outlined in Fig. 11.1.

However, some of the formal features reveal minor differences

Developmental line Interactional/functional focus	Formal features
(1) keep up conversation agree/disagree with NS – one information per utt. (mainly referents/actions) – in case of several ref./act. – in case of background inf.	repetitions of NS invariable word order SVO/det er NP (old-new) loose concatenation topic–comment structure external negation
(2) propositional meaning – some modality/backgr. inf. – in case of several prop.	word order governed by case roles adverb-preposing parataxis internal negation (pre- and post-verbal)
(3) fluency – breaking up complex inf. into chains of utterances – adv. placed in the prop.	parataxis 'det er ... det er ...' variable word order nominal morphology
(4) longer and more complex utt. – causal, temporal etc. relations	co- and subordination verbal morphology serial verbs
(5) communication of complex inf. – advanced grammatical rules – advanced pragmatic rules	possible through the use of inversion, placeholders, placement of negation passive, cleft sentences

Figure 11.1. A developmental line for the acquisition of Danish L2

between the learners: only V1 and V2 produce topic–comment structures at stage 1 (but very few), A1 and A2 use a slightly different word order at stages 2 and 3, e.g. leaving out anaphoric pronouns, and finally A1 produces only a few subordinate clauses and A2 none. These features may all be explained by transfer from the different L1s, and the absence of subordinate clauses may also be seen as a matter of degree of learning, i.e. A1 and A2 have not yet reached the relevant stage.

The learners do indeed differ in rate of learning: within the first 3 conversations A2's IL only develops from stage 1 to stage 2 (he did not take part in the last data collection). A1 and V2 both include stage 3, and V1 develops to stage 4. E1 and E2 enter stage 5.

DISCUSSION

When comparing the six learners, Ellis' (1985) distinction between rate, sequence, and order of development seems useful. There is a clear difference in acquisitional rate, and some minor differences in the formal features (order of development, possibly influenced by L1 and other linguistic and non-linguistic factors). There is no difference in sequence of development (Fig. 11.1). Altogether it seems that the acquisition of Danish L2 is a fairly uniform process.

On the other hand, the similarity in the IL development may also be due to the fact that the study deals with early acquisition. The developmental line thus reflects the general conditions for learners communicating in a very limited language.

It is possible that the use of two basic sentence structures at the early stage(s) should be seen as a means of simplifying the processing burden for the learners, i.e. as a production strategy, and not as a proper stage in the acquisitional process. The same applies to the use of chains of paratactic structures at stage 3.

The two basic sentence structures serve the double purpose of expressing case roles and information structure unambiguously. Apparently, this works because the utterances are so short and the learners can lean on the discourse as a whole. However, they hardly produce any of the broken-down, presyntactic structures known from early child language and pidgins (which also draw heavily on the context). Maybe the present finding is a consequence of the age of the second language learners and of their concomitant wider knowledge of the world, of communication etc. The semantic simplification which they produce does not relate to the propositional string, but to modality features in the utterance. This supports Ellis' view of simplification and of the difference between first and second language learning.

The use of fixed sentence structures is one aspect of the developmental process which is not included in Givón's syntacticization process. There are hardly any examples of proper topic–comment structures in the data, and the development of word order seen here covers a wider range of structures and pragmatic functions than the mere formation of subject–predicate structures. However, the majority of features that are considered characteristic of the syntacticization process are found in the present study, i.e. subordination, faster rate of delivery, larger chunks, and use of grammatical morphology (noun–verb ratio will not be discussed here).

It is quite clear that the development of Danish IL moves along a continuum of increasing complexity, and that this involves all linguistic levels. However, it seems that semantics carries a greater weight than expected in most grammatical studies (including Givón's). Apparently, an important motivation for change along the continuum is the amount of information expressed by the learners and their need/wish to put more and more into words in the L2. Related to this is the learners' need/wish to talk about more and more complex matters and their finding linguistic means of doing that. Neither should one forget the role played by the production process as such. This might explain the semantic simplification and the use of basic sentence structures at the early stage plus the emphasis on fluency (and not on complexity) at a later stage. Finally, part of the development may be ascribed to the learners' growing awareness of the target language – self-repair does not appear until the second stage, from which point it increases – and to the grammatical requirements of a well-developed language system.

REFERENCES

Chafe, W. L. (1976), Givenness, contrastiveness, definiteness, subjects, topics, and point of view. In Li, C. N. (ed.), *Subject and topic*. New York: Academic Press.

Corder, S. P. (1978), Language-learner language. In Richards, J. C. (ed.), *Understanding second and foreign language learning, issues and approaches*. Rowley, Mass.: Newbury House.

   (1983), A role for the mother tongue. In Gass, S., and Selinker, L. (eds.), *Language transfer in language learning*. Rowley, Mass.: Newbury House.

Dik, S. C. (1978), *Functional grammar*. North Holland Linguistic Series, 37. Amsterdam: North Holland.

   (1989), *The theory of functional grammar*. Dordrecht: Foris.

Ellis, R. (1982), The origins of interlanguage. *Applied Linguistics*, 3:3; 207–23.

   (1985), *Understanding second language acquisition*. Oxford: Oxford University Press.

Fillmore, C. J. (1968), The case for case. In Bach, E., and Harms, R. T. (eds.), *Universals in language*. New York: Rinehart and Winston.

Færch, C. (1979), Describing interlanguage through interaction. Problems of systematicity and permeability. *Working Papers on Bilingualism*, 19, 59–78.

Færch, C. and Kasper, G. (eds.) (1983), *Strategies in interlanguage communication*. London: Longman.

Givón, T. (1979), *On understanding grammar*. New York: Academic Press.

   (1984), *Syntax. A functional–typological introduction*, I. Amsterdam: Benjamins.

   (1985), Function, structure and language acquisition. In Slobin, D. (ed.), *The crosslinguistic study of language acquisition*, II. New York: Lawrence Erlbaum.

Hatch, E. M. (1978), Discourse analysis and second language acquisition. In Hatch, E. (ed.), *Second language acquisition*. Rowley, Mass.: Newbury House.

Holmen, A. (1988), Syntax and information structure in learner language. *Journal of Multilingual and Multicultural Development*, 9:1–2; 85–96.

—— (1990), Udviklingslinier i tilegnelsen af dansk som andetsprog. Ph.D. thesis, University of Copenhagen. *Københavnerstudier i tosprogethed*, 12. København: Danmarks Lærerhøjskole.

Huebner, T. (1983), *A longitudinal analysis of the acquisition of English*. Ann Arbor, Michigan: Karoma.

Hyltenstam, K. (1978), Variation in interlanguage syntax. *Working Papers from Department of General Linguistics*, Lund University 18.

Larsen-Freeman, D. (ed.) (1980), *Discourse analysis in second language research*. Rowley, Mass.: Newbury House.

McLaughlin, B. (1978), *Second language acquisition in childhood*. New York: Lawrence Erlbaum.

Sato, C. J. (1990), *The syntax of conversation in interlanguage development*. Tübingen: Guntar Narr Verlag.

Schachter, J. (1983), A new account of language transfer. In Gass, S., and Selinker, L. (eds.), *Language transfer in language learning*. Rowley, Mass.: Newbury House.

Tarone, E. (1982), Systematicity and attention in interlanguage. *Language Learning*, 32.

12 · The weaker language in bilingual Swedish–French children

SUZANNE SCHLYTER

BACKGROUND[1]

Bilingual children

Studies of grammatical development in young bilingual children have mostly concentrated on the cases where the children have a more or less balanced proficiency in two languages (cf. De Houwer, 1987, and most of the papers in Meisel, 1990). There are however studies of bilingual children aged 1–5 which mention that the two languages are not quite in balance during their development, but that, at least for periods of time, one of the languages is weaker (e.g. Leopold, 1939–49; Arnberg, 1981; Lanza, 1988). Normally the majority language will be the stronger one, whereas the minority language is weaker.

Studies of bilinguals also indicate that if the two languages are both equally strong (Meisel, 1989), each language develops in the same way as the same language of a monolingual child. We do not know very much, however, about the quality of the weaker language. Does it develop like a normal first language, but with some retardation? Or does it develop more like a second language? According to some authors (e.g. De Houwer, 1987; Berman, 1979; Parodi, 1990) the weaker language is retarded in relation to the stronger one, and later follows the same development as a normal first language.[2]

However, owing to the fact that the child may have acquired

289

certain concepts in the stronger language, we can also expect him/her to be influenced by these in the acquisition of the weaker, i.e. the later, one, and thus transfer this similarly to a second language.

Differences in the acquisition of L1/L2

Before going into the question of whether the weaker language behaves like L1 or L2, we need to establish what the differences are between these two types of acquisition.

Even though it is evident that there are similarities between first and second language acquisition, as far as e.g. similar developmental sequences of specific morphemes (cf. Wode, 1981) are concerned, there are also differences.

First language acquisition is often reported to be practically error-free, whereas second language acquisition is rich in errors, especially in language-specific morphology, such as agreement, gender etc. Thus, Andersson and Strömqvist (1990), on the acquisition of gender in Swedish L1 and L2 (p. 19), conclude that 'child L1 acquisition is strikingly error-free, whereas adult L2 acquisition is error-intense'.

The special word order phenomena in subordinate clauses are reported as being acquired practically error-free in L1, but not in L2: in German, the finite verb is sentence-final (cf. Clahsen, 1988); in Swedish, the negation is before instead of after the finite verb (cf. Plunkett and Strömqvist, 1990; Hyltenstam, 1977. However, cf. Håkansson, 1989, for counter-examples.)

According to Clahsen (1988), and also Meisel (1991) specific phenomena concerning word order and inflection in German are acquired in clearly different ways in L1 and in L2.

Meisel (1991:272) summarizes the linguistic differences relevant to his hypothesis (cf. below) on the acquisition of German in the following way:

L1 development	L2 acquisition
· initially prefer pronominal subjects	· initially marked preference for nominal subjects
· once subjects are used, frequency of use rises rapidly to approach 100%	· frequency of use varies over time; omissions constrained by situational and structural context
· rapid development of agreement; soon 100% correct	· some learners: no agreement; others: limited success
· if there is a subject, V agrees with it; virtually no errors	· over the entire period studied: numerous errors
· non-finite verbs always in final position; acquisition of inflection triggers V-second	· position of V independent of $+/-$ finite distinction; non-finite V in second position

In French acquired as an L2 (e.g. Harley, 1984) there are similar differences: subject–verb agreement and gender agreement are the most difficult, and last acquired, morphological items. In French L1 (in monolinguals or in balanced bilinguals, cf. Meisel, 1990), on the other hand, these phenomena are acquired early and correctly.

Differences between L1 and L2 acquisition have been accounted for as being due to differences in cognitive development (McLaughlin, 1978). Similar views are held by Wode (1981), Felix (1987), for whom the similarities are evidence of operation of the same linguistic–cognitive principle, and the differences due to differences in cognitive maturity. Andersson and Strömqvist also account for their facts in terms of cognitive differences in the 2 types of learners, in the sense that rote learning (in unanalyzed units) plays a more central role in young children.

At present, there is an intense discussion in the framework of GB theory as to whether a second language is acquired following the principles of Universal Grammar (UG) or not. Whereas these principles per definition govern the acquisition of a first language, functioning as (at least a part of) the Language Acquisition Device, it is not evident that this also is the case for a second language (cf. e.g. White, 1989; Eubank, 1991).

Many scholars argue in favour of some kind of biogenetic programming operating in childhood only (cf. Long, 1990), and related to the principles of UG (cf. Clahsen, 1988: Meisel, 1991), whereas at least adolescent and adult L2 learning follows other principles.

Some of the arguments in favour of such an approach concern the facts that all healthy and normal children acquire language, rapidly and all in a similar way, going through the same developmental stages, independently of their IQ, motivation, attitude etc. In L2 acquisition, on the other hand, there is great variability according to these factors: some learners may acquire a second language almost as well as children, others will never acquire it in spite of much exposure, most learners acquire a second language in some way but slowly and with many errors (cf. Long, 1990).

Other arguments are of a more detailed linguistic nature (cf. Clahsen, 1988; Meisel, 1991), indicating that L1 development – but not L2 learning – can be accounted for as the setting of language-specific parameters, cf. the linguistic data given above. The fact that these different phenomena are acquired simultaneously with one another, rapidly and correctly, indicates that they are 'triggered' in L1 and thus should be considered as a case of parameterized language development, according to UG principles.

Lundin and Platzack (1988) account, in a similar way, for the rapid and correct acquisition of finiteness, V2 word order, subordinate clauses – with correct placement of the negation as an instance of the setting of the 'V2-parameter' in Swedish.

In this paper, I will show that, in spite of many evident similarities between the stronger language and the weaker language, there are certain specific differences between them, concerning the facts crucial for the 'UG only in L1' position.

PRESENT INVESTIGATION

The present study is part of a larger project[3] which aims at discussing, among other things, questions such as those presented above. In this project, 6 bilingual French–Swedish children were investigated longitudinally over a period of 2 years from the age of about 2. The parents are middle class, living in the suburbs of Stockholm. In each family one parent is Swedish-speaking, the other is French-speaking. The children were recorded every fourth month. In each recording session, they played and talked spontaneously with each of their parents, for half an hour in French and half an hour in Swedish.

The recordings were transcribed and coded on computer. The linguistic level was measured with the help of MLU (= Mean Length of Utterances) calculated in words. The general linguistic profile for each speech sample was calculated with the help of the computer, along the lines of the 'Profile Analysis' of Clahsen (1986), adapted to French (cf. the DUFDE project, as described in Meisel, 1990) and to Swedish. The profile thus obtained makes it possible to (a) define the developmental level of each sample qualitatively; (b) observe whether there are differences between a sample of a 'weaker language' and a sample of a 'stronger language' of corresponding level.

The developmental level is accounted for in terms of stages, along the lines of Clahsen (1986). Roughly, these stages can be described as follows:

Stage I = the one word stage; Stage II = the two word stage; Stage III = the stage where grammatical morphemes appear, such as auxiliaries, articles, personal pronouns, prepositions etc.; Stage IV = the stage where language specific word order etc. of main clauses is established; Stage V = the stage where subordinate clauses of different kinds, narratives etc. appear.

In this study, samples of the stronger and of the weaker language have been matched on two grounds: MLU and qualitative analyses, i.e. according to features characteristic of a certain stage of development. Whereas it was relatively easy to state the developmental stage for each sample of the stronger language, the elaboration of a profile for each speech sample often turned out to be more difficult in the weaker language, since typical indicators of a higher level could be found alongside indicators of a lower level, in a sort of 'mixed-stage' pattern. Developmental level has therefore been defined as a combination of MLU and of certain stage indicators, even if the child does not combine all of them. These partial 'Stage Criteria', which thus constitute the similarities between the stronger and the weaker language, are described here:

At 'Stage III' in both the stronger and the weaker language, the children studied here start using articles, auxiliary verbs, finite verb forms, and prepositions. Sentences with SVO or SVX structure appear. Except for PPs (and, partly, NPs), these phenomena are however unstable and variable in the weaker language. MLU is roughly between 2 and 3 (but with certain individual variations).

At 'Stage IV' in both the stronger and the weaker language, the utterances become longer and more complex. In Swedish there is often inversion after a preposed adverb, in French we find preposed adverbs and dislocated subjects or objects. Typical of French, at this level, are object clitics (eg: je *le* vois). Possessive pronouns, paratactic constructions and relative clauses of 'cleft' type are found in both languages.

At 'Stage V' we find, in the stronger and in the weaker language, subordinate clauses with conjunctions, also marking for past and future tense, where the child starts speaking about what is not 'here-and-now,' and attempts to tell stories.

RESULTS

General tendencies

At the time of investigation, the children in this project were not all dominant in Swedish, the majority language, but 3 of them had

French as the stronger language, as follows:

	stronger language	weaker language
Paul	Swedish	French (only some words)
Léo	Swedish	French (some words and formulas)
Jean	Swedish	French
Dany	French	Swedish (only slightly weaker)
Mimi	French	Swedish
Anne	French	Swedish

We can observe that:
— one of the languages was always acquired without problems;
— there is great variation as to the acquisition of the other language: one child, Dany, learned it almost perfectly, whereas some children dropped the second language after initial bilingualism at the one- and two-word stage (Paul, Léo). Still others had a more or less parallel, but clearly weaker, language over a long period of time.

These general observations are congruent with other cases cited in the literature on unbalanced bilingualism (cf. above).

This variation is similar to what has been observed for L2 acquisition, as opposed to L1 acquisition.

Finiteness, pronominal subjects and word order in the stronger and weaker language

The factors which have been studied most intensively as far as the difference between L1 and L2 is concerned are finiteness, pronominal subjects, agreement, and word order. Further, these factors have been examined in a clear theoretical framework, namely the possible access to UG in L2. These phenomena have, therefore, been concentrated on here.

In the *stronger language,* just as Meisel (1989, 1991) points out for L1 in German and French, the children studied here started using personal pronouns in combination with finite verbs, in their correct form and with a correct word order, in a systematic and productive way, e.g.:

il a fini 'he has finished'	dom kommer	'they come'
elle est là	hon är här	'she is here'
je veux manger	jag vill äta	'I want to eat'

Earlier, in Stage II, the grammatical subjects were normally lexical (e.g. teddy, mamma), the verbs were infinite, and the subject could occur before or after the verb.

In a corresponding sample of the *weaker language*, however, the children had problems with these phenomena, of the following kinds:

(A) The child may use just some single (non-functional) words of the language (in the cases where the language is very weak).

(B) The child may avoid the combination subject + verb altogether, which gives a profile with an unusually high frequency of PP's and NP's.

Examples:

Jean 5F:	dans la coquille	'in the shell'
	dans les pieds	'in the feet'
	pas des oursins dans le pied!	'no sea urchins in the foot!'

In these cases, the rest of the sentence (i.e. pronominal subject + finite verb — often auxiliary or copula) may be replaced by items from the stronger language. This results in sentences of the following type (the words from the 'incorrect,' i.e. stronger language, are italicized):

Léo 2F:	*biter* vach*en*	'*bites, the* cow'
	det är en dame.	'*that is a* lady'
	sönder, dame	'*broken,* (the) lady'

| Léo 3F: | *och det är också* soleil | '*and that is also* (the) sun' |
| | *jag* dormir dans la fauteuil | '*I* (to) sleep in the chair' |

(Cf. the weaker language in a child studied by Parodi (1990), which is of a similar type).

(C) If the language is only slightly weaker, the child 'may use personal pronouns, but place them in an incorrect position, and/or combine them with a verb which is not marked for finiteness. He/she may use the correct verb form to mark past or future tense, but fail to mark person/number agreement correctly. The word order may be more incorrect than in a corresponding sample of the stronger language.

Quantitative and qualitative evidence for points (B) and (C) will be given here, based on a detailed analysis of 3 of the children of this project (Jean, Mimi and Anne):

Quantitative analysis of some of the samples. 'Correct finiteness' has been calculated according to the following criteria:
− correct finite verb form (correct for tense and person marking)
and
− explicitly stated subject (normally personal pronouns)
and
− correct word order (in Swedish: verb-second, in French: (X)SV.)

If one or more of these criteria are lacking, the sentence is counted as having 'incorrect finiteness'. The number of sentences with correct finiteness is calculated here in comparison with all comprehensible utterances (except yes/no), in order to account for both 'incorrect finiteness' and for the cases where the subject + verb is avoided by the child or replaced by items in the stronger language.

Language samples are matched with one another with the help of MLU and stage criteria. Since there are certain individual differences concerning the extent to which the children structure the finiteness of their language, the most revealing comparison is between the stronger and the (retarded) weaker language of the same child.

In Table 12.1, the number after the name refers to the recording, the F or S to the language. Stage level in inverted commas means mixed or irregular stage criteria. The dotted line indicates the level at which comparison has been made: since the recordings are rather sparse, we do not always have a recording of exactly comparable level, but the comparison must be a constructed level between the 2 documented here.

Table 12.1. *Percentage of 'correct finiteness' per
comprehensible utterances*

Anne:				
Anne 3F (2;7 years)		————————	Anne 5S (2;11 years)	
Stage III, MLU 2,7:	40%		Stage III, MLU 2,5:	6%
Anne 5F (2;11 years)				
St. III+, MLU 3,2:	55%			
		————————	Anne 7S (3;3 years)	
			St. 'IV,' MLU 2,9:	34%
Anne 7F (3;3 years)				
St. IV, MLU 2,9:	47%			
Mimi:				
Mimi 1F (2;0 years)				
St. III. MLU 2,1:	18%			
		————————	*Mimi 2S (2;2 years)*	
			St. 'IV,' MLU 2,6:	*14%*
Mimi 2F (2;2 years)				
St. IV, MLU 3,2:	52%			
Jean:				
Jean 3S (2;2 years)		————————	Jean 5F (2;6 years)	
St. III, MLU 1,7:	12%		St. III, MLU 2,0:	9%
Jean 5S (2;6 years)		————————	Jean 8F (3;1 years)	
St. IV, MLU 2,7:	58%		St. IV-V, MLU 3,0:	5%

As can be seen in Table 12.1, the proportion of correct finiteness is
smaller in a sample of a weaker language than of a stronger language.
More precisely, it can be observed that, when the stronger language
of a child has entered Stage III, and attained an MLU of c. 2.5 (in
words), the percentage of 'correct finiteness' calculated in this way
increases rapidly to about 50%, whereas this proportion is smaller in
the weaker language of a corresponding level, i.e. at a somewhat later
age. (The proportion varies depending on the degree of weakness of
the weaker language.)

Qualitative analysis of some of the samples. Here, the language of different children will have to be compared, because the qualitative comparison must be between two samples of the same language.

Comparison (A), Swedish at Stage III:
  Stronger lg: Jean 3S (Stage III, MLU 1,7, age 2;2)
  Weaker lg; Anne 3S (Stage III, MLU, 1,9, age 2;7):

Jean 3S: Here Jean speaks his stronger language Swedish very willingly, and does not use any French words in a Swedish-speaking situation. Of the 43 verbs used, 28 have the present tense ending '-r.' Of these, 14 have a pronominal subject, which is systematically placed after the verb. There are no instances of a personal pronoun combined with an incorrect verb form, which supports the findings of Meisel (1991) (cf. above). Examples:

bygger dom	'build they'
pumpar dom	'pump they'
klipper man	'cuts one' 3 occurrences
åker dom	'ride they'
onglar dom	'? they'
a ritar dom	'draw they'
målar dom	'paint they'
brinner dom	'burn they'
där står den	'there stands it'
där var den	'there was it'

The personal pronoun is systematically placed after the verb, which is perfectly correct in the last 2 cases, where an adverb is preposed, but in the other cases constitutes a target-deviant word order. I have considered it as representing 'correct finiteness', since it seems to be a normal step in the development in at least some Swedish children. The child is, in any case, now developing a productive system, concerning finiteness, by using pronominal subject and finite verbs.

Anne 3S: At this age, the French of Anne is very fluent, and has a very elaborate finiteness (40%, cf. Table 12.1). Her Swedish is clearly weaker. She is also unwilling to speak, often answers with 'mm' or 'nej', or uses French words.

In contrast to Jean 3S, and to her own French language, Anne 3S does not have a very regular system of 'subj-pron + finite Verb' structures in Swedish. Anne uses only 2 precursors to the '-r' ending on verbs – both with a precursor to a personal pronoun:

n kissa(r)	'n pee(s)'
n titta(r)	'n look(s)'

The copula, är, is used most times without subject:

*nej är Mimmi, den där.	'no is Mimmi, that one'
*ja, är Mimmi.	'yes, is Mimmi'

An * is here put before utterance which are incorrect not only according to the adult norm, but presumably also to the 'child language norm,' in the sense that utterances of this type have not been found in the samples of the same language as the stronger language in this material.

Anne may omit the subject which is obligatory in Swedish after the finite verb when an object, adverb etc. is preposed:

*den där vill inte ha!   'that one want not (to) have'.

There are also instances of correct finiteness, often with the verb 'vill' (= wish, want to), but these are less systematic than those of Jean 3S.

Comparison (B) Swedish at Stage IV.
   Stronger lg: Jean 5S (Stage IV, MLU 2,7. age 2;6)
   Weaker lg: Mimi 2S (Stage IV, MLU 2,6, age 2;2):

The children Jean and Mimi are well suited for comparison with each other because of their similarities: both are early learners, both structure their stronger language very well, both speak the weaker language rather well and normally quite willingly.

Jean 5S: Jean has a very well-structured Swedish as stronger language at this stage. Of the 77 verbs he uses, almost 90% have correct finiteness in the sense defined above. Only 8 are in non-finite form, and none of these occurs with a subject pronoun. All other verbs are in finite forms and take a pronominal subject, e.g.:

det är bara mattan	'it's only the mat'
jag vill inte	'I want not'
dom gungar	'they swing'
man sprutar vatten	'one sprays water'
han gräver, pappan	'he digs, the father'
hon har ta' skenorna	'she has take' (sic) the rails'
vad ska vi ha i där?	'what shall we have in there?'
hur ska man öppna då?	'how shall one open then?'

Tense is well marked, in the sense that Jean uses the correct Swedish morphology for present, past and future tense. (This is a good illustration of the systematic acquisition of finiteness, such as Meisel (1991) has shown for other children.)

Mimi 2S: At this age, the French of Mimi shows perfect structuring, and its profile is very similar to the Swedish profile of Jean 5S. (Cf. also the quantitative data above.) As for her weaker language, Swedish, Mimi is not unwilling to speak, and she uses rather complex utterance types, but the profile of her Swedish differs from Jean's Swedish at the comparable level.

Mimi uses 63 verbs in this speech sample. Of these, only 19, i.e. 30% of them, have correct finiteness, in the sense defined above. These are of the following type:

det är vatten	'that is water'
den är min	'that is mine'
jag vet inte	'I don't know'
det är där han springer	'that's where he is running'
titta vad jag gör!	'look what I am doing'

The last two utterances, with a simple kind of subordination,

indicate quite a high developmental level – Stage IV or V – as do the
preterite forms below. Still, Mimi makes a great number of errors
concerning finiteness: often she aims at the finite form of the verb,
but does not mark present with '-r' – except in the one case cited
above. (Mimi articulates very clearly, so it cannot be the case that the
-r disappears for phonetic reasons.) Examples:

> (Mimi is describing the pictures of 'Alice in Wonderland,' where a
> rabbit is running.)
> *kanin spring sådär   'rabbit run like that'
> *ja sådär han spring   'yes like that he run'
> *titta han spring sådär   'look he run like that'

After inversion, Mimi often omits the subject (cf. Anne 3S above):

> *så, så där ska vara.   'so, like that shall be'
> *titta vad gör!   'look what does!'
> *titta vad gjorde!   'look what did!'

Mimi also makes errors in word order:

> *den också är grön   'this also is green'
> *och den också sån är grön   'and this also such is green'
> *där jag skrivit   'there I written'
> *titta vad gjorde Nat bollen! 'look what did Nat the ball!'

Errors of these types have not been observed in this material in
Swedish as a stronger language.

Comparison (C) French Stage IV:
  Stronger lg: Mimi 2F (St. IV, MLU 3,2, age 2;2)
  Weaker lg: Jean 6F (St. IV, MLU 3,5, age 2;9)

  Stronger lg: Mimi 3F (St. IV, MLU 3,5, age 2;6)
  Weaker lg: Jean 8F (St. IV-V, MLU 3,0, age 3;0)

In these samples, the French of Mimi has a qualitatively somewhat
lower developmental level than the matched sample of Jean – which
only makes the grammatical differences more interesting. Both

children have acquired tense marking for immediate past and future, i.e. they have a productive use of 'passé composé' and 'futur proche'. Subordinate clauses, reference to remote past, and 'imparfait' (indicators of Stage V in French) start to appear in Jean 8F.

In Mimi 2F, the child starts marking person/number agreement between subject and finite verb:

où il est le avion?	'where is it, the aeroplane?'
ils sont là (talking about points)	'they are there'
j'ai trouvé!	'I have (1ps) found!'
t'as vu?	'you have (2ps) seen?'
il a écrit comme ça	'he has written like that'

In Mimi 3F, the subject–verb agreement is further developed, and she now also marks plural agreement with the copula:

(speaking about puzzle parts)	
ils sont là, les yeux!	'they are there, the eyes'
là il est, le rouge!	'there it is, the red one!'
ils sont là, les souliers!	'they are there, the shoes'
il est là, là!	'he is there, there!'

Jean 6F: Jean now uses most of the typical structures of Stage IV in French. However, there are certain small differences from the otherwise very similar Mimi 2F, which concern subject–verb agreement. Although he knows the pronoun 'je' and uses it for verbs which do not change forms in 1st and 3rd person sing (je sais, je veux), he incorrectly uses 'il' in speaking about himself in the past or future, with the auxiliary verb (which according to the norm should vary in person):

*il a trouvé (=j'ai . . .)	'he has (=I have) found'
(cf. Mimi, who uses the same phrase correctly)	
*il a fait caca, maman	'he has (=I have) done poo-poo, mummy.'
*il va pas la mordre (=je vais pas . . .)	'he (=I) will not bite her'

Jean 8F: Before this recording, Jean has only spoken French with his mother, and his French is in certain respects less, but in others more advanced than in Jean 6F. It is more advanced in the sense that he uses subordinate clauses, a conditional construction, one 'imparfait,' and he sometimes refers to the remote past, all typical features of Stage V. In this sense, his language is more advanced than that of Mimi 3F.

However, he seems unable to mark subject-verb agreement correctly for the plural:

(speaking about more than one ice-cream:)
*où il est, les glaces?   'where is it, the ice-creams?'

He still does not use 'je' with the verb 'vais/va' when referring to himself, but avoids the pronoun altogether, using the verb incorrectly in the 3sg form:

va acheter des bonbons (=je vais...)
va parler à papa (=je vais)
va chez papa (=je vais...)

Negation

Another example of weaker language incorrectness is Mimi's placement of negation when she starts using subordinates. As mentioned above, this position is acquired differently in L1 and L2, and proposed as evidence for the 'UG in L1 only' position.[4] In the Swedish of Mimi (weaker language), no negation is correctly placed in subordinates, it is always in the incorrect position, after the finite verb.

Mimi 3S:
*som ramlar inte   'who falls not'
*därför hon vill titta inte 'because she wants to look not Alice
Alice här bak...   here back'

Mimi 4S:
*att man kan inte	'that you can not'
*att man får inte gå	'that you may not go'
*som var inte bra	'which was not good'

Mimi 5S (3;2 years):
*nån som har inte drog eh 'someone who has not pulled my
drog mitt hår.   hair'

Mimi 7S (3;10 years)
*om du skakar inte på   'if you shake not your hand'
handen

DISCUSSION

I have tried to show that if a sample of the stronger language of a
bilingual child is compared to a sample of the weaker language (of
the same or of another child) of a corresponding linguistic developmental level, then – independently of whether French or Swedish is
the stronger language – the following can be observed:

· the *stronger language* exhibits all characteristics of normal L1
development, as regards the central grammatical phenomena
such as finiteness, word order, and placement of negation;
whereas
· the *weaker language* exhibits great variation in these respects,
from complete non-existence of the grammatical phenomena
mentioned to a lower occurrence of them than in a corresponding sample of the stronger language.

This indicates that the stronger language in a bilingual child is
exactly like a normal first language in monolingual children,
whereas the weaker language in these respects has similarities with a
second language. This also implies that, if a rapid and correct
development of finiteness in L1 is taken as an argument in favour of
access to UG, in contrast to L2 where finiteness is acquired slower,

with errors, and with much variation, then this reasoning could also be applied to the distinction stronger language – weaker language. I will not, however, go into the question of whether this approach is the best way to account for L1 – L2 differences, or whether a cognitive approach is preferable.

NOTES

1 An earlier version of this paper has appeared in Davies and Adelswärd: *På väg mot ett nytt språk*. Linköping 1990.
2 I owe much of the inspiration for this chapter to discussions with T. Parodi in Hamburg on the nature of the weaker language.
3 'The weaker language in bilingual children', financed by the Swedish Council for Research in the Humanities and Social Sciences, 'Humanistisk-Samhällsvetenskapliga Forskningsrådet'.
4 There is however one recent study, Håkansson (1989), which shows that the author's young daughter – Swedish monolingual – uses negation in the incorrect position in subordinates when the finite verb is a copula or auxiliary.

REFERENCES

Andersson, Anders-Börje, and Strömqvist, Sven (1990), Adult L2 acquisition of gender. A cross-linguistic and cross-learner type perspective. Gothenburg Papers in Theoretical Linguistics, 61.

Arnberg, Lenore (1981), *Early childhood bilingualism in the mixed-lingual family*. Linkoeping Studies in Education, Dissertation no. 14. Department of Education, Linkoeping University.

Berman, Ruth (1979), The (re)emergence of a bilingual: Case study of a Hebrew–English speaking child. In *Working Papers on Bilingualism*, 19, 21–39.

Clahsen, Harald (1986): *Die Profilanalyse*. Berlin: Marhold.
    (1988), Parameterizised grammatical theory and language acquisition: A study of verb placement and inflection by children and adults. In Flynn, S., and O'Neill, W. (eds.), *Linguistic theory in second language acquisition*. Dordrecht: Reidel.

De Houwer, Annick (1987), *Two at a time: An exploration of how children acquire two languages from birth.* Doctoral thesis, Free University of Brussels.

Döpke, Susanne (1988), *One parent – one language: An interactional approach.* Doctoral thesis, Department of German, Monash University, Australia.

Eubank, Lynn (ed.) (1991), *Point counterpoint: Universal grammar in the second language.* Amsterdam/Philadelphia: Benjamins.

Felix, Sascha (1987): *Cognition and language growth.* Dordrecht: Foris.

Håkansson, Gisela (1989): The acquisition of negative placement in Swedish. *Studia Linguistica,* 43:1, 47–58.

Harley, Birgit (1984): Mais apprennent-ils vraiment de français? *Langue et Société,* 12, 57–62.

Heinen, Sabine, and Kadow, Helga (1990): The acquisition of French by monolingual children. A review of the literature. In Meisel, J. M. (ed.), *Two first languages. Early grammatical development in bilingual children.* Dordrecht: Foris.

Hyltenstam, Kenneth (1977): Implicational patterns in interlanguage syntax variation. *Language Learning,* 27, 383–411.

Lanza, Elizabeth (1988), Conversations with bilingual two-year-olds. Paper presented at the Eleventh Annual Meeting of the American Association for Applied Linguistics, 27–29 December 1988.

Leopold, Werner (1939–1949), *Speech development of a bilingual child.* Evanston, Chicago.

Long, Michael (1990), Maturational constraints on language development. *Studies in Second Language Acquisition,* 12:3, 251–85.

Lundin, Barbro, and Platzack, Christer (1988), The acquisition of verb inflection, verb second and subordinate clauses in Swedish. *Working Papers in Scandinavian Syntax,* vol. 42.

McLaughlin, Barry (1984), *Second-language acquisition in childhood: Vol. 1 Preschool children.* Hillsdale, N.J.: Erlbaum.

Meisel, Jürgen (1989), Early differentiation of languages in bilingual children. In Hyltenstam, K., and Obler, L. (eds.), *Bilingualism across the lifespan: Aspects of acquisition, maturity, and loss.* Cambridge: Cambridge University Press.

(ed.) (1990), *Two first languages. Early grammatical development in bilingual children.* Dordrecht: Foris.

(1991), Principles of universal grammar and strategies of language learning: Some similarities and differences between first and second language acquisition. In Eubank, Lynn (ed.), *Point counterpoint. Universal grammar in the second language*. Amsterdam: Benjamins.

Parodi, Teresa (1990), The acquisition of word order and case. In Meisel, J. M. (ed.), *Two first languages. Early grammatical development in bilingual children*. Dordrecht: Foris.

Plunkett, Kim, and Strömqvist, Sven (1990), *The acquisition of Scandinavian languages*. Gothenburg Papers in Theoretical Linguistics, 59.

White, Lydia (1989), *Universal grammar and second language acquisition*. Amsterdam/Philadelphia: Benjamins.

Wode, Henning (1981), *Learning a second language. An integrated view of language acquisition*. Tübingen: Narr.

13 Four operating principles and input distribution as explanations for underdeveloped and mature morphological systems

ROGER W. ANDERSEN

INTRODUCTION

Background

After a series of reports on the study of the acquisition of Spanish by English-speaking children and adults, in which I began to describe and seek explanations for the linguistic characteristics of these learners' Spanish (Andersen, 1983, 1984b, 1986a, 1986b, 1986c, 1990e) within a crosslinguistic framework (Andersen, 1984c), I began to find the available theoretical and methodological resources to be seriously lacking for the task at hand.[1] Part of this project included a body of data on my 2 daughters' Spanish at 3 time periods: (1) at ages 4 and 7 after living in their mother's home-town in Puerto Rico for 4 years and just before moving to Los Angeles, (2) after 3 years in Los Angeles (at ages 7 and 10), and (3) after 7 years in Los Angeles (ages 11 and 14). In this substudy I was as interested in their original acquisition of Spanish (as part of the pool of data on 14 children, ages 4–18, and 2 adults[2] in the larger study) as I was in their gradual loss of control of Spanish once they were removed from a Spanish-speaking environment. I also made a series of video and audio recordings of 2- and 3-year old Puerto Rican children, for purposes of comparison.

Recently, however, I decided to postpone further data analysis in order to focus my attention on theoretical and methodological issues that had to be dealt with before I could continue with direct analysis

309

of the data. By this time I had decided to focus on one particular linguistic domain for which there has been considerable research in several fields – tense and aspect – in order to sharpen the theoretical linguistic framework of the study. This area was one of the two[3] main areas I have focused on since my earlier research on second language acquisition of English (e.g., Andersen, 1978) and is also the focus of a related project I am currently engaged in on tense, mood, and aspect in Papiamentu, a Spanish and Portuguese based creole language of the Caribbean (Andersen, 1987, 1990b). Within the scope of research on tense and aspect, I have tried to understand the linguistic literature on tense and aspect in native languages as used by fully proficient adults (e.g., Andersen, 1990c) and the literature on the acquisition of tense and aspect (Andersen, 1990d). Concurrently I have also developed further (in Andersen, 1988 [1990a] and 1989a) the theoretical framework for language acquisition that I am assuming for this research – a cognitive–interactionist theory of language acquisition.

This paper develops an area of the theoretical framework for this work that has been neglected, and which requires serious attention if we are to understand the conflicting claims in the literature on acquisition of morphological marking of categories of tense and aspect – that of the use of verb inflections by proficient native speakers.

The issue

At almost any point in a learner's development from no knowledge of the language to native or native-like competence in the language, his morphological systems will be underdeveloped. That is, whatever the morphological systems in fully developed native language, the learner on his way 'up' towards this level or on his way 'down' from it will use fewer of the grammatical morphemes, and will use them less often and in more restricted ways than the fully competent native speaker (Andersen, 1989b). The most appealing explanations for the nature of these underdeveloped morphological systems are in areas of cognitive and linguistic universals. For example, it could be that, for cognitive reasons, the learner is initially incapable of perceiving, processing, and internalizing certain form–meaning relationships, but quite capable of dealing with others. On the linguistic side, of the various meanings encoded by verbal inflections, the subset of morphological forms we are concerned with in this chapter, the least marked meanings would be more accessible to learners and the most marked far less accessible.

In spite of various controversies within the literature on first language acquisition of morphological encoding of tense and aspect, there is a strong empirical basis for concluding that children between the ages of 18 months and two and a half years restrict their use of the verb morphology of the language they are acquiring such that each inflection is used with a separate and distinct semantic class of verbs (Andersen, 1990d). Past and perfective inflections are restricted primarily to telic and punctual verbs. Progressive inflections are restricted primarily to activities. And imperfective inflections are slower to emerge and, when they do appear, they are initially restricted to activities and states. Viewed from the perspective of the semantic categories, states seldom get inflected in early stages, activities most typically receive progressive and/or imperfective inflections, and punctual and telic events typically receive past and/or perfective inflections.[4]

These correspondences[5] are given schematically in Table 13.1. A distinction is made between earlier and later inflections because, in languages with explicit imperfective marking, use of this inflection is a late development. When imperfective inflections appear in Spanish and Portuguese, they first appear with states and activities (in addition to the earlier inflection for progressive on activities).

Most of authors of the studies reviewed in Andersen (1990d) appear to assume that, except for any language-specific restrictions, there is an equal distribution of verbal inflections across the various semantic classes in native speech. We thus assume something like the array in Table 13.2 for a language like Spanish or Portuguese. For ease of exposition, I am ignoring the marking of present time

Table 13.1. *Distribution of inflections by verb class for first language acquisition*

	States	Activities	Telic/punctual events
Earlier inflections:	uninflected	progressive	past/perfective
Later inflection:	imperfective	imperfective	

Table 13.2. *Assumed distribution of inflections by verb class for native language use*

States	Activities	Telic/punctual events
*	progressive	progressive
perfective	perfective	perfective
imperfective	imperfective	imperfective

Note:
* States do not usually inflect for progressive

reference, since much use of so-called present inflections in acquisition data is really of the unmarked default form, usually the third person singular in highly inflected languages like Spanish.[6]

These findings are so consistent across different studies that it is no wonder that they have generated so much discussion in the literature concerning the forces that create such distributions of verbal inflections in first language acquisition. However, there is evidence that the real distribution of inflections in adult native language use is actually much closer to that found among language learners than is usually assumed. If this is indeed the case, then we need to reconsider the conclusions drawn from the language acquisition studies. In this chapter I will first outline briefly the terminological and conceptual framework assumed in this' work. Then I will summarize the empirical findings from several representative first language acquisition studies. Next I will summarize the evidence that the distribution of inflections in adult native language use is also biased in the same direction as found in the language acquisition studies. Finally, I will offer a uniform explanation for these apparently conflicting sets of empirical evidence and suggest a direction for future research.

Tense, aspect, and aktionsart

Since the terminological and conceptual framework for this paper cannot be assumed to be common knowledge for all readers, I will briefly summarize the major concepts needed to deal with the issues dealt with here. TENSE relates the time of an event to the time of speaking or some other reference point on a time line: 'I *saw* the accident' (prior to the moment of speaking) vs 'I *am telling* you about it right now' (current at the time of speaking). GRAMMATICAL ASPECT refers basically to aspectual distinctions which are OBLI-GATORILY[7] encoded in a specific language. Thus English progressive ('I'm telling you') and perfect ('I've told you') are cases of grammatical aspect. The example of present tense given above, 'I am telling you about it right now' is also encoded for Progressive ASPECT. INHERENT ASPECT (*AKTIONSART*), on the other hand, is not explicitly encoded in morphology; it is simply an inherent part of the word or construction that expresses the situation or action. More specifically, it is the situation or event that has inherent aspect and the verb or predicate merely represents that situation or event and the aspect inherent in it.

The issue dealt with in this chapter has to do especially with categories of inherent lexical aspect. In this term, 'aspect', as with grammatical aspect, refers to the internal nature of the situation or event (as opposed to the time it takes place, as in tense). 'Lexical' means that it is usually assumed that each individual verb – each lexical item – has associated with it some type of aspect, i.e., whether the verb refers to a state or an action and, if an action, whether it is durative or momentary, or possibly a combination of both. 'Inherent' means that this aspect belongs to the situation or event and is an intrinsic part of it. Thus 'run' is inherently durative in aspect and 'break' is inherently nondurative (more specifically 'punctual' or momentary).

Vendler (1967) has divided inherent aspect into four categories, as shown in Example (1). The terms in capitals are his. I will use the terms in parentheses throughout the remainder of this chapter.

(1) STATE	ACTIVITY	ACCOMPLISH-MENT	ACHIEVE-MENT
(state)	(activity)	(telic event)	(punctual event)
have	run	paint a picture	recognize (someone)
possess	walk	make a chair	realize (something)
desire	swim	build a house	lose (something)
want	push	write a novel	find (something)
like	pull	grow up	win the race

'States' continue without change without any additional energy. In fact, it takes energy to change a state. The other three categories are non-stative or, as sometimes referred to, 'dynamic'. Dynamic situations or events require energy to keep them going, as with 'activities' like 'run', for them to take place at all, as in 'punctual events' and then, once they have taken place, they are over, e.g. 'recognize someone', or, finally, to begin and continue an activity and then bring it to completion, in 'telic events' like 'run a mile'. The term 'telic event' (Vendler's accomplishment) refers to an activity such as 'to make a cake' or 'to run a mile', which leads up to an end-point or conclusion. If the end-point is not reached, then the event has not been accomplished. Thus, if you stop in the middle of making a cake, you haven't made a cake. If you stop in the middle of walking, an activity, you have, however, walked.

To speak of inherent lexical aspect gives one the impression that the aspect is inherent in a single lexical item. This is true of most states (e.g. 'want') and activities (e.g., 'run'), but in many cases the aspect is associated not with a single verb, but with the entire predicate or even the entire proposition. In many cases a single particle will make a difference: 'eat' is different from 'eat up'. For this reason the examples of telic and punctual events require more than simply a verb. To sum up, each of these categories of meanings differs according to the aspect inherent in the situation: states are simply that, 'stative'. Activities have inherent duration. Punctual events are momentary in duration. They may be thought of as being reduced to a point. Telic events share aspects of activities (the duration) and punctual events (the punctual end-point). As Mourelatos (1981:193) explains it, telic events 'involve a product, upshot, or outcome.'

LEARNERS ARE CONSERVATIVE IN THEIR USE OF VERBAL INFLECTIONS

In a recent paper (Andersen, 1990d) I reviewed evidence from seven studies that deal with the question of whether children between the ages of 18 months and two and a half years restrict their early use of verbal inflections to a different semantic class of verbs for each inflection. I concluded that even the study that finds fault with one major interpretation for the findings of the earlier studies – Weist Wysocka, Witkowska-Stadnik, Buczowska and Konieczna, 1984 – actually provides evidence in favour of such a conservative use of inflections. I will not repeat the argumentation here. Instead I will summarize some of the quantitative findings from these studies and one additional study so that the reader can better understand the issues and claims made in this chapter. For this purpose I have chosen Antinucci and Miller's (1976) study of the acquisition of English and Italian, Weist, et al.'s (1984) study on Polish child language, and Eisenberg's (1982) report on the acquisition of Spanish (as reanalyzed in Gonzales, 1989).

Table 13.3 summarizes some of the results of Antinucci and Miller's (1976) study of the acquisition of English and Italian as first languages. The authors themselves do not quantify their data. This table is based on my own quantification from their complete lists of verbs used by the children. With the exception of the two activity verbs with past inflections, in both the Italian and the English data,

Table 13.3. *Summary of findings in Antinucci and Miller (1976).*
Number of different verb types with past tense inflections

	State	Activity	Telic/punctual
(1) *Italian*:			
No Inflection:	7	20	4
Past Inflection:	0	2	18
(2) *English*:			
No Inflection:	10	26	6
Past Inflection:	0	0	18

Table 13.4. *Summary from Eisenberg (1982) (Source: Gonzales*
1989). Number of different verb types with each inflection

	State	Activity	Telic	Punctual
(1) *Nancy*:				
Perfective:	0	0	9	43
Imperfective:	1*	0	0	0
Progressive	0	12	0	0
Present	12	6	7	15
(2) *Gabriela*:				
Perfective:	0	0	4	19
Imperfective:	1*	0	0	0
Progressive	0	2	0	0
Present	10	7	9	24

Note:
* = estaba 'was'

the only verbs to receive past inflections are telic or punctual verbs.
States and activities go uninflected.

The 'past' inflections in the Italian data in Table 13.3 are actually
cases of past *perfective*. Spanish also has a perfective–imperfective
contrast. Table 13.4 displays the equivalent count of different verb
types for Spanish data from two Spanish-speaking children who

Table 13.5. *Summary from Weist et al. (1984) Distribution of past perfective and imperfective forms in children's Polish (= Average number of verb phrases in each category in 45-min caretaker–child interaction)*

	State	Activity	Telic	Punctual
Perfective:	0.3	6.3	20.6	22.7
Imperfective:	11.7	20.2	2.6	0.9

were raised bilingually in California. In the data from both children, the perfective inflection is used only with telic and punctual verbs, the progressive exclusively with activity verbs, and the imperfective hardly at all and then only with a stative verb. The distribution of forms in Table 13.4 is especially noteworthy because Clark (1985:750) cites Eisenberg's work as an exception to the tense-aspect studies on first language acquisition. Clark based her assessment on Eisenberg's conclusion that the semantic Aktionsart categories did not explain the appearance of the verb inflection. Eisenberg did not use the same criteria for establishing these categories, however, that the other studies used. When her data are reinterpreted in terms of the Vendler (1967) and Mourelatos (1981) categories of states, activities, telic events, and punctual events, they fit the patterns found in other studies, as I have shown here.

Although Weist et al. (1984) argue strongly against one of the interpretations given to findings such as those reported by Antinucci and Miller (1976), their Polish data nevertheless present the same general picture we have found so far in the English, Italian, and Spanish data. Some of these findings are summarized in Table 13.5 (from Andersen, 1990d). Although all cells are filled in this summary (in contrast with the previous tables), the Polish data are similar to the Spanish and Italian data in that the past perfective marker appears almost exclusively with telic and punctual verbs. The Spanish data produced minimal uses of imperfective verb forms and then only with stative verbs. The Polish data shows that the imperfective is used almost exclusively with state and activity verbs. There are independent reasons for the greater use of the imperfective forms by Polish-speaking children (see Andersen, 1990d; Bloom and Harner, 1989; and Bybee and Dahl, 1989, for details). The point being made here is that perfective and imperfective morphological marking is distributed unequally across the four semantic categories such that perfective marking is found primarily on telic and punctual verbs, and imperfective marking primarily on state and activity verbs.

All three of these studies and the quantitative summaries displayed here provide quantitative empirical support for the claim made earlier in this chapter: in early stages of first language acquisition (roughly between the ages of 18 months to two and a half years) past and perfective inflections are restricted primarily to telic and punctual verbs, progressive inflections are restricted primarily to activities, and imperfective[8] inflections are slower to emerge and, when they do appear they are initially restricted to activities and states.

FULLY PROFICIENT NATIVE SPEAKERS EXHIBIT A SIMILAR DISTRIBUTIONAL BIAS IN THE CLASSES OF VERBS TO WHICH THEY ATTACH VERBAL INFLECTIONS

Background

In my own work on Spanish as a second language, I concluded that second language learners follow the same path as first language learners: they restrict perfective inflections initially to telic and punctional verbs and, after a long period of using the unmarked third person singular present form for the imperfective, they first use the imperfective inflection on stative activity verbs (Andersen, 1985, 1986a, 1986b, 1990e). Since native Spanish allows perfective and imperfective inflections to be used on all four verb types, this seemed to be a significant finding.

Table 13.6. *Past inflected stative verbs by native and nonnative speakers of Spanish*

Native Speaker			Anthony-1	Anthony-2	Annette-1	Annette-2	
PFV	IMP		IMP	IMP	PFV	IMP	
1 estuvo	17 estaba	están	25 estaba	67 estaba	–	37 estaba	
6 tuvo	14 tenía	tiene	14 tenía	25 tenía	1 tuve	62 tenía	
1 quiso	5 quería	quiere	6 quería	9 quería	–	2 quería	
–	5 sabía	sabe	5 sabía	4 sabía	–	15 sabía	
2 pudo	5 podía	puedo	6 podía	1 podía	–	7 podía	

Note:
The five stative verbs are *estar* 'be,' *tener* 'have,' *querer* 'want,' *saber* 'know,' and *poder* 'be able'.

However, when I made a preliminary comparison with a sample of native Spanish speech collected as part of the original study, I found that even in native Spanish speech (in this case, the Spanish of a 16-year-old) perfective and imperfective inflections are distributed unequally across the four semantic types in ways similar to the first and second language learners' distributions. I will give only one example here, from Andersen (1986c). Table 13.6 displays all cases of all stative verbs that were used at least once in a past context by each of three speakers: a native speaker and two non-native speakers, Anthony and Annette, at two time periods. Anthony-1 and Annette-1 represent data from the first period after 2 years of residence in Puerto Rico and Anthony-2 and Annette-2, 2 years later. Anthony, at time 1, used only the unmarked 'present' form in past contexts and Anthony, at time 2, and Annette, at time 1, used only imperfective marked forms, even though statives can be inflected for perfective also. Annette, at time 2, used only one stative verb inflected for perfective. This distribution matches the predictions made from the first language acquisition studies. However, the native speaker used each of these verbs far more often with imperfective marking than with perfective marking, as can be seen in Table 13.6. In spite of the obvious limitations of these being individual case studies, these figures suggest that the learners' preference for imperfective marking on statives may be a direct reflection of the same relative distribution in the native input. Another possibility is that the native and the learner distributions are both due to the same factors.

Some recent case studies of distribution of inflections in native speech

In the Spring of 1990, a group of students and I studied the distribution of verb inflections in native speech according to semantic type, in order to test the Distributional Bias Hypothesis, which is that native speakers will tend to use past or perfective inflections more with telic and punctual events than with states or activities, progressive inflections primarily with activities, and imperfective inflections more with states and activities than with telic and punctual events (Andersen, 1989a:53, 1990a:58–9). That is, that proficient native speakers will exhibit in relative quantitative terms the same distributional bias found in more absolute terms in the acquisitional data. Here I will report the results of this inquiry.[9] I will not use any statistical tests of significance for 2 reasons: (1) given the preliminary nature of these studies and the fact that they were based on convenience samples, it seems inappropriate to use statistics; (2) the most appropriate statistical test for frequency counts would probably be the chi-square test. It is unclear, however, whether the required condition of independence of measures is met by such data.[10]

Simple examples of each type of morphological marking of tense and aspect in each language are given in (2). Only the verb form, in third person singular, without any subjects or objects, is given. English equivalents are meant to be only a rough approximation, since there is not a simple one-to-one equivalence between languages. (In the three cases where progressive was studied, we limited our analysis to past progressives.)

(2)

Language	Category	Example	English Equivalent
English	past	jumped	
	progressive	was jumping	
Spanish	perfective	habló	spoke
	imperfective	hablaba	used to speak/was speaking
	progressive	estaba hablando	was speaking
Italian	perfective	ha lavorato	worked/has worked
	imperfective	lavorava	used to work/was working
	progressive	stava lavorando	was working
	present	lavora	works
Japanese	perfective	mita	saw
	imperfective	miru	see

Table 13.7 displays the distribution of past and progressive inflections in the two English studies according to the four semantic categories (S = state, A = activity, T = telic event, P = punctual event). The study by Yap is based on an interview with a young musician. The study by Shirai, on the other hand, comes from a native English-speaking child interacting with a non-native child during play activities. If the Distributional Bias Hypothesis is valid, we would expect past inflections to occur most frequently with telic and punctual verbs and the progressive inflection mainly with activities in adult native speech. Each of these tables presents the results in two different counts. A token count treats each instance of a verb separately, whereas a type count treats multiple occurrences of the same verb with the particular inflection as one instance. It is not clear whether the DBH should be based on one or the other measures, so both are used here. For ease of exposition I will discuss the token count figures and only enter into the type count if the distribution differs considerably from the token count. The figures in the table are percentages rounded off to the nearest whole number and total 100% from left to right across the four semantic categories.

Yap's data in Table 13.7 fit the prediction only in the case of the

Table 13.7. *Two English case studies (Yap and Shirai). Distribution of past and* ing *forms in token and type counts*

(In percentages; raw scores given below)

	Token counts				Type counts			
	S	A	T	P	S	A	T	P
	%	%	%	%	%	%	%	%
YAP								
PAST	31	11	[17]	[42]	33	15	[19]	[33]
ING	16	[62]	10	11	27	[42]	15	15
SHIRAI								
PAST	21	1	[4]	[74]	30	3	[9]	[58]
ING	9	[59]	6	25	9	[52]	9	30

	Raw scores									
	Token					Type				
	S	A	T	P	Total	S	A	T	P	Total
Y-PAST	37	13	20	51	*121*	18	8	10	18	*54*
Y-*ING*	10	38	6	7	*61*	7	11	4	4	*26*
S-PAST	14	1	3	50	*68*	10	1	3	19	*33*
S-*ING*	3	19	2	8	*32*	2	12	2	7	*23*

Note:
[ ] indicate PREDICTED highest frequency

progressive inflection, whereas Shirai's data fit both predictions. The main differences between these two sets of data is that in the Yap data there are many more cases of past inflections on stative, activity, and telic event verbs. At this point we can only speculate that this is because the data come from an interview in contrast with the more spontaneous conversation during play among children in the Shirai data. Yap's data contain frequent cases of past-time reference for typical and habitual situations in the past of the type, 'when I was a

Table 13.8. *A Spanish case study (Gonzales). Distribution of past and progressive forms in token and type counts*

(In percentages; raw scores given below)

	Token counts				Type counts			
	S	A	T	P	S	A	T	P
	%	%	%	%	%	%	%	%
Perfective	24	3	[1]	[71]	15	8	[3]	[74]
Imperfective	[58]	[11]	1	30	[33]	[28]	2	37
Past progressive	13	[53]	3	33	4	[46]	4	36

	Raw scores									
	Token					Type				
	S	A	T	P	Total	S	A	T	P	Total
PFV	51	6	3	149	*210*	12	6	2	58	*78*
IMP	244	46	4	128	*422*	28	24	2	32	*86*
PRG	5	21	1	13	*40*	4	13	1	10	*28*

Note:

[ ] indicate PREDICTED highest frequency

boy, I did such and such', where each past-inflected verb refers not to a unitary event but to typical situations or events, which tends to increase use of statives and activities.

Table 13.8 summarizes data from several Spanish interviews and conversations analyzed by Patrick Gonzales. Since there are so few cases of telic verbs, I will not consider them in the discussion. The predictions hold for the perfective and progressive inflections. For the imperfective, the greater than expected number of punctual verbs with imperfective marker is counter to our predictions. These cases are primarily uses of the imperfective for past habitual situations, as was the case for the Yap data on English.

The summary in Table 13.9 from an interview with an Italian speaker recorded and analyzed by Paola Leone again supports the

Table 13.9. *An Italian case study (Leone). Distribution of past and progressive forms in token and type counts*

(In percentages; raw scores given below)

	Token counts				Type counts			
	S	A	T	P	S	A	T	P
	%	%	%	%	%	%	%	%
Perfective	0	3	[6]	[91]	0	5	[5]	[90]
Imperfective	[24]	[48]	14	14	[29]	[29]	21	21
Past progressive	0	[0]	100	0	0	[0]	100	0
Present	60	11	15	15	53	12	12	24

Raw scores

	Token					Type				
	S	A	T	P	Total	S	A	T	P	Total
PFV	0	1	2	32	*35*	0	1	1	20	*22*
IMP	5	10	3	3	*21*	4	4	3	3	*14*
PRG	0	0	2	0	*2*	0	0	1	0	*1*
PRES	16	3	4	4	*27*	9	2	2	4	*17*

Note:
[ ] indicate PREDICTED highest frequency

hypothesis for perfective inflections, but much less so for imperfective inflections. It is true that the largest percentages are for states and activities as predicted, for the token counts, but the type counts are very close to an even distribution across all verb types. This is the only study that includes a frequency count of verbs with present inflections. It is interesting that the greatest frequency for present inflections is with states. The cases of past progressives are too small to discuss, although they are in a semantic category which does not match the prediction.[11]

The Japanese data in Table 13.10 appears to fit the predictions for perfective inflections, although the telic event verbs are much lower

Table 13.10. *Two Japanese case studies. Distribution of perfective and imperfective forms in token and type counts*

(In percentages; raw scores given below)

	Token counts				Type counts			
	S	A	T	P	S	A	T	P
	%	%	%	%	%	%	%	%
Study-1								
Perfective	19	21	[13]	[48]	20	21	[12]	[47]
Imperfective	[23]	[65]	2	10	[13]	[63]	3	20
Study-2								
Perfective	20	14	[14]	[52]	25	17	[13]	[45]
Imperfective	[38]	[17]	12	33	[29]	[20]	10	41

	Raw scores									
	Token					Type				
	S	A	T	P	Total	S	A	T	P	Total
1-PFV	21	23	14	53	*111*	13	14	8	31	66
1-IMP	14	39	1	6	*60*	4	19	1	6	*30*
2-PFV	7	5	5	18	*35*	6	4	3	11	*24*
2-IMP	25	11	3	25	*66*	12	8	2	19	*41*

Note: [ ] indicate PREDICTED highest frequency. Study-1 by Takahashi. Study-2 by Takashima and Kamibayashi

than predicted, and state and activity verbs much higher. The cases with imperfective inflections are less clear. Study 1 fits the predictions better than study 2, and the type count for study 2 clearly does not fit the predictions. Study 1 consists of five 'stories' retold by adult native speakers of Japanese based on a storybook for children. Study 2 is from an interview with an elderly Japanese woman born in Japan, but who had lived most of her life in the United States.

Table 13.11. *Summary across studies*

(Percentages)

	Token counts			Type counts		
	S	A	T/P	S	A	T/P
	%	%	%	%	%	%
(1) Past/perfective						
Yap-past	31	11	59	33	15	52
Shirai-past	21	1	78	30	3	67
SPN–PFV	24	3	72	15	8	77
ITL–PFV	0	3	97	0	5	95
JPN-1 PFV	19	21	61	20	21	59
JPN-2 PFV	20	14	66	25	17	58
(2) Progressive						
Yap-*ing*	16	62	21	27	42	30
Shirai-*ing*	9	59	31	9	52	39
SPN–PROG.	13	53	36	14	46	40
(3) Imperfective						
SPN–IMP	58	11	31	33	28	39
ITL–IMP	24	48	28	29	29	42
JPN-1 IMP	23	65	12	13	63	23
JPN-2 IMP	38	17	45	29	20	51
(4) Present						
ITL–PRES	60	11	30	53	12	36

In our working group discussions, we became increasingly aware of the fact that telic event verbs were generally less frequent than other verb types. Given this lower frequency, the failure of the prediction that a high percentage of past- and perfective-inflected verbs will be telic verbs could be simply a consequence of this low frequency of telic verbs in general. Telic events and punctual events can be viewed as sharing a higher level category, which we might call simply 'event' (Mourelatos, 1981). What they share is that the event has a momentary end-point or, in some cases, starting-point, as with 'leave, take off'. Many of the acquisition studies treat telic events and punctual events as one category. Given the lower frequency in general of what I have called telic events up to this point, it may be that the more functional category is that which combines telic and punctual events.

In Table 13.11 the four semantic categories have been reduced to three, with telic and punctual events combined into one. Table 13.11 summarizes across these studies in four groups – (1) past and perfective inflections as one category, (2) the progressive as a second, (3) imperfectives as a third, and (4) a single present category left over as the fourth group.

This display allows us to see that (1) a greater proportion of telic and punctual verbs (as a combined category) receive past or perfective inflections than the other three categories and (2) a greater proportion of activity verbs receive the progressive inflection than is the case for past, perfective, and present forms. Perhaps the best generalization concerning the imperfective inflections is that a lower proportion of the imperfective inflections are on telic or punctual verbs than was the case for the perfective inflections. The distribution across states and activities is less clear across these four sets of data. Although we have data from only one of the studies on present inflections, the best generalization here is that the present tense inflections occur most frequently with stative verbs. This is quite logical. 'Present' really means in many languages 'not restricted to any past time frame'. So-called 'present' situations are true at any time and thus continue to be true unless some change in the situation occurs. Similarly, states continue without the input of additional energy to keep them going. Present inflections are thus congruent with the semantic category 'stative'.

HOW CAN WE RECONCILE THESE TWO SETS OF EMPIRICAL OBSERVATIONS?

I believe that the acquisitional data can be explained by four acquisitional principles and a conceptual prime. Let me begin with the conceptual prime. The perceptual systems of humans and other animals allow or perhaps we might say force us to distinguish an important or foregrounded entity or event from all of the unimportant or less important events or situations or the background to the entity or the situation. Thus we are able to see a familiar face in a crowd, or we can carry on conversation in a crowded noisy party by filtering out all sound (chatter, shouting, music, street noise, fans, etc.) that is not relevant or important and taking in the significant sound or the person or persons we are conversing with, in contrast to a microphone, which will treat all sounds as equal. According to this basic notion of distinguishing figure from ground, we would say that the learner perceives the punctual or telic events as key, important, foreground, and learns to mark them as such and to not mark the background events or situations.[12]

Bybee (1985) and Slobin (1985) discuss a Relevance Principle (see also Woisetschlaeger (1976), cited by Bloom, Lifter and Hafitz, 1980). According to this principle, a grammatical morpheme, such as a verb inflection, will be placed closer to the verb stem the more relevant the meaning of the morpheme is to the meaning of the verb. Thus, assuming that each morpheme is independent (which is often not the case), an aspectual morpheme would be placed closer to the stem than a tense morpheme, because aspect is more relevant to the meaning of the stem than the time when the event occurred, and a tense morpheme would be placed closer to the stem than an agreement morpheme, because the time of occurrence of the event is more relevant to the meaning of the stem than is information about the subject (encoded as an agreement marker). The Relevance Principle thus predicts that learners will initially attach an inflection to a verb stem according to the inherent aspect of the verb. This also indirectly explains why inflections that mark tense in the adult language (past markers in English, for example) are initially used by learners according to aspectual notions such as completed, terminated – such a notion is implied in the tense notion, past, but the aspectual notion is more relevant to the meaning of the verb.

However, it appears that the operation of the Relevance Principle is mediated by what I will call a Congruence Principle: a grammatical morpheme is used by learners according to how congruent the meaning of the morpheme is with the meaning of the lexical item to which it is attached. Progressive morphemes are especially relevant to activities, which have inherent duration like the duration conveyed by the morpheme itself, and past and perfective inflections are especially relevant to punctual and telic events. 'Past' can be conceptualized as referring to an event that is finished, over with, as can 'perfective', and both apply most logically to telic and punctual events, which by their very nature are finished and over with once they have occurred. Present morphology typically refers to situations that are continually true and present inflections are logically more relevant to states (as well as, perhaps, activities) than to telic and punctual events, since states continue to exist and are timeless. Thus, the first inflections that children use are those that are most relevant to the meaning of the verb (the Relevance Principle) and of these inflections, it is the inflection whose meaning is most congruent with the meaning of the verb stem that will be attached to a particular verb (the Congruence Principle).

A third principle that appears to account for the acquisitional data is the One-to-One Principle (Andersen, 1984a), which guides the learner to assume that each grammatical morpheme he discovers has one and only one meaning, function, and distribution. Combined with the Relevance Principle and the Congruence Principle, the 1:1 Principle would guide the learner to assume that a verbal inflection is attached *only* to verbs that are congruent in meaning with the meaning of the inflection.

A fourth and related principle is the Subset Principle (see Hyams, 1986: 24, footnote 7) and also Pinker's related Continuity Assumption (Pinker, 1984:6–9). According to the Subset Principle, learners will assign a more conservative form:meaning relation to a morpheme or syntactic structure than fully proficient native adults in such a way that the learner's form–meaning relation is a logical subset of the proficient adult's form–meaning relation. Thus, using past or perfective inflections only on telic and punctual events is a logical subset of using the inflections on any verb type in that the learner can gradually extend the applicability of the inflection from the more conservative subset of verb types progressively to a wider and wider range until it can be used with all verbs.

Learners – both first and second language learners – are therefore conservative in their initial use of verb inflections along the lines discussed here because they follow the perceptual and conceptual need to distinguish figure from ground and are guided by the Relevance Principle, the Congruence Principle, the One-to-One Principle, and the Subset Principle in constructing minimal logical form:meaning relations and systems.

But what then of the apparent similarity between fully proficient adult speakers' use of these inflections and the learner's initial conservative use of the same inflections? I believe that the same principles that apply to learners apply to fully proficient native speakers with two additional developments: (1) The more diverse speech of the proficient speakers includes additional marked meanings and functions for forms that learners initially internalize in more conservative unmarked uses. (2) Fully proficient native speakers at some time have added to their repertoire new and more marked forms that are beyond the reach of less experienced language learners. These 'acquisitional' principles appear to be relevant only to underdeveloped morphological systems typical of language learners. However, once we take into account the later acquisition of more marked uses of pre-existing forms and acquisition of new but more marked forms, it is not so counterintuitive to suggest that these same principles apply to normal language use by fully proficient speakers.

The samples of native speech used here are samples based on convenience and overrepresent one particular type of speech event – the open-ended interview – primarily because this is one of the most logical speech events to participate in when the two participants are seated next to a tape recorder with the purpose of getting one of the participants to 'talk'. I would speculate that the type of speech event which would be more representative of the type of speech event learners more typically participate in would be highly concrete, non-abstract, non-specialized conversation about real and realized unitary events and activities. Most of the samples I have used are from a more specialized speech genre and include a greater number of marked uses of verb forms than would be found in conversation.

In conversations – which I would assume would be more like the naturalistic child language data, which is also conversational – I believe the distributional bias in use of inflections with different verb types would be even more in the direction of the acquisition data, precisely because the speakers would have fewer occasions to use more marked forms typical of higher education levels, professional jargon, complex abstract discussion, hypothetical reference, etc. For example, each use of a past form for contrary to fact reference (*If I knew that . . .*) is a move away from the distributional bias we expect, as is each use of past forms in English and imperfective forms in Spanish to talk about typical past situations rather than one particular unitary action or event.

I believe that the Congruence Principle is especially important in explaining the similarities in distribution of inflections in learner speech and the speech of fully proficient native speakers. Most language use is highly redundant and has a high degree of predictability such that even without the particular verb inflection the listener could interpret the time reference and aspect for each proposition. Let us assume that a speaker is about to say something about part of an event that took place prior to the moment of speaking. He would choose a verb appropriate for reporting the event and, almost simultaneously, the appropriate verb inflection for that verb. If he is reporting a real event, he is highly likely to choose a telic or punctual verb to report it and, depending on the language he is speaking, a past or perfective inflection for the verb. Both choices – the particular verb and the inflection attached to it – are motivated by the information the speaker intends to convey. It is perhaps in this way that inflections most congruent with the meaning of the verb get attached to verbs.

Because of this type of redundancy, the verb inflection attached to the verb would be, in most cases, the one that is the most congruent with the inherent semantics of the verb in 'normal, non-specialized conversation'. Thus we would expect that most verbs used to report real events that took place in a past time frame would be verbs that depict situations that have an end-point inherent in the meaning of the verb, and thus past morphemes would be more naturally associated with punctual and telic verbs; and progressive morphemes would occur most naturally with verbs that depict events that are in themselves already durative.[13] The grammatical morpheme thus adds little, if any, totally new information.

The cases where the verb morpheme has a high information load would be where the morpheme is *least expected*: for example, a progressive morpheme on a punctual verb, since without the progressive inflection we would have to assume a non-durative interpretation; and a past morpheme on a stative verb since, as states continue without interruption, without the past morpheme we would not normally understand that the state *only* existed in a past time frame. Thus a small number of uses of the verb morphemes in the speech of fully proficient adult native speakers would be extremely important in conveying the speaker's perspective – those uses where the meaning of the verb morpheme is not at all congruent with the meaning of the verb and not at all predictable from the context.

Following this argument, an overall frequency count (whether type or token counts are best is not yet clear) would show that each morpheme occurs most frequently with verbs that are congruent with the meaning of the morpheme. Therefore the distribution of the verb morphemes in adult native speech and in child language learners and non-native learners all have the same source: a Congruence Principle which operates in conjunction with the figure–ground distinction, the Relevance Principle, the One-to-One Principle, and the Subset Principle discussed earlier with regard to acquisition. The *real* development in language learning and the real virtuosity in native speaker language use occurs when the speaker or learner gains expressive control over the use of each morpheme so that he can intentionally (although presumably subconsciously) *impose* his own perspective on each proposition through the use of the morphology. For the learner's repertoire this would include adding the marked uses of existing forms to the more conservative uses of these forms. In addition, he will acquire marked forms that did not exist in his earlier repertoire.

CONCLUSION

The implications of these findings and the explanation offered here are far-reaching. Most if not all of the studies on acquisition of verb inflections seem to assume that language learners are doing something different with these inflections from what fully proficient native speakers do with them. Proficient native speakers use past markers to convey the notion of past time reference, whereas novice learners apparently use the same markers to encode a notion of completion or end point. If it is true, however, that the distribution of these inflections across verb types in native speech is not quantitatively very different from the distributions in learner speech, then this finding calls such an assumption into question. This still leaves unresolved the ultimate source of such a similarity. There are at least two logical possibilities: (1) Learners and proficient users are both subject to the principles I have discussed and thus the distribution of forms in learner speech is not due so much to some 'process of acquisition' by itself as to operation of the same set of principles that govern normal adult language use (the Relevance Principle and the Congruence Principle) interacting with principles that are more relevant to novices, such as the One-to-One Principle and the Subset Principle. (2) Proficient native speakers modify their speech in interaction with learners in such a way that they model for the learners the more limited distribution of inflections across verb types, but use a less restricted distribution in speech with other native speakers. The one study I know of that reports data relevant to this question (Stephany, 1981)[14] clearly shows that mothers' use of tense-aspect inflections in speech to their children is indeed simplified in the direction of the distributional bias discussed in this paper, in comparison with the same mothers' speech to their adult peers. However, even in their speech to their adult peers, these adult native speakers exhibit a quantitative distributional bias in the use of verbal inflections. Even if caretakers modify their speech in this way to inexperienced learners, and even if this is a partial source of the distribution of the inflections in the learners' speech, the distribution of the inflections in the speech of the mothers to other adults still remains to be explained, as does the distribution of forms in adult native language use reported in this paper.

There are thus three possible sources of the limited distribution of inflections reported in the summaries of child language acquisition studies in Tables 13.3–5 of this paper: (1) principles such as the One-to-One Principle and the Subset Principle cause learners to restrict the distribution of inflections in their own speech even if the speech addressed to them is not so severely restricted, (2) principles such as the Relevance Principle and the Congruence Principle, which apply to proficient (i.e., natives and near natives) and novice speakers (i.e., learners) alike, independently motivate such a distribution without any need to posit special acquisitional processes to account for them, and (3) learners receive modified input that provides misleading models for the learners: the learners are simply matching the distribution of forms in the input they receive. Since the second source, which applies to normal native language use as well as learner speech, requires explanation regardless of the importance of the other two sources that are specific to the language acquisition setting, I would consider that this source requires the most serious attention in further research.

NOTES

1 This chapter is one part of a series of studies of tense, mood, and aspect in language acquisition and use, with a special focus on creole languages. Portions of this chapter have benefited from research grants from the UCLA Academic Senate Research Committee and the US

National Science Foundation (grant no. BNS 88-12750). I am grateful to the students whose work is reflected in this chapter for their insightful questions and contributions. I have benefited from comment and criticisms by the following friends: Marianne Celce-Murcia, Patrick Gonzales, Sally Jacoby, Charlene Polio, John Schumann, and Yas Shirai.

2 Fathers of two of the children.

3 The two areas are verbal and nominal morphology and their semantic and discourse-pragmatic counterparts of tense, mood, aspect, and agreement (for verb morphology) and nominal reference (for nominal morphology). The ultimate goal is, of course, to investigate relationships across the two areas.

4 Languages vary considerably with regard to the particular categories they encode for tense and aspect. It is misleading to group 'past' and 'perfective' together as if they were similar. This general statement is based on the observation in the literature that past forms in languages like English, and perfective forms in languages like Spanish and Italian, are treated in similar ways by learners. See Andersen (1990d) for further details.

5 Different accounts in the literature explain these findings in different ways. I will not go into each account here. For more details, however, see Andersen (1990d) and Weist et al. (1984) and the series of exchanges between Rispoli and Bloom (1985), Smith and Weist (1987), and Bloom and Harner (1989).

6 See Bybee (1985) for independent reasons for third person singular present being the least marked verbal form in languages in general. The marked nature of English third person singular present is exceptional crosslinguistically.

7 For our purposes here, 'obligatorily' means that, when the conditions for that particular aspectual distinction in that particular language are met, an explicit linguistic device (usually an auxiliary or inflection) must be used.

8 Imperfective marking in Polish is really partly lack of marking, the unmarked verb in many cases and suppletive derivation in other cases, which gives the impression that children acquire marking for imperfectivity much earlier when acquiring Polish than when acquiring languages like Spanish, Portuguese, and French. The differences between Slavic languages and non-Slavic languages in marking aspect

deserve better treatment than is given here. But this would take us far beyond the purpose of this chapter.

9 The English studies were done by Foong Ha Yap and Yasuhiro Shirai, the Spanish study by Patrick Gonzales, the Italian study by Paola Leone, and the two Japanese studies by Kazumi Takahashi (Study-1) and Hideyuki Takashima and Keiko Kamibayashi (Study-2).

10 I owe this observation to Evelyn Hatch (personal communication).

11 Since telic events share the feature 'durative' with activities, these two occurrences of past progressives with telic event verbs do not really violate the predictions. At any rate, the number is too small to deal with.

12 Yas Shirai (p.c.) has pointed out to me that while figure-ground is good for accounting for early acquisition of past or perfective inflections on telic or punctual verbs, it does not appear to explain the early acquisition of progressive -ing or -ndo in English and Spanish.

13 This applies to activities (and possibly to telic events), but not to states, even though both activities and states are 'durative' in one sense. Perhaps we need to be more precise in specifying that the progressive -ing inflection and activities are durative, but also *dynamic*.

14 I am indebted to Yas Shirai, who made me aware of the importance of Stephany (1981) to the issue discussed here.

REFERENCES

Andersen, R. W. (1978), An implicational model for second language research. *Language Learning*, 28, 221–82.

(1983), Transfer to somewhere. In Gass, S., and Selinker, L. (eds.), *Language Transfer in Language Learning*. New York: Newbury House.

(1984a), The one to one principle of interlanguage construction. *Language Learning*, 34, 77–95.

(1984b), What's gender good for, anyway? In Andersen, R. W. (ed.), *Second languages: A cross-linguistic perspective*. New York: Newbury House.

(ed.) (1984c), *Second languages: A cross-linguistic perspective*. New York: Newbury House.

(1985), Interpreting data. Plenary address. Los Angeles Second Language Research Forum.

(1986a), El desarrollo de la morfología verbal en el español como segundo idioma. In Meisel, J. M. (ed.), *Adquisición de lenguaje/ Aquisição da linguagem*. Frankfurt/M.: Vervuert.

(1986b), Interpreting data: second language acquisition of verbal aspect. Unpublished manuscript.

(1986c), The need for native languages comparison data in interpreting second language data. Unpublished MS. Invited Forum Lecture, 1986 TESOL Summer Institute, University of Hawai'i.

(1987), Mood and modality in Papiamentu. Unpublished MS.

(1988), Models, processes, principles, and strategies: Second language acquisition in and out of the classroom. *IDEAL*, 3, 111–38.

(1989a), The theoretical status of variation in interlanguage development. In Gass, S. et al. (eds.), *Variation in second language acquisition: Psycholinguistic issues*, pp. 46–64. Clevedon, England: Multilingual Matters.

(1989b), The 'up' and 'down' staircase in second language development. In Dorian, N. (ed.), *Investigating obsolescence. Studies in language contraction and death*, pp. 385–94. Cambridge: Cambridge University Press.

(1990a), Models, processes, principle, and strategies: Second language acquisition in and out of the classroom. In Van Patten, B., and Lee, J. F. (eds.), *Second language acquisition – Foreign language learning*, pp. 45–78. Clevedon and Philadelphia: Multilingual Matters. (Revised version of Andersen 1988.)

(1990b), Papiamentu tense-aspect, with special attention to discourse. In Singler, J. (ed.), *Pidgin and creole tense-mood-aspect systems*, pp. 59–96. Amsterdam: John Benjamins.

(1990c), Verbal virtuosity and speakers' purposes. In Burmeister, H., and Rounds, P. L. (eds.), *Variability in second language acquisition*, pp. 1–24. Proceedings of the Tenth Annual Second Language Research Forum, University of Oregon. Department of Linguistics, University of Oregon, Eugene, Oregon.

(1990d), La adquisición de la morfología verbal. *Lingüística* 1, 89–141. (Original English version, written August, 1988 as Acquisition of verbal morphology, available from author.)

(1990e), Developmental sequences: the emergence of aspect marking in second language acquisition. In Huebner, T., and

Ferguson, C. A. (eds.), *Cross-currents in second language acquisition and linguistic theories*. Amsterdam and Philadelphia: John Benjamins.

Antinucci, F., and Miller, R. (1976), How children talk about what happened. *Journal of Child Language*, 3, 169–89.

Bloom, L., and Harner, L. (1989), On the developmental contour of child language: a reply to Smith and Weist. *Journal of Child Language*, 16, 207–16.

Bloom, L., Lifter, K., and Hafitz, J. (1980), Semantics of verbs and the development of verb inflection in child language. *Language*, 56, 386–412.

Bybee, J. (1985), *Morphology*. Amsterdam and Philadelphia: John Benjamins.

Bybee, J., and Dahl, Ö. (1989), The creation of tense and aspect systems in the languages of the world. *Studies in Language*, 13:1; 51–103.

Clark, E. (1985), The acquisition of Romance, with special reference to French. In Slobin, D. (ed.), *The crosslinguistic study of language acquisition*. I; pp. 687–782. *The data*. Hillsdale, New Jersey: Lawrence Erlbaum.

Eisenberg, A. R. (1982), Language acquisition in cultural perspective: Talk in three Mexicano homes. Unpublished Ph.D. thesis, University of California, Berkeley.

Gonzales, P. (1989), The emergence of verbal morphology in early child language: a reanalysis of Eisenberg 1982. Unpublished term paper, Applied Linguistics, University of California at Los Angeles.

(1990), The imperfect–past progressive distinction in Spanish discourse: An aspectual analysis. Unpublished MA thesis, University of California at Los Angeles.

Hyams, N. M. (1986), *Language acquisition and the theory of parameters*. Dordrecht and Boston: D. Reidel.

Leone, P. (1990), Tense and aspect in Italian: A bias in the distribution of verbal inherent semantics and verb morphology. Unpublished term paper Applied Linguistics, University of California at Los Angeles.

Mourelatos, A. P. (1981), Events, processes, and states. In Tedeschi, P. J., and Zaenen, A. (eds.), *Syntax and semantics. Volume 14:*

tense and aspect, pp. 191–212. New York: Academic Press.

Pinker, S. (1984), *Language learnability and language development*. Cambridge, Mass.: Harvard University Press.

Rispoli, M., and Bloom, L. (1985), Incomplete and continuing: theoretical issues in the acquisition of tense and aspect. *Journal of Child Language*, 12, 471–4.

Shirai, Y. (1990), The defective tense hypothesis: Is there a distributional bias in the input? Unpublished term paper, Applied Linguistics, University of California at Los Angeles.

Slobin, D. I. (1985), Crosslinguistic evidence for the language-making capacity. In Slobin, D. I. (ed.), *The crosslinguistic study of language acquisition*. II, pp. 1157–256. Hillsdale, New Jersey: Lawrence Erlbaum.

Smith, C. S., and Weist, R. M. (1987), On the temporal contour of child language: a reply to Rispoli and Bloom. *Journal of Child Language*, 14, 387–92.

Stephany, U. (1981), Verbal grammar in Modern Greek early child language. In Dale, P., and Ingram, D. (eds.), *Child language: an international perspective*, pp. 45–57. Baltimore: University Park Press.

Takahashi, K. (1990), A study of tense-aspect marking in Japanese narrative. Unpublished term paper. Applied Linguistics, University of California at Los Angeles.

Takashima, H., and Kamibayashi, K. (1990), Superman and PTA. Is there a distributional bias in Japanese? Unpublished term paper, Applied Linguistics, University of California at Los Angeles.

Vendler, Z. (1967), Verbs and times. In *Linguistics in Philosophy, Zeno Vendler*, 97–121. Ithaca, N.Y.: Cornell University Press.

Weist, R. M., Wysocka, H., Witkowska-Stadnik, K., Buczowska, W., and Konieczna, E. (1984), The defective tense hypothesis: on the emergence of tense and aspect in child Polish. *Journal of Child Language*, 11, 347–74.

Woisetschlaeger, E. (1976), A Semantic theory of the English auxiliary system. MIT thesis.

Yap, F. H. (1990), Semantic categories in an adult speech sample: A case against the distributional bias hypothesis? Unpublished term paper, Applied Linguistics, University of California at Los Angeles.

14   Crosslinguistic perspectives
on lexical organization and
lexical progression[1]

ÅKE VIBERG

This chapter will be concerned with lexical progression at the individual level, that is with first and second language acquisition. In the conclusion, the relation of these areas to other types of progression and to regression will be briefly discussed. The chapter will open with a brief presentation of a general framework for studying the organization of the lexicon from a crosslinguistic perspective, since a proper understanding of language structure is a prerequisite for any deeper understanding of the learning process and more general explanatory factors.

THE ORGANIZATION OF THE BASIC LEXICON

Frequency ranking and semantic field classification

The fundamental problem with the lexicon is its size. In any full-blown natural language, the number of lexical items which are actively commanded by a native speaker is in the tens of thousands. In order to give a holistic account of lexical structure, a method must be found to delimit a set of basic words which represent the lexical core of a given language.

A simple method which has been shown to be very useful is frequency ranking within word classes. Words within each of the four open word classes are ranked with respect to frequency and classified into semantic fields. It is then possible to compare languages with respect to the meanings of the words belonging to a

340

certain part of speech at different frequency ranks (e.g. the 10, 20, 50, or 100 most frequent verbs). From studies I have carried out based on frequency dictionaries for 11 European languages, it can be shown that a small number of fields cover most of the highest ranked words within each part of speech and, furthermore, that there are many striking similarities with respect to the basic meaning of the most frequent members of these fields across languages. Several of these meanings are typologically unmarked and appear at the top of universal lexicalization hierarchies.

A (lexical) semantic field is defined as a set of words which belong to the same word class and which are closely related in meaning. In order to delimit a field, reference has often been made to a superordinate term covering all and only the words belonging to the field. Thus 'tool' is superordinate to words such as *hammer, tongs,* and *screwdriver* and 'colour', although not strictly a superordinate term since it is a noun, covers a field of adjectives such as *white, black, red,* etc. In several cases, however, words which are often regarded as members of the same semantic field cannot be subsumed under a superordinate term, e.g. verbs of possession such as *own, receive, give,* and *sell.* A more powerful definition is to say that a semantic field is organized around a core concept. This approach is taken in Miller and Johnson-Laird (1976), who, for example, assume that verbs of possession are organized around the abstract predicate POSSESS (x,y) and verbs of motion around TRAVEL (x). Superordinates can be looked upon as a special case of core concepts.

A brief view of English lexical structure

Many of the most basic characteristics of English lexical structure are typical of European languages in general. An areal typological characteristic of European languages is that all the four open parts of speech (N, V, ADJ, ADV) are well developed, in the sense that they are distinguished formally in a clear way, and that they form large classes with several thousand members. Several groups of non-European languages do not have special classes of adjectives and adverbs or have very small classes of such words, while nouns and verbs probably can be distinguished in all languages (Schachter 1985). Table 14.1 shows the result of applying the method of frequency ranking to the four open word classes in English.

It is more or less an established practice to talk about fields such as dimensional adjectives, motion verbs, possession verbs, and verbal communication verbs. But, actually, the semantic fields form a hierarchical structure. To take just a few examples, motion verbs together with position verbs such as *live, stay* (in a place) are included in a field, which can be referred to as spatial verbs. The more extensive fields can be referred to as macro-fields. At the same time, traditionally recognized fields can be divided into sub-fields. Within the field of motion verbs, for example, there is a primary division between reflexive and objective verbs of motion. The first category refers to verbs where the moving entity appears as subject (*go, rise, fall*) and the second to verbs where it appears as object (*put, raise, throw*). It is also possible to make further divisions within these sub-fields. The reflexive motion verbs, for example, can be divided into sub-fields such as deictic verbs (*come, go*), directional verbs (*rise, sink, fall, descend, enter* etc) and verbs of bodily locomotion (*walk, run, creep, swim* etc). Sometimes even smaller fields are recognized such as verbs of walking (*stroll, waddle, shuffle, strut, trip,* etc). Where to cease making further divisions is of course arbitrary from a strictly logical point of view. In principle, it is possible to talk about fields with only a few members such as verbs of stealing (*pinch, bone* etc). For some special purpose such as a study of criminal argot, such a classification can make sense, but for general purposes, the system of semantic fields has a basic level which has been more or less established in linguistic practice. In general, I refer to groups of words at this level simply as 'fields', but sometimes 'field' is used as a neutral term. If confusion arises, the term basic field can be used in the more restricted sense. In Table 14.1, some macro-fields have been indicated followed by a colon above the names of the (basic) fields that are recognized in this study.

As is obvious from the table, some macro-fields such as Spatial,

Temporal and Modal are so general that concepts belonging to these fields are realized as several different word classes. For example, partonymic nouns, dimensional adjectives, verbs of motion, and spatial adverbs represent different subtypes of spatial concepts. Even grammatical categories realized as bound inflection (e.g. local cases) or closed word classes (e.g. spatial adpositions) belong to such macrofields. Fields, which are so general that they cut across the boundaries of the open word classes, or even between lexicon and grammar, should perhaps rather be regarded as conceptual fields.

As has already been mentioned, only words belonging to the same word class form (lexical) semantic fields. In this way, it is possible to specify a number of basic semantic fields which tend universally to be realized as noun, verb or adjective roots. As Dixon (1977) has shown, if a language has adjectives, Dimension, Age, Value, and Colour are realized as adjectives in the unmarked case. Such generalizations, of course, apply only to root morphemes and not to derived words. Through derivation a certain root can often be recategorized as some of the other open word classes: *wide* (Dimensional adjective) – *widen* – *width* – *widely*.

Frequency is especially useful as a tool to identify the most basic types of verbs and adjectives. Among nouns, the most frequent words in general are not the most typical ones. Within the prototypical and large fields called Person and Physical object, only a few of the most generic nouns are found in Table 14.1. At least in European languages, temporal units such as *year*, *day*, and (often) *week* are found among the ten most frequent nouns, obviously due to their use in temporal adverbial phrases. Among the most frequent adverbs, finally, temporal and spatial concepts tend to dominate.

Lexical markedness

A further hypothesis, which it has been possible to substantiate to a relatively high degree at least for verbs and adjectives, is that the meanings of several of the most frequent words within a specific part of speech are typologically unmarked and appear at the top of

Table 14.1. *English Top Twenty. The 20 most frequent words within the open word classes in English (based on Francis and Kučera, 1982)*

Noun

Person	Physical object	Part: bodypart	Spatial: general	Temporal	Other
1 man	12 thing	11 hand	4 state	2 time	6 way
7 people			8 world	3 year	9 life
			17 place	5 day	10 work
					16 number
					19 course
		OTHER PART	BUILDING	COGNITION	VERBAL COMMUNICATION
		15 part	13 house	20 problem	18 word
			14 school		

Adjective

Spatial: dimension	Temporal: age	value	colour	nationality	Other
5 great	1 new	4 good	18 white	9 American	2 such
7 small	6 old				3 own
8 long	11 young				13 important
10 high					15 social
14 large			MODAL		16 general
17 big					19 national

Verb

General dynamic	Modal	Spatial: motion	Possession	Production
1 be	3 will	9 go	2 have	7 make
4 do	5 can	11 come	10 take	
19 use	8 may		14 give	
	16 shall		15 get	
	18 must			

Verbal Communication	Perception	Cognition
6 say	12 see	13 know
	17 find	20 think

Adverb

Spatial	Temporal			Value	Other
6 here	2 then	10 never	18 often	9 well	1 only
11 back	3 now	13 again	20 ever		4 also
14 there	7 just	15 always		ORDER	5 even
16 away	8 still	17 once		19 first	12 so

Table 14.2. *Basic verbs in European languages*

a Reflecting universal tendencies: The nuclear verbs

Motion	Possession	Production	Verbal communication	Perception	Cognition	Desire
GO (10)	GIVE (11)	MAKE (10)	SAY (11)	SEE (11)	KNOW (9)	WANT (8)
COME (8)	TAKE (11)					

b Areally specific basic verbs

c Subareally specific basic verb

General dynamic	Modal verbs		Possession /State
BE (11)	CAN (11)		HAVE (8)
	MUST (9)		

The figures within parentheses state the number of languages in which a verb with the given meaning belongs to the twenty most frequent ones. *Languages*: English, German, Swedish; French, Spanish, Italian, Rumanian; Russian, Polish; Finnish, Hungarian.

universal lexicalization hierarchies. To begin with, there is a striking similarity between European languages. In Viberg (in progress), a comparison is made between the 20 most frequent verbs in 11 European languages. The result is shown in Table 14.2. It turns out that 6 basic meanings are realized by one of the 20 most frequent verbs in all 11 languages (BE, CAN, GIVE, TAKE, SAY, SEE) and that 2 meanings are realized within this frequency range in all but one language (GO, MAKE). The absence of one of these meanings from one language each is primarily due to the arbitrariness of the cut-off point 20. Several of the verbs with the meanings given in Table 14.2 belong to the most basic or unmarked verbs in several groups of non-European and completely unrelated languages. These verbs are shown in section (a) of Table 14.2 and will henceforth be referred to as nuclear verbs. The nuclear verbs are the typologically least marked verbs within their respective semantic fields. This is reflected in lexicalization hierarchies based on implicational univer- sals of the type discussed in Greenberg (1966). In Viberg (1984), a markedness hierarchy is presented for the verbs of perception based on data from approximately 50 languages. In slightly simplified form, this hierarchy can be stated as follows:

SEE > HEAR > FEEL > TASTE, SMELL

If a language has only one verb of perception, the basic meaning is 'see'. If it has two, the basic meanings are 'see' and 'hear' etc. As can be seen, the first step of the hierarchy is reflected in the frequency of the verbs of perception in European languages. 'See' is the most frequent verb of perception in all eleven European languages in the sample.

For reasons which are discussed in Viberg (in progress), it can be claimed that the presence of the verbs GO, GIVE, TAKE, MAKE, SEE, and SAY among the most frequent verbs represents an unmarked feature. These meanings seem to be the most unmarked within their respective fields even in many non-European languages. The claim is substantiated by frequency data from Chinese, Arabic, and Didinga (Nilo-Saharan, Sudan) and data on the meaning of the simple verbs in languages with minimal verbal systems (10–40 simple verbs). In Viberg (in progress), descriptions are compared of languages such as (U)ngarinjin, Walmatjari, and Mangarayi (Australia) and Kalam and Kobon (Highlands Papua New Guinea), in which a small set of simple verbs are used extensively to form compound verbs (verb + noun or particle) or serial verb complexes. The meanings of these verbs, with some interesting exceptions, show striking similarities to the meanings of the most frequently used verbs in European languages.

Actually, it seems as if some meanings should be added to the list of nuclear verbs in Table 14.2a such as HIT (Physical contact), and that some of the verbs given there such as COME, KNOW, and WANT are somewhat more marked typologically than the rest of the verbs in 14.2a. However, for the purposes of this chapter, the verbs given in 14.2a will be regarded as the set of nuclear verbs without further distinctions.

Typologically unmarked lexical terms such as the set of nuclear verbs tend to form a subset of the basic words in all languages. There will also be some basic words which are language-specific. Using frequency of occurrence as a diagnostic trait of basicness, there are some basic verbs in European languages which do not have a typologically unmarked status, but rather represent important areal-specific characteristics of European languages. The most frequent verb in practically all European languages is the copula BE, which clearly is such an areal-specific characteristic. In many languages outside Europe, 2 noun phrases are simply juxtaposed in equational sentences or linked with a morpheme that lacks many or all verbal characteristics (Li and Thompson, 1977). The existence of a particular group of modal verbs is another important areal-specific characteristic of European languages. As is stated by Palmer (1986), similar meanings are often expressed by bound inflection (mood) or clitics and particles in other languages.

The second most frequent verb in a large group of languages in the centre of Europe is HAVE. But actually, this verb is completely missing from the Celtic languages at the western fringe of Europe and from languages to the east such as the Finno-Ugrian languages. As is well known, relatively few languages outside Europe have developed an equivalent of HAVE (Ultan, 1978), which makes the presence or absence of HAVE in a large group of European languages an important sub-areal characteristic.

Certain types of polysemy tend to appear independently in many genetically and areally widely separated languages. Such universal tendencies will be referred to as natural polysemy. Verbs in general, and especially the most frequent verbs, tend to belong to the most polysemous elements in a language. One reflection of this is the tendency of verbs with certain meanings to give rise to grammatical markers. COME and GO, for example, tend to develop inchoative and future meanings, while SAY tends to develop into a general subordinator ('that') and MAKE into a morphological causative marker. The meaning extensions typically proceed in steps which form a kind of hierarchy, like the following one for KNOW:

KNOWLEDGE > PRACTICAL COMMAND > ABILITY > POSSIBILITY

The extension of KNOW to PRACTICAL COMMAND is quite common and is reflected synchronically in many European languages, such as the use of French *savoir* 'know' in examples such as *Pierre sait nager* 'Pierre can swim'. In Turkish, where the verbal suffix *-ebil* 'be able to' is transparently related to the lexical stem *bil-* 'know', the extension reaches ABILITY and POSSIBILITY.

The semantically motivated hierarchies also have syntactic and morphological reflexes. Unmarked elements at the top of the hierarchies tend to have greater possibilities syntactically and appear in a wider range of syntactic constructions. The verb 'see', for example, tends to take a wider range of sentential complements than the other verbs of perception. Verbs connected to sight also tend to be more productive in word formation and appear in more derivations and compounds (Viberg, 1984). The different aspects of markedness which have been discussed in this section are summed up in Table 14.3. Language-specific basic words can share several or all of these characteristics except the first one. (Thus, it would be possible to speak about language-specific markedness in addition to

Table 14.3. *Characteristics of typologically unmarked lexical items*

Typologically unmarked lexical items tend to:
—be lexicalized in a greater number of languages and to be implied (in Greenberg's sense) by more marked elements

—be more frequent in individual languages

—be lexicalized in a simpler way

—be more polysemous and be dominant in hierarchies of polysemy

—have more irregular inflection (automatized inflected forms)

—give rise to grammatical markers

—show more possibilities syntactically

—show more possibilities in word formation

—be stylistically (or diatypically) neutral and have a wide collocational range

typological markedness, which is the type of markedness that primarily is considered in this chapter.)

In the analysis of English lexical structure, basic words have also been referred to recently as core words (Carter, 1987) or nuclear words (Stubbs, 1986). Several of the criteria in Table 14.3 have direct counterparts in the two papers referred to. The most important difference is the typological basis of markedness theory as it is conceived of here and the attempt to form explicit hierarchies of basicness/markedness. Carter and Stubbs also consider stylistic (or diatypical) factors, and stress the fact that basic vocabulary is neutral with respect to field or mode of discourse and with respect to connotations, and that basic words have a wide collocational range.

The meanings of the nuclear verbs are rooted in human principles of categorization. Cognitively, the event-space seems to be partitioned into a restricted number of basic semantic fields such as Motion, Production, and Perception. Each field is associated with one or two semantic foci, which have a strong tendency crosslinguistically to be lexicalized as one of the nuclear verbs in Table 14.2a. The verb in general plays an important role for the syntactic structure of the clause, in particular its argument structure. A further characteristic of the nuclear verbs in Table 14.2a is that they are highly differentiated with respect to the types of argument structures they can take. In English, *make* is a typical monotransitive verb and *give* a typical ditransitive verb, while *go* can take a variety of spatial complements such as *from* NP and *to* NP and be combined with spatial particles such as *up*, *down*, *in*, and *out*. With respect to sentential complements, *say* and *know* can take *that*-S- or WH-complements and *see* can alternate between sentential complements and raised structures (*I saw him coming*). The verb *want* takes different types of *to* + Infinitive complements (*I want (him) to come*). Further below, I will argue that the nuclear verbs tend to function as syntactic prototypes in first and second language acquisition. When a certain argument structure first becomes productive, its characteristic nulear verb tends to be favoured in production. This combination then can serve as a model to produce and interpret new combinations by substituting a more specific verb for the nuclear one.

Progression at the lexical level

As is stressed by Berman (1993) and Wode (1993) in their contributions to this volume, language acquisition cannot be properly understood unless general areas such as phonology and syntax are broken down into smaller, functionally integrated areas which are studied in detail. The same appears to be true about the lexicon and, accordingly, I will concentrate on one such functionally integrated area: the semantics and syntax of basic verbs. How verbs are related to the rest of the lexicon will be briefly discussed at the end of this chapter.

The centrality of verbs for language progression in general has often been emphasized. In first language acquisition, the number of different verbs is small in the single-word period, but increases with the onset of two- and multi-word speech. In this period between 2 and 3 years of age according to Bloom (1981), the verb system is 'the central feature of the target language' that influences the acquisition of increasingly complex structures. In a number of studies collected in Bloom (1991), the verb is shown to play a central role for the acquisition of a variety of structural areas such as simple sentence structure, verbal inflections, wh-questions, and complex sentences. Bloom's studies were based on extensive longitudinal data from four children. Using a psychometric design, Bates, Bretherton, and Snyder (1988) arrived at a similar conclusion concerning the centrality of verbs for the passage from single words to grammar. In particular, a shift was observed with respect to individual differences in vocabulary composition. Precocious children at 13 months tended to specialize in object names ('nouns') but at 20 months, precocity was associated with a proportional emphasis on verbs.

The centrality of verbs for progression in L2 is evidenced by a global, quantitative study of lexical development applied to a longitudinal corpus of adult untutored learners representing five different Western European target languages and a number of different source languages (Broeder, Extra, van Hout, Strömqvist, and Voionmaa 1988). A relative increase in the number of verbs (both with respect to lemmas and tokens) was correlated with a general increase in lexical richness, while no clear developmental patterns emerged for the proportion of nouns. In many respects, verbs patterned together with function words, while nouns patterned like adjectives, quantifiers and adverbs, which indicates that the current division between content and function words may have to be refuted.

In the remainder of this chapter, I will try to show how the outline of lexical structure presented in the previous section can serve as a general framework for studying progression in this area. Even if most of the relevant earlier work has been concerned with first language acquisition, I will start with second language acquisition since this is my own area of specialization. First language acquisition will be discussed later in the article.

The acquisition of basic verbs in Swedish L2

The data presented in this section were collected within the project 'Evaluation of methods for Swedish as a second language in the preschool'[2] (Arnberg and Viberg, 1991). Recordings were made with 23 6-year-old immigrant children and 12 native Swedish controls of the same age. Thirteen first languages were represented (all non-Germanic) and the proficiency of the immigrant children covered a relatively broad spectrum of intermediary levels. All recordings were carried out individually by a researcher according to a specific plan including free conversation mixed with the retelling of short video clips and informal play with two sets of flannel boards representing different scenes such as a hospital or a shop. In this way, it was possible to obtain relatively equivalent recordings across informants at the same time as relatively great variation was brought about within the individual recordings with respect to topics.

The frequencies of all verbs were calculated, first in each individual recording and then summarized for each group. At the group level, the verbs were ranked in descending frequency. There were approximately twenty verbs that were used by all or most of the informants in both groups. (The variation was somewhat greater within the immigrant group.) Even if the exact cut-off point is arbitrary, it is only meaningful to compare frequencies in approximately this range, at least in a corpus of this size. In Table 14.4, the twenty most frequent verbs in the recordings with the native controls are rank-ordered ('the native top 20') together with information about their frequencies in the recordings with the native children and the corresponding frequencies in the recordings with the immigrant children.

A similar list was prepared based on the rank order of the 20 most frequent verbs in the recordings of the immigrant children ('the

Table 14.4. *The 20 most frequent verbs: Six-year-olds*

Rank			Swedish control		Immigrant children		Over- and underrepresentation
			n/F	%V	n/F	%V	
1	vara	'be'	12/508	14.34	23/877	14.69	
2	ska	'shall'	12/340	9.60	21/665	11.14	
3	ha	'have'	12/267	7.54	22/406	6.80	
		Aux	12/111	3.13	22/215	3.60	
		Main	12/156	4.40	21/191	3.20	
4	få	'get; may'	12/178	5.02	18/102	1.71	Under
5	komma	'come'	12/126	3.56	21/245	4.10	
6	veta	'know'	12/115	3.25	23/201	3.37	
7	sitta	'sit'	12/109	3.08	20/82	1.37	Under
8	ligga	'lie'	11/101	2.85	16/33	0.55	Under
9	kunna	'can'	11/84	2.37	20/260	4.36	
10	ta	'take'	11/73	2.06	22/224	3.75	
11	gå	'go; walk'	11/73	2.06	23/276	4.62	Over
12	stå	'stand'	9/73	2.06	14/59	0.99	(Under) *
13	göra	'make; do'	9/71	2.00	21/287	4.81	
14	tro	'think/believe'	11/53	1.50	12/34	0.57	(Under) *
15	bli	'become'	11/53	1.50	15/61	1.02	

			Immigrant children		Swedish control		
16	finnas	'there is'	10/51	1.44	15/63	1.06	Under
17	sätta	'put/set'	12/48	1.35	7/25	0.42	
18	se	'see'	11/48	1.35	20/98	1.64	
19	heta	'be called'	10/47	1.33	16/68	1.14	
20	åka	'ride, travel'	11/36	1.02	6/24	0.40	
10	titta	'look'	23/174	2.92	8/16	0.45	Over
11	vilja	'want'	21/112	1.88	9/13	0.37	Over
15	leka	'play'	19/75	1.26	5/12	0.34	Over
17	säga	'say'	17/67	1.12	6/12	0.34	Over
20–21	kasta	'throw'	19/60	1.01	6/20	0.56	
20–21	ramla	'fall'	18/60	1.01	6/5	0.14	

n = number of informants who use the verb

F = number of tokens

%V = the proportion (in %) of the total number of verbs

Under = statistically significant underrepresentation

Over = statistically significant overrepresentation (two-tailed t-test, $p < 0.05$)

* = Near-significant ($p < 0.06$)

Table 14.5. *General measures of verb usage by the Swedish control group in comparison to the immigrant children*

Number of children	Total number of verbs:		Accumulated %V		Nuclear verbs %	Language-specific verbs %
	Tokens	Types	1–10.	1–20		
Swedish control 12	3543	263	53.67	69.28	14.99	15.38
Immigrant children 23	5969	221	60.56	73.77	25.29	5.44

non-native top 20') and at the bottom of the table, information is given about the verbs in this list which are not included in the native top 20. In Table 14.5, the differences between the groups are shown at a more general level.

The material is organized in such a way that it is possible to make an exact, quantitative comparison between the usage of basic verbs by the non-native and the native children. The native top 20 is actually a fairly representative cross-section of the basic verbal lexicon in Swedish in general. I will start by characterizing the native top 20 from this perspective. The most frequent verbs cover a large proportion of the total number of verbs. The native children produce 263 different verb types. Out of these, the 10 most frequent ones cover 54% and the 20 most frequent ones 69% of the total number of running verbs. As has already been shown, this dominance of a small number of the most frequent verbs is characteristic for the verbal lexicon in general, even if this tendency is reinforced by the relatively small size of the corpus and perhaps also by the range of topics.

In Allén (1971), which is based on one million running words of Swedish newspaper text, the 10 most frequent verbs cover 38%, and the 20 most frequent ones 46% of the total number of running verbs, which is still a very high proportion. (There were 4,649 verb types.) A look at the individual verbs appearing among the top 20 is even more revealing. Out of the native top 20, 13 verbs appear also among the top 20 in Allén (1971). Most of these verbs have a meaning equivalent to the basic verbs of European languages presented in Table 14.2. Actually, the majority of the most basic verbal semantic fields are represented among the native top 20, which is shown in Table 14.6, where the verbs have been classified into semantic fields.

The ranks of *ska* 'shall' and of the Postural verbs seem to be exceptionally high, which obviously depends on the activities with the flannel board. (The children tend with only small variations to say: *'This one should lie here and this one should stand here'*. In Swedish, the present tense form *ska* is used.)

I will now turn to a characterization of the non-native children's

Table 14.6. Semantic field classification of the control top 20 verbs

General dynamic	Modal	Postural	Motion	Possession
1 vara 'be'	2 ska 'shall'	7 sitta 'sit'	5 komma 'come'	3 ha 'have'
15 bli 'become'	9 kunna 'can'	8 ligga 'lie'	11 gå 'go'	4 få 'get'
		12 stå 'stand'	17 sätta 'put, set'	10 ta 'take'
			20 åka 'ride (in a conveyance)'	

Production	Cognition	Perception	Metalinguistic
13 göra 'make'	6 veta 'know'	18 se 'see'	19 heta 'be called'
	14 tro 'think/believe'		

Existence
16 finnas 'there is'

use of basic verbs. To begin with, it would be expected that the non-native children should rely even more on the most frequent verbs than the native children, something which turns out to be true; the 10 most frequent verbs according to the non-native rank cover 61% (versus 54% for the native children) and the 20 most frequent ones cover 74% (versus 69%). Interesting as this finding may be, its significance is hard to evaluate more precisely. Fortunately, it is possible to observe a number of tendencies which can be characterized more exactly:

1 The learners will tend to favour the typologically unmarked, nuclear verbs.

2 By and large, the learners will tend to avoid verbs expressing language-specific semantic patterns and/or neutralize the semantic distinctions between verbs representing language-specific semantic contrasts. (Contrastive relationships between L1 and L2 is a further complication in this case. See below.)

The favouring of nuclear verbs is reflected in 2 ways: by a higher frequency than in native speech (overrepresentation) and by overextension in meaning. The problematic nature of language-specific semantic contrasts in the most straightforward cases leads to avoidance, which can be observed as a lower frequency than in native speech (under-representation). Often language-specific factors bring about more complicated patterns, but the discussion of such cases will be postponed until later.

These hypotheses can be tested by comparing the overall frequencies of nuclear and language-specific verbs. It turns out that all the nuclear verbal meanings listed in Table 14.2a are found among the control and/or non-native top 20 except GIVE. The nuclear verbs (except GIVE) cover 25% of the verbs in the learner data and 15% in the native control data. Among the native top 20 verbs, *få* 'get; may', *åka* 'ride (in a vehicle)', the Postural verbs (with respect to their frequent use with inanimate objects) and *sätta* 'put in a fixed position' clearly represent language-specific differentiation patterns. Together, these verbs cover only 5% in the learner data versus 15% in the control data.

The frequencies of individual verbs can also be compared. The comparison can be based on the coverage of a certain verb in terms of the percentage covered of the total number of running verbs (%V in Table 14.4). The difference is sometimes very striking. The verb *få* 'get; may', for example, covers 5.02% of the total number of verbs used by the native controls, while the same verb covers only 1.71% of the verbs used by the non-native children. The number of informants who use a verb (n in Table 14.4) is another basis of comparison. The verb *sätta*, for example, is used by all the 12 native children, while only 7 of the 23 non-native children use this verb. This seems to imply that many of the non-native children have not acquired any representation of this verb. In many cases, however, a verb is used by most children in both groups but with different frequencies. This indicates that the non-native children have acquired the verb in principle but that the representation is different from that of native children in some respect, for example range of meanings or functions or availability/degree of automatization. The exact characterization, of course, still remains to be seen, and may turn out to vary from case to case. In order to identify such cases, a t-test was carried out for each verb comparing the individual frequencies of the native with those of the non-native children. Significant differences ($p < 0.05$) are marked OVER and UNDER in Table 14.4. OVER means that the verb is over-represented by the non-native children and UNDER that it is under-represented.

Recordings built around similar types of activities were carried out with the same groups of children one year later at the end of their first year at school. In Table 14.7, the patterns of over- and under-representation in these recordings (Time 2) are compared with the patterns in the earlier recordings (Time 1). The patterns are very similar, which implies that such patterns are relatively stable over time (once the learners have passed a certain early level) and develop in the direction of native usage rather slowly.

I will turn now to a discussion of the findings in more general

Table 14.7. *Over- and under-represented verbs*

Field/ verb		Time 1 Preschool	Time 2 School
a. Nuclear verbs			
Motion			
gå 'go'		OVER	OVER
Production			
göra 'make'		n.s.	OVER
Perception			
titta 'look'		OVER	OVER
Verbal Communication			
säga 'say'		OVER	OVER
Desire			
vilja 'want'		OVER	n.s.
b. Verbs representing language-specific differentiation			
Postural			
ligga	'lie'	UNDER	few ex.
sitta	'sit'	UNDER	n.s.
stå	'stand'	(UNDER)	UNDER
Motion			
åka	'ride'	n.s.	UNDER
sätta	'put, set'	UNDER	UNDER
lägga	'put, lay'	few ex.	OVER
Possession/Modal			
få	'get, may'	UNDER	(UNDER)

few ex. = too few examples in both groups for drawing any conclusions terms. In this connection, the results of other relevant studies are brought in for comparison.

The role of nuclear verbs in second language acquisition

Among the nuclear verbs in Table 14.7, *gå* 'go', *säga* 'say' and *göra* 'make' are strongly favoured by the non-native children on both occasions. This conclusion is motivated also by the patterns of overextensions accounted for in greater detail in Viberg (1991). The verb *gå*, for example, appears in a great number of clear overextensions where it replaces other motion verbs with meanings such as 'fly', 'rise', and 'ride (in a vehicle)'. The appearance of *göra* 'make' in many overextensions at Time 1 motivates regarding the non-significance of the over-representation at this time as sporadic. The verb *säga* 'say', actually, does not appear very frequently in clear overextensions, but this is obviously due to the fact that the verb has such a general meaning that it can replace most other verbal communication verbs without being directly unacceptable. (In other materials, decompositions such as 'say very loudly' for 'shout' have been found (Viberg, 1987).) The inclusion of *titta* 'look' among the nuclear verbs will be discussed below. At this point, it will simply be noted that this verb is strongly overrepresented on both occasions. (As for *vilja* 'want', I will leave it open how great importance should be attached to the over-representation at Time 1.) The favouring of several of the nuclear verbs is a striking phenomenon in this study and follows a clear pattern of overrepresentation in combination with overextension.

An interesting parallel based on a different kind of data is found in Håkansson's (1987) study of Swedish teacher talk. The lexical part of the study is concerned with the way the teachers use verbs belonging to 3 verbal semantic fields, namely Perception, Cognition, and Verbal communication. Verbs from these fields were frequency ranked in transcriptions of lessons given by six teachers, who taught Swedish to adult immigrants in courses for beginners. The verbs presented in Table 14.8 turned out to be the most frequently used

Table 14.8. *Nuclear verbs in Swedish teacher talk.*
Based on Håkansson (1987)

Verbal Communication	Cognition		Perception	
säga 'say'	veta	'know'	titta	'look'
	tänka	'think'	(se	'see')

within their respective fields. Håkansson refers to them as 'core verbs' within their respective fields, which can be equated to the term 'nuclear verbs'. The verbs *säga* 'say', *veta* 'know' and *tänka* 'think, reflect' were even overextended in some cases. The results were experimentally controlled in a second study, where a number of teachers were asked to retell a written story orally, once to a group of learners and once to a native speaker. The text was specially prepared and contained several instances of verbs from the three verbal fields. The 'core verbs' were used more frequently in the retold versions than in the original text and replaced more specific verbs in the original. Actually, this turned out to be true under both conditions. But the 'core verbs' were used more frequently in the versions directed to learners than in those directed to native listeners.

The favouring by learners of certain basic verbs was observed also by Harley and King (1989), who compared the verbal lexis in written compositions of grade 6 French immersion children in Canada with similar data from French-speaking children. The immersion children tended to use high-coverage verbs to a greater extent than their native peers. Such verbs were characterized as having high frequency and/or utility. By and large, they seem to coincide with the nuclear verbs in French, even if no complete list or criteria were provided.

A very strong predominance of one or two verbs within some basic verbal semantic fields has been observed in so-called early or basic learner varieties of untutored adult learners. The first studies of this type were produced within the Heidelberg-project (Klein,

Table 14.9. *Strongly favoured verbs in early learner varieties of German. Based on the Heidelberg-project*

Modal	Motion	Verbal Communication	Perception
müssen 'must'	1. kommen 'come' 2. gehen 'go'	1. sprechen 'speak' 2. sagen 'say'	gucken 'look'

1979), which was based on a cross-sectional study of interviews with 48 Spanish and Italian migrant workers in Western Germany, who had acquired German L2 without explicit teaching. In order to make it possible to draw inferences about developmental trends, the learners were divided into four proficiency levels on the basis of a syntactic index. The favoured verbs are summed up in Table 14.9, where they have been arranged into semantic fields. A very clear preference for one verb was found with respect to the verbs of Perception (HPD V, 1979). Similar to what was found in Swedish L2, this verb meant 'look' and not 'see'. *Gucken* 'look' was almost the only perception verb used by learners at the lowest level and predominated strongly even with learners at the intermediary levels. Only at the highest proficiency level the learners commanded a wider repertoire of perception verbs. The verb *gucken* showed a strong tendency to be overextended. Most frequently it replaced *sehen* 'see' but it also tended to acquire more general cognitive meanings ('control', 'find'). This tendency was further supported by the results of a translation test. There were relatively strong tendencies to use *gucken* as a translation for Spanish verbs such as *ver* 'see', *controlar* 'control', *buscar* 'look for' (German: *suchen*) and *encontrar* 'find'. These meaning extensions obviously cannot be interpreted as transfer. They should rather be explained with reference to natural polysemy, since they seem to follow universally valid hierarchies of polysemy. Verbs of perception show a strong tendency crosslinguistically to acquire cognitive meanings (Viberg,

1984), but 'look' in these early learner varieties have taken over the role typically played by the nuclear verb 'see' in native language varieties.

A parallel case was found by Dittmar (1984). Among learners at the lowest stage in the Heidelberg-project, two verbs dominated clearly with respect to frequency of occurrence, namely *sagen* 'say' and *sprechen* 'speak'. Three learners, who had acquired only one verb within this field, used *sprechen*, which was used with a clear overextension. Sometimes it even replaced *sagen*, which is the nuclear verb in native German. Within the Motion-verb field, the major finding in the Heidelberg-project was that *kommen* 'come' was dominant for learners at the lowest stage, while there was a shift (indicated by numbering the verbs in Table 14.9) in this respect towards *gehen* 'go' in the varietes of learners at the more advanced stages (HPD IV, 1978). Close parallels to the findings of the Heidelberg-project were found in a study of basic varieties of uninstructed learners of Swedish (Kotsinas, 1983, 1984).

These findings clearly indicate that one verb tends to be dominant within several verbal semantic fields in early learner varieties. I will henceforth refer to this as the nuclear verb strategy. As for the choice of exponent, the same verb is not always treated as nuclear as in native usage. This can probably be explained with reference to factors having to do with input salience. Verbs meaning 'look' and 'talk' refer to concrete activities, which can be directly observed in the speech situation, while nuclear verbs such as 'see' and 'say' often have a more abstract meaning. This phenomenon can be referred to as referential salience, which is characteristic of concrete objects and concrete activities. The formal salience of nuclear verbs also tends to be low (short and irregular words). Once the nuclear verbs of the target variety have been acquired and established, they will tend to be favoured for rather long periods of time due to their great utility, both semantically and syntactically.

One more complicating factor will be briefly discussed. Klein and Perdue (1988) have observed a tendency in very early learner varieties to leave verbs with certain meanings implicit. The

Table 14.10. *Implied verbal meanings in early learner varieties.*
Based on Klein and Perdue (1988)

General dynamic	Motion	Possession	Verbal communication
State: 'be/have'	'move'	'give'	'say'
Inch.: 'become'	($\approx$ 'go')		

meanings to a great extent coincide with the meanings of some of the nuclear verbs, as can be observed in Table 14.10, where I have arranged these verbal meanings into semantic fields. At first glance, this seems to contradict the claim that nuclear verbs will tend to be favoured, but this phenomenon is rather a reflection of the centrality of the meanings of the nuclear verbs. The nuclear verbs function as syntactic prototypes (see below), each one appearing as the unmarked realization of the verb slot in one of the basic syntactic frames of the language. Since learners at this stage exploit redundancy to the maximum, the verbal slot will primarily be left empty when it is semantically close to the unmarked value.

The role of the nuclear verbs for grammatical development

The material from the pre-school children in my own study is also suitable for studying the interaction between lexical and syntactic development. An important characteristic of the nuclear verbs which can only be touched on briefly in this chapter is their role as syntactic prototypes. One of the clearest examples of that is the use of *veta* 'know', which is dominant among the verbs which govern indirect questions (WH-complements). At time 1, 82% of the WH-complements were governed by the verb *veta* 'know' in the speech of the immigrant children. In the speech of the NS controls, the corresponding proportion was 57%. The learners relied more heavily than the native speakers on the syntactic prototype. A similar pattern has been found in a study of adult learners of

Swedish (Viberg, 1990, 1993), where low proficiency learners relied more on *veta* than high proficiency learners. The proportion of *veta* also decreased over time, especially for low proficiency learners, from the first to the third (and final) interview. The learning mechanism behind these patterns seems to be that learners initially acquire 'know' + a specific WH-complement as a holophrase, which becomes productive in two steps. First, the complement is varied and later other verbs are substituted for 'know', which serves as a model for other verbs taking the same kind of complement. For that-S-complements (introduced by *att* in Swedish), there seem to be two prototypes in Swedish L2: *tro* 'think-believe', which is the prototype for verbs indicating propositional attitude and *säga* 'say', which is the prototype for verbs expressing different types of indirect report. The closest semantic equivalents of these verbs seem to play a similar role in English L2. According to Sato (1988), the three verbs *say, think* and *know* (in negative form: *dono*) served as 'lexical entry points' for sentential complements in the speech of two Vietnamese boys acquiring English L2. The verbs meaning 'know' and 'say' in Swedish and English provide clear examples of nuclear verbs serving as syntactic prototypes. (The status of 'think' is more complicated. In Swedish, for example, there are three language-specific equivalents, which belong to the 50 most frequent verbs. Arguably, *tro* is more basic than the other two verbs.) The emergence of sentential complements following a small number of verbs, most of which clearly belong to the set of nuclear verbs, has earlier been demonstrated for English first language acquisition by Bloom (1981, 1991).

The favouring of nuclear and other basic verbs in discourse is important also for an understanding of the development of verbal morphology (to be exact: morphophonology or the choice of the correct allomorphs). The majority of the 20 most frequent verbs in Table 14.4 are irregular. Among the native top 20, only 2 (*tro, åka*) are regular. The other 18 verbs cover close to 67% of the running verbs and since the majority of these verbs tend to reach a high percentage in spoken conversation in general, this means that the mastery of the correct inflected forms of these verbs by a learner would boost overall accuracy in this area considerably. On the other hand, the most productive of the 3 regular conjugations (the ar-verbs) covers only a little more than 10% of the total number of tokens, but almost 50% of the types. To some extent the result is an effect of the restricted size of the corpus, but the same trends are found in the frequency dictionary (Allén, 1971). Eighteen of the 20 most frequent verbs are irregular and cover together approximately 45% of the total number of tokens. The textual frequency of the ar-verbs is 25% and the lexical frequency 67%.

The great utility of a small number of verbs in terms of semantic coverage, syntactic prototypicality and morphological accuracy may contribute to the explanation for the experience of 'plateaux' in second language acquisition. Once the most basic verbs have been acquired, this will provide the learner with a communicatively effective solution in a large number of cases. Even if I have no hard data on this, the mastery of the nuclear verbs in their most typical uses seems to coincide with the achievement of basic fluency and mastery of the most fundamental aspects of clause structure. To progress from here to native or near-native command seems to be a very time-consuming process. Native speakers also favour nuclear and other basic verbs, but on a number of occasions they opt for a more specific verb. The basic verbal semantic fields typically contain several hundred such verbs, which often differ from one another in rather subtle and language-specific ways. A native-like mastery of the nuclear verbs also requires the command of a complicated pattern of secondary meanings and functions or uses, many of which can be language-specific.

The role of nuclear verbs in first language acquisition

The tendency to favour a small set of verbs with high frequency and very general meaning was first observed in connection with first language acquisition. Clark (1978) refers to such verbs as general purpose verbs, which are characteristic of a stage English-speaking children seem to pass through around age 2;0 to 2;6 (MLU 2.5).

Table 14.11. *General purpose verbs in early child language from approximately age 2;0–2;6. Based on Clark (1978)*

General dynamic	Motion		Possession	Production
	Reflexive	Objective		
do	go	put	get take	make

According to Clark, a small set of such verbs can be applied to a great number of different actions and are used much more frequently than other verbs at this stage. From a semantic point of view, several of these verbs are equivalent to one of the nuclear verbs. Like these, they cover the foci of some of the most basic verbal semantic fields as can be demonstrated by classifying the verbs into semantic fields as in Table 14.11. We will turn now to the question of the relative order of appearance of the nuclear verbs. Relevant data are available in particular for Hebrew, whose status as a non-European language make parallels to the system of basic verbs in European languages all the more interesting. Berman (1978) gives a description of the productive verbal vocabulary of a 2-year-old Hebrew–English bilingual child. At 23 and a half months, the child actively used only 10 words that could be regarded as verbs, all in Hebrew, which clearly was the dominant language. In Table 14.12, these verbs are classified into semantic fields. The structure of this early verbal system in many ways reflects universal tendencies. Verbs of motion predominate, a characteristic which is further emphasized if we look at the next 10 verbs to be acquired. (Even these were all in Hebrew.) Six of these were verbs of motion. One language-specific feature, however, was the early appearance of motion verbs incorporating direction ('get down', 'get up'; 'put down', 'pick up'). Among the verbs of Possession, the 2 nuclear verbs 'give' and 'take' were acquired first, and among the verbs of Perception, 2 sight verbs ('look' and 'see'). Among the 20 first verbs, one more nuclear verb appeared: *roca* 'want'.

A very systematic case study, which covers the development of

Table 14.12. *The verbal system of a Hebrew-speaking child at 23 and a half months. Based on Berman (1978)*

| Motion | | Possession | Perception | Physiological |
Reflexive	Objective			Condition
bói	sími	(t)ni	tistakli	lisšon
'come!'	'put!'	'give!'	'look!'	'to sleep'
larédet		(k)xi	tiri	
'to get down'		'take!'	'see!'	Nourishment
zuzi				
'move over!'				le?exol
				'to eat'

the entire lexicon of one Hebrew-speaking child during the single-word stage, has been presented by Dromi (1987). The total number of productive words turned out to be 337, acquired between the ages of 10 and 17 months. Among these, only a small proportion (13%) correspond to verbs in adult language. For our present purposes, it will be satisfactory to look at the meanings of all the equivalents of adult verbs (listed in the complete cumulative lexicon in appendix A). The nuclear verbs were not acquired before all other verbs which appeared during this period, but by the end of the single-word stage, most of them had emerged. The first verb to appear at the beginning of month 14 was *lištot* 'drink', which is a non-nuclear basic verb. Relatively soon after this at the end of the same month, the two nuclear possession verbs *tnili* 'give (me), and *tax* '(you) take' emerged and replaced what actually had been the first action word to be acquired, the situational formula *toda* 'thank you', which had been used to request objects. Other nuclear verbs were *ba* 'come', *halax* 'go', *lirot* 'see' and *roca* 'want'. As in Berman's study, a rather large proportion of motion verbs were also acquired, among them several of the language-specific direction-incorporating verbs but also some manner-incorporating ones with meanings such as 'run', 'climb', and 'spill, pour'. The majority of the nuclear verbs had emerged already during the one-word stage. To be exact, 6 of the 9 nuclear verbs in Table 14.2a had been acquired. The only exceptions were MAKE, KNOW and SAY.

Judging from English data, MAKE actually seems to appear rather early (cf. 'general purpose verbs', above), but KNOW and SAY seem to be established a little later than the rest of the nuclear verbs. This, however, is true in general of the fields to which these verbs belong. It seems as if the nuclear verbs are dominant once the fields have been established. This is well documented for KNOW and the field Cognition. According to Shatz, Wellman & Silber (1983), the first verbs belonging to the field Cognition appear in English L1 at some time during the third year, well into the multiword stage. The nuclear verb *know* was among the first to appear and very soon was dominant in terms of frequency of occurrence.

Detailed information concerning the order of appearance of the nuclear verbs belonging to the Mental macro-field (SEE, KNOW, WANT) can also be gained from Bretherton and Beeghly (1982). In this study, data on the appearance of internal state terms among 30 28-month-old children were collected by means of detailed questionnaires given to the mothers. The instrument was highly correlated with data obtained through direct observation. Within the field Volition, *want* was dominant (93%), and among the perceptual verbs, verbs of vision came first (*see, look, watch*). Among the cognition verbs which tended to appear after the vision verbs, *know* appeared first.

To sum up, there is strong evidence that children acquire most of the nuclear verbs of adult language very early and, in particular, that the nuclear verbs in many respects are dominant within their respective fields. In this respect, there is strong similarity between first and second language acquisition.

It must be stressed, however, that children often have not acquired the full adult meaning and range of syntactic uses. The piecemeal nature of the acquisition of the semantic representation of the nuclear verbs is well illustrated by a study of perception verbs by Edwards and Goodwin (1986). The visual verb(s) which appear already in the one-word stage initially have a deictic function rather than referring to a mental state. Edwards and Goodwin describe the development of one child in the following way: 'Alice initially used *see*, accompanied by gestures and directed gaze, as a deictic term, within the context of Sheila (her caretaker) asking her to find named objects. The use of *see* was then extended to situations in which vision is either difficult or novel, such as suddenly seeing a reflection on the screen of a switched-off television. It seems probable that children do not start to understand *see* as a mental verb until they experience situations in which either their caretaker can see something but they cannot, or vice versa.' (op. cit. p. 271). The path towards the full lexical representation of the nuclear verbs probably can be rather different for small children and older L2 acquirers due to both cognitive maturation and to transfer effects.

The role of language-specific factors

Nuclear verbs reflect strong universal tendencies in lexical structure. In order to strike a reasonable balance, I will give a short sketch of the role of language-specific factors, even if space will not allow any full treatment.

The term 'language-specific' will be used rather loosely as a general opposite of 'universal', which has often been used in a strong ('absolute universals') and various weaker senses ('tendential,' 'variational' universals). In its strongest sense, language-specific refers to features which are more or less unique to an individual language (or group of closely related languages) and in a weaker sense it refers to typologically marked features. 'Specific' can also be restricted with respect to areally and/or genetically delimited groups of languages. When clusters of specific features are found in areally and genetically separated languages, it can be motivated to talk about lexical types. In studies of second language acquisition, where a number of different source languages are involved, language-specific features of the L2 can be operationally defined as 'unique in relation to the source languages'. At the lexical level, this is often the only practical method.

Four different types of language-specific lexical patterns will be distinguished with respect to (1) conflation, (2) differentiation (3) polysemy, and (4) grammaticalization.

The difference between motion verb systems of the Germanic and the Romance type probably represents the most far-reaching typological division in the verbal lexicon of European languages and is basic even from the perspective of general typology (Talmy, 1985).[3] This typological difference is obviously reflected very early in child language. Children acquiring a Germanic language start using directional particles already at the one-word stage, while direction-incorporating verbs start appearing during the same stage in languages of the opposite type (see e.g. data from Hebrew in the previous section and Berman, this volume; Choi and Bowerman, 1991). For L2 acquisition, the evidence are equivocal at present.[4] At any rate, this represents a case of typologically contrasting conflation patterns. Basically, in the Romance type, notions such as 'up'/'down' or 'in'/'out' are conflated with the verb and in the Germanic type these notions are realized as independent particles. The notions as such are approximately as important in both types of languages.

This does not apply in the second type of lexical pattern, which will be referred to as a language-specific pattern of differentiation. In this case, two or more words contrast semantically in the target language, while most other languages (or at least the source languages) have a single equivalent. An important example in Swedish, is the contrast between the three verbs of putting *ställa* 'put in a standing position', *lägga* 'put in a lying position' and *sätta* 'put in a fixed position'. (This is an area-specific pattern, which, roughly, is found in Slavonic and Germanic languages with an optional status in English.) Many other languages primarily have one equivalent meaning simply 'put' (or a set contrasting with respect to direction). In Swedish L2, it is common that learners neutralize the contrast and use one of the verbs as if it meant simply 'put'. The data from the pre-school children in Table 14.7b show that *sätta* 'put in a fixed position' is under-represented, while *lägga* 'put, lay' is overrepresented.

In order to characterize cases like this one exactly, contrastive relationships between L1 and L2 must be controlled for. This was done in an earlier study of 60 adult learners of Swedish L2, who were evenly divided between Polish, Spanish, and Finnish. The informants were required to give instructions illustrated with video recordings. In this way a number of realizations were elicited of instructions requiring one of the placement verbs *sätta*, 'put in a fixed position', *ställa* 'put, stand' and *lägga* 'put, lay'. Roughly, Polish has semantic equivalents of the last two verbs, while Finnish and Spanish make no equivalent distinctions. The design of the study made it possible to test a number of specific hypotheses. Simplifications were independent of source language (e.g. 'file on table', 'file go table' for *lägg* 'put, lay the file on the table'), while overextentions of one of the placement verbs showed a very strong effect for contrastive relationships. Several of the Spanish and the Finnish learners used one of the Swedish verbs as a generalized placement verb as if it meant only 'put' (Viberg, 1985).

Language-specific lexical differentiation patterns of this type seem to be acquired in a markedly different way in first language acquisition. In an interesting comparison of the acquisition of contrasting semantic patterns in English and Korean child language, Bowerman (1989) concluded that children were able to form language-specific categories from the late one-word period and possibly earlier. In particular, there was one case that forms a clear parallel to the acquisition of placement verbs in Swedish L2. In Korean, there is an obligatory differentiation between different types of attachment in such verbs and their reversals, corresponding to the single pair *put*/*take* (*away*, *apart*) in English. One basic pair is used if there is a tight fit, for example putting a hand in a glove and its reversal, while other verbs must be used if there is a loose fit (e.g. apples in a bowl). The language-specific meanings were clearly grasped by Korean children at least by 20 to 22 months of age, and the verbs were not overextended to situations of loose fit, where other appropriate verbs were used. This stands in sharp contrast to what was found in Swedish L2, where many learners tended to replace the whole set of placement verbs by one of these verbs. In second language acquisition, contrastive relationships play a major role, which is noticeable in particular with respect to language-specific but basic words in the target language.

The third type of lexical pattern will only be briefly exemplified. The under-representation of *få* 'get; may' in the Swedish L2 of pre-school children (Table 14.7b) is classified as a language-specific case. The motivation is that *få* represents a case of language-specific polysemy. The basic meaning of the verb is 'get, receive' (field: Possession), for example: *Peter fick en bok* 'Peter got a book'. The verb is also frequently used as an auxiliary with a number of modal meanings connected to Obligation: *Får vi komma in?* 'May we come in?' (This polysemy is a Nordic, areal specialization found in Norwegian, Swedish and in Finnish. The combination of meanings is not completely without parallel, however. It follows a general rule of natural polysemy: Possession > Obligation. Cf. English: *have to* with parallels in other European languages).

The last lexical pattern distinguished here is grammaticalized verbs. The grammaticalization of lexical verbs is a universal process. However, the most frequent grammaticalized verbs in European languages BE, HAVE, and the Modals represent a typologically relatively marked, area-specific characteristic. These verbs in many respects have a special status. In several languages, they are crucially involved in strictly grammatical processes such as inversion (part of the place-holder constraint in Hammarberg and Viberg, 1977).

The grammaticalized verbs are obviously acquired later than the majority of the nuclear verbs in first language acquisition. In spite of the fact that *be* and *have* are the two most frequent verbs in adult native English, these two verbs are not among the first to appear and are not used very frequently in early multi-word speech. The different forms of *be* do not appear regularly in obligatory contexts until the end of the third year in the four children studied by Brown (1973). The modals also appear rather late and in a piecemeal fashion, form by form in English. According to one representative study quoted by Stephany (1986), the modal auxiliaries were still one of the 'main areas of growth' in the ages between 3–5. The late acquisition of these verbs may partly be due to factors such as low referential and formal salience and high redundancy. But an important factor is also that these verbs form an integrated part of language-specific syntax such as inversion and negation in English.

It seems as if second language acquisition can follow a rather different path in this case. I will only mention one, relatively well-documented case. In SLA, grammaticalized verbs can appear in early and strong overextensions. The most extreme example of verbal over-extension has been reported by Yoshida (1978) in a case study of a Japanese child's acquisition of English L2 during the first 7 months (from age 3;5). At the end of this period, the child still used verbs only in memorized phrases such as *sit down* and *please push me*. The only productively used verb was different forms of the copula which substituted for any main verb. In early recordings, the verb slot was filled with an /iz/ sound, which may have been a form of the English copula or merely a filler sound. An example is: *Miki /iz/ lunch today* with the intended meaning: 'I am going to stay for lunch today'. In later recordings, several different forms of the copula were used as a kind of generalized verbs: *I am parade* 'I saw a parade in Disneyland'; *You are submarine?* 'Have you ever seen a submarine?'. This type of over-extension obviously serves a strictly grammatical function by bringing the syntactic form of the clause closer to the target norm. The explanation for this behaviour must be related to the fact that the learner already has acquired knowledge in L1 about basic aspects of clause structure such as the existence of a verb slot. According to HPD IV (1978), the German modal *müssen* 'must' tended to be used by certain adult untutored learners as a substitute for morphological tense markers of the verb in order to avoid unmarked verb forms which represent a socially stigmatized feature. The overextensions of the nuclear verbs are in general semantically motivated and derivable from the core meaning of the verb.

To sum up, there seems to be a fundamental difference between first and second language acquisition with respect to language-specific factors. In first language acquisition, language-specific conflation and differentiation patterns start to emerge early, while in second language acquisition, at least language-specific differentiation patterns tend to be neutralized unless the same pattern happens already to have been established in the L1. Grammaticalized verbs (BE, HAVE, Modals) in importants respects are acquired differently from basic lexical verbs. Part of the explanation for this is that these verbs in several respects form an integrated part of language-specific syntax. At early stages, second language learners can utilize general knowledge of syntax in a way that sets them off from first language learners.

The relationship of the verb lexicon to the lexicon in general

I will end by briefly discussing some broader issues. First, what is the relationship of verbs to other parts of the lexicon? As has been mentioned, verbs do not follow the same developmental path as nouns. It has often been noted that nouns are learnt before verbs in both first (Gentner, 1982) and second language acquisition (Dietrich, 1990). This actually covers several phenomena such as the verb-to-noun ratio in running text and the size of the learner's vocabulary. Only the last one will be discussed here.

The relatively slow growth of the verb lexicon in comparison to the noun lexicon is a direct reflection of the lexical organization of full-blown, adult languages. Verbal semantic fields are typically organized around one (or a few) nuclear verb(s) as described earlier, while nominal semantic fields typically contain a large number of words at the basic level. The most extensive ones, such as animal and plant taxonomies, readily contain several hundred terms at the basic level. In spite of that, the differentiation patterns across languages are similar to an amazing degree. Berlin (1978), for example, estimates that more than 60% of the folk plant and animal terms in Tzeltal, a Mayan language, correspond in a one-to-one fashion with scientific species at the basic ('generic') level. More general terms within these fields such as 'mammal' or 'bush' and 'flower' (herb), which could be equated in semantic generality to the nuclear verbs, are rather marked and have evolved only in some of the languages of the world (Brown, 1979). The referents of basic level nouns in general have salient perceptual (in particular visual) characteristics such as a distinctive shape, to which the principles of human categorization are highly sensitive. These characteristics also promote acquisition (referential salience).

Adjectives typically develop later than both nouns and verbs in first language acquisition. Before around age 3, children use only a few adjectives, which are learned as contrastive sets such as 'big'-'small' (Berman, 1988). Second language learners also have a tendency to favour some of the adjectives with a typologically unmarked meaning such as 'big' (Size) and 'good' (Value) as shown by Axelsson (1991) in a study of adult learners acquiring Swedish in a semiformal context (i.e. combined instructed and naturalistic acquisition). The favouring of one (or a few) adjective(s) within the most basic adjectival semantic fields forms a parallel to the use of nuclear verbs, but in contrast to verbs a very large proportion of the adjectives in a language such as Swedish belong to non-basic fields containing derived (denominal etc) adjectives, which do not appear in any great numbers until rather advanced stages.

To sum up this section, it should not be expected that the lexicon develops in a uniform way. Basic verbs, nouns, and adjectives are organized very differently in the lexicon and non-basic members of the major word classes in many respects differ from basic members.

A short note on lexical regression

The second broader issue that will be briefly touched on is the relation of progression to regression. It is reasonable to expect that the nuclear verbs should turn out to be among the most resistant words in all types of regression except certain types of selective, pathological loss. The motivation for this is both their high frequency which indicates rather directly that their accessibility is high and their lexical coverage and syntactic prototypicality. When the nuclear verbs are given up, basic clause structure will probably also break down. Even if certain other types of lexical elements can be retained after this point has been passed, it is doubtful whether what is left could still be referred to even as a reduced language system.

Actually, there is even some evidence that nuclear verbs can be overextended by learners of an L2, who once have known the correct, more specific word. An example of this kind is found in Berman and Olshtain (1981) in a study of the attrition of English L2 in Israeli-born children, who had spent 2 or more years in an English-speaking country and then returned to Israel. The nuclear verb *go* was often used instead of *walk*, even by children who 'quite certainly knew (or had known) the word *walk*' (p. 228). In this particular case, attrition seems to be a mirror of acquisition. However, the parallelism does not always extend that far. In a study of regression in a community of speakers of Dyirbal, an Australian language, Schmidt (1985) observed how the young generation were on the way to losing the language. At the lexical level, there was a tendency to replace more specific words with more basic words, which forms a parallel to acquisition, but, contrary to what is common in that case, this happened only if the basic word completely covered the replaced word in meaning. Thus, semantic overextensions which are characteristic of acquisition did not appear. When basic words were not appropriate, a word borrowed from English was used instead. This means that simplification (favouring of basic vocabulary) is combined with restructuring to a greater extent than in second language acquisition, where borrowing or transfer of complete words plays a prominent role primarily when two very closely related languages are involved as L1 and L2 or when formally related cognates are acquired in the less basic strata of the vocabulary which contain many international and other borrowed words.

Borrowing, which in many languages is a source of constant change, can be regarded both as progression and as regression. At the societal level, when bilingualism is restricted among speakers of the borrowing language, borrowing is in general restricted to nonbasic vocabulary and can often be regarded as an expansion of the lexical resources, but when contact is more intensive and bilingualism is more extensive even basic vocabulary can be replaced. Several cases of this type are documented in Thomason and Kaufman (1988) who refer to this process as 'contact-induced change in language shift', which in combination with heavy structural borrowing eventually can lead to a complete abandonment of the heritage language and language death.

NOTES

1 This research has been carried out within my professorship in 'Lexical research' financed by The Swedish Council for Research in the Humanities and Social Sciences.

2 The linguistic part of this project on which the present account is based has been supported by The Swedish Council for Research in the Humanities and Social Sciences (grant no. F 537/89).

3 My position is that the verbs which are the closest equivalents of 'go' and 'come' in the Romance languages are nuclear verbs also in these languages, even if their domain is not as extensive as in European languages of the Germanic type. These verbs have a higher frequency than the direction-incorporating verbs and show patterns of polysemy in accordance with the universal tendencies for these verbs.

4 Becker, Carroll, and Kelly (1988) studied adult untutored acquirers of four Germanic languages and French. As for motion verbs, the basic findings were that the acquirers of a Germanic language primarily followed a nuclear verb strategy, even if individual learners could choose various non-nuclear verbs as exponents of that function. Learners of French, however, followed a completely different strategy. Several of the language-specific direction-incorporating verbs such as *arriver*, *partir*, *entrer* emerged more or less from the beginning. These findings contrast with those of Harley's (1989) study of the use of motion verbs in L2 French by L1 English immersion children, in which strong evidence for transfer strategies was found. There were also some signs that the nuclear verbs *aller* 'go' and *venir* 'come' were favoured. The studies are, however, based on different types of learner and data-gathering

techniques. In particular, the motion verb systems in the L1s of the learners in the Becker et al. study (Arabic and Spanish) both were of the direction-incorporating type like French (short typological distance). In addition, the distance is short between Spanish and French along the interlinguistic lexical transparency parameter.

REFERENCES

Allén, Sture (1971), *Frequency dictionary of present-day Swedish*. Almqvist and Wiksell, Stockholm.

Arnberg, L., and Viberg, Å. (1991), *Utvärdering av skolförberedelse-grupper i Rinkeby. Rapport 1. Sammanfattning*. Centre for Research on Bilingualism, Stockholm University.

Axelsson, M. (1991), The acquisition of Swedish adjectives by adult second-language learners. In Herberts, K., and Laurén, C. (eds.), *Multilingualism in the Nordic countries and beyond*. Institutet för finlandssvensk samhällsforskning, P.B. 311, SF-65101, Vasa, Finland.

Bates, E., Bretherton, I., and Snyder, L. (1988), *From first words to grammar. Individual differences and dissociable mechanisms*. Cambridge: Cambridge University Press.

Becker, A., Carroll, M., and Kelly, A. (eds.) (1988), Reference to space. Second language acquisition by immigrants. Final report. Vol. IV. Strasbourg: European Science Foundation.

Berlin, B. (1978), Ethnobiological classification. In Rosch, E., and Lloyd, B. (eds.), *Cognition and categorization*. Hillsdale, N.J.: Lawrence Erlbaum.

Berman, R. (1978), Early verbs: comments on how and why a child uses his first words. *International Journal of Psycholinguistics*, 5, 21–39.

(1988), Word class distinctions in developing grammars. In Levy, Y., Schlesinger, I. M., and Braine, M. (eds.), *Categories and processes in language acquisition*. Hillsdale, N.J.: Lawrence Erlbaum.

(1993), Crosslinguistic perspectives on native language acquisition. This volume.

Berman, R., and Olshtain, E. (1983), Features of first language transfer in second language attrition. *Applied Linguistics*, 4:3, 222–34.

Bloom, L. (1981), The importance of language for language development: linguistic determinism in the 1980s. In Winitz, H. (ed.), *Native language and non-native language acquisition*. New York: Academy of Sciences, New York.

(1991), *Language development from two to three*. Cambridge: Cambridge University Press.

Bowerman, M. (1989), Learning a semantic system: What role do cognitive predispositions play? In Rice, M. L., and Schiefelbusch, R. L. (eds.), *The teachability of language*. Baltimore and London: Paul H. Brookes.

Bretherton, I., and Beeghly, M. (1982), Talking about internal states: the acquisition of an explicit theory of mind. *Developmental Psychology*, 18, 906–21.

Broeder, P., Extra, G., van Hout, R., Strömqvist, S., and Voionmaa, K. (eds.) (1988). Processes in the developing lexicon. *Second language acquisition by adult immigrants. Final report. Vol. III*. Strasbourg: European Science Foundation.

Brown, C. (1979), Folk zoological life-forms: Their universality and growth. *American Anthropologist*, 81.

Brown, R. (1973), *A first language: the early stages*. Cambridge, Mass.: Harvard University Press.

Carter, R. (1987), Is there a core vocabulary? Some implications for language teaching. *Applied Linguistics*, 8, 178–93.

Choi, S., and Bowerman, M. (1991), Learning to express motion events in English and Korean: the influence of language-specific lexicalization patterns. *Cognition*, 41, 83–121.

Clark, Eve (1978), Discovering what words can do. In *Papers from the Parasession on the Lexicon*. Chicago Linguistic Society.

Dietrich, R. (1990), Nouns and verbs in the learner's lexicon. In Dechert, H. W. (ed.), *Current trends in European second language acquisition research*. Clevedon: Multilingual Matters.

Dittmar, N. (1984), Semantic features of pidginized learner varieties of German. In Andersen, R. (ed.), *Second languages. A cross-linguistic perspective*. Rowley, Mass.: Newbury House.

Dixon, R. M. W. (1977), Where have all the adjectives gone? *Studies in Language*, 1, 19–80.

Dromi, E. (1987), *Early lexical development*. Cambridge: Cambridge University Press.

Edwards, D., and Goodwin, R. (1986), Action words and pragmatic function in early language. In Kuczaj, S., and Barrett, M. (eds.), *The development of word meaning*. New York: Springer-Verlag.

Francis, W. N., and Kučera, H. (1982), *Frequency analysis of English usage. Lexicon and grammar*. Boston: Houghton Mifflin Company.

Gentner, D. (1982). Why nouns are learned before verbs: linguistic relativity versus natural partitioning. In Kuczaj, S. A. (ed.), *Language development: language, cognition and culture*. Hillsdale, N.J.: Lawrence Erlbaum.

Greenberg, J. (1966), Language universals with special reference to feature hierarchies. *Janua Linguarum. Series minor LIX*. The Hague: Mouton.

Hammarberg, B., and Viberg, Å. (1977), The place-holder constraint, language typology, and the teaching of Swedish to immigrants. *Studia Linguistica*, 31:2, 106–63.

Harley, B. (1989), Transfer in the written compositions of French immersion students. In: Dechert, H. W., and Raupach, M. (eds.), *Transfer in language production*. Norwood, N.J.: Ablex.

Harley, B., and King, M. L. (1989), Verb lexis in the written compositions of young L2 learners. *Studies in Second Language Acquisition*, 11:4, 415–39.

HPD IV: Heidelberger Forschungsprojekt 'Pidgin-Deutsch'. Zur Erlernung des Deutschen durch ausländische Arbeiter. Wortstellung und ausgewählte lexikalisch-semantische Aspekte. Arbeitsbericht IV. Germanistisches Seminar der Universität Heidelberg. 1978.

HPD V: As above. Studien zum Spracherwerb ausländischer Arbeiter. Arbeitsbericht V. 1979.

Håkansson, G. (1987), *Teacher Talk*. Lund: Lund University Press.

Klein, W. (1979), Untersuchungen zum Spracherwerb ausländischer Arbeiter. Tätigkeitsbericht für die Gesamtdauer des Projektes.

Klein, W., and Perdue, C. (eds. 1988), Utterance structure. *Second language acquisition by adult immigrants. Final report. Vol. VI*. Strasbourg, European Science Foundation.

Kotsinas, U-B. (1983), On the acquisition of vocabulary in immigrant

Swedish. In Ringbom, H. (ed.), *Psycholinguistics and foreign language learning*. Publications of Research Institute of the Åbo Academy Foundation, Åbo/Finland.

(1984), Semantic over-extension and lexical over-use in immigrant Swedish. *Scandinavian Working Papers on Bilingualism 2*, 23–42.

Li, C., and Thompson, S. A. (1977), A mechanism for the development of copula morphemes. In Li, C. (ed.). *Mechanisms of syntactic change*. Austin: University of Texas Press.

Miller, G. A., and Johnson-Laird, P. N. (1976), *Language and perception*. Cambridge, Mass.: Harvard University Press.

Palmer, F. R. (1986), *Mood and modality*. Cambridge: Cambridge University Press.

Sato, C. (1988), Origins of complex syntax in interlanguage development. *Studies in Second Language Acquisition*, 10, 371–95.

Schachter, P. (1985), Parts-of speech systems. In Shopen, T. (ed.), *Language typology and syntactic description. Vol. I.* Cambridge: Cambridge University Press.

Schmidt, A. (1985), *Young people's Dyirbal. An example of language death from Australia*. Cambridge: Cambridge University Press.

Shatz, M., Wellman, H., and Silber, S. (1983), The acquisition of mental verbs: A systematic investigation of the first reference to mental state. *Cognition*, 14, 301–21.

Stephany, U. (1986), Modality. In Fletcher, P., and Garman, M. (eds.), *Language acquisition*. 2nd edn. Cambridge: Cambridge University Press.

Stubbs, M. (1986), Language development, lexical competence and nuclear vocabulary. Ch. 6 in *Educational linguistics*. Oxford: Blackwell.

Talmy, L. (1985), Lexicalisation patterns: semantic structures in lexical forms. In Shopen, T. (ed.), *Language typology and syntactic description. Vol. III.* Cambridge: Cambridge University Press.

Thomason, S. G., and Kaufman, T. (1988), *Language contact, creolization, and genetic linguistics*. Berkeley: University of California Press.

Ultan, R. (1978). Toward a typology of substantival possession. In Greenberg, J. H. (ed.), *Universals of human language. Vol. 4. Syntax*, 11–49. Stanford: Stanford University Press.

Viberg, Å. (1984), The verbs of perception: a typological study. *Linguistics*, 21, 1.

(1985), Lexikal andraspråksinlärning. In *SUM-rapport 2*. Centre for Research on Bilingualism, Stockholm.

(1987), Explaining some aspects of second language lexical development. Paper distributed at the conference Explaining Interlanguage Development, La Trobe University, Melbourne, August 1987. (32 p.) (MS.)

(1990). Bisatser i inlärarperspektiv. In Tingbjörn (ed.), *Andra symposiet om svenska som andraspråk*. Skriptor förlag, Stockholm.

(1991). En longitudinell djupstudie av språkutvecklingen. *Utvärdering av skolförberedelsegrupper i Rinkeby. Rapport 4*. Centre for Research on Bilingualism, Stockholm University.

(1993), The acquisition and development of Swedish as a first and as a second language: the case of clause combining and sentential connectors. In: Kettemann, B., and Wieden, W. (eds.), *Current issues in European second language acquisition research*. Tübingen: Gunter Narr.

(in progress). The lexical profile of European languages.

Wode, H. (1993). The development of phonological abilities. This volume.

Yoshida, M. (1978), The acquisition of English vocabulary by a Japanese-speaking child. In E. Hatch, (ed.), *Second language acquisition: a book of readings*. Rowley, Mass.: Newbury House.

15 · Attrition or expansion? Changes in
the lexicon of Finnish and American
adult bilinguals in Sweden

SALLY BOYD

INTRODUCTION

It is within the lexicon that bilinguals report the most dramatic changes in their first language (L1) after acquiring a second language (L2). On the one hand, they report word-finding problems. On the other hand, they are appalled by the L2-origin words that creep into their speech in L1 in various forms. This paper will discuss the second of these phenomena, and contrast the patterns of incorporations of Swedish-origin lexemes into the English and the Finnish of adult bilinguals living in Göteborg.

In several recent studies, researchers claim that there are general, structural constraints on certain types of incorporation, notably code-switching. In a relatively early study of incorporation, Hasselmo (1974: ch.5) proposes the 'hypothesis' that incorporation of English lexemes in American Swedish follows an 'ordered choice' hierarchy (see below). He makes no strong claims of generality, however. DiSciullo, Muysken, and Singh (1986) claim that structural constraints on code-mixing (what I and others prefer to call *code-switching*) follow the general principle of government. Poplack (1980 and later papers) claims that code-switching, narrowly defined, follows a general 'equivalence constraint' (see below). While the debate on ways of characterizing candidates for structural constraints on code-switching, borrowing or both goes on, the role of the social context of language contact seems to have been neglected. The purpose of this chapter is to examine some of these claims of universality or predictability of patterns of incorporation

386

in relation to data of incorporation of Swedish lexemes in the Finnish and English of Finnish and American first generation immigrants in Sweden. I suggest, in this connection, that it may be premature to propose universal structural constraints on code-switching. Rather, social factors in the context of language contact play at least as important a role as language-internal structural factors do, and may help to explain why different pairs of languages in contact seem to follow different strategies in incorporation.

SOME PROPOSED UNIVERSALS OR GENERAL CONSTRAINTS ON INCORPORATION

In this chapter, I will concentrate my analysis of incorporations of Swedish lexemes into American English and Finnish to comparisons with Poplack's equivalence and free morpheme constraints (1980:585–6. See also Sankoff and Poplack, 1981) on the one hand and with Hasselmo's (1974) ordered selection hierarchy on the other. Poplack's constraints were originally formulated to describe the extensive code-switching typical of Spanish–English bilinguals in New York City. These constraints are perhaps the most commonly mentioned ones in the literature.

Free morpheme constraint: Codes may be switched after any constituent in discourse provided that constituent is not a bound morpheme.

In other words, Poplack predicts that switches will not occur between a bound morpheme and a free morpheme, or between 2 bound morphemes.

Equivalence constraint: Code-switches will tend to occur at points in the discourse where juxtaposition of L1 and L2 elements does not violate a syntactic rule of either language, i.e. at points around which the surface structures of the two languages map onto each other.

In other words, if two elements are normally ordered in the same way by the grammars of both languages, then switching is permitted.

In his earlier study of American Swedish, Hasselmo suggests (as a

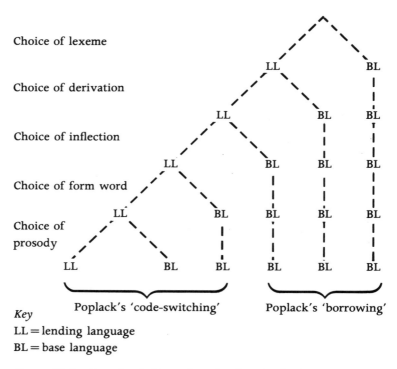

Choice of lexeme

Choice of derivation

Choice of inflection

Choice of form word

Choice of prosody

Key
LL = lending language
BL = base language

Figure 15.1   Hasselmo's hierarchy of ordered selection

hypothesis), a hierarchy of ordered choice, when bilingual speakers incorporate items from English into their Swedish. These involve a number of morphological choices, some of which would seem to violate Poplack's equivalence constraint. In some respects, however, Hasselmo's hierarchy can be seen as an earlier and more detailed version of Poplack's free morpheme contraint (see Figure 15.1).

In this figure, and in the following discussion, the abbreviation *BL* is used for *base language* (i.e. the language of the discourse prior to the incorporation) and *LL* for *lending language* (i.e. the language of origin of the incorporated material, at least historically). As will be seen below, the identification of BL and LL, and of stretches of speech as being in BL or LL, is in itself not unproblematic.

On the first level of Hasselmo's hierarchy, a choice can be made between lexemes originating either in LL or in BL. Once this choice is made, if LL is chosen, a derivational suffix originating either in LL or BL may be chosen. If a BL lexeme was chosen, however, then only BL derivations are possible. The same is true at each successive level. If BL was chosen at the previous level, then only BL can be chosen at the current level; if LL was chosen at the level above, then BL or LL may be chosen at the current level. No claims of universality are made, however. Hasselmo's hierarchy of ordered choice is particularly interesting to us, since it is based on switching between Swedish and English (although the roles of BL and LL are reversed).

DEFINITIONS

One of the problems of comparing the various universal constraints that have been proposed is that the constraints generally apply to something called code-switching, which is defined differently by different people proposing the constraints (cf. Clyne, 1987). Many researchers distinguish between *code-switching* and *borrowing*, some make finer distinctions within these categories. In this paper, I will question the usefulness of these universals, not by citing a number of counter-examples to them – this has been done by others working in the field (see e.g. Clyne, 1987). Rather, I intend to question the distinction between code-switching and borrowing as clearly different phenomena, which seems to underlie most of the suggestions for universal constraints on code-switching. In addition, I would like to suggest that the pattern for incorporation into a language of 'other language' material is different in different bilingual communities. The structures of the languages in contact may play an important role, but the social and historical aspects of the language contact situation are, I will argue, at least equally important.

Rather than compare and contrast the existing definitions of code-switching and borrowing, I will begin the discussion of definitions by presenting definitions of both terms as ideal types, which I believe capture what 'everyone' intuitively believes to be the ideal difference between the concepts.

Borrowing (cf. Poplack, Wheeler, and Westwood, 1987:4–5) is ideally incorporation of LL material in a BL discourse such that the LL material is

a   phonologically,
b   morphologically, and
c   syntactically integrated into the BL.
d   Use of the same LL material, integrated in similar ways, and occurring in similar contexts is widespread in the BL speech community, including among BL monolinguals, who may be unaware of its origins in LL.
e   Borrowing is usually limited to stretches of only one lexeme.

Code-switching is ideally incorporation of LL material in a BL discourse such that the LL material is *not*

a   phonologically,
b   morphologically or
c   syntactically integrated into BL.
    That is, the phonology, morphology, and syntax of the LL material follows LL grammar, rather than BL grammar.
d   No claims are made as to recurrence of switching in the wider community.
e   Code-switching often involves longer stretches of speech in LL, but in a limiting case may also be applied to single words.

In their ideal forms, these definitions clearly delimit different phenomena. However, there are certain interesting assumptions underlying both definitions. For example, we can see in both definitions the ideal of what might be called 'preservation of the (monolingual) norms of language X'. The assumption is that languages are not (or cannot be, or ought not to be?) *really* mixed. In the case of borrowing, material from LL is 'made over' to follow the grammar and phonology of BL. In the case of code-switching, speakers switch from BL to LL, but preserve the grammars of each on either side of the switch point. Poplack's (1980) equivalence constraint strengthens the assumption of grammatical integrity of the two languages in code-switching.

These definitions also seem to assume that there is little or no phonological, morphological or syntactic convergence between languages in language contact. If there is any substantial convergence, it becomes impossible to determine whether a specific form belongs to LL or to BL. Of course, this is simply another instance of the old problem of the difficulty of determining the boundaries between one language and another, which I and others have discussed elsewhere (see Boyd, 1988; LePage and Tabouret-Keller, 1985).

If it is the case that most researchers would accept the characterizations given above of borrowing and code-switching as ideal types, then we can see that disagreements arise when particular cases of incorporation do not fit the ideal cases. I proposed that ideal borrowing calls for phonological, morphological, and syntactic integration, as well as widespread use in the community. How should we regard examples of incorporation where only 1, 2, or 3 of these conditions are met? Different researchers (or groups of researchers) have chosen to give priority to different criteria in the ideal definitions above when faced with cases which do not fulfil all the criteria in the ideal.

The criteria of phonological and morphological integration

DiSciullo et al. (1986:2, ftn3) use 'lack of phonological adaptation' as 'the crucial criterion' for distinguishing code-mixing (their term denoting what comes closest to my ideal concept of code-switching as defined above) from borrowing. In other words, incorporations which are phonologically adapted are borrowings, and those which are not are code-switches. Poplack, Sankoff, and their associates, on the other hand, explicitly deny the usefulness of phonological integration as a distinguishing criterion of borrowing as opposed to code-switching. Instead, their primary criterion seems to be mor-

phological integration (e.g. Poplack et al., 1987:6) if an LL lexeme is
inflected using BL affixes and occurs together with BL function
words, it is a borrowed lexeme; if it is inflected using LL affixes, it is a
one-term code switch. Problems arise however, using either of these
criteria.

First of all, it is easy to see when we examine actual cases of
incorporation that both phonological and morphological integration
are often partial, thus making difficult or arbitrary the use of either
of these criteria, alone or in combination for distinguishing between
borrowing and code-switching. Since we can note different degrees
of integration of the same Swedish lexeme between speakers in the
same community (see exs. in Table 15.2), the rules of phonological
integration must be considered to be variable rules. Of course the
skill of the individual speaker in producing Swedish forms with
near-native phonology is another variable factor in phonological
integration, as well as the degree of overlap of the phonological
systems of the two languages, which renders certain forms indeterminate as to the occurrence of or degree of phonological integration.

In both our Finnish and American data, we also find examples of
incorporations with mixed or indeterminate morphology. The same
form can include a Finnish derivational suffix and a Swedish particle,
(e.g. *helssa-ta poo* for Swedish *hälsa på* 'visit') or Swedish definiteness suffix and Finnish inflection. In a few cases, American
informants mark Swedish-origin nouns for definiteness with both an
English article and a Swedish suffix. Hasselmo (1974:147) reports
that partial morphological integration is also common among
American Swedes.

Not only can phonological and morphological integration be
partial or duplicated, but, as many LL items occur in morphologically unmarked form, their assignment as cases of code-switching or
borrowing on morphological grounds becomes indeterminate. When
the phonological or morphological systems of the 2 languages
happen to overlap, it may also be indeterminate as to which system a
speaker is applying in a specific case. This is the case for many
unmarked contexts, as well as e.g. for English and Swedish genitive

suffix, which coincides after voiceless non-sibilants. Another problem is presented by 'international' learned words (Andersson, 1990), which like established loan words may exist in the speech of monolinguals, in which case we would not like to consider them to be incorporations at all; on the other hand, many appear in a variety of phonological or morphological forms in the speech of bilinguals, which make them look more like nonce loans.

In sum, I think it is clear that a sharp distinction between borrowing and code-switching is a dubious one. Rather than a dichotomy, it seems more accurate to think of code-switching and borrowing, as characterized above, as end-points on a continuum. Especially when dealing with single-word switches, it seems not only possible, but in many cases more accurate, to think of the integration process as a gradual one, which, when specific items are in the process of becoming established, leads incorporation to be a highly variable phenomenon. Our data on incorporations of Swedish lexemes into Finnish and English support this view, especially when they are compared to other data of language contact.

OUR DATA

In this section, I will present an overview of the data of incorporation of Swedish lexemes into Finnish and American English by bilingual speakers who have lived 10 years or more in Sweden. The data analyzed so far comes from interviews with 12 informants in the American group, and 14 in the Finnish group, carried out within the project Variation and Change in Language Contact. The Finnish material was collected, transcribed, and analyzed by Paula Andersson.

The informant groups studied in this project differ in many respects. The Finns in Göteborg comprise by far the largest immigrant group in the city. The group is dominated by working-class individuals, many of whom work in local industries such as Volvo. For many however, moving to Sweden has led to further education and consequent upward social mobility. The Finns tend to live in working-class or upper working-class apartment areas of the north and east of the city (De Geer, 1989). Cultural similarity between Finns and Swedes leads to relative ease of contact between the groups, and e.g. a high rate of marriage between Finns and Swedes. There is also a long history of contact between the languages both in Finland and Sweden. Finns are probably the best-organized immigrant group in Göteborg. Elementary schooling is, for example, available for Finnish children in Finnish, and about half of the Finnish children in the city take advantage of this opportunity.

The American group in Göteborg is much smaller, and lives scattered in different parts of the city (De Geer, 1989). Their occupations tend to be middle class, and many language-related jobs as e.g. teachers or translators. A large majority of those who are living in Sweden for a longer period of time are married to Swedes, and can be considered to be well integrated into Swedish life (Brady, 1989). Many express problems in raising their children to be bilingual in English and Swedish.

Incorporations from Swedish to Finnish

The entire set of incorporations from Swedish into Finnish in our corpus totals 458 relatively clear cases. Can these 458 cases be considered as cases of borrowing or code-switching, and what grammatical properties do they display? Can we identify any norm or set of norms for incorporation of Swedish lexemes into Finnish among our informants?

The 458 cases can be divided into different word and phrase types as follows (see Table 15.1). Single words, particularly single nouns dominate the examples. A certain number of other word classes and longer items do occur, however. Based on the length alone, our first guess would be that most of these items are borrowings, or what Clyne calls lexical transfers.

Now the question is, to what extent are these items integrated phonologically and morphologically into Finnish, which has a

Table 15.1. *Word and phrase types: Swedish incorporations into Finnish*

Single nouns	286	62.6%
Single verbs	65	14.2%
Single adjectives	41	9.0%
Interjections, feedback etc.	29	6.3%
Adverbs	10	2.2%
NP	10	2.2%
VP	6	1.3%
Conjunctions	5	1.1%
Other	5	1.1%
Total	457	100.0%

Table 15.2. *Phonological (including prosodic and phonotactic) integration of Swedish lexemes in Finnish, 14 informants*

Finnish phonology (ex:/'ropleemi/) 'problem')	96	21.0%
Mixed phonology (ex/'propleemi/)	174	38.0%
Swedish phonology (ex:/pro'bleem/)	188	41.0%
Total	458	100.0%

characteristic phonological system, and a well-developed system of nominal case marking (see Table 15.2)? As mentioned above, it was difficult to code many of the cases, as the items showed certain adjustments to Finnish phonology, (especially initial syllable stress) while retaining some features of Swedish phonology (especially segmental and phonotactic). The category 'Finnish phonology' was reserved for cases where adjustment to Finnish phonology was more or less total; the 'mixed' cases included degrees of integration which were similar to that of newer loans into Finnish, where e.g. *f* and voiced stops are retained. Most of the examples coded for Swedish phonology were unmarked morphologically, or marked with Swedish inflections, so that (in accordance with the ideals for code-switching and borrowing) phonological integration tended to go hand in hand with morphological.

Table 15.3. *Phonological integration among 12 Finnish informants*

Finnish phonology	71	31.7%%
Mixed phonology	79	35.2%
Swedish phonology	74	33.0%%
Total	224	100.0%

This is a somewhat unclear picture, with the different phonological patterns rather evenly divided, and the largest number of cases with mixed phonology. If we look at the group of informants excluding for a moment the 2 informants who showed the lowest rates of phonological integration in their incorporations, and the greatest variation in different word and phrase classes types, Riitta and Tuulikki, we get a distribution with a somewhat greater proportion of integration (see Table 15.3).

I will return to Riitta and Tuulikki in a discussion below. In general, I think we can say that there is plenty of variation in the degree of phonological integration, with about a quarter of all the cases phonologically integrated, and over a third unintegrated. In other words, only a quarter of the cases would qualify as loans using a strict phonological criterion. However, I will argue later that at least a certain degree of phonological integration is the norm for incorporation in this community.

The question of morphological integration is equally interesting, but here the picture is somewhat different (see Table 15.4). Here, we can see that of the 458 cases, 224 were clearly marked with a Finnish inflection. An additional 58 had either a Finnish derivational suffix, were part of a Swedish–Finnish compound or were phonotactically integrated, e.g. with a vocalic suffix. At the Swedish end of the continuum of marking, 50 showed Swedish morphology or syntax (e.g. plural marking, verb + verb particle, or a prepositional phrase). The majority of these also had Swedish phonology, and many were longer stretches of speech, so they would seem to be rather clear cases of intra-sentential code-switching.

Table 15.4. *Morphological integration of incorporations of Swedish lexemes in Finnish*

Finnish inflection (e.g. case, finite verb morphology)	224	48.9%
Other Finnish morphology (e.g. deriv. + compounding) besided inflection	58	12.7%
Unmarked	126	27.5%
Swedish inflection or syntax	50	10.9%
Total	458	100.0%

Ex: Tuulikki 58: Ruotsissa ei ollu vielä rasismia eikä + ja todella tuli tänne ninku tämmönen *ärad gäst* + 'There wasn't any racism in Sweden yet + and you really came here as an *honored guest*'.

The remaining 126 cases consist of morphologically unmarked items, all but 26 of them are nouns in nominative singular contexts. Because they occur in a context which is unmarked in both languages, this group is ambiguous as to morphological marking, and thus, if we take the morphological criterion for code-switching as crucial, they are ambiguous as to their status as code-switches or nonce loans. (See Andersson, 1990, for a more detailed discussion of morphological and phonological integration of Swedish incorporations in Sweden-Finnish.)

The results show that a majority of the Swedish items which should have received morphological marking were marked with Finnish inflections or derivations, rather than Swedish ones. The greater part of the unmarked items occurred in nominative singular contexts. Thus, the general tendency clearly seems to be one of morphological integration. If we categorize our incorporations as we think Poplack et al. (1987) have done, a total of 84.4% would be considered as nonce borrowings, rather than code-switches. This is a significantly greater share than in the Canadian Finnish material, and may perhaps be explained by the social network structure of the majority of our informants, compared to the Canadian Finns (see further below).

In our analysis of morphological integration we noted again that the same two informants who showed a lower rate of phonological integration, Riitta and Tuulikki, were responsible for about $\frac{3}{4}$ of all the cases of Swedish inflection (i.e. code-switching). Riitta, Tuulikki and another informant Jussi also had the lowest rates of inflection in Finnish of Swedish-origin items. I will return to a discussion of these informants below.

To sum up, the general picture for incorporations of Swedish lexemes into Finnish is one where

1   Single items dominate, especially single nouns.
2   There is a variable tendency to integrate phonologically. Only about a third clearly have Swedish phonology. About $\frac{2}{3}$ have been adapted at least partially to Finnish phonology.
3   There is a stronger but variable tendency to integrate morphologically. About $\frac{2}{3}$ are clearly morphologically integrated.

How do these results compare with the definitions, and Poplack's and Hasselmo's predictions? A majority seem to qualify as borrowings, or at least nonce borrowings, using the morphological criterion as primary, but there are a large number of ambiguous cases, and a significant minority which seem to be code-switches. In comparison with Hasselmo's hierarchy, the majority of the cases follow one of the allowed paths indicated in Figure 15.2. Exceptions exist (where lines cross), however, which violate Hasselmo's predictions, e.g. examples with Finnish inflection and Swedish form word. The paths that are favoured are those towards the 'borrowing end' of the decision tree.

Incorporations from Swedish to English

In our corpus of interviews with 12 American informants, we have collected a total of just over 200 cases of incorporation. This rate of

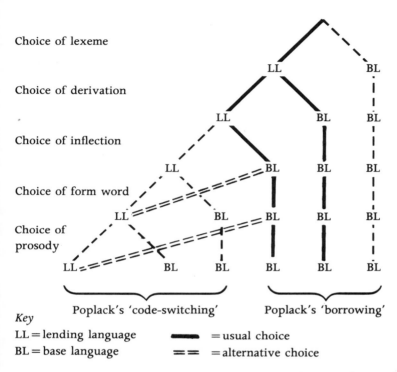

Choice of lexeme

Choice of derivation

Choice of inflection

Choice of form word

Choice of prosody

Poplack's 'code-switching' Poplack's 'borrowing'

Key
LL = lending language   **——** = usual choice
BL = base language   **==** = alternative choice

Figure 15.2   Incorporations from Swedish to Finnish: norm for Sweden Finns

use of Swedish words is significantly lower than that of the Finnish informants, and contrasts strongly with Poplack's over 1,200 examples of incorporations for 8 interviews with Canadian Finnish women. Although Hasselmo doesn't provide any total figures for his corpus, his discussion leaves the strong impression that the overall rate of use of English words in American Swedish is higher than what we have found in our Gothenburg corpus.

The 207 examples can be categorized as follows in relation to word and phrase type (see Table 15.5). The set of incorporations are clearly dominated by single nouns, even more strongly dominated than was the Finnish corpus. Other word classes occur, but in significantly fewer numbers, as compared to the Finnish material. It is

Table 15.5. *Incorporations of Swedish lexemes into American English by word/phrase type*

single nouns	178	86.0%
single verbs or verb + prt	3	1.4%
single adjectives	14	6.8%
noun phrases	3	1.4%
vocatives	3	1.4%
other + indeterminate	6	2.9%
Total	207	99.9%

Table 15.6. *Occurrence of compounds among incorporations from Swedish in English*

Compound nouns Swe + Swe	133	64.3%
Compound nouns Swe + Eng	4	1.9%
Compound nouns Eng + Swe	5	2.4%
All other cases	65	31.4%

furthermore interesting to note the domination of compounds in the English corpus (see Table 15.6). Over two-thirds of all cases of incorporation of Swedish material into English involve Swedish or partly Swedish compounds. This suggests that Swedish words are resorted to primarily for semantically 'heavy' concepts which in many cases do not have a direct English equivalent.

To what extent are these incorporations phonologically and morphologically integrated? If we begin with phonological integration (keeping in mind the problems of partial integration, interlanguage and phonological overlap mentioned above) we see the following pattern among the American informants (see Table 15.7). The domination of Swedish phonology is overwhelming. In fact, it comes close to be a defining characteristic of incorporation in our American material. For the Americans, it has been easier to code for phonological integration: any case which shows Swedish segmental or prosodic features is counted as unintegrated. This was the case for the vast majority of the incorporations, and is in stark contrast with

Table 15.7. *Phonological integration of Swedish incorporations in English*

Swedish	194	93.7%
English	11	5.3%
Other cases	2	1.0%

Table 15.8. *Morphological integration of Swedish incorporations into English*

Swedish	21	77.8%
English	4	14.8
No marking at all	2	7.4%
Total	27	100.0%

the Finnish incorporations, which tended to be at least partially integrated phonologically.

I will discuss morphological integration in two stages. First of all, morphological marking other than definiteness. This affects only a small number of examples, (especially in comparison with the incorporations into Finnish) primarily nouns in the plural and a few tense markings on verbs. Below, I will discuss definiteness marking, which shows a more complex pattern.

There are only 27 items of the 207 which ought to have received some sort of morphological marking, other than definiteness (see Table 15.8).

This table shows a clear tendency towards *not* integrating morphologically, but not as overwhelming a tendency as for phonological integration. There were, in other words, a few cases like the one below:

Jean B011 but there were +I think four or five foreign lecturer *tjänst*s ('positions')

This evidence, together with that of the preceding section, suggests that what we have here must be considered as one-word

Table 15.9. *Incorporation of Swedish nouns in definite contexts into English*

English def marking only	22	25.0%
ex: the *folkhögskola*		
Swedish def marking only	40	45.5%
ex: *folkhögskolan*		
Both Swedish and English marking	3	3.4%
ex: the *folkhögskolan*		
No marking at all	7	7.9%
ex: *folkhögskola*		
Demonstrative without suffix	14	15.9%
ex: this *folkhögskola*		
Demonstrative with suffix	2	2.3%
ex: this *folkhögskolan*		
Total	88	100.0%

code-switches, rather than borrowings. In that case, they should conform to the equivalence constraint.

When we turn to the set of Swedish nouns in definite contexts incorporated into English among the American informants, we see immediately that the equivalence constraint does not hold. Recall that the equivalence constraint predicted that no switches would occur between elements which are ordered differently in the two languages. In Swedish, definiteness of single nouns is marked by a suffix (*-en* or *-et*). In English, it is marked by a pre-posed article. This should then block all incorporations with an English article followed by a Swedish noun.

A total of 88 cases of semantically definite Swedish-origin single nouns occurred in the corpus. These were treated in the manner shown in Table 15.9 by the American informants.

It should perhaps be added that the indefinite Swedish origin nouns were categorically marked with the English indefinite article a/an. (Since Swedish has a preposed indefinite article, this does not

Table 15.10. *Definiteness marking of definite single nouns incorporated from Swedish*

	Namey nouns	%	Common nouns	%
English def marking only	3	6.1%	19	48.7%
Swedish marking only	31	63.3%	9	23.1%
Both Swedish + English marking	2	4.1%	1	2.6%
No marking	4	8.2%	3	7.7%
Dem + 0	7	14.3%	7	17.9%
Dem + suffix	2	4.1%	0	0.0%
Total	49	100.1%	39	100.0%

create problems for the equivalence constraint.) Except for the 16 cases in which a demonstrative pronoun +/- Swedish definite suffix is used (where Swedish also allows an optional definite suffix), the equivalence constraint would seem to be violated.[1]

In general, we don't seem to get such a clear pattern with the definite nouns as with other cases of morphological integration, probably partly because of the fact that the solution which is used for indefinite nouns (Eng. art + Swe. noun) violates the equivalence constraint for definite nouns. Some clarity is provided, however, when we distinguish between common nouns and what I would like to call namey nouns, i.e. near-proper nouns such as *bostadsförmedlingen* 'the housing exchange' and *fortbildningsavdelningen* 'the department for further education' (see Table 15.10).[2] The namey nouns total 49 cases out of the 88 above.

This table shows there to be a clear preference for using Swedish definiteness for the 'namey nouns', but this use is certainly not categorical. For the common nouns, there is a preference for English marking, but there is certainly a lot of variation, especially if we compare with indefinites, which all used English marking.

Can we then sum up the general pattern of incorporation of Swedish lexemes into English? The tendency seems to be:

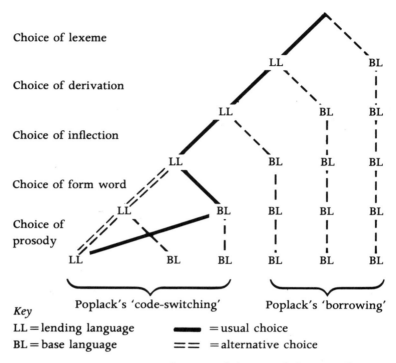

Key
LL = lending language   ━━ = usual choice
BL = base language   ══ = alternative choice

Figure 15.3   Incorporations from Swedish to English: norm for
Americans in Sweden

1   Single, semantically heavy items (especially Swedish com-
    pounds) are incorporated.
2   They are not phonologically integrated.
3   They tend not to be morphologically integrated, but definiteness
    tends to be marked with English articles, except for namey
    nouns, which tend to get Swedish definite marking.

Now, how do these results compare with Hasselmo's hierarchy of
choice (Figure 15.3)?

A comparison of the most favoured paths in Hasselmos's hierarchy of choice for incorporations from Swedish into English shows
one clear set of violations, i.e. 'choice of form word' which (if we

include definiteness here, which Hasselmo explicitly does (1974:144)) normally is English, while prosody, along with phonology is normally Swedish. In any event, incorporations from Swedish into English tend to follow paths towards the left side of Hasselmo's hierarchy, in contrast to incorporations from Swedish to Finnish.

Deviations from the American pattern of incorporation. In Table 15.5 we see that there are 29 instances of incorporations from word classes other than single nouns occurring in the corpus. Two or 3 of these seem to be slips of the tongue. Except for 4 informants with one case each, all the other 22 cases arise in the interviews with 4 of the other informants: Harry, Jean, Don and Eleanor. Especially Harry and Eleanor use both verbs and adjectives more freely than other informants.

In Table 15.7, there were 11 cases of phonological integration in the corpus as a whole. One of these 11 cases I would regard as a slip of the tongue. Of the remaining 10, 2 occurrences might be excluded as being a vocative, the other 8 examples come in one case from Harry and the other 7 are all Eleanor's. In the case of morphological integration (Table 15.8), there was a total of only 4 cases. Harry and Eleanor are responsible for one case each, while Jean, Harry's wife, had 2 cases (one of which is exemplified above). So the exceptions to the pattern outlined above tend to come from the same informants: Harry, Jean, Don, and particularly Eleanor. Harry and Eleanor were also the informants with the highest overall number of incorporations. Is there any explanation for the fact that the same informants deviate from the general pattern in several different respects?

COMPARISON OF FINNISH AND AMERICAN INCORPORATIONS FROM SWEDISH

I have argued in the preceding sections that the general pattern of incorporations from Swedish in the 2 groups is that Finns tend to incorporate Swedish items in a manner approaching ideal borrowing, while the Americans' norm approaches ideal code-switching.[3] The norm for *both* communities seems to be to keep the number of

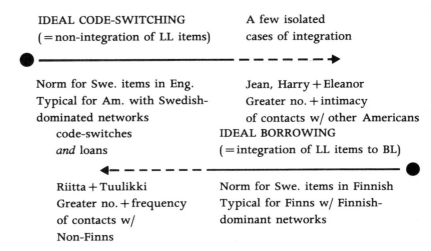

Figure 15.4   Norm and deviation for incorporations from Swedish into English and Finnish

incorporations to a minimum. Deviations from these norms occur in both groups, both in number and degree of integration. We might summarize the pattern of integration of Swedish lexemes in the 2 groups as follows (see Figure 15.4).

In the Finnish group, 2 or 3 informants, Riitta, Tuulikki, and, to a certain extent, Jussi, use a large number of incorporations, in a larger number of word and phrase classes, but tend less often to integrate them phonologically and morphologically. In other words, their incorporations are more similar to ideal code-switches than those of the rest of the group. Mirja, another informant with a relatively large number of incorporations, represents the other extreme: almost all of her incorporations are integrated both phonologically and mor-phologically, i.e. they approach the borrowing end of the spectrum.

In the American group, we can observe a tendency to treat incorporations like (usually single-word) code-switches. The deviations from the norm of limited use of Swedish lexemes, and non-integration phonologically and morphologically come from 3–4 informants: Jean, Harry, Eleanor, and, to a lesser extent, Don. Their incorporations show some minor tendencies towards both phono-logical and morphological integration. Is there anything these small groups of 'deviants' have in common?

Compared with the rest of the Finnish informants, Riitta and Tuulikki have an unusually mixed social network. Both have learned Swedish to a relatively high level of skill, and associate with Swedes as well as with immigrants from other backgrounds, but not so much with Finns. Both speak Swedish at home. The remainder of the informant group have networks more highly dominated by Finns, and tend to have a lower level of skill in Swedish. The fact that Riitta and Tuulikki are more skilled in Swedish could explain quite directly why they tend to incorporate more often than the other Finnish informants, but not why their incorporations tend more to resemble code-switches. In contrast, Mirja's network of contacts is more Finnish-dominated; among other things, she worked for several years at Volvo, where she had many Finnish-speaking workmates.

In the American group, Jean, Harry, and Eleanor are unusual in that they are married to other English speakers. Jean and Harry are a married couple, and Eleanor is married to an Englishman. All 3 of them have social networks which tend to be more dominated by non-Swedes, in comparison to the rest of the American informants. Eleanor has a brother living in Sweden, another close relative from the US living with her, and has many contacts with other immigrants, many of whom she speaks English with. Jean and Harry have many contacts with English speakers as close friends and through their work.

In her study of sociolinguistic variation in Belfast, Milroy (1980) claims that an informant's degree of integration in a locally based social network will have a rather direct relation to her/his adherence to local speech norms. In the cases described here, the Finnish informants whose networks were most Swedish dominant, seemed to deviate most from the conservative Finnish norm of phonological and morphological integration of Swedish items. In the case of the American informants, the ones with relatively many English-speaking contacts, especially in the family, tended to deviate from the American norm of phonological and morphological non-integration of Swedish items. Both of these 'deviant' groups tended to incorporate more often than the rest of the informants did. In both groups, we find a stronger tendency to integrate Swedish items among the speakers who have close contacts within the minority language group. It may be the case that without such close contact, the possibility of establishing common patterns of integration of LL items is more limited. The Volvo plant in Göteborg is probably a good example of an environment where integration patterns, as well as specialized terms, can be established and learned by new Finnish employees. There, there seems to be a large number of established loan words specific to the work situation at the plant, such as *paani* for Swedish *bana* 'assembly line' and *templa-ta* for Swedish *stämpla*, 'punch in/out'. This type of environment does not exist for Americans in Göteborg.

It seems to us quite plausible that the 'deviant' informants represent the beginnings of possible long-term changes in the lexicon of Finnish and English as spoken in Sweden. Unsystematic, but daily, observation of incorporations of Swedish items into English and Finnish among second generation speakers lead us to believe that the patterns of Riitta and Tuulikki on the one hand and Jean, Harry, and Eleanor on the other have the possibility of becoming more general in the future. If this is the case, it fits in nicely with J. and L. Milroys' later claims (1985) that the leaders of a change process can be found among the speakers with good contacts in several different speaker groups. It is another question as to whether this change process actually can be carried out in the American group, where the language survives as a minority language mainly by a continued immigration of new speakers, and not so much by transmission from generation to generation.

CONCLUSION

In this paper, I have argued that it is difficult, when confronted with a set of actual incorporations, to draw a clear distinction between code-switching or borrowing. Ideal cases are clearly different, but many examples don't fit the ideal cases. Instead it seems more accurate to view the pattern of incorporation as variation along a continuum, with norms for different bilingual communities tending to approach one endpoint or the other of the continuum. The end-point a particular community seems to favour (i.e. ideal code-switching or ideal borrowing) may depend on a range of factors, including language typologies, but probably also other factors, such as the history and present social context of the language contact. Deviations from the norms of different communities may also fruitfully be related to the patterns of social contact within and between speaker groups.

NOTES

The support of the Council for Research in the Humanities and Social Sciences, who funded the project Variation and Change in Language Contact is gratefully acknowledged. Special thanks are also due to Paula Andersson, my co-worker on the project, who collected, transcribed, coded, and analyzed the Finnish data, and who has given me many helpful comments on the manuscript as a whole.

1 The results for definiteness marking of Swedish nouns in English is not presented primarily as counter-evidence for the universality of the equivalence constraint. Rather, it could be argued that these results show the dilemma speakers are placed in, when the equivalence constraint (perhaps best viewed as a strong tendency) makes switching in an otherwise favoured context (Det + noun) more difficult (cf. Sankoff and Poplack 1981).

2 These and other examples of 'namey nouns' come so close to being proper nouns that the question is raised as to whether they should be counted as incorporations at all. It is true that it was often difficult to draw the line between true proper nouns and what I have called 'namey nouns'. In fact, a certain amount of variation occurred with several of the most common 'namey nouns' e.g. *kursverksamheten*, the name of a local evening school occurred a few times as *kursverksamhet*. And the names of various *folkhögskolor*, particularly *kvinnofolkhögskola*, which occurred with both Swedish, English and no definite marking at all. Another

informant consistently translated *folkhögskola* to *folk high school* (the latter were not counted as incorporations). A general principle of variation studies within sociolinguistics has been that the scope of occurring variation should determine the definition of a variable.

3 By using morphology as a criterion for distinguishing code-switching and borrowing, the results from the 2 informant groups may appear more different than they are, looked at in another way. It could be claimed that both languages tend to retain BL grammar, and incorporated only content from Swedish. Because Finnish is a more agglutinating language, in order to retain its grammatical structure, it tends to integrate Swedish lexemes morphologically (which qualifies the incorporations as nonce borrowings, using the morphological criterion). English is more isolating, so that little morphological integration of Swedish lexemes is necessary, if the goal is to preserve English grammatical structures. The lack of morphological integration makes incorporations from Swedish to English qualify.as code-switches, again if we take the morphological criterion as primary.

In both groups, one could also say that there is a puristic norm for treating incorporations from Swedish. For the Finns, it is to transform Swedish lexemes into Finnish, so as to preserve Finnish grammar and phonology in the discourse as a whole. For the Americans, it is to retain Swedish phonology and morphology in Swedish lexemes, in order to preserve the grammar and phonology of each language in the discourse.

REFERENCES

Andersson, P. (1990), Blandat och klart. Paper presented at the symposium on Finnish outside of Finland. Stockholm. Dept of Finnish. September 1990.

Boyd, S. (1988), Texanska: ett hemspråk? In Strömqvist, S., and Strömqvist, G. (ed.), *Kulturmöten, kommunkation, skola*. Stockholm: Norstedts.

Brady, P. (1989), *Americans in Sweden. An assimilation study*. Ph.D. thesis. Uppsala: Uppsala university.

Clyne, M. (1987), Constraints on code-switching: How universal are they? *Linguistics*, 25, 739–64.

De Geer, E. (1989), Göteborgs invandrargeografi. De utländska medborgarnas regionala fördelning. Uppsala multiethnic papers 16. Uppsala: Centre for Multiethnic Research. Uppsala University.

DiSciullo, A., Muysken, P., and Singh, R. (1986). Government and code-mixing. *Journal of Linguistics*, 22, 1–24.

Hasselmo, N. (1974), *Amerikasvenska. En bok om språkutvecklingen i Svensk-Amerika*. Skrifter utgivna av Svenska språknämnden 51. Stockholm: Esselte Studium.

Le Page, R., and Tabouret-Keller, A. (1985), *Acts of identity. Creole-based approaches to language and ethnicity*. Cambridge: Cambridge University Press.

Milroy, J., and Milroy, L. (1985), Linguistic change, social network and speaker innovation. *Journal of Linguistics*, 21, 339–84.

Milroy, L. (1980), *Language and social networks*. Oxford: Blackwell.

Poplack, S. (1980), Sometimes I'll start a sentence in Spanish Y TERMINO EN ESPAÑOL: Towards a typology of code-switching. *Linguistics*, 18:7–8, 581–618.

Poplack, S., Wheeler, S., and Westwood, A. (1987), Distinguishing language contact phenomena: Evidence from Finnish–English bilingualism. In Lilius, P., and Saari, M. (eds.), *The Nordic languages and modern linguistics 6*. Helsinki: University of Helsinki Press.

Sankoff, D., Poplack, S., and Vanniaranjan, S. (1986), The case of the nonce loan in Tamil. Technical Report 1328 Centre de recherches mathématiques. University of Montreal.

The linguistic perspective 2

Phonology

16 · The development of phonological abilities

HENNING WODE

INTRODUCTION

The key assumption behind this chapter is that humans are endowed with specific abilities that allow them to acquire natural human languages. Some of these abilities may be available at birth, others may develop later in interaction with the input provided by the ambient language(s). It is the state of development of a given individual's acquisitional abilities that determines how s/he will master a particular language, e.g. as a monolingual (L1) learner, as a bilingual L1 learner, as a L2 or L3 learner, or when relearning some language. The implication is that, if a given learner's state of development is known, it should be predictable how s/he will acquire a given language. The approach is illustrated via a summary of the development of speech perception. First, apart from specialists on speech perception, this research tends not to be well known to most acquisition researchers, although it is basic to language acquisition. After all, learners need to tune into the language in order to be able to learn it. Second, the development of speech perception can be traced, although presently only in its major outlines, from infancy to adulthood. And, third, speech perception, at the present time, appears to be the only area which can be considered from both the point of view of its anatomical and functional biological substrates as well as the resulting cognitive system(s). The theoretical framework is the universal theory of language acquisition (UTA).

Before turning to speech perception I need to enlarge on why a theory of language acquisition needs to be universal. This is done by considering the domain of a theory of language acquisition, and by making explicit certain implications with respect to the nature of the language learning abilities.

The domain of a theory of language acquisition

Ever since L2 acquisition began to attract the attention of researchers during the early 1970s there has been a consensus that it is the underlying abilities rather than the surface products that are of primary interest. However, for methodological reasons the study of the latter needed to be given priority, because the former are not open to direct inspection, but they can only be inferred from the observable surface phenomena. Closely linked to the above methodological problem has been the issue of whether or not the L2 acquisitional abilities are the same as those activated for L1 acquisition (e.g. Ervin-Tripp, 1973; Hatch, 1974; Wode, 1974). I have always adopted a more radical view. Namely, that all types of language acquisition should be considered, and that they must be based on one universal learning system (e.g. Wode, 1974, 1981, 1988). If this assumption is not made, then it needs to be explained how L1 acquisition by children could ever result in the same kind of linguistic knowledge arrived at by L2 children, adolescents or even adults, and how all of this should ever fit in with the general properties of natural human languages, such as language change, language typology, or language universals. Some of the difficulties, it seems, are artefacts of the original assumptions. What they share is a discontinuity view concerning people's psycholinguistic basis for natural human languages.

Continuity

The term continuity is to capture the fact that language abilities apply across a range of domains, including language acquisition (Wode 1990). To illustrate what is meant consider the role of speech perception in language acquisition, language change, and people's ability to monitor their own speech.

Continuity in language acquisition research

Assume, for a moment, that for each new learning situation, such as L1 vs. L2, or L2 vs. L3, new learning abilities are developed or activated which are unrelated to any of those utilized before. This is a *discontinuity* view. The *continuity* view, on the other hand, assumes that abilities activated in a new situation may (a) be the same as used previously in other situations, (b) develop in a continuous fashion out of earlier ones, or (c) they may have been present all along but have been dormant.[1]

From the acquisitional point of view the discontinuity view appears to be rather unlikely. For one thing, an individual may be faced with so many different situations in the course of her/his life that the number of different abilities must be close to infinite, which is beyond anybody's capacity. In contrast, the continuity view does not meet with such difficulties. Learners are able to react to so many differences in the learning situations, because they can adapt their original acquisitional abilities to cope with new tasks. (For details cf. Wode, 1981, 1988, 1990.)[2]

In terms of counter-evidence, for the discontinuity view to be acceptable it must meet the requirement that there be at least one property that categorically differentiates the acquisitional types, such as L1 vs. L2. Age is probably the most likely factor to meet this requirement, because there are many studies which report differences between child L1 learners and (adult) L2 learners. (For recent overviews cf. Harley, 1986; Wode, 1988; Long, 1990, and this vol.). In fact, adherents of the critical period hypothesis (Lenneberg, 1967) claim that adults cannot learn L2's in the same way as children.[3]

However, as pointed out in more detail in Wode 1990, for methodological reasons even age will not do. If one compares adult L2 acquisition to child L1 acquisition, then the age difference is so obvious that it may be hard not to regard age as a property that sets these two groups of subjects apart. But this procedure involves an artefact. Age is a gradient. The issue, therefore, is to determine at which point in time one or more properties occur only with one age group. In order to solve this problem the origin and the development of the respective abilities must be traced from infancy through childhood, adolescence, and adulthood and the comparison needs to include L1 acquisition as well as other acquisitional types, such as L2 acquisition or the relearning of a language.

Note that the continuity view does not require that every language acquisitional ability necessarily changes over time. There is ample evidence to suggest that some abilities do not do so. Recall the notorious pre-verbal negation NP NEG VP. Utterances like *me no close the window* meaning 'I'm not going to close the window' have been found with L1 monolingual, L1 bilingual and L1 trilingual children, child and adult L2 learners, in L2 relearning, and in foreign language teaching (survey in Wode, 1988). Note, however, that it will be assumed that age-related differences do not constitute counter-evidence to the continuity view as long as the differences can be shown to be due to learning abilities that develop out of abilities in existence before.

It is a well-established assumption that linguistic theories should also cover language acquisition. By the same logic it is important to bear in mind what should be a truism, namely, that there should be no discontinuity between the language learning abilities and those required for other domains of language use. Therefore, language change and the ability of humans to monitor their own speech are briefly considered from the point of view of (dis)continuity.

Continuity in language change

One fundamental property of natural human languages is their potential for change. Socio-linguistic studies of large urban populations have yielded many insights into the details of diachronic changes in general, and on sound changes in particular. For example:

Who initiates sound change? Who is liable to propagate it? Are there any phonological properties that cannot be subject to change?

The general pattern of results can be illustrated by Labov's pioneering studies on English in New York City (1966) and on Martha's Vineyard (1963). Recall that in the New York City study Labov investigated the phonological variation of post-vocalic /r/ and other variables as a function of age, social class, gender, and style. From the point of view of this paper, the following results are of particular interest. All age groups were sensitive to the most prestigious variant, namely, post-vocalic /r/, and they could produce it, although the frequency of usage differed systematically across the age ranges as a function of age, gender, social class, and style. The subgroup most sensitive to post-vocalic /r/ turned out to be the females of the lower middle class aged around 40. They had the highest rate of hypercorrections.

Labov suggested that this synchronic pattern was a reflection of a sound change in progress. It is obvious from his findings that this change did not originate with children, nor were they the ones to primarily propagate it. At best, credit has to go to the middle-aged females. They were the most sensitive, although no age group proved totally insensitive to post-vocalic /r/. This finding goes counter to any assumptions to the effect that sound change originates with children (e.g. Halle, 1962; Kiparsky, 1965. Survey in Baron, 1977. Cf. Wode, 1984 for more details on this counter-argument against such traditional views).

For the purpose of this paper, it is important to notice that in order to be able to adjust one's own speech to ongoing sound change one needs to be able to perceive the changes in the pronunciation of the speech community. Since the speakers of all age ranges investigated by Labov were able to do so, it follows that all of them must have retained at least some of their original sensitivity for this type of contrast. Furthermore, the fact that the middle-aged females of the middle class excelled in hypercorrections does not mean that females are more sensitive to sound change on any biological grounds, because in Labov's study on Martha's Vineyard the males were the most advanced with respect to adapting to the sound changes. It follows, therefore, that people, throughout their entire life span, retain their ability to adjust to sound changes in their environment. Moreover, there is no indication at present that the perceptual abilities activated by adults for language change are different from those needed to perceive the phonic patterns of any unfamiliar language(s). There is no discontinuity with respect to these abilities. Consequently, it would be a strange result if the perception research would, in fact, show that adults cannot perceive non-native phonological contrasts.

Continuity and self-control[4]

The abilities required to adapt to language change can be regarded as a special case of yet another even more general ability of speakers, which, at the same time, constitutes a basic requirement for communication to be successful. Speakers need to be able to check on their own speech whether they are still in tune with the norms of their speech community. This is the metalinguistic function of languages (Jakobson, 1960). Just like the ability to adapt to sound change, the requirement that metalinguistic abilities be available to speakers throughout their life span is not consistent with any discontinuity claim.

The above remarks on language change, self-control, and age in language acquisition present evidence which is inconsistent with any radical discontinuity view with respect to the underlying abilities. It is from this vantage point that I want to look at speech perception across age ranges.

SPEECH PERCEPTION

Speech perception is rooted in the human auditory system. This system is capable of two modes of perception: the categorical mode and the continuous mode. The categorical mode operates on an all-or-none basis. For example, for a phone to be interpreted as /b/ no attention is paid to the degree of voicing, i.e. whether fully voiced, partly voiced, or whether there is only very little voicing. Obviously, speech perception and speech processing could not possibly work as fast as they do if they were not based on a categorical mode.

On the other hand, humans can discriminate very minute sound differences, such as levels of loudness or pitch height, e.g. when listening to non-speech sounds. This is achieved via the continuous mode.

The bimodal character of the auditory system is neither specific to the species of *homo sapiens*, because categorical perception has also been found in non-humans (e.g. Kuhl/Miller, 1978); nor is it restricted to speech, because non-speech sounds may also be perceived categorically (e.g. Miller, et al., 1976; Pisoni 1977). Moreover, the interaction of the two modes constitutes the mechanism that allows human beings to control, adjust, and create the categories of the target language(s). That is, the categorical mode provides for the categories; and the continuous mode allows human beings to monitor their own speech, to adjust the categories to any sound change, and to develop the category boundaries in those locations required by the target language(s) (Wode, 1990).

Methodologically, the investigation of speech perception is a highly technical matter. It is important to briefly review the basic cut of the experimental techniques in order to be able to appreciate the research results.

Experimental techniques

Speech perception can be said to be categorical if an acoustic continuum is perceived discontinuously. Two abilities are required, namely, discrimination and identification. Discrimination allows stimuli to be heard as being different; identification is required to recognize them as members of a specific category, e.g. the phoneme /b/ or /p/. The basic cut of the experimental designs to investigate categorial perception are still much like the ones during the late

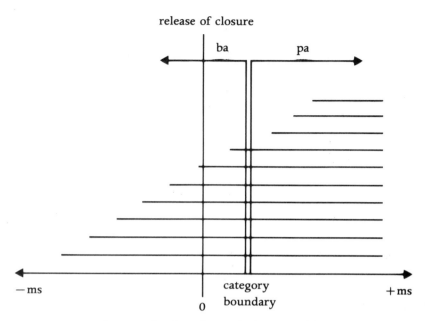

Figure 16.1   Schematic display of stimuli (horizontal lines) used for the detection of boundaries between perceptual categories, e.g. between /b/ and /p/. The stimuli (horizontal lines) are synthesized to differ in VOT by small margins each. Taken together, these stimuli form a continuum. Played to listeners they are perceived categorically according to the phonemes of the language. — indicates periodic vibration setting in before the release of the closure; + after the release.

1960s and 1970s (e.g. Liberman, et al., 1957; overview and references in Repp 1984; Wode 1990.) Figure 16.1 is a schematic illustration via the contrast voiced /ba/ vs. unvoiced /pa/.

The stimuli, represented by the horizontal lines, differ as to VOT (voice onset time). VOT marks the point at which voicing sets in relative to the release of the closure, e.g. before, after, or at the time of, the release. The stimuli are synthesized in such a way that the individual tokens differ only by a very small margin, say, 10 ms, so that the entire range of stimuli presents a (pseudo-)continuum. The tokens are randomized for presentation. Subjects are asked to discriminate the tokens and/or to identify them as /ba/ or /pa/. In general, discrimination scores are poor, i.e. random, for those stimuli which belong to the same category, but high for stimuli belonging to different categories. Similarly, within-category stimuli are identified as the same; across-category ones as different. The borderline between two categories is called the category boundary or the phoneme boundary. It is marked by an abrupt changeover in the judgements of the informants as to which category a stimulus belongs to.

The learnability of perceptual categories

Suppose the L1 learner is faced with an array of stimuli as in Figure 16.1. How is s/he to learn where to locate the phoneme boundary? Note that in this respect real speech is much like the situation represented in Figure 16.1. Consider final voiced fricatives in English. Some tokens may be fully voiced, others somewhat voiced, and still others may be completely devoiced. In such situations the category boundaries cannot be detected in any direct way from the acoustic properties of the speech wave. What, then, is the origin of these perceptual categorization abilities?

The ontogeny and the development of speech perception

Categorical perception

Assume, as a starting point, that the mature state is characterized by the perception of adult monolingual speakers. With them the category boundaries recur at values that are fairly stable. These values are language-specific, i.e. every language has its own values. There may be some variation as to their location across individual speakers (e.g. Simon/Fourcin, 1978; Gass 1984) and within the same speaker, the latter sort, however, only within narrow margins (e.g. Howell/Rosen, 1984). The term categorical, therefore, must be taken as referring to a high degree of categoriality. Moreover, it may take until age 16–18 before speakers arrive at the values for the perceptual categories of adults (e.g. Zlatin/Koenigsknecht, 1976; Flege/Eefting, 1986).

The initial state: The contribution of genetic endowment

At the present time, it appears that all the distinctions utilized for phonological purposes in natural languages are available to infants before they begin to speak. Some of these distinctions have been shown to be available with children as young as 4 weeks of age; other distinctions become available subsequently before the onset of speech. (For details and additional references cf. surveys like Jusczyk, 1981, 1986, Kuhl, 1987.) Apparently, children are born with the same abilities for speech perception irrespective of the language of their environment. Consider English, Spanish, and Kikuyu, a Bantu language of Kenya. They differ as to how voicing is made use of. English contrasts voiced unaspirated stops vs. voiceless aspirated stops; Spanish has prevoiced vs. voiceless unaspirated stops; and Kikuyu contrasts voiced vs. prevoiced stops, except for the labial place of articulation. Kikuyu has only one labial stop and it is prevoiced (Streeter, 1976). Pre-speaking infants, no matter which language they are exposed to, at first discriminate three different VOT ranges, namely, prevoiced, voiced, and voiceless, and the VOT boundaries are much the same for all children irrespective of the ambient language. Streeter, 1976, for example, found the three categories with Kikuyu children, although, as just noted, Kikuyu has only one labial stop which is prevoiced. Similarly, English infants are, at first, sensitive to prevoicing although it is not a distinctive feature of the phonological system of English (e.g. Lasky, et al., 1975; Aslin, et al., 1983).

Subsequent developments: the impact of external stimulation

These original abilities subsequently give rise to the category values of the input language. The major highlights of this development are summarized in Table 16.1.

Table 16.1. *The perception of two place-of-articulation contrasts by infants, children, and adults from L1 monolingual English environments as well as native adult speakers of Hindi and Thompson. Part (a) perception; (b) effect of training. Part (a) is based on Werker, et al., 1981, Werker/Tees, 1983; 1984; (b) on Tees/Werker, 1984 (adapted from Burnham, 1986:224).*

(a)

	infants			children			adults		
reached criterion	0;7	0;9	0;11	4;0	8;0	12;0	native English	trained English	native Hindi
/t̪/vs./ʈ/ YES	11	8	2	0	0	1	1	0	5
NO	1	4	10	12	12	11	9	10	0

(b)

	untrained English adults	trained English adults	native English-speaking adults with 5 years Hindi experience	students of Hindi with early exposure of Hindi language when tested		students of Hindi with no early exposure of Hindi language when tested	
reached criterion				1–2 wks.	1 yr	1–2 wks.	1 yr
/t̪/vs./ʈ/ YES	1	6	5	9	10	16	23
NO	14	8	0	1	0		15

The impact of the ambient language is already noticeable before the onset of speech. For example, the contrast between the retroflex/ṭ/ and the dental /ṭ/ is phonemic in Hindi, but not in English. Until age 0;7 the infants from monolingual English-speaking environments had the same ability to perceive /ṭ/ vs. /ṭ/ as infants growing up in a monolingual Hindi environment. Subsequently, the behaviour of the subjects changed. By age 0;9 only one-third of the English-environment subjects were successful up to criterion; by age 0;11 only 2 out of 12; and at age 4;0 none distinguished /ṭ/ vs. /ṭ/.

Whereas Table 16.1 provides data on what looks like total loss of perceptual abilities, other distinctions may be affected too, but not necessarily as radically as /ṭ/ and /ṭ/. Consider the Hindi contrast /t^h/ vs. /d^h/. Based on Werker, et al., 1981, Werker/Tees, 1983, and Tees/Werker, 1984, Burnham, 1986 points out that children and adults retain some ability to discriminate /t^h/ and /d^h/ even without training or exposure. In addition, it may take as little training as 1–2 weeks for adult students to be able to perform up to criterion in the discrimination of /d^h/ and /t^h/. This contrasts with the poor performance of the adults even after training for /ṭ/ and /ṭ/ (as summarized in Table 16.1). Note that training was successful only with those students who had had some prior exposure to Hindi early in life. In fact, these subjects were relearning Hindi rather than being exposed to it for the first time as their L2.

The development of non-native contrasts

How, and to what extent, can the perceptual abilities of learners be activated for the purpose of learning additional languages? Note that it is only via contact with additional languages that the true potential of the speech perception system of humans is revealed.

To date, there still is much less research on L2 than on L1 perception. (For an L2 overview cf. Flege, 1988). None the less, the available evidence is consistent with the following highly tentative view: People approach the task of learning an L2 on the basis of the state of development of their perceptual system, i.e. including their

L1 phonological system. According to equivalence theory (Wode, 1981, Flege, 1988), the latter forms the grid according to which L2 speech is at first processed. One possibility is that, as the L2 learner begins to make progress, some category boundaries developed through the L1 are gradually modified to serve both languages. For example, it has been observed by Caramazza, et al. (1973) and Williams (1979, 1980) that their fairly advanced speakers used a VOT boundary for stops that was a compromise intermediate between the L1 and the L2 and that matched neither one. This compromise boundary was used by the speakers for both their L1 and L2. At the present time, the status of such compromise categories is still unclear. For example, are they necessarily used to perceive and/or produce both the L2 and the L1? Flege/Hillenbrand (1984) and Flege (1987) have reported such compromise VOT boundaries also for production. What is their place in the developmental sequence? Are they due to lack of appropriate L1 input and hence due to unlearning the L1 distinctions? Do the compromise boundaries arise with all categories or only with certain ones? Unfortunately, not enough contrasts have been examined so far to suggest definite answers. In any event, in the subsequent course of development such compromise values need to be revised in such a way that the L1 is perceived and produced according to the appropriate L1 and L2 values. Can people do this?

One popular view is that at least adults cannot (e.g. Lenneberg, 1967). I have argued elsewhere that this claim is too strong and that the presently available explanations in terms of some critical period for language acquisition are not consistent with the evidence (Wode, 1981, 1990 cf. also Harley, 1986). As far as categorical perception is concerned, the evidence reviewed below suggests that the answer is not simply yes or no. It is important, however, to first briefly consider the continuous mode.

Continuous perception

Note that those crucial issues raised with respect to the categorical mode need to be applied to the continuous mode too. Two issues are particularly important: Does the continuous mode change as a function of age; and are there any age-dependent changes in the interplay between the categorical and the continuous mode? Recall that it was suggested above that the interaction between the continuous and the categorical mode functions as the mechanism that allows people to create, adjust, and/or maintain the categories of their ambient language(s). In particular the metalinguistic control function and people's ability to adapt to sound changes makes it very unlikely that the continuous mode changes as a function of age. I am not aware of any research that specifically investigates the development of the monitoring function of the continuous mode, but there is such evidence for the categorical mode.

Loss or accessing difficulties?

It begins to appear from recent experiments (notably, Werker/Tees, 1984, Werker/Logan, 1985, Best, et al., 1988) that the original categorical sensitivities do not cease to exist. For example, Werker/ Tees, 1984 ran a series of experiments to check on 3 alternative explanations: Are the differences in the perceptual behaviour of adults due to (a) a decline or a loss of sensory abilities after being exposed to a language that lacks these contrasts; (b) to a shift in attentional focus; or (c) to changes in the processing strategies? The subjects were adult speakers of English. They were tested on their ability to discriminate natural tokens of the Hindi retroflex vs. dental stop contrast and the glottalized velar vs. uvular stop contrast of Thompson, an Amerindian language of British Columbia, Canada. The stimuli were presented in two different conditions. In one condition, the interval between the stimuli was 500 ms, and in the other 1500 ms. All subjects, including the adults, were able to discriminate the contrasts in the 500-ms condition; the 1500-ms condition yielded the results summarized in Table 16.1.

Obviously, the original abilities are still in existence, but access to them is made difficult or blocked via the rise of the categories associated with phonemic perception. An analogous experiment with synthetic stimuli produced the same results (Werker/Logan, 1985). Since then additional evidence is becoming available (Best, et al., 1988 for Zulu clicks; Polka/Werker, under review, for vowels). These studies are consistent with Werker's original result in so far as the original sensitivities remain available, but may become increasingly difficult to access. However, Polka's and Werker's findings on the perception of vowels by 6–8 and 10–12 month old infants suggest that the developmental sequences may differ depending on the categories involved, for instance, whether consonants or vowels. Obviously, there is a great need for more research of this sort and caution is required with respect to any premature generalizations.

Speech perception within UTA

Integrating the individual aspects discussed above, speech perception in humans can be said to develop out of their auditory system. This system is genetically endowed and constitutes the biological foundation for speech perception.

The auditory system is characterized by areas of heightened sensitivity and it provides for 2 modes of perception. Both are required for the development of speech perception. They constitute the genetically endowed prerequisites for speech perception in humans (Eimas, et al., 1971). The continuous mode functions as a control device for the development of the categories of the categorical mode, and it remains unchanged throughout life.

As for the speech perceptual categories, they develop out of those perceptual contrasts for which human beings are particularly sensitive. These abilities allow infants to respond to the sounds of the target language already during the prelinguistic period, i.e. while the child does not understand the language(s) yet. As Table 16.1 suggests, during this time infants create a perceptual–cognitive system of categories as a reflex of the phonic pattern of the ambient language(s). This category system is prephonemic, because, as Werker/Pegg, 1992 point out, infants at that time do not have phonemes yet. At this stage, therefore, the developments in the categorical mode are due to the fact that those phonetic properties not exploited for distinctive purposes are either rare in the input or they do not occur there at all. This pre-phonemic system allows prelinguistic infants to desensitize to those distinctions that are not needed in the ambient language(s), and become more sensitive to those that are needed without any loss of the original categorical sensitivity. Moreover, the prephonemic system makes sure that, when children begin to speak, they already have a first approximation towards the target categories. As children develop after the onset of speech, their distinctions continue to be shaped towards the target. The mature state may not be reached until age 16–18.

In monolingual situations, the development results in the fact that those original sensitivities not required by the target become less readily available. The degree of availability differs depending on the category involved. Some contrasts, at least with some speakers, cannot be activated immediately upon first contact with an additional language. Recall the difficulty that the English-speaking adults had in identifying the retroflex vs. dental stops of Hindi (Table 16.1). The abilities for other contrasts may remain more readily available, for example, the relative retention of the ability to identify the Hindi voiced vs. voiceless aspirated stops by speakers of English.

It is the state of development of the individual learner's speech perceptual system that determines how its various functions are met, namely, self-control, adaptation to language change, and language contact. I use the latter term to draw attention to the fact that L2 acquisition is merely a special case of the more general phenomenon of what may happen in language contact situations. This also subsumes pidginization and borrowing. As for their psycholinguistic basis in general and the perceptual one in particular, there is no reason to assume that L2 acquisition, pidginization, and borrowing, are based on a different perceptual machinery.

As for the details of learning additional languages, e.g. L2, L3, etc., one of the major problems is to explain the systematic nature of the phonological substitutions including transfer. Here I rely on equivalence theory (Wode, 1978, 1981; Flege, 1987, 1988, 1992). If a new language has phonological elements that are identical with some already developed by the speaker, then they are handled via the pre-existing categories. In the case of totally new elements, i.e. categories which are perceived as not resembling any category of the L1, no pre-existing category will do. The learner needs to go back to her/his original categorical sensitivities and develop the new target. Since the particular area of sensitivity is not preoccupied by other categories, learners tend to be successful, although it may take some time (Flege, 1992). What they activate is their original categorical and continuous sensitivities.

Similar elements, i.e. categories perceived as similar though not identical to the L1 categories, present the most difficult case. The L2 elements feed into pre-existing categories. As a consequence the similar elements are handled easily and fairly consistently in borrowing as well as in pidginization and L2 acquisition. Since the areas of sensitivity are preoccupied by other categories, the original categorical sensitivity is difficult to access, because language processing is based on the categorical mode.

CONCLUSIONS

UTA is an attempt to integrate prior work and to overcome undesirable discontinuities, such as the implausible idea that totally different learning abilities should be activated for different acquisitional types. UTA is based on a restatement of the domain of the theory of language acquisition. The basis for UTA is the biological apparatus of *homo sapiens* and certain functional abilities common to all of humankind. UTA attempts to reconstruct and specify them at birth and traces their development as a function of age and/or experience.

For the purpose of this paper the domain of speech perception was chosen for illustration. The biological basis is the auditory system. It was shown to provide, at birth or probably before, certain abilities indispensable to the learning and functioning of natural human languages. These original abilities constitute the biological substrata for speech perception. They interact with external stimulation to create the speech perceptual categories of the ambient language(s).

The present state of the art requires caution with respect to any generalizations and many issues that may immediately come to mind cannot be answered yet. For example, how many category systems can be created by the auditory system? This question is important in view of the fact, that languages tend to have different phonological systems and that, to date, there is no principled reason such as based on biology, that restricts the number of languages that individuals can learn.

Another issue is the relationship between perception and production. The details are anything but clear. None the less, the perception research holds great promise. For instance, the fact that infants create some kind of pre-phonemic category system long before they begin to speak explains why the structure of babbling may change towards the phonic pattern of the ambient language(s), and why babbling can function as a precursor to phonemic development without the infant having recourse to phonemic principles (cf. Wode, in press, for details of this argument).

At the present state of the art, it is probably the age issue that is likely to benefit more than any other issue. Most of the previous approaches to age are not specific enough. There is, for example, the idea that there should be some period when the acquisition of an additional language becomes difficult or impossible, e.g. puberty (Lenneberg, 1967) or age 6;0 (Long, 1990, this volume). Others have suggested that there is an optimal age, although differing for phonology, morphology, syntax, or other domains (e.g. Ervin-Tripp, 1974. For an overview cf. Harley, 1986; Wode 1988). Such suggestions do not answer the question of what may cause these differences. The presently available findings for speech perception clearly indicate that no satisfactory understanding is likely to be forthcoming if we continue to analyse the development of learning abilities in terms of looking at the entire language. We need to single out, and study in detail, the individual abilities that it takes to master specific domains, such as speech perception, production phonology, or the various areas of morphology, syntax, or semantics.

Hopefully, we may then be in a position to generalize on the nature and the cause of what on the surface looks like age-dependent differences. There is no need to assume that all language learning abilities follow the same pattern as the auditory abilities. Some alternatives to consider are whether the acquisitional abilities available at birth

(a) give rise to the L1('s) and then cease to exist;
(b) give rise to the L1('s), continue unchanged and remain re-activatable for the acquisition of additional languages;
(c) give rise to the L1('s), but change in the process;
(d) give rise to the L1('s), continue to exist unchanged, but become increasingly difficult to access and/or activate as a function of the way linguistic information is stored and/or retrieved in memory?

There is no a priori reason at all that any of the above options must be ruled out in principle. I am further assuming that not all components of the human language learning capacity should be subject to the same explanation. In fact, speech perception appears to follow option (d) above, developmental structures like NP NEG VP appear to follow (b).

In a more general perspective, perhaps the most important challenge growing out of UTA in conjunction with the development of speech perception is a methodological one. To really understand the true nature of the language learning capacity of human beings it is necessary to go beyond monolingual L1 acquisition and study other acquisitional types. Recall that only by going beyond L1 perception was it possible to clarify the status of the original perceptual abilities over time.

NOTES

1 There are other uses of the term continuity with reference to language acquisitional abilities. Pinker, 1984, for example, excludes from the above readings the possibility of developmental changes by assuming that learning abilities remain unchanged throughout life. But note that Pinker is only concerned with L1 acquisition.

2 Discontinuity views used to be popular in foreign language teaching research (e.g. Lane, 1962). The idea was that since the situation in the classroom is so radically different from non-classroom situations the learning abilities had to be different, too. In addition, discontinuity is implicit in a general way in approaches to linguistics that look only at monolingual situations, which is true for most of the current linguistic approaches.

3 By now there are several versions of the general idea that there is a critical period for language acquisition. See Harley, 1986 for a recent survey. For the purpose of this discussion it is immaterial whether one adopts a strong version, i.e. claiming biologically based age-dependent changes, or a weaker one assuming some reduction in the sensitivity or flexibility of the functional potential.

4 I use the term self-control to avoid confusion with the term monitor in Krashen's sense (e.g. 1981).

REFERENCES

Aslin, R. N., Pisoni, D. D., and Jusczyk, P. W. (1983), Auditory development and speech perception in infancy. In Haith, M., and Campos, J. (eds.), *Handbook of child phonology infancy and developmental psychobiology*, II. New York: Wiley.

Baron, N. S. (1977), *Language acquisition and historical change.* Amsterdam: North-Holland Publ. Co.

Best, C. T., McRoberts, G. W., and Sithole, N. M. (1988), Examination of perceptual reorganisation for nonnative speech contrasts: Zulu Click discrimination by English-speaking adults and infants. *Journal of Experimental Psychology*, 14, 345–60.

Burnham, D. K. (1986), Developmental loss of speech perception: Exposure to and experience with a first language. *Applied Psycholinguistics*, 7, 207–40.

Caramazza, A., Yeni-Komshian, G., Zurif, E., and Carbone, E. (1973), The acquisition of a new phonological contrast. The case of stop consonants in French-English bilinguals. *Journal of the Acoustical Society of America*, 54, 421–8.

Eimas, P. D., Siqueland, E. R., Jusczyk, P., and Vigorito, J. (1971), Speech perception in infants. *Science*, 171, 303–6.

Ervin-Tripp, S. M. (1973), Some strategies for the first two years. In

Moore, T. E. (ed.), *Cognitive development and the acquisition of language*, 261–86. New York, London: Academic Press.

(1974). Is second language learning like the first? *TESOLQ*, 8, 111–27.

Flege, J. E. (1987), The production of 'new' and 'similar' phones in a foreign language: evidence for the effect of equivalence classification. *Journal of Phonetics*, 15, 47–65.

(1988), The production and perception of foreign language speech sounds. In Winitz, H. (ed.), *Human communication and its disorders: A review 1988*, 224–401. Norwood, N.J.: Ablex.

(1992), The intelligibility of English vowels spoken by British and Dutch talkers. In Kent, R. (ed.), *Intelligibility in speech disorders: Theory, measurement and management* I, pp. 157–232. Amsterdam: John Benjamins.

Flege, J. E., and Eefting, W. Z. (1985), Linguistic and developmental effect on the production and perception of stop consonants. *Phonetica*, 43, 155–71.

Flege, J. E., and Hillenbrand, J. (1984), Limits on pronunciation accuracy in adult foreign language speech production. *Journal of the Acoustical Society of America*, 76, 708–21.

Gass, S. (1984), Development of speech perception and speech production in adult second language learners. *Applied Psycholinguistics*, 5, 51–74.

Halle, M. (1962), Phonology in generative grammar. *Word*, 18, 54–72.

Harley, B. (1986), *Age and second-language acquisition*. Clevedon: Multilingual Matters.

Hatch, E. M. (1974). Second language learning – universals? *Working Papers in Bilingualism*, 3, 1–17.

Jakobson, R. (1960), Linguistics and poetics. *Sebeok*, 350–77.

Jusczyk, P. (1981), Infant speech perception: A critical appraisal. In Eimas, P. D., and Miller, J.-L. (eds.), *Perspectives on the study of speech* (113–64). Hillsdale, N.J.: Lawrence Erlbaum.

(1986), Toward a model of the development of speech perception. In Perkell, J. S., and Klatt, D. H. (eds.), *Invariance and variability in speech processes*, pp. 1–19. Hillsdale, N.J.: Lawrence Erlbaum.

Kiparky, P. (1965), *Phonological change*. Ph.D. thesis. MIT.

Krashen, S. D. (1981), *Second language acquisition and second language learning*. Oxford: Pergamon Press.

Kuhl, P. K. (1987), Perception of speech and sound in early infancy. In Salapatek, P., and Cohen, L. (eds.), *Handbook of infant perception II*, pp. 275–381. New York: Academic.

Kuhl, P. K., and Miller, J. D. (1978), Speech perception by the Chinchilla: Identification functions for synthetic VOT stimuli. *Journal of the Acoustical Society of America*, 63, 905–17.

Labov, W. (1963), The social motivation of a sound change. *Word*, 19, 271–309.

(1966), *The social stratification of English in New York City*. Washington, DC: Center for Applied Linguistics.

Lane, H. (1962), Some differences between first and second language learning. *Language Learning*, 12, 1–14.

Lasky, R. E., Syrdal-Lasky, S., and Klein, R. E. (1975), VOT discrimination by four to six and a half year old infants from Spanish environments. *Journal of Experimental Child Psychology*, 20, 215–25.

Lenneberg, E. (1967), *Biological foundations of language*. New York: Wiley.

Liberman, A. M., Harris, K. S., Hoffman, H. S., and Griffith, B. C. (1957), The discrimination of speech sounds within and across phoneme boundaries. *Journal of Experimental Psychology*, 54, 358–68.

Lisker, L., and Abramson, A. (1964), A cross-language study of voicing in initial stops: Acoustic measurements. *Word*, 230, 384–422.

Long, M. H. (1990), Maturational constraints on language development. *Studies in Second Language Acquisition*, 12, 251–85.

Miller, J. D., Wier, L., Pastore, R., Kelly, W., and Dooling, R. (1976), Discrimination and labeling of noise-buzz sequences with varying noise-lead times: An example of categorical perception. *Journal of the Acoustical Society of America*, 60, 410–17.

Pisoni, D. B. (1977), Identification and discrimination of the relative onset time of two component tones: Implications for voicing perception in stops. *Journal of the Acoustical Society of America*, 61, 1352–61.

Polka, L., and Werker, J. (under review), Developmental changes in perception of non-native vowel contrasts. (Submitted to *Journal of Experimental Psychology: Human Perception and Performance*).

Repp, B. H. (1984), Categorical perception. Issues, methods, findings. In Lass, N. (ed.), *Speech and language: Advances in basic research and practice*, X, pp. 243–335. New York: Academic Press.

Simon, S., and Fourcin, A. J. (1978), Cross-language study of speech-pattern learning, *Journal of the Acoustical Society of America*, 63, 925–35.

Streeter, L. A. (1976), Kikuyu labial and apical stop discrimination. *Journal of Phonetics*, 4, 43–49.

Tees, R. C., and Werker, J. F. (1984), Perceptual flexibility: maintenance or recovery of the ability to discriminate non-native speech sounds. *Canadian Journal of Psychology*, 38:4, 579–90.

Werker, J., Gilbert, J., Humphry, I., and Tees, R. (1981). Developmental aspects of cross-language speech perception. *Child Development*, 52, 349–55.

Werker, J., and Tees, R. (1983), Developmental changes across childhood in the perception of non-native speech sounds. *Canadian Journal of Psychology*, 37:2, 278–86.

(1984), Phonemic and phonetic factors in adult cross-language speech perception. *Journal of the Acoustical Society of America*, 75, 1866–78.

Werker, J. F., and Logan, J. S. (1985), Cross-language evidence for three factors in speech perception. *Perception and Psychophysics*, 37, 35–44.

Werker, J., and Pegg, J. (1992), Infant speech perception and phonological acquisition. In Ferguson, C. A., Menn, L., and Stoel-Gammon, C. (eds.), *Phonological development: models, research, implications*, pp. 285–311. Timonium, MD: York Press.

Williams, L. (1979), The modification of speech perception and production in second-language learning. *Perception and Psychophysics*, 26, 95–104.

(1980), Phonetic variation as a function of second-language learning. In Yeni-Komshian, G., Kavanagh, J., and Ferguson, C. A. (eds.), *Child Phonology, 2, Perception*, pp. 185–216. New

York: Academic.

Wode, H. (1974), Natürliche Zweisprachigkeit: Probleme, Aufgaben, Perspektiven. *Linguistische Berichte*, 32, 15–36.

(1978), The beginnings of L2-phonological acquisition. *IRAL*, 16, 109–24.

(1981), *Learning a second language: An integrated view of language acquisition.* Tübingen: Narr.

(1984), Psycholinguistische Grundlagen sprachlicher Universalien: Möglichkeiten eines empirischen Paradigmas. *Folia Linguistica*, 18, 345–77.

(1988), *Einführung in die Psycholinguistik. Theorien, Methoden, Ergebnisse.* Ismaning: Hueber.

(1990), Continuity in the development of language acquisitional abilities. In: Burmeister, H., and Rounds, P. L. (eds.), *Variability in second language acquisition. Proceedings of the 10th meeting of the Second Language Research Forum, vol. 1,* 85–116.

(1992), Categorical perception and segmental coding in the ontogeny of sound systems: A universal approach. In Ferguson, C. A., Menn, L., and Stoel-Gammon, C. (eds.), *Phonological development: models, research, implications,* pp. 605–631. Timonium, MD: York Press.

(in press), Perzeption, Produktion und die Lernbarkeit von Sprachen. In Ramers, K. H., Vater, H., und Wode, H. (eds.) *Universale phonologische Strukturen und Prozesse.* Wiesbaden: Niemeyer.

Zlatin, M., and Koenigsknecht, R. (1975), Development of the voicing contrast: Perception of stop consonants. *Journal of Speech and Hearing Research*, 18, 541–53.

(1976), Development of the voicing contrast: A comparison of voice onset time in stop perception and production. *Journal of Speech and Hearing Research*, 19, 93–111.

17 · The course of development in
second language phonology
acquisition: a natural path or
strategic choice?

BJÖRN HAMMARBERG

Modern theories of second language acquisition (SLA) have put
emphasis on the learner's active creative role and on natural
linguistic constraints which govern the acquisitional process. The
two notions of learner creativity and natural constraints are
generally, in one form or another, considered to be essential aspects
of the process of SLA. Yet it is not always clear how they are thought
to interrelate. Obviously, there is an inherent dualism in viewing the
learner on the one hand, as an active operator, and on the other, as
subject to constraints which make him follow preconditioned paths.
In SLA research, one of these aspects will often seem more central to
the purpose of study than the other, and will therefore be focused
more. Thus, in some areas of L2 research, typically studies in a
communicational and interactional perspective, the learner's pur-
posefulness has generally been foregrounded, and options, strategies, and choices have been matters of central interest. In other
areas, typically studies dealing with developmental patterns and
acquisitional routes, the focus has rather been on the 'constraint'
aspect, and the concern has been more with uniformity, predictability, and conditioning factors. The hypothesis of a 'natural route of
interlanguage development' has become a central notion here. The
linguistically inherent constraints on the shaping of the learner
language have been analyzed in terms of notions such as markedness
relations, simplification, and transfer.

The standpoint taken here is that we are dealing with the same general process of SLA in all the cases mentioned, and that it is important to join together the two perspectives of 'strategic creativity' and 'natural constraint' into an integrated view. This means that the learner must be seen as both 'purposeful' and 'constrained,' that each of the two aspects has an essential role to play in the L2 acquisition process, that they function together, and that the interrelation between them is a crucial matter. The aim of this chapter is to discuss some aspects of this choice–constraint interface within the domain of L2 phonology acquisition, particularly on the basis of how learners' solutions vary and develop with regard to specific points in L2 segmental phonology. The data will be drawn from a more extensive study of learner solutions in the early stages of adult L2 acquisition in which German learners of Swedish were investigated. A full account of that study is given in Hammarberg (1988).

Within the larger project, 5 adult Germans (3 women and 2 men, aged 18–25) acquiring Swedish in daily life in Sweden were observed individually at 3 points of time during their initial stages of contact with Swedish: in their first, second, and fourth month of stay, respectively. On each occasion, a combination of phonetic tests and conversations was carried out. At Time 1, the attempts to start simple conversations in Swedish merely confirmed that the subjects at that point knew no Swedish. But, at Time 2 and 3, a conversational corpus totalling about 40 minutes for each subject could be recorded. The subject and myself, a native speaker of Central Swedish, were the participants.

The relevant parts of the test and conversational data will be presented below.

STRATEGIC ACTION AND NATURAL CONSTRAINTS

What is at issue here is the formation of the learner's phonological *solutions* on specific points in the second language. The learner is faced with the need to establish (mental representations of) sound segment categories as well as phonotactic and prosodic structures, acquire the adequate perceptual and articulatory routines for their precise phonetic realization, and come to grips with the patterns of speech style and lectal variation encountered in the target L2 community. These various tasks may be identified as *problems* to which solutions are sought. The learner, who is the actor in the process, is then looked upon as a problem-solver in the sense used in cognitive psychology (cf. Anderson, 1990) with the combined aim of (a) processing messages and acting in communicative situations, and (b) acquiring the linguistic code and continuously adjusting his own version of it to match that of the target language speakers as adequately as possible.

In accordance with what has been said above, L2 phonological development can be assumed to be purpose-driven and constraint-governed (in some combination). On a general level, we may identify the need to expand communicative resources and the need to integrate socially with the target language environment as motives which drive progression in L2 phonology. Both these ambitions may of course be more or less strong in a particular learner; however, I will not attempt to explore this aspect of variation in the present chapter.

Within an information-processing framework, McLaughlin (1987, 1990) describes SLA as the learning of a complex cognitive skill by a combined process of developing automaticity and restructuring acquired information. In the present context of focusing on the formation of learner solutions, it is especially the 'restructuring' aspect of this process which is of prime interest. It could (and should, as I see it) be taken to include the structuring underlying the very early solutions in the initial phase of L2 acquisition. In the framework proposed by McLaughlin, restructuring takes place when an automated skill at the previous stage has made the learner ready for it. The central question in our context is what guides the (re)structuring process and shapes the resulting solutions.

Working empirically from the manifestations of learner solutions in observed L2 performance, we may try to identify *strategies* employed by the learner to produce the solutions. A 'strategy' will here be understood in the sense of a plan which the learner constructs and executes in order to handle encountered problems, as proposed by Færch and Kasper (1980). The kind of strategies we have to do with here can be characterized with Færch and Kasper's terminology as 'psycholinguistic learning strategies', or using Ellis' (1986) terms as 'cognitive strategies for learning L2'.

Variant solutions in L2 sound identification and pronunciation can in many cases be interpreted as the outcome of alternative learner strategies. For example, a Swedish sound type which is unfamiliar to most non-Swedes is the voiceless dorsopalatal–dorsovelar fricative [ɧ], used e.g. in *sjö* 'lake,' *sked* 'spoon', *choklad* 'chocolate'. An imitation test with Germans yielded the variants [ç] (dorsopalatal), [ʃ] (predorsoalveolar), [x] (dorsovelar), and [f] (labiodental), each reflecting a different strategy (or line of action) taken by the learners in order to approximate the target sound.

Examining the learning strategies becomes crucial in those cases where we have evidence for *strategic choice* in the formation of learner solutions, i.e. where a choice between alternative strategies can be identified. Strategies are purposeful in the sense that they are goal-oriented, i.e. in our case directed towards the phonological problems at hand, yet I see no point in assuming that the choice of strategy for a particular task is a matter of which the learner must be consciously aware.

Various types of learning strategies have been defined according to the source of information on which they are based. Thus, following Færch and Kasper (1980) (but with certain changes in terminology made here), we may distinguish *inductive* (input-based), *deductive* (based on previous knowledge), and *inferential* strategies (based on both input and knowledge); a knowledge-based (deductive or inferential) strategy may be intralingually based (*L2-generalization*) or interlingually based (cross-language *transfer*), or both. I will give some illustrations of such types in the following.

As McLaughlin (1987) points out, a cognitive skill theory is not in itself sufficient to explain the choice of solutions and the course of development in SLA. It 'needs to be linked to linguistic theories of second-language acquisition. By itself, for example, the cognitive perspective cannot explain such linguistic constraints as are implied in markedness theory or that may result from linguistic universals... Similarly, an account of transfer phenomena requires linguistic considerations.' (McLaughlin, 1987:150.)

In other words, it is necessary to analyze the learning problems linguistically in order to account for the language-dependent constraints or influences which may condition the choice of strategies and the shape of learner solutions. 'Natural' linguistic solutions derive from the ways 'natural' processing factors act upon the various kinds of linguistic structures that the learner has to interpret and render. Such factors are typically related to the simplicity dimension (leading to target-simplifying solutions) and/or the familiarity dimension (yielding transfer solutions, notably from L1).

Generally speaking, a natural tendency in early L2 phonology will be for the learner to produce phonetically motivated and structurally uncomplicated solutions. If the target structure is unmanageable (complex, marked) or involves phonetically unmotivated alternation of form, the learner will tend to set out with a corresponding simpler/less-marked solution, or one that ignores the alternation. Basically the same principle applies to transferability. The learner will transfer categories and rules from L1 to the extent that they are 'psychologically real' for him as a speaker of L1, which in turn has to do with their being phonetically motivated and not limited by lexical exceptions, morphological environment conditions etc. (Cf. Hammarberg 1988, 1989, 1990 for discussions of the simplicity/familiarity and naturalness issues in the present context.)

Our question then is to what extent the learner, when tackling problems in L2, can choose freely between potentially available strategies, and to what extent this choice is preconditioned by language-dependent natural factors. We will first examine some variant solutions and their development.

SOME TEST DATA FOR VARIATION
AND DEVELOPMENT

Available research findings show that variation is abundant in L2 phonology. This is shown very clearly in L. Dickerson's (1974) investigation of 10 Japanese learners' development of their English pronunciation. (Cf. also L. Dickerson, 1975; W. Dickerson, 1976.)

Basing her study on a Labovian model of phonological variation, Dickerson demonstrated that interlanguage pronunciation varies in a patterned way and develops over time by shifting gradually to variants that come closer to the target norm. That is, the coexistence of variant solutions constitutes a normal state and a basis for development; by and by, the learner introduces 'better' variants and uses them with increasing frequency, thus gradually replacing the 'worse' variants, which are used less frequently and are eventually abandoned (if development reaches this point). This general pattern can be traced for a given speaker, phoneme, phonetic environment, and contextual style with great regularity in Dickerson's data. It was demonstrated in a parallel way with read material (word lists, sentences) and free speech.

Although this study certainly contributed important insights, the picture it produces is somewhat problematic. There seems to be a built-in bias for a uniform natural route hypothesis because of the method of evaluating variants. These are ranked on the basis of the degree of phonetic similarity with the target variant, and an index score is calculated for the coexisting variants at each point of time in order to measure progress. In this way the variants of each variable are (for each speaker, phonetic environment, and contextual style) ordered on a uniform, linear scale according to how close to the target they are found to be, and the progress over time, if any, is also viewed as a gradual development along a line. But the ways in which the variants differ in type from the target and from each other are not considered.

The ranking of variants seems to work rather well with the English consonant phonemes that Dickerson chooses to examine as variables. But other cases can be found where it is striking that the occurring variants are very different in type and may not be so easy to order. In the previously mentioned German–Swedish study, this is true of certain phonotactic structures, such as word-final /lj/, /rj/ and /ŋn/ which German learners find difficult to render. ([lj] here symbolizes a voiced palatal fricative or glide.) These items tend to produce a rich repertoire of variants both in spontaneous production and in tests. Thus, for example, one learner within a time span of a few minutes during a conversation produced the following instances of the word *familj* [faˈmɪlj] 'family':

[ən stuᵉ fəmijˀ]	*en stor familj*	'a large family'
[ən stuᵉ fəmiljə]	*en stor familj*	
[ən fəmijə po landn̩]	*en familj på landen*	'a family in the country'
[ən stuᵉ famɪlj]	*en stor familj*	
[ən fəmɪlç fʁon afʁɪka]	*en familj från Afrika*	'a family from Africa'

In the German–Swedish learner data, the following main types of variants for final /lj/ can be distinguished:

(1) Reduction to [l] or [j]
(2) Syllabization: [li]
(3) Epenthetic vowel: [ljə]
(4) Final devoicing: [lç]
(5) Target variant: [lj]

We may try to rank them according to a natural principle by placing them on various points along a scale of simplification/elaboration. Then the reductive variants (1) should be placed lowest since they miss out a whole consonant segment; after this we place (2) which vocalizes [j] and changes the syllable structure; then (3) which preserves [lj] but simplifies the syllable structure of the word by adding a syllabic element; then (4) which preserves the syllable structure but replaces the voiced [j] with the less marked, voiceless [ç]; finally (5), the target variant.

But we should also notice the fact that these various learner solutions do not form a phonetic continuum, but rather apply a range of different phonetic ways of finding a substitute for the target structure /lj/. We may describe them as approaching the target from a number of alternative directions:

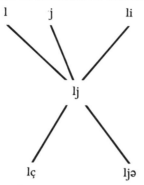

These phonotactic structures are not very frequent in free speech, particularly not in the speech of beginners, so, in order to get an adequate amount of data to study variation patterns, we have to elicit learner responses. For that purpose, items with word-final /lj/, /rj/ and /ŋn/ were included in a mixture with other items in an imitation test where the task was to listen to phonotactically well-formed Swedish nonsense words and to repeat them in a standard phrase. The test was given to the 5 German subjects at Time 1, and then repeated at Time 2 and 3, so that a version from each stage was recorded for each subject. The answers were evaluated orally and transcribed by me. Table 17.1 shows the distribution of the occurring variants of /lj/ by subject and time.

The table shows variation both intra- and interindividually, as well as change over time. Let us focus on the issue of learner choice vs. natural route.

To obtain a rank order of variants, I have assigned index values according to the principle of simplification/elaboration mentioned above. Before going into the problems involved with this ranking, let us look at the version shown in the table. The epenthesis variant ([ljə]) here gets the lowest value, O. It is then followed by a variant with a weaker syllabic element ([ljᵊ]), variants with devoicing *and* an

Table 17.1. *Learner imitations of word-final /lj/. Frequency distribution of variants.*

Subject	Time	Variants with index values		lçə	lç		Number of test	Index
		ljə	ljᵊ	ljə	lj̬	lj	items	score
		0	1	2	3	4		
KG	1	4	1				5	1
	2	5					5	0
	3	2	3				5	3
WG	1	4				1	5	4
	2	3	1			1	5	5
	3	2	1			2	5	9
HH	1	5					5	0
	2	1	3			1	5	7
	3	2	2			1	5	6
GS	1	5					5	0
	2	5					5	0
	3	4				1	5	4
WW	1	3		1	1		5	5
	2	1	1		1	2	5	12
	3		1	1	2	1	5	13

epenthetic vowel ([lçə, ljə]), final devoicing variants ([lç, lj̬]), and the target variant ([lj]). An index score for each line in the table is obtained by multiplying the frequency of each variant with its index value and adding up those totals. The index score in this case may vary between 0 and 20. Progress over time should then be reflected by an increasing index score from one time to the next for the learner in question. Equal scores indicate stagnation, and decreasing scores regression. Progress can also be seen in the table as a tendency for variant frequency values to move from the top left towards the bottom right for a given subject. In general, the table shows a clear tendency for all subjects to shift gradually from lower-ranked to higher-ranked variants. This general pattern agrees with the one found by Dickerson.

Another observation can be made that makes the picture more complicated, however. Besides the variation between epenthesis and devoicing variants, there is a scale of variants within each of these types, each forming a phonetic continuum of approaching the target: [ljə ... lj^{ə} ... lj] and [lç ... lj̥ ... lj]. Obviously, we have to distinguish *variation of type* (where learner solutions apply different phonetic means) from *variation of degree* (where there are various degrees of approximation to the target along the same phonetic dimension). (The variation of type only occurs with WW in this table, but more evidence for it is found in the data for /rj/ and /ŋn/ which are left out here for reasons of space.) This makes the ranking of variants problematic. Is strong devoicing ([lç]) 'better' than a weakly articulated epenthetic vowel? In the table I have adhered to the principle of not interrupting continua of degree, but this is clearly a somewhat crude solution to the problem. The strong and light devoicing variants are rather difficult to delimit safely in each instance, but with the epenthesis variants it is clear that the ones with a weaker vowel increase over time. In analogy with the figure given above, we may represent this complex variation in the following way:

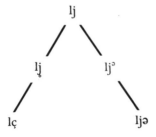

The interpretation I would suggest in order to account for these observations is that the variation of degree is a matter of approximation to the target along a linear continuum of development, whereas the variation of type rather reflects alternation of learner strategies. The learner (here WW), as it were, bets on different horses and gradually works out which one is best.

A further fact which I think supports this conclusion is the existence of variants with both devoicing and epenthesis ([lçə, ljə]. These are peculiar: on the one hand, final devoicing is motivated as a transfer solution because German has a rule of final devoicing of obstruents which has proved to be quite productive in L2 acquisition, but on the other hand the epenthetic vowel destroys the proper phonetic environment for this rule, and thus would seem to cancel the motivation for devoicing. Thus, [lçə, ljə] cannot be explained as an intermediate stage in a phonetic development from [ljə] to [lç, lj]. Rather, they must be understood as hybrid solutions, reflecting the combined application of two strategies which the learner has established and also uses separately. Here they are accessed and activated simultaneously. We may incorporate this in our figure, indicating this interference between strategies with dotted lines:

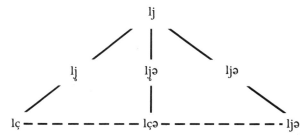

It thus seems that variation is of a complex kind, involving alternation between strategies which produce variants of type, some mechanism of evaluating co-occurring solutions, and continua of phonetic approximation within variants of type, resulting in variants of degree.

The synchronic coexistence of target and non-target variants within an individual learner, and WW's alternation of epenthesis and devoicing variants, suggests that the learner in question at that time identifies the target structure perceptually as /lj/, and that the problem here is one of production. The alternation of strategies may then reflect the learner's feeling that his production is still inadequate, which makes him try various ways.

FREE OR GOVERNED CHOICE

If variants of type result from the application of alternative phonetic strategies, how free is the learner to choose?

Obviously the choice of variants for /lj/ in our example above is constrained in some ways by natural conditions. For one thing, we saw that the learner solutions are explainable in terms of simplification/elaboration, and that more elaborate solutions tended to increase over time. Also, all the variants except the target and its close approximations comply with L1 phonotactic restrictions. This provides evidence for a transfer effect.

There is evidence that the status of the particular phonological regularity which is involved may affect the extent to which the learner is forced to simplify or to comply with L1. Learner pronunciation of /r/ constitutes a case where this can be illustrated.

In German, /r/ shows a complex pattern of phonetic variation. An extensive empirical investigation has been made by Ulbrich (1972). Concise descriptions can be found in handbooks such as Moulton (1962), Kohler (1977), and Benware (1986). Briefly stated, there is (1) a dialectal dimension of variation in that some speakers use a uvular fricative or approximant [ʁ] or trill [R] whereas others use an apical trill or flap [r, ɾ]. We may label them *R speakers* and *r speakers*, respectively. There is (2) a positional dimension of variation in that /r/ in most dialects is usually vocalized to [ɐ] in positions postvocally in the syllable (i.e. in the syllable coda), but not prevocally in the syllable (i.e. in the onset). Vocalization is a form of articulatory reduction, and here some phonetic environments thus favour this process more than others. Finally (3), there is a stylistic dimension of variation in that trills tend to be used in slow, careful speech and the more reduced variants in casual speech.

Swedish /r/ varies in a partially similar way. There is a dialect

Table 17.2. *Learner pronunciation of /r/ in free speech recorded at Time 2 and 3. Frequency distribution of variants.*

Subject; r/R speaker in Ll		Environment	Variants (%)			Number of occurrences
			Uvular	Vocalized	Apical	
KG	r	Prevocalic	—	—	100	137
		Postvocalic	—	34	66	269
WG	r	Prevocalic	—	—	100	56
		Postvocalic	—	38	62	127
HH	r	Prevocalic	—	—	100	125
		Postvocalic	—	10	90	303
GS	R	Prevocalic	100	—	—	123
		Postvocalic	1	99	—	258
WW	R	Prevocalic	47	—	53	85
		Postvocalic	3	88	9	211
Total						1694

difference between R speakers and r speakers. In Stockholm Swedish which is the target dialect in our case, apical /r/ is used. There is a stylistic reduction continuum which for the Stockholm apical /r/ runs roughly from trill [r] to fricative [ʐ] to approximant [ɹ] to zero. But /r/ is not vocalized to [ɐ].

Tests with groups of Germans who were examined before the five case studies indicate that German R speakers who acquire Swedish in Stockholm may take various lines of action with /r/: they may either choose to keep their uvular /r/ or try to use the apical variants they hear from native Stockholmers.

To study this more in detail with the five subjects under discussion here, all the instances of /r/ in the conversational corpus were listened to carefully, and sorted according to subject, time, environment and phonetic variant. Table 17.2 shows the result in a broad summary; it turns out that for the purpose of dealing with our problem here, we may add together Time 2 and 3, distinguish only pre- and post-vocalic syllable positions, and summarize the variants as uvular, vocalized, and apical.

Of the 5 subjects, KG, WG, and HH are r speakers, and GS and WW are R speakers in German. In Swedish, the 3 r speakers continue using apical variants consistently in prevocalic position. But post-vocalically they vary between the more or less target-like apicals and the non-target-like vocoids, HH being somewhat more capable than the other 2 of avoiding vocalization. GS displays an entirely German R-speaking pattern, using uvulars consistently in prevocalic position, and vocalizing post-vocalically. If GS is an 'R retainer', then WW is an 'R→r switcher'. Using uvulars in L1, he attempts apicals in L2, which he achieves about half the time in prevocalic position, in alternation with uvulars. Yet post-vocalically he by and large retains the German R speaker's pattern, using mostly vocalized variants.

The interesting thing here is that the subjects behave differently with pre- and postvocalic /r/. Prevocalically, there are alternative courses of action, as suggested earlier. The German r speakers, who already possess an /r/ which matches the target fairly well, have of course no reason to switch. The other 2 make different choices. GS decides that her uvulars will do for /r/ in Swedish as in German. She apparently *infers* this from her familiarity with the dialect pattern of L1 (judging from the fact that she was already using uvulars in test performance at Time 1, before she was at all acquainted with the Swedish language community). WW decides to try the apicals, a solution which he obviously *induces* from the way he hears /r/ spoken by Swedes.

Postvocalically, as we saw, the non-target-like, vocalized variants are used by all the subjects. GS and WW use them nearly all the time, and KG, WG, and HH less often, in variation with the apicals. At least with the 4 subjects who aim at apicals (KG, WG, HH, and WW), we have no reason to assume that vocalized variants are chosen on purpose. We must conclude that vocalization occurs because it is difficult for the subjects to control and avoid. It is clear that the

German /r/ vocalization process is productive for the subjects in acquiring Swedish, and for the 'R→r-switcher' WW it is apparently much harder to avoid vocalization than to avoid using uvulars prevocalically.

If we look at the types of phonological regularity represented in German /r/, it becomes clear that different kinds of rules are involved here. The unreduced consonantal variant (uvular or apical, depending on speaker) must be taken to be the underlying form. It can actually be used postvocally, too, in overly articulated speech, but vocalization cannot be applied prevocalically. Distinctive features for /r/ in its basic form include the uvular or apical property (or equivalent categories, say, [−coronal, +back...] and [+coronal, −back...], respectively). Choosing uvular or apical is a matter of identifying the basic form of a sound segment. The difference between these two types is of a fairly salient kind and should normally be perceptually familiar to adult German speakers, especially since it functions as a dialectal marker.

The interdialectal correspondence of uvular and apical /r/ can be described with an 'adaptive rule' (cf. Wurzel, 1977), converting (for R speakers) primary dialect [R] into secondary dialect [r]. The possession of such a rule will enable R speakers to interpret apical /r/ cognitively, and (if they want to, and have the skill) to produce it in the place of the uvular.

Postvocalic /r/ vocalization has a different functional status. It represents what Linell (1979) in a functional rule typology defines as an 'articulatory reduction rule'. Whereas the rules defining the underlying segment /r/ and the correspondence between the uvular and the apical types are rules on a more abstract level of phonology, postvocalic /r/ vocalization displays a range of properties characteristic of a concrete rule (see Linell, 1979:214). Rules of this latter type are natural in the sense that they are phonetically motivated (by demands for articulatory economy), and a number of empirical criteria show that they may be difficult to control and suppress for the speaker for whom they are operative. Thus, for example, they are often found to be transferred in L2 acquisition.

Returning to the issue of learner choice vs. natural constraint, we may conclude that for our German learners of Swedish, uvular and apical /r/ types are alternatives that can be chosen, whether or not the learner is then capable of realizing them consistently in a target-like fashion. Vocalization, on the other hand, is not chosen but forced upon the learner by natural conditions.

PRONOUNCING SOUNDS OR PRONOUNCING WORDS?

Another context where it is obvious that different strategies for pronunciation are available, are those cases where learners find alternative cues for pronunciation at different levels of language structure, e.g. when phonetically based and lexically based interpretations compete. The latter type, the lexically based interpretation, tends to occur when words in the target language have close form-equivalents in L1. Examples can be drawn from a picture-naming test with German learners in which variant solutions occurred for certain Swedish vowels which lack close phonetic equivalents in German.

Here, Swedish [ʉː], a high, front vowel with so-called 'in-rounding' (i.e. narrow vertical constriction of the mouth opening without lip-protrusion) was mostly rendered as a high, front, rounded vowel, varying between something like the German [üː] as in *Lübeck* and the target [ʉː]; but sometimes it was rendered as a high, back, rounded [uː]. The back variant was predominant in the word *tub* 'tube', and the front variants in the words *hus* 'house' and *gul* 'yellow'.

Swedish [ɑː], a low, back, slightly rounded vowel was rendered either as a back vowel [ɑː] or [ɔː], or as a low, central, unrounded [aː] like the corresponding sound used in German. This central variant was predominant in the words *radio* 'radio' and *blad* 'leaf', and the back variants in the words *gata* 'street' and *barn* 'child'.

This distribution of variants correlates with the fact that some of the words have close form-equivalents in L1 whereas the others do not. The learner can recognize *tub* as being similar to German *Tube* ['tuːbə], *radio* to German *Radio* ['raːdi̯o], and *blad* to *Blatt* [blat], which may guide him in interpreting the sound shape of these words. With the other words, there is no such striking similarity of form: cf. *hus – Haus; gul – gelb; gata – Straße; barn – Kind*. Here, the learner apparently is more observant of how the target language speakers pronounce the words.

In the case of a pronunciation solution being established by way of association with a lexical form-equivalent in L1, the learner can be said to apply an inferential, predominantly knowledge-driven strategy. That is, he applies his already existing knowledge rather than observing the phonetic input. In the latter case, his strategy is to a greater extent inductive, or input-driven.

It seems that learners at the initial stages tend to make systematic use of lexical form-equivalence. In an experiment described in Hammarberg (1985), learner variants for the difficult Swedish retroflex sounds [ʈ ɖ ɳ] were elicited with a test of repeated picture-naming (regarding the test type, see below), and the proportion of phonetically based vs. lexically based solutions were examined. It turned out that the test words could be placed along a scale of frequency of lexically based solutions which correlated very well with a scale of judgements by language experts as to how lexically transparent the word-form would be for a German listener with no previous contact with Swedish.

Thus at least during an initial period it seems that there are cases where an inductive-phonetic and an inferential-lexical strategy of phonological interpretation alternate, and that a governing factor in favour of the latter is perceived lexical form-equivalence. The lexical cues in this experiment tended to take precedence over phonetic cues where they applied. However, the choice was not an entirely automatic affair, for often a learner did not treat a word consistently according to the same strategy. Apparently the various strategies coexist and compete in the learner's mind.

The lexically based solutions are in a way analogous to the 'holophrastic' or 'formulaic' solutions frequently observed in syntax at early stages. They are unanalyzed items from the point of view of the learner's interlanguage phonology, and are acquired item by item. One development to be expected would be that the learner, with more target language input, will start to 'analyze' and 'regularize' the phonology of such words as he becomes more observant of their phonetic form.

COMPETING VARIANTS IN THE PERFORMANCE SITUATION

As a final point in this discussion, we shall look at some detailed evidence for the competition between variants in the L2 performance situation. The data here come from the test of repeated picture-naming that I already mentioned briefly. This test was given to the 5 German subjects introduced above, starting at Time 1. A number of cards, each illustrating a word by means of a picture, were first shown to the subject, one by one, and the target word was pronounced by the test leader (i.e. by me). After this preparation, the set of cards was run through again and the subject was required to name the word if he or she could remember it. If the subject failed to recall the word or produced it in the wrong lexical form, the test leader would say it once again; usually, the subject would then spontaneously repeat the word after the test leader. If the subject recalled the word by himself, the test would simply proceed. The cards were then run through again a few times until the subject could render practically all the words in the set. In this way about five rounds were obtained. At Time 2 the elicitation part was repeated again in the same way, and at Time 3 the pictures were again run through once. The test was recorded on tape and the answers were transcribed by me. This produced for each test word a series of learner pronunciations at 3 different lengths of interval: immediate succession, a couple of minutes, and 1 to 2 months.

Table 17.3 shows the sequence of trials on the target word *säng*

Table 17.3. *Attempts by 3 learners to render the word* säng [sɛŋ] *'bed' in a test of repeated picture-naming.*

WG		GS		KG	
1:1	sɛŋ	1:1	zɛŋ	1:1	bɛd # en zɛŋ
2	sɪŋ # sɛŋ, sɛŋ	2	zɛŋ	2	bɛd # sɛŋ
3	zɪŋ	3	zɛŋ	3	bɛd, skɛn # sɛŋ, sɛŋ
4	zɪŋ, zɪŋ # zɛŋ, zɛŋ	4	zɛŋ	4	beːt, skɛŋ, ʃɛŋ
5	sɛŋ	5	zɛŋ		# sɛŋ, sɛŋ
				5	bɛd, ʃɛŋ
2:1	zɛŋ	2:1	ʑɛŋ	2:1	bɛd̪, # sɛŋ
2	zɛŋ	2	zɛŋ	2	sɛŋ, bɛd
3	zɛŋ	3	zɛŋ	3	zɛŋ
4	zɛŋ	4	sɛŋ	4	zɛŋ
5	zɛŋ	5	sɛŋ	5	zɛŋ
3	zɛŋ	3	sɛŋ	3	sɛŋ

[sɛŋ] 'bed' by the 3 subjects WG, GS, and KG. The phonological problem here is to pronounce the initial prevocalic voiceless [s]. German learners tend sometimes to replace it with a voiced [z] due to a phonotactic rule in German which requires an alveolar fricative to be voiced initially before a vowel. Even if initial [s] is really not difficult for German speakers to pronounce and has proved to be readily achieved in imitation tests, the /z/ rule shows some productivity in spontaneous free speech in L2. Thus, the two main competing variants in this material are the inductive, phonetically based [s] and the inferential, L1-phonologically based [z].

In the table, '1:1' means Time 1, Round 1, etc., and '#' marks when the test leader intervenes and says the word. Looking first at WG's series we see that she starts by pronouncing [s] at Time 1:1. In the subsequent rounds she uses the wrong form of the word (the wrong vowel) and gets corrected. At Time 1:3 she switches to the inferential solution [z] which she maintains in spite of fresh input at Time 1:4. Then at Time 1:5 she resumes the inductive solution [s] (from her memory, without immediate intervention by the test leader). At Time 2 she uses [z] again, retaining this variant consistently through Time 2 and 3.

GS rather follows an opposite course. She settles consistently on [z] at Time 1. But at Time 2, perhaps after fresh input in the meantime but without any intervention by the test leader, she begins to vary, using a slightly devoiced [z] at Time 2:1, then resuming [z] at Time 2:2 and 2:3, and finally using [s] from Time 2:4 onwards.

Even though WG and GS end up with different results in this early period, there are similarities in their behaviour. In both cases we can observe an unstable phase in the development, for WG at Time 1 and for GS at Time 2, alternating with stable phases. It is clear that with both subjects, the two variants are established as separate solutions and are stored parallel in the subject's mind for some time, competing with each other. That the two solutions are simultaneously active, at least during the unstable phases, is evidenced by the fact that the learners exchange them spontaneously, rather than by repeating after the test leader. Either the inferential or the inductive solution may win the competition for the time being.

The two solutions appear to differ in the way the learner's access to them works. Whereas [z] has been taken over from L1 and is thus automated beforehand, [s] apparently requires a certain amount of control before it is mastered automatically. Thus there seem to be 2 factors at work determining the two solutions: a processing control factor which determines whether the learner chooses [s] or resorts to [z], and an L1 rule factor which conditions the shape of the latter solution.

The series from KG provides some additional illustration of these phenomena. In the beginning, KG has difficulties recalling the word *säng*. Not until Time 2:3 has he gained full control of this lexical item. It is interesting to see that it is precisely at this point that he shifts to [z] and from then on sticks to [z]. Apparently his efforts to memorize the word-form direct his attention to the phonetic input, but when the lexical item is mastered, this attention weakens. The more automatic phonological solution then prevails. The same interpretation is applicable to the way WG acts at Time 1 and 2. This also explains why a less target-like phonological solution may well end up predominating after an unstable phase.

CONCLUSION

The issue here has been the role of purposeful choice versus natural conditioning in the formation of the learner's acquisitional solutions in second language phonology.

It is clear that both simplification–elaboration hierarchies and L1 rule constraints play an essential part in determining phonological solutions and ordering them in time. The case of final /lj/ provided an illustration of this. But as we saw, such constraining factors do not necessarily eliminate alternatives. There may still be some scope for a choice procedure in which the learner tries out different phonetic strategies.

The natural constraints may vary in strength, and hence the learner's possibility to exert control over his choice of solution may vary. As the case of German postvocalic /r/ vocalization indicated, a phonetically motivated process which governs the speaker effectively in L1 tends to be difficult for the learner to control at will, unlike L1 phonological regularities of a more abstract nature. And as we could see in the example of initial prevocalic /s/ (*säng*), where the transfer constraint is weaker than with postvocalic /r/, a competition may arise between a constraint-based and a learner-chosen variant, and there may be room for the learner to put in effort to monitor and control his choice of solution – variably, depending on the strength of the constraint. (For discussions of factors determining the strength of the transfer constraint, see Hammarberg, 1988 and 1990.)

There is also a link to semantic aspects even in segmental phonology. Identifying the phonological shape of words and morphemes is an important part of the learning of vocabulary. The unequal phonological interpretation of cognate and non-cognate word-forms which we saw examples of above, suggests that attention to what 'makes sense' is a motive in acquiring L2 pronunciation (cf. Hammarberg, 1985, 1988). As a result, a lexically based identification of a word form (or else, for example, a morphophonologically or orthographically based interpretation) may compete with a phonetic-phonological interpretation.

In sum, what we see is a variety of motives and conditions which may interact in determining second language phonological solutions. One conclusion to be drawn from this is that, in the phonological domain, the 'natural route of interlanguage development' is an oversimplified notion, which does not reflect the real complexity of the matter. In particular, we cannot expect the development of an L2 structure always to proceed along a single line, describable on the basis of a single criterion of progress. Rather, an interplay between factors of strategic choice and factors of natural conditioning will be the normal state in many cases, and the resulting variation of solutions will often be of a complex kind.

How well can we predict the outcome of this interplay in specific cases? By its nature, strategic choice is a flexible factor which can be 'stretched' by the learner's own effort, or manipulated by directive teaching. On the other hand, the potential of the linguistic constraints, which operate on a regular basis, can be assessed, which can give an indication of the scope of the learner's own choice in each case. At present, a good deal is known about the accessibility of target phonological structures and the transferability of L1 phonological rules. But there is still a need for studies which aim at quantifying more carefully the relative strength of these factors with regard to particular phenomena in L2 phonology, and the relative degree of influence which they tend to exert on learner solutions under given conditions of L2 acquisition.

REFERENCES

Anderson, J. R. (1990), *Cognitive psychology and its implications*. 3rd edition. New York: Freeman.

Benware, W. A. (1986), *Phonetics and phonology of Modern German*. Washington D.C.: Georgetown University Press.

Dickerson, L. J. H. (1974), *Internal and external patterning of phonological variability in the speech of Japanese learners of English*. Thesis, University of Illinois, Urbana-Champaign.

(1975), The learner's interlanguage as a system of variable rules. *TESOL Quarterly*, 9, 401–7.

Dickerson, W. B. (1976), The psycholinguistic unity of language learning and language change. *Language Learning*, 26, 215–31.

Ellis, R. (1986), *Understanding second language acquisition*. Oxford: Oxford University Press.

Færch, C. and Kasper, G. (1980), Processes and strategies in foreign language learning and communication. *Interlanguage Studies Bulletin*, 5, 47–118.

Hammarberg, B. (1985), Learnability and learner strategies in second language syntax and phonology. In Hyltenstam, K., and Pienemann, M. (eds.), *Modelling and assessing second language acquisition*. Clevedon: Multilingual Matters.

(1988), *Studien zur Phonologie des Zweitsprachenerwerbs*. (Acta Universitatis Stockholmiensis, Stockholmer Germanistische Forschungen 38.) Stockholm: Almqvist and Wiksell International.

(1989), Is it possible to predict phonetic difficulty in a second language? In Hammarberg, B. (ed.) *Language learning and learner language*. (Scandinavian Working Papers on Bilingualism, 8, 11–19.) Stockholm: Stockholm University, Centre for Research on Bilingualism.

(1990), Conditions on transfer in second language phonology acquisition. In Leather, J., and James, A. (eds.), *New Sounds 90. Proceedings of the 1990 Amsterdam symposium on the acquisition of second language speech*. Amsterdam: University of Amsterdam.

Kohler, K. J. (1977), *Einführung in die Phonetik des Deutschen*. Berlin: Schmidt.

Linell, P. (1979), *Psychological reality in phonology*. Cambridge etc.: Cambridge University Press.

McLaughlin, B. (1987), *Theories of second-language learning*. London: Edward Arnold.

(1990), Restructuring. *Applied Linguistics*, 11, 113–128.

Moulton, W. G. (1962), *The sounds of English and German.* Chicago and London: University of Chicago Press.

Ulbrich, H. (1972), *Insrumentalphonetisch-auditive r-Untersuchungen im Deutschen.* Berlin: Akademie-Verlag.

Wurzel, W. U. (1977), Adaptionsregeln und heterogene Sprachsysteme. In Dressler, W. U., and Pfeffer, O. E. (eds.), *Phonologica 1976.* Innsbruck: Institut für Sprachwissenschaft der Universität Innsbruck.

18 · Sociolinguistic factors in loss and acquisition of phonology

ROY C. MAJOR

First language loss or language attrition can refer to the diminishing competence in a language, varying in degree from complete loss, such as language death (Dressler, 1972), to loss of proficiency (Sharwood Smith, 1983a and 1983b), to change in language contact situations (Weinreich, 1953; Clyne, 1972, 1980; Weltens, de Bot, and van Els, 1986). Although L1 loss can occur in cases of isolation from all language use, in most cases L1 loss includes concomitant learning of an L2 and integration into the L2 culture. Thus, second language acquisition and first language loss seem to be inextricably linked. In general, it is reasonable to assume that the better one does at L2 language and culture the more likely that person will undergo L1 loss. That this is true seems readily apparent when one contrasts extreme cases. An American who learns three words in Japanese is unlikely to suffer loss of English while one who has spent the last 20 years in Japan probably will.

A number of social and affective factors have been linked to second language acquisition such as cultural identity, attitude, motivation (integrative vs. instrumental, Gardner, 1985), accommodation (Beebe and Giles, 1984), ego permeability, the affective filter, and risk-taking. Because a high degree of proficiency in L2 has been linked to L1 loss, it would be reasonable to investigate whether these factors mentioned above also relate to L1 loss. For example, if x and y are correlated with L2 acquisition, but only y is correlated with concomitant L1 loss, this would tell us something important about the differences of these factors in L1 loss and L2 acquisition. On the other hand, if the factors in L1 loss and L2 acquisition turn out to be the same, then this indicates the unitary nature of the 2 processes, acquisition and loss.

The following study documents L1 loss and L2 acquisition, and then speculates on some of the causes of the widely different behaviour of the different subjects, by profiling the subjects' background, including means of learning the L2, motivation, attitudes toward the L1 and L2 culture, and other socio-affective considerations.

METHODS

The study investigates one aspect of the English and Portuguese pronunciation of five adult native speakers of American English who had immigrated to Brazil. This investigation examines the subjects' VOT (voice onset time) in English and Portuguese voiceless stops (/p t k/). It is hypothesized that there will be a positive correlation between L2 proficiency and L1 loss. The perception of an accent as native or non-native is obviously governed by a composite of factors, VOT being just one of them. Although VOT may at first seem to be a relatively minor aspect of native or foreign accent, there is good evidence that it is highly correlated with overall foreign accent or what I have called global foreign accent (Flege and Eefting, 1986, and 1987; Major, 1987a). Furthermore, since VOT is so amenable to objective measurement, it seems to be a worthy factor to be investigated in a study of loss and acquisition of native accent.

Subjects

The five adult female subjects (35–70 years of age) were native speakers of American English who had immigrated to Brazil as adults, and had been living in Brazil from 12 to 35 years (Table 18.1). They had arrived in Brazil between 22 and 36 years of age. Individuals were selected who might be expected to have very

Table 18.1. *Subject profile*

Subject	Age	Years in Brazil	Age of arrival
B1	70	34	36
B2	59	35	24
B3	42	20	22
B4	45	23	22
B5	35	12	23

compelling reasons to learn Portuguese as well as to maintain their native English. For these reasons, subjects were chosen who had Brazilian spouses, had raised children speaking Portuguese, had large extended families of Brazilians, and were employed at a large English-language institute as teachers and/or administrators.

In addition to the American immigrant subjects, 2 control groups were chosen: 3 native spakers of American English residing in the US, and 5 native speakers of Brazilian Portuguese in Brazil.

Materials and procedure

The speech materials consisted of words with initial voiceless stops preceding a vowel (interspersed with words with voiced stops), and sentences composed by the speakers using these words. The words contained initial stress, and were monosyllabic or disyllabic. The English data also included a conversation portion of 30–45 minutes, and the words selected also were monosyllabic or disyllabic with initial stress containing initial voiceless stops. The subjects were recorded producing four tokens of each word before proceeding to the next word: twice in isolation and twice in an original sentence (composed by each subject) containing the word. After this, the subjects spoke informally to the author for 30–45 minutes. The same procedures for the control groups were utilized. The bilinguals and Brazilians were recorded in Brazil and the Americans recorded in the US.

For the purposes of this analysis, the English word and sentence lists were analyzed together and considered as FOR (Formal) style, and the conversation portion was labelled CAS (Casual) style. Only the formal style of Portuguese was elicited. Sixty stops (20 for each place of articulation) were chosen for each subject for the FOR and CAS styles of English and 60 stops for the Portuguese utterances. VOT measurements were made from spectrograms (a total of nearly 2,000) and then t-tests and Pearson regression correlations were performed to determine possible significant differences between the bilingual and NS subjects.

RESULTS

The mean VOTs are indicated in Figures 18.1 and 18.2, which treat all three stops together.[1] The VOTs for NSs of English for FOR are similar to other data on English VOTs (Lisker and Abramson, 1964, 1967; Caramazza, Yeni-Komshian, Zurif, and Carbone, 1973; Flege and Eefting, 1986, 1987), although there appears to be no published study dealing with English CAS for comparison. The results of NS Portuguese are consistent with Major (1987a; there appears to be no other published data on native Portuguese).

There is a great deal of variation in the ability of the subjects to learn Portuguese as well as to retain English. B1 and B2 produced Portuguese poorly, but lost English only slightly (barely significant at $p < 0.05$). B3 and B4 were significantly different in everything – both their FOR and CAS English and Portuguese, compared to NSs ($p < 0.001$). Thus, they appear to be NSs of neither language. In contrast, B5 retained FOR English, and her Portuguese was native-like (no significant differences with NSs) but her English CAS demonstrated severe loss ($p < 0.001$).

Regression correlations (Pearson correlation coefficients) were utilized to determine any possible correlations between Portuguese and FOR and CAS English. There was no significant correlation between Portuguese proficiency and English FOR; however, a highly significant correlation between Portuguese proficiency and‘English

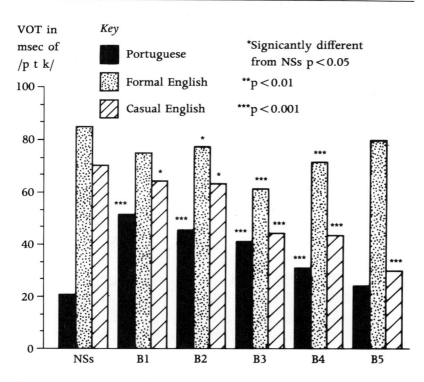

Figure 18.1   Native speaker and bilingual /p t k/

CAS (R = 0.94, F = 20.92, p < 0.05). This means that learning Portuguese had no influence on loss of English FOR, while, on the other hand, learning Portuguese had a large impact on losing English CAS. That means the better a subject mastered Portuguese, the greater the chances for losing English CAS.

DISCUSSION

One of the most obvious conclusions one could make from the data is that L2 influences L1, and that the greater the mastery of L2 the more likely it is to influence the L1. Contrast, for example, B1 with B5.

More specifically, L1 loss in the casual style is highly correlated with the relative mastery of the L2 while the formal style of the L1

VOT in msec of /p t k/

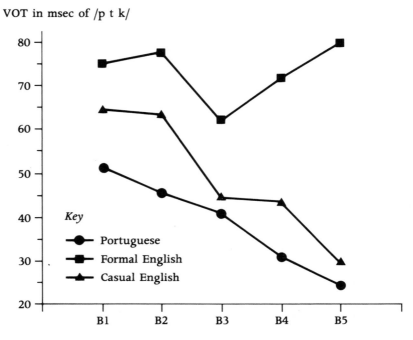

Figure 18.2   Bilingual /p t k/

may or may not be influenced by the L2 (e.g. B3 vs. B5). The correlations regarding the degree of mastery of L2 with L1 loss as well as the stylistic patterning follow logically from what we already know about language behaviour and human behaviour in general. One would expect the influence of the L2 on L1 to be greater in a speaker with a high degree of proficiency in L2 than for one with a low degree of proficiency.[2] To make an analogy, if tennis players A and B take up racket ball, but player A achieves a high degree of proficiency in racket ball while B does not, then one might expect to see the influence of racket ball strokes more in player A than B, especially in the heat of competition.

Furthermore, this study also suggests that the amount of attention paid to speech (monitoring) also is important. Generally the more monitoring there is, the more target-like the production is in L2 situations (Dickerson and Dickerson, 1977; Schmidt, 1977; Tarone, 1979, 1988; Major, 1987b, 1988; Preston, 1989), and in L1 monitoring, the more closely the production approaches the perceived standard (Fischer, 1958; Labov, 1963, 1972). The results of this study follow from these known tendencies: the speakers were able to more closely monitor their formal L1 speech and therefore were able to dampen the effect of the L2.

Although the factors discussed above, stylistic considerations and the relative mastery of L2, are useful in explaining the general behaviour among the five subjects, they do not explain the disparate individual behaviour of the subjects, for example why B1 learned Portuguese so poorly and B5 learned it so well.

One factor which was not measured or controlled for in this study was phonetic mimicry ability.[3] However, it is quite probable that this factor can interact with other social and psychological factors, e.g., confidence, motivation, and willingness to integrate. Success at mimicking phonetically may increase a person's self-confidence in the L2, which in turn can cause the learner to become motivated to further his or her ability in the language and to want to try to become integrated with the L2 culture. On the other hand, being aware that one is poor at pronouncing foreign sounds can cause the person to give up early and withdraw. In other words, success breeds success while failure breeds failure. As Beebe and Giles (1984:23) put it: '...the interaction between *ability* and *motivation* is at the heart of SLA research on both use and development'. It is quite plausible that the subjects with poorer phonetic mimicry ability did more poorly at Portuguese for 2 reasons: lack of aptitude *per se*, and the interaction of aptitude with other factors, e.g. motivation.

Subject profile

Although phonetic mimicry aptitude was not measured, and therefore is a speculative at this point, it is possible to give a brief profile of each of the speaker's background, including the means by which they learned Portuguese, their attitudes about Brazilian and

American culture, their self-assessment of their Portuguese proficiency, and several other individual characteristics. While the
following description does not purport to exhaustively explain the
behaviour of the subjects, perhaps it can provide some insight into
the reasons for the disparate behaviour regarding L2 mastery and L1
loss in the various subjects.

Subjects B1 and B2 were 70 and 59 years old and had been living in
Brazil, for 34 and 35 years respectively, longer than any of the other
subjects (Table 18.1). Neither had studied Portuguese formally; they
learned Portuguese informally as 'street learners' do. When they
first came to Brazil, neither of them used Portuguese frequently. In
fact, one of them often spoke French[4] with others and had very
limited exposure to Portuguese. Neither had to use Portuguese
extensively, since during their initial stage of acquisition neither
worked outside the home. My impression of these subjects'
Portuguese was that it was atrocious in all aspects — accent, grammar,
fluency, and vocabulary. This is also the impression of others;
frequently comments were heard such as, 'Please don't talk
Portuguese; we have visitors at the institute'. 'This is x. She's been in
Brazil for 30 years and still can't speak Portuguese.' 'Only her maid
can understand her Portuguese.' Such scathing remarks certainly
have an effect on even a thick-skinned person, and undoubtedly are
not the kind of comment that tends to build self-confidence about
speaking Portuguese. Quite possibly, constantly hearing about their
failure might have caused the subjects to believe that they had no
ability to learn the language, i.e. the self-fulfilling prophecy may
have been in effect: 'you are what you think you are'.

On the other hand, these 2 subjects' success at retaining English
might be attributed precisely to their failure with Portuguese: since
Portuguese was mastered poorly it would not be expected to exert
much influence on their English. Furthermore, failure at one thing
often causes a defence mechanism in persons so that they seek out
things with which they can be successful. In this case it was the L1.
Perhaps the two subjects were thinking unconsciously, 'At least I
can speak English well so I better hold onto that'. In addition, these

two subjects identified more with American culture than any of the other subjects. One question I asked the subjects in the interview was, 'Do you feel more like an American or Brazilian?'[5] Both the subjects mentioned that they were comfortable living in Brazil, but they definitely felt American. One of them even referred to the strong American identity she felt when she hears the American national anthem, The Star-Spangled Banner.

Subject B3 was 42 years of age and had lived in Brazil for 20 years; B4 was 45 and had been in Brazil for 23 years (Table 18.1). Both had worked since their arrival in Brazil, studied Portuguese formally, taken a number of college courses, taught in Portuguese, and were completing Ph.D.s in Brazil. Thus, they both were required to use Portuguese extensively with a high degree of accuracy. With regard to their sense of identity, they both said they felt bicultural – somewhat American and Brazilian, although not completely either. B3 even said that when she travels back to the US some people ask her where she is from, and remark that she must have been gone a long time. This dual identity is reflected in these two subjects Portuguese and English – all of their productions (all styles) of English and Portuguese are significantly different ($p < 0.001$) from NSs of both languages, approaching an intermediate point between the two languages. That is, their Portuguese was non-native in the direction of English, but their English was non-native in the direction of Portuguese. This is perhaps an example of what Flege (1987) called *equivalence classifications,* where subjects somehow classify sounds from the L1 and L2 as 'equivalent'. This tendency can also extend to broader areas, and seems to be very common in bilinguals: linguistically and culturally they are participants in both communities x and y, but are never completely members of either. Thus, their x is coloured by y, and their y coloured by x.

Speaker B5, 35 years of age, had been living in Brazil for only 12 years. She is a remarkable case of an excellent language learner. Her Portuguese VOTs were not significantly different from NSs, and by her own self-assessment she passed for native. Other Brazilians I talked to confirmed that she spoke Portuguese like a native, including accent, syntax, and semantics. Impressionistic as these remarks are, they are certainly congruent with her native-like VOTs. What is also remarkable is that she did not study Portuguese formally. However, she mentioned that as she was learning Portuguese, she carefully paid attention to linguistic forms and pronunciation and took mental notes of things, which later became part of her competence. Her success with this language acquisition strategy would tend to support Schmidt (1990) concerning the role of consciousness in L2 learning, namely that 'noticing' and 'paying attention' is probably necessary for certain kinds of learning.

Notice that B5's English FOR was native-like, but that her CAS was not. In fact, her English CAS was closer to her Portuguese than to her English FOR. Comparing B5 to B1 and B2, we seem to have the flip-side of the coin. While B1 and B2 had little success with Portuguese and, perhaps as a defence mechanism, maintained a strong L1 identity, B5 was successful with Portuguese and perhaps just neglected her English casual speech, thinking that it always would be intact. Her formal English did remain intact, illustrating the tendency that greater accuracy is achieved in monitored situations. When I talked to her informally my impression was that she had a Brazilian accent. Her first name is a common Brazilian and American name, and when I met her I was not aware of whether she was American or Brazilian. After talking to her for a while, and noticing that her English was so good, I thought that she must have lived in the US for several years. When she said she was American I was surprised, and, in fact, she mentioned when she travelled to the US that many people found it hard to believe that she was American.

During our interview I found out some information about her sense of identity. She said that in the past she had felt quite Brazilian, but lately she had been feeling less and less Brazilian and more disillusioned with the country, partly because of the economy, government, crime, and other social conditions. Within a few months after recording her speech, she moved to England and, after a year or so there, moved back to the US. I talked to her in the US about a year after the recording in Brazil (she had been living in

England) when she mentioned that shortly before leaving Brazil she started noticing her own Portuguese taking on an American accent. This parallels her increasing disillusionment with Brazil. Furthermore, when I talked to her in the US, my impression was that her English sounded American, and when I saw her again a year after that it also seemed not to have any traces of Brazilian accent (this was 2 years after the recording). A colleague of mine saw her in Brazil (she was living in the US but visiting Brazil) $2\frac{1}{2}$ years after the recording and his impression was the same as mine – she sounded perfectly American. Although 'sounded American' is just an impression, it would suggest that her L1 language loss was not permanent, something a lot of NSs may be wondering about as they contemplate living in a foreign country for a period of years.

Speech accommodation theory

It has long been known that speech varies according to social situation. Examples from style and register shifting are legion. Speech Accommodation Theory (SAT), developed by Giles and his associates and elaborated by others (Giles, 1973; Thakerar, Giles, and Cheshire, 1982; Beebe and Giles, 1984; Giles and Johnson, 1987; Giles, Mulac, Bradac, and Johnson, 1987), attempts to uncover the motivations and constraints for speech shifts and the social consequences. The terms *convergence* and *divergence* describe this process. Speakers will often *converge* with the interlocutors when they seek social approval, desire communicational efficiency, and wish to maintain positive social identities with the interlocutors. They will often *diverge* from the interlocutors when they wish to emphasize their differences, such as communicate a contrastive self-image or dissociate personally from the interlocutors.

Usually SAT is used in connection with short-term speech shifts, such as adjusting one's style or accent depending on the interlocutor. For example, Beebe (1980) found Thai speakers adjust their accent according to whether the interlocutor is Chinese or Thai. However, SAT can also be thought of in terms of long-range accommodation, such as the learning of a new dialect or second language. When people move to a new region, e.g. from Alabama to Minnesota, during the course of years they may gradually adjust their speech towards the norm. These individuals have lost their first dialect because when they go back to visit Alabama they do not pass for native Alabaman anymore. The present study may be viewed in similar terms: during the course of second language acquisition the speakers have lost the native accent of their first language in acquiring a second.

There appear to be at least two important mutually reinforcing causal factors for the L1 loss: L2 transfer and accommodation. L2 (Portuguese) interfered with the subjects' native English (just as L1 transfer to L2 is widely known). However, it is also quite plausible that the subjects accommodated, consciously or unconsciously, to what we may consider a second dialect – Brazilian English. The speakers adjusted their speech toward the direction of the Brazilian norm, namely Brazilian-accented English. That is, the subjects appear to be *converging* toward some perceived societal norm, which is far different from North American English. Thus, we may say that some long-term accommodation has taken place. However, we do not know during the recording session whether there was any short-term accommodation in the subjects toward my own speech. Although subjects' VOTs were much shorter than standard US English,[6] it is not known whether their English VOTs in conversation with other Brazilians changes significantly. This was an area not investigated in the study, but would certainly be worth pursuing in some future study. If the subjects' speech pattern does change in the direction of native Portuguese when talking to other Brazilians, and towards the American norm when talking to Americans, it would appear to be a case of double convergence: the subjects converge toward the Brazilian norm when talking to Brazilians, but likewise converge with the American norm when talking to Americans. On the other hand, if the subjects show no differences in VOTs when talking to Americans or to Brazilians, we could say the subjects diverged when talking to Americans for the purpose of setting themselves apart – i.e. they no longer considered themselves exclusively Americans, but rather hybrids (this was suggested in the section above under subject profile).

CONCLUSION

The subjects showing the greatest loss in their native accent in English were those who approached native Portuguese more closely and closely identified with Brazilian culture. Two important mutually reinforcing factors were suggested: L2 transfer to L1 and accommodation. The change in VOTs in the subjects' English toward the direction of Brazilian Portuguese appears to be a clear-cut case of L2 transfer. Furthermore, it is suggested that the subjects have undergone long-term accommodation to another variety of English, namely Brazilian English.

The study indicates an individual's languages (L1 and L2) are dynamic fluid entities and can vary over time. Although to some it may seem unfortunate that these immigrants lost their native accent as they learned Portuguese, there are some very positive aspects that outweigh the loss. The fact that they learned Brazilian culture and Portuguese has enabled them to gain more empathy with Brazilians learning English, and, even though the subjects suffered some loss of their English, this loss was not severe enough to impair their effectiveness as native models for their students. Furthermore, it appears that the native accent can be recovered if the subjects move back to the US, as evidenced by Subject 5. Therefore, rather than being a curse, losing one's first language is a clear manifestation of how remarkably human beings can adapt to different situations.

NOTES

1 For an expanded discussion of the three stops treated separately see Major (1992).
2 However, when an L3 is involved the picture becomes less clear, since it has been observed that an L2 can have more influence on the L3 than the L1, even though the L2 is incompletely mastered.

3 I thank Richard W. Schmidt for pointing this out, and for his other comments on an earlier version of this paper.
4 In order not to reveal the subjects identity, the two subjects, whose performance in English and Portuguese was similar, will be discussed together.
5 I attempted to investigate the subjects' consistency in this area by asking several related questions throughout the interview, such as 'How do you feel about living in Brazil?' 'How do you like it here?', etc.
6 In the conversation with subjects, I took a short sample from my own speech and found my VOTs to be equivalent to NS English.

REFERENCES

Beebe, Leslie (1980), Sociolinguistic variation and style shifting in second language acquisition. *Language Learning*, 30, 433–47.
Beebe, Leslie and Howard Giles (1984), Speech accommodation theory: a discussion in terms of second-language acquisition. *International Journal of the Sociology of Language*, 46, 5–32.
Caramazza, A., Yeni-Komshian, G. H., Zurif, E. B., and Carbone, E. (1973), The acquisition of a new phonological contrast: The case of stop consonants in French–English bilinguals. *JASA*, 54, 421–8.
Clyne, Michael (1972), *Perspectives on language contact*. Melbourne: Hawthorn.
    (1980), Typology and grammatical convergence among related languages in contact. *ITL*, 1980, 49–50.
Dickerson, Lonna J., and Dickerson, Wayne B. (1977), Interlanguage phonology: current research and future directions. In *Actes du 5ième Colloque de Linguistique Appliqué de Neuchâtel, the notions of simplification, interlanguages, and pidgins, and their relation to second language pedagogy*, pp. 18–30. Geneva: Droz.
Dressler, Wolfgang U. (1972), On the phonology of language death. *CLS*, 8, 448–57.
Fischer, J. L. (1958), Social influences in the choice of a linguistic variant. *Word*, 14, 47–56.
Flege, James Emil. (1987), The production of 'new' and 'similar' phones in a foreign language: Evidence for the effect of equivalence classification. *Journal of Phonetics*, 15, 47–65.

Flege, James Emil, and Eefting, Wieke (1986), Linguistic and developmental effects on the production and perception of stop consonants. *Phonetica*, 43, 155–71.

(1987), Cross-language switching in stop consonant perception and production by Dutch speakers of English. *Speech Communication*, 6, 185–202.

Gardner, R. C. (1985), *Social psychology and second language learning: The role of attitudes and motivation*. London: Edward Arnold.

Giles, Howard (1973), Accent mobility: a model and some data. *Anthropological Linguistics*, 15, 247–52.

Giles, Howard, and Patricia Johnson (1987), Ethnolinguistic identity theory: a social psychological approach to language maintenance. *International Journal of the Sociology of Language*, 68, 69–100.

Giles, Howard, Mulac, Anthony, Bradac, James J., and Johnson, Patricia (1987), Speech accommodation theory: the first decade and beyond. In McLaughlin, Margaret L. (ed.), *Communication Yearbook*, pp. 10, 13–48. Sage: Beverly Hills.

Labov, William (1963), The social motivation of a sound change. *Word*, 19, 273–309.

(1972), *Sociolinguistic patterns*. Philadelphia: University of Pennsylvania Press.

Lisker, Leigh, and Abramson, Arthur (1964), A cross-linguistic study of voicing in initial stops: acoustical measurements. *Word*, 20, 384–422.

(1967), Some effects of context on voice onset time in English stops. *Language and Speech*, 10, 1–28.

Major, Roy C. (1987a), English voiceless stop production by Brazilian speakers of English. *Journal of Phonetics*, 15, 197–202.

(1987b), A model for interlanguage phonology. In Ioup, Georgette, and Weinberg, Steven H. (eds.), *Interlanguage phonology: The acquisition of a second language sound system*, pp. 101–124. New York: Newbury House/Harper and Row.

(1988), Variation in second language phonology. In Miller, Ann, and Powers, Joyce (eds.), *ESCOL '87: Proceedings of the Fourth Eastern States Conference on Linguistics*, pp. 40–51. Columbus: Ohio State University.

(1992), Losing English as a first language. *The Modern Language Journal*, 76, 190–208.

Preston, Dennis R. (1989), *Sociolinguistics and second language acquisition*. New York: Basil Blackwell.

Schmidt, Richard W. (1977), Sociolinguistic variation and transfer in phonology. *Working Papers in Bilingualism*, 12, 79–95.

(1990), The role of consciousness in second language learning. *Applied Linguistics*, 11, 129–58.

Sharwood Smith, Michael (1983a), On explaining language loss. In Felix, S., and Wode, Henning (eds.), *Language development at the crossroads: Papers from the interdisciplinary conference on language acquisition at Passau*, pp. 49–59. Tübingen: Gunter Narr.

(1983b), On first language loss in the second language acquirer: problems of transfer. In Gass, Susan, and Selinker, Larry (eds.), *Language transfer in language learning*, pp. 222–31. Rowley, Mass.: Newbury House.

Tarone, Elaine (1979), Interlanguage as chameleon. *Language Learning*, 29, 181–91.

(1988), *Variation in interlanguage*. London, Baltimore, Melborne, Auckland: Edward Arnold.

Thakerar, Jitendra N., Giles, Howard, and Cheshire, Jenny (1982), Psychological and linguistic parameters of speech accommodation theory. In Fraser, Colin, and Scherer, K. (eds.), *Advances in the sociology of language*, pp. 205–55. Cambridge: Cambridge University Press.

Weinreich, Uriel (1953), *Languages in contact*. New York: The Linguistic Circle of New York.

Weltens, Bert, de Bot, Kees, and van Els, Teo (eds.) (1986), *Language attrition in progress*. Dordrecht: Foris.

Index

Abu, 54f
accommodation 166, *see also* linguistic
    accommodation
accretion, 4
acquisition
    affective factors, 153
    and behavioural theory, 148
    bilingual first language (BLIA), 5
        balanced/unbalanced, 5
    and cognitive theory, 149
    and cognitive-interactionist theory,
        310
    and communitive intent, 157
    and expressive children 161
    and innatist theory, 148
    linguistic complexity, 6
    and linguistic theory, 148
    patterns of, 171
    and referential children, 161
    and social interactionist theory, 149
acquisitional path, 254
acquisitional principles 327ff
acrolect, 124, 126, 136
activation, 237
    threshold of, 238
activities, 312, 314ff
Adjora, 118
Afrikaans, 65
age of onset (AO), 197ff

aktionsart, 313ff
Albanian, 267
Alzheimer's dementia, 183, 222–40
    in bilinguals 222, 225–240
    phases of deterioration, 224f
American English, 126
American Sign Language (ASL), 166,
    198
angular gyrus, 150f
AO, *see* age of onset
aphasia, 5, 169–171, 179ff
    Broca's aphasia, 169, 179
    conduction aphasia 169f
    in polyglots 183
    Wernicke's aphasia, 152, 170
Arabic, 347
arcuate fasciculus, 150f
areal-specific characteristics, 348
ASL, *see* American Sign Language
aspect, 313ff
    inherent, *see* aktionsart
attrition
    environmental, 26, 28
    global (vs. specific), 187f
    in the lexicon, 386–410
    pathological (*see* aphasia and
        (Alzheimer's) dementia)
    related to old age 189ff
        in L1 189ff

attrition (*cont.*)
   in L2 189ff
   of specific words 187
   specific (vs. global) 187f
autism 167
automatization, 239
availability, 247ff

babytalk (BT), 156
background information, 279
balanced proficiency, 289
base language (BL), 388ff
basic lexicon, 340
basic sentence structures, 286
basic verbs, 346, 353
basilect, 123ff, 126, 131, 134
bilingualism
   balanced/unbalanced, 295
bilinguals
   Albanian
      and Danish 267, 272ff
   Chinese
      and English, 182
      and Thai, 473
   Danish
      and Albanian, 267, 272ff
      and English, 267, 272ff
      and Vietnamese, 267, 272ff
   Dutch
      and English, 182, 225
   English
      and Chinese 182
      and Danish, 267, 272ff
      and Dutch, 182, 225
      and Hebrew, 369
      and Japanese, 444
      and (Brazilian) Portugese, 464ff
      and Spanish, 182, 309ff, 387
      and Swedish, 386–410
      and Yiddish, 226
      and errors, 202ff

Finnish
   and Swedish, 202, 226ff, 374ff,
   386–410
French
   and Swedish, 289–306
German
   and Itialian 364ff
   and Spanish, 364ff
   and Swedish, 226, 445ff
Hebrew
   and English, 369
Italian
   and German, 364ff
Japanese
   and English, 444
Mexicano
   and Spanish, 74, 76
Polish
   and Swedish, 374ff
Portuguese
   and English, 464ff
Spanish
   and English, 182, 309ff, 387
   and German, 364ff
   and Mexicano, 74, 76
   and Swedish, 202, 374ff
stronger language, 289, 293ff
Swedish
   and (American) English, 386–411
   and Finnish, 202, 226ff, 374ff,
   386–410
   and French, 289–306
   and German, 226, 445ff
   and Polish, 374
   and Spanish, 202, 374ff
Taiap
   and Tok Pisin, 94ff
Thai
   and Chinese, 473
Tok Pisin
   and Taiap, 94ff

Vietnamese
   and Danish, 267, 272ff
   weaker language, 289, 293ff
   Yiddish
   and English, 226
Bislama, 45
BL, see base language
BLIA, see acquisition, bilingual first
      language
blood-flow studies, 191
bootstrapping 245ff, 260
   multiple sources of, 246
borrowing, 226, 239f, 279ff, 386ff
   as enrichment, 30
   as interference, 30
Brazilian Indian languages, 61
Broca's area 150f
BT, see babytalk
Buang, 41f

casual style, 466ff
CDS, see child directed speech
Celtic languages, 348
centrality of verbs, 351ff
   in first language acquisition 351
   in second language acquisition,
      351ff
child directed speech, (CDS), 156
   prohibitives, 162
   socialization messages, 162
Chinese, 347
Chinookan, 77, 80
code contextualization, 69
code definition 70
code differentiation, 69, 73
code-switching, 77, 86, 100ff, 226,
      239f
   and the equivalence constraint
      386ff
   and the ordered choice hierarchy,
      386

cognitive universals 311ff
communicative mode, 269
competition model, 245
compounds, 400ff
conceptual prime, 327
conflation 373, 377
Congruence Principle, 328ff
construction types, 254
continuity, 417ff
   in language acquisition, 417f
   in language change, 418–20
   and self-control, 420
core grammar, 246
cortical stimulation, 181ff
creole (languages), 39–67, 122–39
   Guyanese, 124
   Haitian, 65
   Hawai'i Creole English 123ff, 206
creole continuum, 122–39
creolization, 6, 29, 45, 57
critical periods, 184ff, 434
   in L2 acquisition, 184ff
crosslinguistic acquisition research,
      245ff
crosslinguistic perspectives, 340–381
Czech, 171

Danish, 267–87
DBH, see Distributional Bias
      Hypothesis
deactualization, 26, 28
deafness, 165f
decrement, 4
decreolization, 29f, 122–39
   patterns of, 123
   in individuals, 126–32
   the sociopolitical context, 132
definiteness, 401ff
demarking, 7
dementia (see Alzheimer's d.)
derailment, 240

deterioration, 229ff
developmental continuum, 269ff
developmental line for Danish
    L2–acquisition, 284
developmental phases, 154ff
developmental route, 271ff
dialect levelling, 29f
dichotic studies, 179
Didinga, 347
differentiation, 373ff
discourse, 254, 256
discourse analysis, 267
Distributional Bias Hypothesis (DBH),
    320, 333
Dobu 51ff
Dyirbal 70ff, 379
dynamism, 3

EC's Bureau for Lesser Used
    Languages, 31
embedding of complex information,
    282
endstate grammars, 245, 247ff
English, 40, 41, 48, 49, 54, 57, 62, 63,
    72, 80, 97, 117, 190, 247, 250ff,
    267, 315ff, 341ff, 419, 424
    American, 126
    Black, 56, 206
    Creole, 56
    Hawai'i Creole (HCE), 123ff, 206
    Indian, 78
    Jambun, 70ff
    Standard (SE), 126ff
    Standard Australian (SAE), 70, 71
equivalence classification, 471ff
equivalence constraint, 386ff
ethnolinguistic diversity (in Hawai'i),
    124ff
exercise hypothesis, 197ff
existential predication, 130
expansion

in the lexicon, 386–410

Finnish, 346
Finno-Ugrian languages, 348
first language acquisition (L1A), 5,
    26ff, 147ff, 311ff
    atypical language development, 26,
    164ff
    crosslinguistic perspectives 250ff,
    340ff
    differences to L2A/SLA, 290ff
    neurolinguistic aspects, 147ff
    normal development 151ff, 291ff
    typical, 26ff
    verb morphology, 311
    verb class inflections, 311ff
    and distributional bias, 318
first language loss (see also language
    loss), 147, 168–72, 180, 463–76
first language maintenence, 208
    and L2 proficiency, 208
form-function relations, 251ff
formal style, 466ff
free morpheme constraint, 387ff
French, 58, 60, 64, 346, 363, 470
frequency ranking, 340f
functional grammar, 267ff

Gaelic, 45
GB theory, see Government-Binding
    Theory
German, 250ff, 290, 295, 346
Germanic languages, 373
Geshwindt and Galaburda hypothesis,
    185
Government-Binding Theory (GB
    theory), 247ff, 291
grammatical aspect (durativity), 251
grammaticalization, 373ff
Greek koiné, 51
Guyanese creole, 124

Haitian creole, 65
Hawai'i Creole English, (HCE), 123ff,
    206
HCE, *see* Hawai'i Creole English
Hebrew 250ff
heterogeneity, 4
heteroglossia, 69f
Hindi, 425ff
Hiri Motu, 41, 48ff
Hungarian, 346

IL, *see* interlanguage
implicational universals, 347
incorporation, 386ff
    equivalence constraint, 387ff
    free morpheme constraint, 387ff
    hierarchy of ordered choice, 386ff
    norms for bilingual communities,
        409ff
    pattern, 389
    and social networks, 407ff
indefinite reference, 127, 129ff
Indian English, 78
information load, 332
information structure, 274ff
inhibition, 237
intercultural communication, 51
interlanguage (IL) development, 268ff
interlanguage interference, 188f
interlanguage (IL) study, 267
Italian, 315ff, 346

Jakobson's regression hypothesis,
    189
Jambun English, 70ff
'jargon' babbling, 158

Kalam, 348
Kanaka English, 39
Kate, 53
Kiksht 77 (*see* Wasco)

Kikuyu, 424
Kobon, 348
Kopar, 118

L1A, *see* first language acquisition
L2A, *see* second language acquisition
LAD, *see* language acquisition device
language acquisition (*see* specific
    terms and acquisition)
language acquisition device (LAD),
    148, 187
language birth, 29
language change, 122
language choice, 183, 223, 226ff
language contact, 4, 122, 389ff
language death, 29, 41ff, 68, 83, 87,
    97
language decay, 29
language development, 253–6
language loss
    first language 147, 168–72, 180,
        463–76
    and SLA, 463–76
language maintenance, 28, 89ff
language maintenance programmes
    88ff
language mixing, 226, 239
language monitor, 183
language obsolescence, 7, 31, 69, 83,
    90
language organization (vs. language
    processing), 181ff
language planning, 29f
    corpus planning, 30
    status planning, 30
language policy, 134
language processing 181
    in bilinguals, 191
language progression 256 (*see also*
    progression)
language separation, 223, 226ff

language shift, 28f, 43, 46ff, 68–91,
    94–118
  practice 68ff
  structure, 68ff
language socialization, 84, 94–118
language spread, 28f
language suicide, 98
language switch, 183ff
language-dependent constraints, 443ff
  and the familiarity dimension, 443ff
  and the simplicity dimension, 443
language-particular factors, 257
language-specific lexical patterns,
    373ff
  conflation, 373ff
  differentiation, 373ff
  grammaticalization, 373, 375ff
  polysemy, 349, 373, 375, 377
laternal dominance, 152ff, 178ff
  in bilingulas, 178ff
Latin, 51
left hemisphere specialization, 151
lending language (LL), 388ff
length of residence (LOR), 199
Lenneberg's critical period
    hypothesis, 197
  the exercise hypothesis, 197ff
  the maturational state hypothesis,
    197ff
lexical acquisition, 340–81
lexical markedness, 343
lexical organization, 340–81
lexical progression, 340–81
lexical regression, 378ff
  contact-induced, 380
Lexical–Functional Grammar, 247
lexicalization, 79
lexicalization hierarchies, 341, 347
lexically based interpretations, 454ff
lingua franca, 40ff
  aboriginal, 56

Lingua Gerale, 61
Linguala, 60
linguistic accommodation, 104
linguistic change, 96
linguistic diversity, 62ff
linguistic ecology, 43, 62
linguistic functions, 245, 250ff
linguistic ideology, 80
linguistic universals, 311ff
linguistic variation, 122
literacy acquisition, 5
LL, see Lending Language
locative trajectories, 251f
longitudinal investigations, 222
longitudinal study, 267, 271ff
LOR, see length of residence

Maccassanese Pidgin, 53
majority languages, 289
Mangarayi, 348
markedness hierarchy, 347, 350
maturational constraints, 196ff
maturational state hypothesis, 197ff
Mayan Quiche, 253, 259
Mean Length of Utterances (MLU),
    275, 293
mbd, see minimal brain damage
mental retardation 166f
  fragile X-syndrome, 166
  Down syndrome, 166
mesolect, 124, 131
methodological issues
  in second language acquisition,
    204–13
metropolitan languages, 61ff
Mexicano, 70, 73ff
  legítimo mexicano, 74
minimal brain damage (mbd), 168
minority languages, 31, 68, 289
  and obsolescence (see language
    obsolescence), 68

MLU, *see* Mean Length of Utterances
modularity, 246
morphological integration, 391ff
motor cortex, 150f
Motu, 51, 57
multilingualism, 45ff, 63
    and urbanisation 55ff

Nahuatl, 70, 73ff
namey nouns, 403ff
narrative development, 250ff
Native American Languages Act, 90
native language acquisition, 245–61
nativism, 245
negation, 304
Neo-Melanesian, 42
neuroanatomical specialization, 152
neurolinguistic aspects
    of first language acquisition, 147ff
    of first language loss, 147ff
    of second language attrition, 178ff
    of second language development,
        178ff
New Guinea Malay, 53
New South Wales Aboriginal Pidgin,
    45
nonce loans, 397ff
Northern Paiute, 78
nuclear verb strategy, 365
nuclear verbs 247ff

One-to-One Principle, 329ff
overextension (in meaning), 359, 376
overrepresentation, 359ff

Papiamentu, 310
parameter-setting, 247
paratactic structures, 280
parts of speech, 341ff
passive voice, 252f
past time reference (for non-stative

verbs), 127, 129ff
perception verbs, 364ff
performance analysis, 267ff
PET scan, 191
petit nègre, 43
phonetic continuum 448ff
    variation of degree, 448ff
    variation of type, 448ff
        free choice, 450ff
        governed choice, 450ff
phonetically based interpretations,
    454ff
phonological acquisition, of, L2
    and concomitant L1 loss, 463ff
    and natural constraints, 440ff
    and strategic action, 440ff
phonological integration, 391ff
phonological variation
    and development, 444ff
phonology acquisition in SLA, 439–60
pidgin (languages), 39ff
Pidgin English, 43, 47, 61, 126
Pidgin Fijian, 53
Pidgin Sango, 56
pidginization, 28f
pidginized English, 125
pidginized Hawaiian, 125
Pijin, 57
Pinker's Continuity Assumption, 329
planum temporale, 151
Plateau 'Penutian' languages, 78
Police, 52
Polish, 335, 346
polysemy, 349, 373ff, 375, 377
prelinguistic development 155ff
premorbid degree of second language
    proficiency, 234ff
pre-syntactic mode, 269
primary auditory area (of cortex), 150
primary visual area (of cortex), 150f
principle of transitivity, 280

principles of acquisition 246ff
productivity of use, 253
profile analysis, 293
progression
  at the individual level, *see*
  acquisition
  at the societal level 5, 29–31, 39ff
pronominal subjects, 295ff
psycholinguistic learning strategies,
  442
punctual events, 312, 314ff
purism, 72, 75

question-formation, 258

rate of development, 198
rate of learning, 285
Red Indian pidgins, 61
regression (*see* attrition, language loss
  etc.)
  at the individual level, 5, 168–72,
  222–40
  temporary, 26f
  at the societal level, 5, 29–31, 39ff
relative clauses, 251ff
Relevance Principle, 328ff
reliability, 211–13
repidginization, 137
restructuring, 441
Role and Reference Grammar, 248
Romance languages, 373
Rumanian, 346
Russian, 346

SAE, *see* Standard Australian English
Sahaptin, 78ff
Sango, 57, 60
SAT, *see* Speech Accommodation
  Theory
Saua, 52
SE, *see* Standard English

second language acquisition, (L2A,
  SLA), 5, 178, 196ff, 267ff
  and basic words, 353ff
  differences to L1A, 290ff
  and first language loss, 463–76
  learner creativity, 439ff
  methodological issues, 204–13
  natural constraints, 439ff
  phonology, 439–60
  talent in, 185
second language attrition, 178ff
second language development 178ff,
  267–87
second language processing, 178
second language regression, 222–40
semantic fields, 340ff
semantic roles, 276, 281
Semitic languages, 261
sensitive period (*see also* critical
  period), 196ff
Sepik-Ramu Phylum, 118
Sesotho, 253, 258, 259
simplification, 270f
simultaneous acquisition, 186
SLA, *see* second language acquisition
Slavonic languages, 373
SLI, *see* specific language impairment
social networks
  and incorporation, 407ff
sodium amytal procedures, 180, 182
solidarity coding, 85, 86, 88
solidarity ideology, 136
Solomon Pijin, 45, 55
Spanish 74ff, 97, 250ff, 316ff, 424
specific language impairment (SLI)
  167f, 170
Speech Accommodation Theory (SAT),
  473ff
  convergence, 473ff
  divergence, 473ff
speech perception, 157, 415ff

and the categorical mode, 420f,
    423ff
and the continous mode, 420–2,
    427ff
and experimental techniques, 421
within UTA, 429
Speech Perception in Noise (SPIN),
    190
SPIN, *see* Speech Perception in Noise
Sranan, 45
Standard English (SE), 126ff
states, 312, 314ff
stronger language (in bilinguals),
    293ff
Stroop colour word test, 190
subject selection, 204f
subordination, 275
Subset Principle, 329ff
subsystem hypothesis, 237
Swahili, 59, 60
Swedish, 346, 353ff, 273ff
Sylvian fissure, 182
syntactic mode, 269
syntactic prototypes, 351, 366ff
syntacticization, 269ff

tachistoscopic presentations, 179
Taiap, 94–118
target categories, 248
task types, 208
telic events, 312, 314ff
temporal plane, *see* planum temporale
tense, 313ff
tense markings, 303
Tok Boi, 56
Tok Pisin, 40ff, 57, 94–118
token counts, 321ff
topic–comment structure, 278ff
Town Bemba, 56, 59
trade languages, 51

transparency of form–meaning
    relations, 255
Turkish, 250, 256, 349
two-word sentences, 161
type counts, 321ff
typological markedness, 350
typology of use, 252
Tzeltal, 377

UG, *see* universal grammar
ultimate attainment, 197ff
(U)ngarinjin, 348
universal grammar, (UG), 292
universal theory of language
    acquisition (UTA), 415ff
urbanisation 55ff
UTA, *see* universal theory of language
    acquisition
Uto-Aztecan languages, 73, 78

validity, 211–13
variation theory, 4
verbal inflections, 310ff
vernaculars, 39ff, 94–118
Vietnamese, 267
voice onset time (VOT), 422ff, 466ff
voices, 69, 70
VOT, *see* voice onset time

Walmatjari, 348
Walpiri, 259
Wasco, 70, 77ff
weaker language in bilinguals, 289,
    293ff
Wernicke's area, 150–2
word order, 295ff
word-formation, 258
words per utterance, 275

Yabem, 41, 53